# The power of pragmatism

Manchester University Press

# The power of pragmatism

Knowledge production and social inquiry

Edited by Jane Wills and Robert W. Lake

Manchester University Press

Published by Manchester University Press
Oxford Road, Manchester M13 9PL
www.manchesteruniversitypress.co.uk

British Library Cataloguing-in-Publication Data
A catalogue record for this book is available from the British Library

ISBN 978 1 5261 3494 3 hardback
ISBN 978 1 5261 6719 4 paperback

First published 2020
Paperback published 2023

Typeset by Sunrise Setting Ltd, Brixham

# Contents

# Figures and table

**Figures**

**Table**

# Contributors

**Trevor Barnes** is Professor and Distinguished University Scholar at the Department of Geography at the University of British Columbia, Vancouver, Canada.

**Clive Barnett** is Professor of Geography and Social Theory at the University of Exeter, UK.

**Gary Bridge** is Professor of Human Geography at the School of Geography and Planning, Cardiff University, Wales, UK.

**Malcolm P. Cutchin** is Professor of Gerontology at the Institute of Gerontology and Professor of Occupational Therapy in the Department of Health Care Sciences, Wayne State University, Detroit, USA.

**Azadeh Hadizadeh Esfahani** is a PhD Candidate at the Graduate School of Geography at Clark University in Worcester, Massachusetts, USA.

**Alireza F. Farahani** is a PhD Candidate at the Graduate School of Geography at Clark University in Worcester, Massachusetts, USA. He is also director of Policy Making and Strategic Planning at Tehran municipality, Iran.

**Crispian Fuller** is Senior Lecturer in Human Geography, School of Geography and Planning, Cardiff University, Wales, UK.

**Klaus Geiselhart** is Senior Lecturer at the Institute of Geography at the Friedrich-Alexander University of Erlangen-Nürnberg, Bavaria, Germany.

**Liam Harney** has a PhD in Geography from Queen Mary University of London. He works as a community organiser in east London, UK.

**Meg Holden** is Professor of Urban Studies and Geography at Simon Fraser University in Vancouver, Canada.

**Alice E. Huff** obtained her PhD in Geography from the University of California, Los Angeles, USA. She is currently a research associate with the Kettering Foundation in Dayton, Ohio, USA.

**Ihnji Jon** is a Lecturer in International Urban Politics at Melbourne School of Design, University of Melbourne, Australia.

**Owain Jones** is Emeritus Professor of Environmental Humanities at the Environmental Humanities Research Centre at Bath Spa University, UK.

**Robert W. Lake** is Professor at the Bloustein School of Planning and Public Policy and a member of the Graduate Faculties in Geography and the Urban Planning at Rutgers University, USA.

**Susan Saegert** is Professor of Critical Social Personality and Environmental Psychology, and Geography, at the Graduate Center of the City University of New York (CUNY), USA.

**Jane Wills** is Professor of Geography at the Centre for Geography and Environmental Science (CGES) and the Environment and Sustainability Institute (ESI), University of Exeter, working on the campus in Cornwall, UK.

# Acknowledgements

This book originated in an international conference on Human Geography and the Pragmatic Tradition organised by Jane Wills and Robert Lake at Queen Mary, University of London, in May 2017. Through two days of presentations and intense discussion, it became apparent that an approach to social inquiry informed by the pragmatic tradition transcends national boundaries and disciplinary specialisations and opens promising new avenues for rethinking the aims, process and practices of knowledge production in the social sciences. This book is the result, and the editors are grateful to conference participants for their productive engagement with the power of pragmatism; for their thoughtful, informative and provocative contributions; and for agreeing to rework their presentations for publication. We thank Queen Mary, University of London, for hosting the two-day conference and for providing a visiting fellowship in support of Robert Lake's participation in the event. We are also very grateful to Trevor Barnes and Clive Barnett for writing for us even though they didn't come to the conference; they have added important depth and breadth to the book.

Thomas Dark at Manchester University Press ably guided the book through publication. We thank the many friends, colleagues and students – too many to count – who have humoured, tolerated and encouraged our engagement with pragmatism over many years and whose enthusiasm and support were integral in bringing this work to publication. We also feel deep appreciation for our families; enduring thanks for your patience, love and support.

Jane Wills
Penryn, Cornwall, UK

Robert Lake
Brooklyn, New York, USA

# Part I

# The power of pragmatism

# Introduction: The power of pragmatism

## Jane Wills and Robert W. Lake

In life we are accustomed to the fact that our most important decisions are often based on uncertainty. We take a punt, follow our nose or listen to our gut. We make decisions without knowing that things will work out. We accept a marriage proposal, blow the whistle on an employer or go out on strike in the hope that it will be for the best. We expect to reach our golden anniversary, receive vindication for our efforts and win collective gains, but we know it could all too easily end in divorce, persecution or unemployment. Even mundane decisions like going for a walk, buying a gift for a relative or accepting a lunch invitation make us vulnerable to unintended and unexpected consequences: one thing leads to another and unanticipated events can occur. Our greatest emotional triumphs and our most dismal failures come from putting our neck on the line. We navigate everyday life learning to expect and manage uncertainty.

When it comes to our approach to social research, however, such insights and practices tend to be lodged in the back of the mind. We deploy theoretical frameworks and abstract concepts to help us reduce the complexity of the world to manageable proportions. Even if we acknowledge that they are simplifications, we approach social inquiry with a predefined lexicon that allows us to find 'gentrification', 'neoliberalism', 'planetary urbanism', 'settler colonialism' or the 'post-political' (to highlight some of the most popular concepts in critical social inquiry today) because those are the things we expect to find. If we use large datasets and analytical models, we look for predictable patterns to find the universal causal processes behind complex activities such as voting choices, knife attacks or rates of obesity. In the search for certainty, not surprisingly, we simplify social life and find evidence that supports our established ideas. Academics pursuing the normal science of social inquiry all too often produce concepts that allow us to see certain things while ignoring others, and, in a circular and self-reinforcing process, the resulting research reproduces prevailing ideas or generates new ones that feed the cycle anew.

Relinquishing what John Dewey (1929) called 'the quest for certainty' has proved extremely difficult in both physical and social research. Predictable causal relationships might appear clear in a laboratory setting, but even there we are likely to ignore the role of confounding factors and the likelihood of unintended consequences. The invention of DDT promised the eradication of mosquito-borne diseases but instead produced a carcinogenic legacy of global environmental contamination. The miracle invention of antibiotics that fight deadly bacteria stimulated new strains of highly resistant 'superbugs' and destroyed the microbiota of the human gut that support good immunity. The laws of economic science that allow markets to flourish also produce income inequality, negative environmental externalities and uneven development. These are just a few examples in a long list of unanticipated consequences of science that are coming home to roost in the Anthropocene (Mitchell, 2002; Polanyi, 1920 [2018], 1944 [2001]). In both the natural and social sciences, belief in certainty has sometimes produced deadly effects.

This book aims to make the case for pragmatism as an approach to social inquiry in which the absence of certainty is an asset rather than a liability for the process of knowledge production in the social world. A practice of social inquiry informed by pragmatism, we argue, leaves open the possibility for the unexpected, the potential joy of one thing leading to an (unexpected) other. It offers an opportunity, as Richard Rorty (1979 [2009], 370) suggests, "to keep space open for the sense of wonder... that there is something new under the sun... something which (at least for the moment) cannot be explained". Pragmatism, Rorty continues, "is not a 'method for attaining truth'" but, rather, "is *supposed* to be abnormal, to take us out of our old selves by the power of strangeness, to aid us in becoming new beings" (1979 [2009], 357, 360, emphasis in the original). In so doing, a pragmatist approach to social inquiry enlarges the possibility of creating new knowledge in the world.

While the body of thought and practice known as pragmatism has been in existence for more than a hundred years (Menand, 1997, 2011; Morris, 1970), its popularity has ebbed and flowed with changing academic fashions and it was largely eclipsed by the ascendancy of analytical philosophy in the twentieth century. Yet there is strong and mounting evidence that pragmatism is again becoming more widely recognised as a promising orientation for social research (Baert, 2005; Boltanski and Thévenot, 2006; Dickstein, 1998; Morgan, 2014; Rogers, 2009). By advocating for the wider adoption of pragmatic ideas in social and spatial research, *The power of pragmatism* offers a possible avenue of escape from the pitfalls and contradictions of prevailing modes of inquiry while cohering with multiple sources of emerging thought and practice. As we discuss further, below, a pragmatist approach to social inquiry offers scope to incorporate parallel and related arguments from intellectual antecedents and companions such as Nietzsche, Heidegger and Wittgenstein and from subsequent social theorists such as Bourdieu, Foucault and Latour who have been influenced by pragmatism or share its convictions (Bernstein, 1992, 2010; Harman, 2014; Mouffe, 1996; Purcell, 2017; Rorty, 1979 [2009], 1989).

A resurgent pragmatism also connects to nascent efforts to develop practice-oriented approaches to the conduct of social research, such as phronetic inquiry (Flyvbjerg, 2001), actor–network theory (Latour, 2005) and non-representational theory (Masumi, 2015; Thrift, 2008). Active experiments to adopt research approaches and methods based on collaboration beyond the academy, such as participatory action research (PAR), citizen science and the practice of co-production, also present strong affinities with pragmatic social research (Fischer, 2009; Kindon et al., 2007; Jasanoff, 2012; Pestoff et al., 2012; Whyte, 1991). In their alignment with pragmatism, these approaches recognise the futility of what Dewey (1916 [2004]) called 'the spectator theory of knowledge', in which the thinker or researcher stands at an objective distance outside the culture or community of which they are part and in which knowledge constitutes a representation of that separately existing, antecedent reality. Social researchers aligned with pragmatism acknowledge the full import of the crisis of representation, the end of the 'God-trick' and the need to embrace uncertainty in the production of knowledge. While the allure of foundational certainty remains strong when rewarded by conventional practices of obtaining grant funding, publishing a journal article or presenting a conference paper, pragmatism provides a way out of the conundrum of searching for the lifeboat of apparent foundations even as we know they cannot exist.

With a commitment to problem-solving and a perspective extending beyond the academy, pragmatism promotes the social value of social research. Its feet are firmly planted in 'the field', in tackling the problems of everyday life and incorporating broad public scrutiny to decide what is the right thing to do. Rather than taking its cue from existing theory, academic debate or prevailing intellectual concerns, pragmatic inquiry reorients the focus of research to working with a particular social group or community. Such research is designed to be useful: in the language of pragmatism, it is about working with publics around their problems through community-based inquiry and, in the process, further building the collective capacity to act. Akin to an anthropologist practising ethnography, a pragmatist researcher starts by listening to the beliefs, or 'truths', that exist in a community and tries to understand the work they are doing for variously situated community members. Comprehending such truths is further aided by a genealogical – that is, geo-historical – appreciation of the particular development of that community, its economy, institutionalised practices and related processes of identity-formation. If community members express an appetite to move forward over a particular concern or problem, the researcher might then work with the community to facilitate inquiry into the situation and to collectively develop the ideas and associated practices needed to produce a desired change. This means shedding *a priori* expectations of what comprises a 'social problem' and instead working with people to define what, from their perspective, constitutes an issue, problem or priority, which may look very different from the long list of public policy issues that regularly feature as recognised public concerns.

Signs of a resurgent pragmatism have been apparent since Richard Rorty, Richard Bernstein and other 'neo-pragmatist' philosophers published their accounts of the power of pragmatism in the 1980s (Bernstein, 1989, 1992, 2010; Rorty, 1979 [2009], 1989; Unger, 2007). The neo-pragmatist perspective has selectively diffused into various areas of social research, such as social psychology (Shibutani, 2017), sociology (Joas, 1993; Shalin, 1986), political science (Bohman, 1999a, 1999b; Festenstein, 1997), public administration (Ansell, 2011; Dieleman, 2014; Shields, 2003, 2008), medical social science (Tolletsen, 2000), human geography (Bridge, 2005; Harney et al., 2016; Wood and Smith, 2008), urban studies (Lake, 2016, 2017), planning theory (Healey, 2009; Hoch, 1984), business studies (Wicks and Freeman, 1998) and economics (Nelson, 2003). Perhaps not surprisingly, take-up has been greatest in the humanities and applied arts, such as law (Posner, 2003), education (Biesta, 2015), history (Kloppenberg, 1989), literature (Mitchell, 1982), theology (West, 1989) and philosophy (Misak, 2002), where the quest for certainty was already much less secure. The contributions in *The power of pragmatism* attempt to build on this ongoing work to further explore its implications for the practice of social inquiry.

In suggesting that pragmatism can be applied across the social sciences to diverse fields of research, *The power of pragmatism* advocates the adoption of a pragmatic approach that can advance the practice of social inquiry while enhancing the public impact of the work that is done. Adopting pragmatism, however, involves major changes in the practice of social science, with significant implications for the ontological status and substantive content of the knowledge produced, as well as for our academic subjectivity and public identity as 'researchers'. This book seeks to elucidate those changes and to address some of the challenges impeding their realisation.

In the remainder of this introduction, we set out the historical development of the pragmatist tradition and its core ideas, before exploring its application to social research, past and present. We then make a strong case for pragmatic social research, outline its key components and highlight its implications for research practice and outcomes. In the penultimate section, we address some of the long-standing concerns about pragmatism in order to provide critical context to the chapters that follow.

## The pragmatic tradition of thought

The pragmatic tradition of philosophy developed in the years just after the American Civil War when a group of friends living in Cambridge, Massachusetts in the 1870s met to talk about ideas. They sought an explanation for, and an alternative to, the chaotic upheaval and violence of civil war, in which, they thought, the vehement adherence to incommensurable convictions had led to incomprehensible barbarity and destruction. The key protagonists were Nicholas St John Green (1830–76), Oliver Wendell Holmes Jr (1841–1914), William James (1842–1910), Charles Sanders Peirce (1839–1914) and Chauncey Wright (1830–75) (Menand, 2011; Mills, 1943 [1964]). They called themselves the Metaphysical Club and exchanged ideas about philosophy, science and law, eventually advocating a new approach to understanding ideas. As Brandom (2009, 31) puts it, they came to believe that society

> needed … a different attitude toward our beliefs: a less ideologically confident, more tentative and critical attitude, one that would treat them as the always-provisional results of inquiry to date, as subject to experimental test and revision in the light of new evidence and experience, and as permanently liable to obsolescence due to altered circumstances, shifting contexts, or changes of interests.

The early pragmatists were resolutely anti-foundationalist, rejecting the grounding of truth on *a priori* principles – human nature, natural law, divine will or similar premises that were themselves without foundation – and the pragmatists understood any such 'truth' to be arbitrary, socially constructed and unverifiable. Rather than searching for metaphysical or immutable truths, pragmatists held that ideas are practical tools and can be best understood in relation to their consequences. Ideas matter not because of their correspondence to an antecedent reality but because of what they allow people to do and to get done in the world. From an ecological and historicist perspective, ideas were understood to be products of particular circumstances and were dependent upon their utility.

Fusing the consequentialist spirit of Bentham's utilitarianism with the new Darwinian science, Peirce was particularly important in arguing that the value of ideas could be understood in relation to their effects, and he first published the term 'pragmatism' in a paper in 1878 (Mills, 1943 [1964]). Pragmatism, according to Peirce, sought "to lay down a method of determining the meaning of intellectual concepts, that is, of those upon which reasoning may turn". In what has become known as the 'pragmatic maxim', Peirce argued that "[i]n order to ascertain the meaning of an intellectual conception one should consider what practical consequences might conceivably result by necessity from the truth of that conception" (quoted in Mills, 1943 [1964], 178). This was a powerful argument about a theory of meaning and the definition of truth. Ideas could be deemed to be true, the pragmatists claimed, when they had useful consequences and this practical application provided their meaning. As such, ideas are related to their social context and particular interests, and it is no longer possible to support a 'spectator theory of knowledge' in which the truth lies in an antecedent reality behind or beyond the grind of everyday life. The grind is the point, and ideas are related to their use in the world.

This new approach presented a startling position that challenged the understanding that had ruled the history of ideas since Plato, running into the European Enlightenment in the seventeenth century, when scientists and philosophers embarked upon the pursuit of a particular kind of knowledge that was understood to be rational – that is, universal rather than particular, general rather than local, timeless rather than timely, and written rather than oral (Toulmin, 2001). Enlightenment reasoning produced a shift away from "*practical* philosophy, whose issues arose out of clinical medicine, judicial procedure, moral case analysis, or the rhetorical force of oral reasoning, to a *theoretical* conception of philosophy" (Toulmin, 2001, 34). The turn from the immediate and practical to the theoretical and abstract offered an escape from a dogmatic political order in which religious intolerance and endless war were at their height. For the scholars of the Enlightenment, the certainty and predictability of universal laws seemed to provide a path to progress in the face of a chaotic and destructive social order. From Descartes and Newton to Ricardo and Marx, the Enlightenment quest for the certainty of universal laws governed the production of knowledge in the physical as in the social world. The promise of progress through knowledge continued unabated in the years leading up to and following the Second World War, when the popularity of logical positivism, abstract formalism in music, art and architecture and the rise of spatial science all reflected a context in which universal ideas were sought and applied regardless of the contextual specificities of history and geography.

The journey towards a 'second enlightenment' (Brandom, 2009) was promoted by pragmatists as they rejected dogmatism and relinquished the quest for certainty (Menand, 2011). This new approach, however, did not reject reason in favour of art, emotion and feeling in responding to the world, as had been advocated by the romantic poets and thinkers who sought to resist the Enlightenment of the seventeenth and eighteenth centuries (Toulmin, 2001). Rather, the pragmatists adopted a new version of reason that focused on practice and application, reflecting their interest in "intelligent doings rather than abstract sayings" (Brandom, 2009, 25). Such 'intelligent doings' were crystallised in pragmatists' appreciation for the new kind of science that reflected the importance of practice and application over metaphysical speculation and abstraction. 'Science', as pragmatists understood it, could not depend on a stance of distanced objectivity – an unattainable position when the inquirer is inescapably situated in the world. Rather, science described a method of democratic experimentation in response to problems encountered in experience. "Science is a *pursuit*," John Dewey observed in 1920, "not a coming into possession of the immutable" (Dewey, 1920, x). It was from this understanding of science as collective experimental problem-solving that pragmatists formulated their notion of 'inquiry', understood as the way in which individuals situated in specific contexts or communities could together confront the limits of their knowledge and deliberate over possible alternative futures on the basis of new ideas for action.

In its first, Peircean, manifestation, the practice of pragmatist inquiry was argued to be relatively limited, stimulated by a particular doubt (or what Dewey later called a 'problematic situation') that prompts the search for new ideas for action. Peirce argued that most beliefs are generally not subject to doubt. Once an idea is established and becomes habituated in systems of thought and action, it can be left to one side. Indeed, Peirce described himself as a 'conservative sentimentalist' who had no need to reflect on the instincts and core beliefs that are required to live. It is only in situations of doubt triggered by new experience, when the individual does not know what to think or how to act, that inquiry is needed to find a new way of thinking and acting. Thus Peirce understood inquiry as a process that necessarily takes place within and among a community of inquirers that, in an adaptation of laboratory science, works through experimentation to verify, or otherwise, a new set of ideas. Writing in 1896, Peirce advocated the "laboratory habit of mind", whereby "[t]he scientific spirit requires a man to be at all times ready to dump his whole cartload of beliefs, the moment experience is against them. The desire to learn forbids him to be perfectly cocksure that he knows already. Besides positive science can only rest on experience; and experience can never result in absolute certainty, exactitude, necessity or universality" (quoted in Mills, 1943 [1964], 163).

In this vision, scientific practice and, by implication, philosophy can never be fixed as 'belief'. In the world of the laboratory, ideas can only ever be provisional and open to the winds of new experience and the inevitable reformulation of thought; and in the next phase of development, this analysis was extended beyond the laboratory to the wider society. Between 1906 and 1907, William James gave a series of lectures on pragmatism that were published as *Pragmatism: A new word for old ways of thinking* (1907). He made powerful arguments about the social character of knowledge and the practical meaning of 'truth' in the wider society, saying that "the whole function of philosophy ought to be to find out what definite difference it will make to you and me, at definite instants of our life, if this world-formula or that world-formula [were] to be the true one" (James, 1907 [2000], 27). Working in the spirit of earlier generations of empirically oriented thinkers, he argued that the pragmatist "turns towards concreteness and adequacy, towards facts, towards action and towards power … It means the open air and possibilities of nature, as against dogma, artificiality, and the pretence of finality in truth" (James, 1907 [2000], 27). This intervention represented a dramatic shift in philosophy as ideas were to be understood as "a program for future work" (James, 1907 [2000], 28) rather than the final answer or ultimate truth. James advocated a pragmatic 'method' that involved understanding the consequences of ideas in the world. He argued that we could get to the bottom of things by understanding the work being done by an idea and its consequences for life.

However, James also highlighted the difficulty of changing our ideas even when we realise they are doing us no good and we want to find something better. Experience, the encounter with the world, might prompt doubt and indecision about what to do, but our old ideas prove remarkably stubborn and difficult to relinquish. As James put it: "The most violent revolutions in an individual's beliefs have most of his old order standing. Time and space, cause and effect, nature and history, and one's own biography remain untouched. New truth is always a go-between, a smoother-over of transitions" (James, 1907 [2000], 31). For James,

> our minds grow in spots; and like grease spots, the spots spread. But we let them spread as little as possible; we keep unaltered as much of our old knowledge and beliefs as we can. We patch and tinker more than we renew. The novelty soaks in; it strains the ancient mass; but it is also tinged by what absorbs it. (James, 1907 [2000], 75)

The instrumental role of ideas underpins human culture in ways that will never be predictable, and we can never be certain that truth will "happen to an idea" nor that it will be "made true by events" (James, 1907 [2000], 88). Indeed, James recognised the immense challenge posed by the social validation of an idea, saying: "We must find a theory that will work; and that means something extremely difficult; for a theory must mediate between all previous truths and certain new experiences" (James, 1907 [2000], 95).

It was the philosopher John Dewey (1859–1952) who took up the challenge of further applying pragmatism to understanding the role of ideas, their place in society and the way in which ideas can and should change for the better. Dewey had not been part of the Metaphysical Club, and he came from a different time, place and background (Westbrook, 1991; Mills, 1943 [1964]). Dewey's early philosophical work was strongly influenced by established traditions of Hegelian idealism, but he was gradually exposed to more practically oriented ideas both through encountering James's approach to psychology in the 1890s and by working with Jane Addams at Hull House in Chicago around the same time (Buxton, 1984; Deegan, 1990). As professor of philosophy and pedagogy at the University of Chicago, Dewey established the Laboratory School in 1896, and it became widely known as the Dewey School. By 1903, it had 140 students and 23 teachers and, informing and reflecting the philosophy he came to write, it focused on teaching children to learn through doing rather than being told and then repeating what to believe. The focus was on concrete rather than abstract learning, and the curriculum was designed to embed ideas in their practical application (Dewey, 1916 [2004]). Moreover, democracy was practised in the classroom as much as in the wider world, and the children were encouraged to develop their character as active participants in the school community. The goal of education, Dewey insisted, is to prepare democratically competent citizens capable of collectively addressing shared problems rather than, as was and still is widely believed, to prepare workers for an insatiable economy or to insert bodies into a prevailing class structure. As a window on to Dewey's philosophy, the school demonstrated his belief in knowledge as a practical tool for getting things done and in setting goals through collective debate and deliberation about the way ahead. Rather than absorbing abstract 'truths', the children were encouraged to learn through practical experiment and to develop their creative intelligence about the world around them. Dewey presented this model as a way to "transform American schools into instruments for the further democratization of American society ... Schools should try to deepen and broaden the range of social contact and intercourse, of cooperative living, so that the members of the school would be prepared to make their future social relations worthy and fruitful" (Westbrook, 1991, 109).

Applying these ideas beyond the institution of the school, Dewey developed an argument about the importance of experience for learning and acting in the world. Whereas children within the setting of the school could be given learning opportunities against which to test their ideas and develop their intelligence, Dewey argued that experience plays a similar role in the world at large as people test their ideas through interacting with the world in which "the organism has to endure, to undergo, the consequences of its own actions" (Dewey, 1917 [1980], 8). Experience, in this approach, is understood as the active mediation between ideas and outcomes, potentially prompting people to change their ideas when, faced with the provocations of life, they have to inquire into new ways of thinking and acting. Whereas Peirce argued that doubt prompts changes in ideas in the context of a particular community of inquirers, Dewey relocated this sense of doubt into the broader concept of experience, suggesting that humans are prompted to rethink ideas when experience teaches them to do so, and particularly when (re)learning in collaboration with others. Moreover, he argued that there is a role for philosophy – via what he called social inquiry – in promoting this process of learning. In an essay titled 'The need for a recovery of philosophy', written in 1917, he suggested that "philosophy recovers itself when it ceases to be a device for dealing with the problems of philosophers and becomes a method, cultivated by philosophers, for dealing with the problems of men" (Dewey, 1917 [1980], 46).

For Dewey, building on Peirce, inquiry is the practice through which people formulate new ideas and develop potential solutions to the challenges posed by experience. Reflecting the focus on practical application, he called for the development of 'warranted assertions' – ideas that can be tested and potentially validated through experiment or practice but that always remain open to subsequent challenge and continued re-evaluation. He developed Peirce's ideas of the 'laboratory method' for application to society, recognising the importance of social complexity and diversity in the testing and validation of ideas: "What purports to be experiment in the social field is very different from experiment in natural science; it is rather a process of trial and error accompanied with some degree of hope and a great deal of talk" (Dewey, 1938 [1988], 109).

Dewey had faith in the capacity of human beings to form intelligent judgments, decisions and action (or Darwinian 'adaptations') in response to changing circumstances, reflecting a basic democratic and relational ethos affirming the intrinsic worth of every socially embedded individual (Lake, 2017; Rogers, 2009; Westbrook, 2005). Rather than considering democracy in relation to its institutional forms, laws and related activities, he argued that democracy reflects what it is to be human, embedded in communities that are able to learn from experience and make collective decisions about the way ahead. Far more than a system for aggregating preferences, democracy can be found in the plurality of social spaces such as family, school, church and government (Honneth, 1998; Lake, 2017; Wills, 2016a). A flourishing democracy, moreover, requires that ordinary people have the opportunity to exercise their capacity for collective judgment, for the good of both the decisions being made and the people making them, and this is to be achieved through the combined processes of public formation and collective social inquiry.

This pragmatic practice of democratic inquiry was understood to be about developing and applying collective intelligence in particular contexts, rather than applying rules or abstractions untethered from place and time. Dewey argued that "[w]e cannot seek or attain health, wealth, learning, justice or kindness in general. Action is always specific, concrete, individualized, [and] unique. And consequently, judgements as to acts to be performed must be similarly specific" (1920 [1957], 166–7). This approach requires energy to be invested in the particularities of situated inquiry rather than in the futile quest for generalities, abstractions and absolute 'truth'. In a harsh criticism that rings true today, Dewey argued that "to set up a problem that does not grow out of an actual situation is to start on a course of dead work ... Problems that are self-set are mere excuses for seeming to do something intellectual, something that has the semblance but not the substance of scientific activity" (1938 [1939], 108).

Dewey's commitment to democratic experimentation and collective problem-solving emerged as a direct challenge to critics who advocated the superiority of experts and expertise in democratic decision-making (Lippmann, 1922, 1927 [1993]). In *The public and its problems*, Dewey (1927 [1954]) mounted a strong defence of the role of ordinary people, conceived as multiple publics, debating and deliberating about shared concerns. For Dewey, democracy needs the people just as much as the people need to have a voice. As he put it: "It is impossible for the high-brows to secure a monopoly of such knowledge as must be used for the regulation of common affairs. In the degree to which they become a specialized class, they are shut off from knowledge of the needs which they are supposed to serve" (Dewey, 1927 [1954], 206). While he recognised the economic, social and political processes that undermine community, and acknowledged the role of the new social scientists who sought to provide expertise on behalf of the growing administrative bureaucracy of an expanding state, Dewey staunchly defended the capacity of ordinary people to make good decisions. If people are unprepared for this task, he held, then this requires conscious and directed effort to provide the spaces and means through which people can deliberate together and act, and to which the process of collective inquiry can make a contribution (Lake, 2017; Westbrook, 1991).

Dewey expressed concern that the 'Great Community' needed protection from being displaced by the 'Great Society'. Without the face-to-face relationships and trusted interactions associated with community, it was hard to see how people could have a role in democratic life and collective decision-making. With a public that was "largely inchoate and unorganised" and "bewildered" in the face of dominant business interests, mass political parties, remote public administration and the demagogic manipulation of public opinion, Dewey advocated much greater attention to the protection of the public (Dewey, 1927 [1954], 109, 116). In words that still resonate, he declared that "It is not that there is no public, no large body of persons having a common interest in the consequences of social transactions. There is too much public, a public too diffused and scattered and too intricate in composition" (1927 [1954], 137). The challenge was thus to organise the public and to find "the means by which a scattered, mobile and manifold public may so recognise itself so as to define and express its interests" (1927 [1954], 146). He highlighted the role of multiple overlapping institutions such as "the family, the school, industry, religion" (1927 [1954], 143) in underpinning public organisation. But more than this, the problem for the public was one of communication: "The essential need," he maintained, "is the improvement of the methods and conditions of debate, discussion and persuasion. That is *the* problem of the public" (1927 [1954], 208, emphasis in the original; see also MacGilvray, 2010).

By the middle of the twentieth century, however, the hegemonic dominance of technical rationality, analytical philosophy, authoritarian modernism, scientific management and quantitative social science (among many other domains) meant that Dewey's work was increasingly "widely honoured and broadly ignored" (Westbrook, 1991, 532). As Toulmin (2001) suggests, the post-war years saw a virulent return to the 'quest for certainty', and pragmatism's commitments to contextuality, provisionality, fallibilism and inclusive democratic experimentation were largely forgotten. If considered at all, Dewey was characterised as naïve, out-of-date and out-of-keeping with the rising currents in analytical philosophy, positivist social theory and calculative social science. A challenge to this ascendant worldview and its renewed quest for certainty did not arise until the social movements of the 1960s and 1970s broke through the barricade of prevailing ideas by demanding greater creative and political freedom for women, people of colour and sexual minorities. These rising social movements demonstrated the diversity of truths in the world and, although they were generally associated with the radical left, triggering a renewed interest in Marxism and anarchism that later proved to be a Trojan horse for new certainties, they also opened the door to revisiting arguments that had been made by the earlier generation of pragmatists. Especially in their early days, the new social movements put great emphasis on collective learning through consciousness-raising, empowerment, deliberation and participation (Stears, 2010).

The renewed attention to democracy had strong echoes of Dewey's earlier work, and the philosopher Richard Rorty recognised the parallels between pragmatism and the new structure of feeling at large in a fast-changing world.[1] Rorty argued that the insights of pragmatism were to be realised through attention to the power of narrative and imagination to remake the world (Malachowski, 2010). He sought to foster solidarity across difference by finding ways to tell new stories through a process he called 're-description', which could help people find common ground (Lester, 2019). Echoing themes introduced by the earlier generation of pragmatists, Rorty rejected dependence on unwavering foundations, welcomed the impossibility of certainty and embraced the social and practical nature of truth. Without the fixed anchor of metaphysical truth, the task of philosophers and intellectuals is to develop a 'new vocabulary' that keeps society together despite its inherent multiplicity and the absence of a singular consensus.

Having nothing outside the social context and the particular community in which we find ourselves provides an imperative against "theory and towards narrative" (Rorty, 1991a, xvi). The goal of Rorty's neo-pragmatist philosophy is "to redescribe lots and lots of things in new ways, until you have created a pattern of linguistic behaviour which will tempt the rising generation to adopt it, thereby causing them to look for appropriate new forms of non-linguistic behaviour, for example, the adoption of new scientific equipment or new social institutions" (Rorty, 1991a, 9). As demonstrated by the social movements of the 1960s and 1970s, the new languages of feminism, environmentalism and civil rights imagined and thus prompted new forms of being and acting in the world (Minnich, 2005, 2017). The task for Rorty was to find ways of intervening in public debate and culture that foster narratives that create wider, richer and stronger forms of social solidarity. Building on Dewey's legacy, Rorty retained a faith in liberal democracy as a space of freedom in which to develop new narratives providing a vehicle for collective solidarity and social hope (Rorty, 1998a, 1999).

In a world of radical diversity in personal beliefs, Rorty argued that politics depends on the ability to develop ideas that appeal across multiplicity and difference. As he put it: "the only test of a political proposal is its ability to gain assent from people who retain radically diverse ideas about the point and meaning of human life, about the path to private perfection" (Rorty, 1999, 173). Despite the many threats posed to democratic institutions and practices, Rorty had a strong faith that democracy is the best thing we have to proceed in the world. Recognising that there is nothing outside human culture, democracy provides a way to reduce exploitation and domination and advance human flourishing. Pragmatism, for Rorty, highlighted the importance of gaining "a renewed sense of community". Recognising "our community" as ultimately encompassing the globe (Rorty, 1997), he insisted that

> our identification with our community – our society, our political tradition, our intellectual inheritance – is heightened when we see this community as *ours* rather than *nature's*, *shaped* rather than *found*, one among many which men have made. In the end, the pragmatists tell us, what matters is our loyalty to other human beings clinging together against the dark, not our hope of getting things right. (Rorty, 1980, 727, emphasis in the original)

For Rorty, then, the focus of intellectual work should be on developing useful interventions in relationship with a particular expanding community, and he thought there was no particular method required to do this. While Dewey had built on Peirce's notion of the practice of inquiry, Rorty wanted to leave things open-ended. As he put it: "If one takes the core of pragmatism to be its attempt to replace the notions of true beliefs as representations of 'the nature of things' and instead to think of them as successful rules for action, then it becomes easy to recommend an experimental, fallibilist attitude, but hard to isolate a 'method' that will embody this attitude" (Rorty, 1991b, 65–6). Indeed, having abandoned representation as the purpose of inquiry, he thought that "the whole idea of … choosing between 'methods'… seems to be misguided" (Rorty, 1982, 195).

Rorty (1996) instead defended Dewey's attention to the 'problematic situation', in which existing ideas are no longer adequate for a particular task and new ones are needed; the role for social sciences is then one of supporting the search for new ideas in tandem with the community of people directly affected by the problem and its solution. As Rorty put it: "Sociologists and psychologists might stop asking themselves whether they are following rigorous scientific procedures and start asking themselves whether they have any suggestions to make to their fellow citizens about how our lives, or our institutions, should be changed" (Rorty, 1998b, 70). "One way of thinking of wisdom as … not the same as … argument," he suggested, is "to think of it as the practical wisdom necessary to participate in a conversation (and) the attempt to prevent conversation from degenerating into inquiry, into a research program" (Rorty, 1979 [2009], 372). Relinquishing the goal of accurate representation, pragmatism seeks engagement in a collective democratic experiment aimed at discerning what Dewey called "a sense for the better kind of life to be led" (Dewey, 1919 [1993], 39).

## Pragmatism and social research: past and present

The take-up of pragmatism has had a long, uneven and at times contentious record in the practice and impact of social research. When Jane Addams and Ellen Gates Starr established the Hull House Settlement on the west side of

Chicago in 1889, their "great experiment in social service" (Commager, 1961, xii) rested firmly on pragmatist principles of community engagement, collective experimentation, anti-foundationalism and problem-orientation. Addams was familiar with William James's writing, and her close and enduring friendship with John Dewey predated his appointment to the philosophy faculty at the newly established University of Chicago in 1894.[2] Reflecting Peirce's 'pragmatic maxim' that the value of ideas relies on their consequences in practice, Addams asserted that "action is the only medium man has for receiving and appropriating truth" (Addams, 1910 [1961], 81). Recollecting her experience at Hull House after two decades, Addams described the Settlement approach in a long passage that easily stands as a manifesto for pragmatism:

> The one thing to be dreaded in the Settlement is that it lose its flexibility, its power of quick adaptation, its readiness to change its methods as its environment may demand. It must ... have a deep and abiding sense of tolerance. It must be hospitable and ready for experiment. It should demand from its residents a scientific patience in the accumulation of facts ... It must be grounded in a philosophy whose foundation is on the solidarity of the human race ... Its residents must be emptied of all conceit of opinion and all self-assertion, and be ready to arouse and interpret the public opinion of their neighbourhood. They must be content to live quietly side by side with their neighbours, until they grow into a sense of relationship and mutual interests ... They are bound to see the needs of their neighbourhood as a whole, to furnish data for legislation, and to use their influence to secure it. (Addams, 1910 [1961], 84–5)

These principles articulated a pragmatist sensibility on multiple grounds. The Settlement championed a method of flexibility, fallibility and experimentation; a willingness to bracket prior expectations and foundational assumptions; an openness to and tolerance of multiple perspectives; the denial of superior expertise and all 'self-assertion'; a status of radical equality between Hull House residents and surrounding neighbours; and a driving commitment to collective and collaborative problem-solving. This last point in particular – the commitment to address problems facing Chicago's most impoverished immigrant residents – constituted the central aim and purpose of the Hull House Settlement. As Addams expressly explained, "the Settlement, then, is an experimental effort to aid in the solution of the social and industrial problems which are engendered by the modern conditions of life in a great city" (Addams, 1910 [1961], 83).

These pragmatist principles were unevenly adopted and retained by the scholars who were launching the new school of urban sociology at the nearby University of Chicago during the same period.[3] However, this new school of academic sociology moved relatively fast to adopt a more "scientific stage in sociology" (Faris, 1970, xiii), and the quest for a 'science' of sociology displaced the earlier commitment to problem-solving and social reform. Similarly, in an otherwise highly adulatory overview of the Chicago School's formative period, Short disparaged the Hull House Settlement as "characterized by highly partisan purposes of immediate social reform … unguided by explicit theoretical premises and hence not productive of generalized, objective statements about urban structure and social life" (Short, 1971, xvi). The identification of universal, generalisable, theoretical statements about the city was elevated as the defining aim of Chicago academic sociology, expressed in the title of the foundational text, *Introduction to the science of sociology,* written by Robert Park and Ernest Burgess in 1921, in distinct contrast to the earlier focus on improving the lived experience of people in cities.[4] Only five years later, Burgess was able to announce that "sociology is being transformed from a social philosophy into a science of society" (Burgess, 1926, viii; see also Burgess and Bogue, 1964) and "the study of the city became divorced from social action and practice" (Deegan, 1990, 37). As Deegan recounts, "Park and Burgess were key figures in disassociating sociology from the appearance of doing social reform" as academic sociology in Chicago "loudly and defiantly separated itself from social reform" (Deegan, 1990, 143).

Chicago was growing rapidly during this period through a combination of industrialisation, mass immigration and urbanisation, and the early academic sociologists viewed the city as a laboratory from which they could extract a science of urban growth and human behaviour (Park, 1916, 1929; Park and Burgess, 1921 [1924]; Park et al., 1925 [1967]). Park's 1929 essay 'The city as a social laboratory' exhorted social researchers to emulate the hard sciences by employing the city as a source of immutable truth (Abbott, 1999; Gross, 2009). The trope of the city as a social laboratory that repeatedly appeared in the writing of the Chicago sociologists of this period presupposed that the city constituted an antecedent reality amenable to discovery through the observational methods of laboratory science, yielding generalisable laws and universal regularities. As a result, as Gieryn points out, "Chicago (was) naturalized to become (an) analytical object (and) the peculiarities of Chicago are elided, as the city is made into a specimen of generic and universal 'urbanism,' describable not in local details but with laws" (Gieryn, 2006, 10–12).

The ambition to observe the city as a sociological laboratory generated an extensive series of ethnographic field studies of Chicago neighbourhoods, institutions and organisations published as volumes in the Sociological Series by the University of Chicago Press in the first decades of the twentieth century (Burgess, 1916; Harney et al., 2016; Wills, 2016b).[5] While these ethnographic studies indeed provided a window on the city as "a spatial pattern and a moral order" (Park, 1916), the detailed description of urban life was primarily used as a means for the elucidation of generalisable principles. Writing the preface to Nels Anderson's *The hobo: The sociology of the homeless man* (1923), Park asserted "[i]t is, in fact, the purpose of these studies to emphasize not so much the particular and local as the generic and universal aspects of the city and its life, and so make these studies not merely a contribution to our information but to our permanent scientific knowledge of the city as a communal type" (Anderson, 1923, vii–viii, quoted in Gieryn, 2006, 31). In his ethnographic account of *The ghetto* (1928), Louis Wirth wrote that the ghetto became a "laboratory specimen" (Gieryn, 2006, 12), and Faris approvingly observed that "Wirth's interests were less in the Jewish ghetto as such than in what Park called the natural history of such settlements" (Faris, 1967, 71).

The academic perspective on urban residents as specimens to be observed in the sociological laboratory was utterly anathema to Jane Addams and her pragmatist colleagues at Hull House. The difference in perspective between university researchers and Settlement workers encompassed but also went well beyond the divergent objectives of sociological science and social change: the fundamental disagreement regarding the position of Chicago's residents as research subjects reflected a basic philosophical as well as political divide. If the residents of Chicago's slums and ghettos provided the academic sociologists with observations on which to develop theorisations about the city, those same residents provided the Settlement workers with co-equal partners in devising solutions to the problems presented by the exigencies of life in the industrial metropolis. For the academic sociologists, people were the subjects being examined; for Addams and the workers at Hull House, people were the experimenters (Gross, 2009).

Describing the *Hull House maps and papers,* the early collection of data published in 1895 that the Settlement workers used to document neighbourhood conditions and the need for reform, Deegan explains that:

> The use of these maps by female Chicago sociologists (at Hull House) was radically different from their subsequent 'scholarly' use by male sociologists (at the University of Chicago). On the one hand, the maps of the 'scholars' were intended to reveal to experts and decision-makers the lives of the people of the neighbourhood. On the other hand, the maps of Hull-House were intended to reveal to the people of the neighbourhood that their lifestyles had patterns and implications that they could use to make more informed decisions. These maps were part of the community and integral to the settlement's goals of democracy and education. (Deegan, 1990, 47)

The two perspectives differed not only with respect to the positionality of subjects but also in regard to the position of researchers. While the academic sociologists aspired to immutable conclusions that would transcend the specificities of place and time (and would simultaneously assure and preserve their status in the academic canon), Addams espoused the intention to become both invisible and unnecessary. "That was exactly what we wanted," she avowed, "– to be swallowed and digested, to disappear into the bulk of the people" (Addams, 1910 [1961], 203).[6] Addams, furthermore, explicitly rejected the academics' assumption of superior expertise and status relative to the subjects of their inquiries. Her experience at Hull House, she reported, had revealed that:

> The daintily clad charitable visitor who steps into the little house made untidy by the vigorous efforts of her hostess, the washerwoman, is no longer sure of her superiority to the latter... She is chagrined to discover that in the actual task of reducing her social scruples to action, her humble beneficiaries are far in advance of her, not in charity or singleness of purpose, but in self-sacrificing action. She reaches the old-time virtue of humility... because she has stumbled and fallen in the road through her efforts to... march with her fellows. (Addams, 1902 [2005], 20)

Finally, for the academic sociologists who viewed the city as a social laboratory, it was a small step to enlist Hull House as their window on the urban neighbourhoods to which they sought entry. This move Addams also rejected, saying "I have always objected to the phrase 'sociological laboratory' applied to us, because Settlements should be something much more human and spontaneous than such a phrase connotes" (Addams, 1910 [1961], 203). As Deegan reports,

> this 'colonization' of social settlements was a popular idea among male sociologists [but] was unacceptable ... to the women sociologists. The latter's resistance to analysing populations as 'specimens' was a fundamental divergence between the male and female sociologists ... It was the view of settlements as 'laboratories' which [they] rejected, believing that the needs of the people took precedence over the needs of researchers ... The women closed their sociological 'windows,' placing the needs of the community first. The view of people as 'objects' and not participants in social studies was rejected by them. (Deegan, 1990, 35–6).[7]

In contrast to the contentious relations between the urban sociologists and the Settlement workers, the close relationship between Addams, Dewey and his departmental colleague George Herbert Mead (Dewey's "closest friend" (Ryan, 1995, 79)) nourished the development of a pragmatist approach that transcended the dualisms between knowledge and action, idealism and realism, social theory and social reform (Bernstein, 1971).[8] In the view of some of the Chicago School sociologists, discovering fundamental scientific knowledge about the urban community was tantamount to finding solutions to its problems. Dewey and Mead, in contrast, rejected the supposition, central to the spectator theory of knowledge, that the individual and society are antecedent to their co-constitution in practice. They sought a more direct route from present experience to future betterment that avoided the retrospective detour of representing a world as it already was. In Mead's view, as quoted by his student Anselm Strauss, "intelligent activity does not seek to know the world but 'undertakes to tell us what we may expect to happen when we act in such and such a fashion'" (Strauss, 1964, xx). Knowledge, for the pragmatists, does not precede action but resides within it.

Mead spent his career trying to understand the development of shared meaning in society, highlighting the importance of intersubjective communication as the medium of social action (Mead, 1934 [2015]). Reflecting pragmatism's concern to understand meaning in its social context, Mead developed new analytical tools for understanding how meaning is created within the communicative co-production of individual and society, focusing on the deployment and interpretation of what he called 'significant symbols', comprising gestures, words, intonations and a shared understanding of intent that allow communication and foster the trust needed to underpin collective action (Faris, 1937; Misak, 2013; Strauss, 1964). This work exemplified a pragmatic approach to understanding society from the ground up, exploring "how humans create meaning in their everyday life and … how this meaning is created and carved out through interactions with others and by use of various symbols to communicate meaning" (Brinkmann, 2017, 106). The meaning created in turn shapes action and the further evolution of social communities, demonstrating the pragmatic connection between ideas and their consequences in a never-ending cycle of experience, experimentation and further interpretation (Blumer, 1969).

Transcending the dualism of *theoria* and *praxis* (Bernstein, 1971) has been a continuing theme in the pragmatic practice of social inquiry. Drawing on Aristotle's distinction between different kinds of knowledge and their associated implications for subjectivity and practice, Flyvbjerg (2001) distinguishes epistemic (*episteme*) and technical knowledge (*techne*) from practical wisdom, or *phronesis*. Rather than aspiring to the creation of abstract epistemic knowledge about society, phronetic inquiry seeks to "restore social science to its classical position as a practical, intellectual activity aimed at clarifying the problems, risks and possibilities we face as humans and societies, and … contributing to social and political praxis" (Flyvbjerg, 2001, 4). Echoing the central tenets of Deweyan pragmatism, phronetic social research is understood as a vocational craft that involves applying and testing ideas in the context of particular circumstances. In parallel with phronetic professions such as law, medicine, ministry, teaching and community organising, practitioners apply their knowledge on a case-by-case basis, working through the problematic situation to find a way forward that is sensitive to the diversity of values, interests and potential outcomes specific to the case.

Thus Flyvbjerg advocates case-study research in which inquirers look at particular situations and work with affected publics to understand what is going on and to highlight the moral and political imperatives involved. Rather than treating the case study as a window on to general processes that are valorised as being more important, as is common in social science, he advocates attention to the case on its own terms (see also Mitchell, 2002; Savage, 2010). Only through immersion in the particular case and its practices, interests and power relations can the collective community of inquirers gain the insight with which to illuminate the practical matters at hand. Rather than producing abstract (epistemic) knowledge, the goal of phronetic research is "not to develop theory, but to contribute to society's practical rationality in elucidating where we want to go, and what is desirable according to diverse sets of values and interests" (Flyvbjerg, 2001, 167).

Based on an intensive case study of a planning decision in Aalborg, Denmark, Flyvbjerg (1998, 2001, 60) developed a four-pronged approach to inquiry comprising the following questions: (1) Where are we going? (2) Is this desirable? (3) Who is gaining and losing from the status quo? and (4) What, if anything, should be done about it? (Lake, 2016). While he roots this approach in Bourdieu's attention to practice via the concept of the habitus, and in Foucault's reading of Nietzsche and the development of genealogy, Flyvbjerg could also call this pragmatic research. His phronetic social science is particularly alert to the importance of working with diverse publics, prioritising the value of public engagement in establishing the focus of research and endorsing, or otherwise, particular arguments or justifications of fact, value and truth. His phronetic research is "done in public for the public, sometimes to clarify, sometimes to intervene, sometimes to generate new perspectives, and always to serve as eyes and ears in our ongoing efforts at understanding the present and deliberating about the future" (Flyvbjerg, 2001, 166).

There is increasing evidence of similar pragmatic themes emerging in various areas of social science, such as political science, economics and public administration. James Bohman has made a particularly strong contribution in applying pragmatism to international relations and political theory, adopting and adapting Dewey's arguments about inquiry into problematic situations (Bohman, 1999a, 1999b, 2002). Bohman (2002) has advocated a multiperspectival approach that seeks to understand problematic situations from the ground up through direct engagement with the people affected, so that: "In the context of inquiry, critical social science treats social actors as knowledgeable social agents to which its claims are publicly addressed ... Social science research helps agents to see their circumstances differently, especially when mounting problems indicate that some change is practically necessary" (Bohman, 1999a, 475). In the field of public administration, Dieleman (2014) has applied the pragmatic principle of fallibilism to assist decision-makers to act in the absence of certainty, and she advocates the practice of pragmatic engagement as a means to democratise the administrative state. Drawing directly from Dewey and Addams, Shields (2003) advocates the method of collective intelligence developed via a community of inquiry as a model of participatory democracy in public administration.

A new body of research has sought to focus on the intersections between pragmatism and the insights of feminism and critical 'race' studies (Kautzer and Mendieta, 2009; Sullivan, 2009). There has been strong interest in the scholarship of W.E.B. Du Bois and Alain Locke (Fraser, 1998) and in creating space for women's voices in democratic debate (Collins, 2012). Several scholars have traced the close affinity between pragmatism and feminism reflected in a shared commitment to pluralism, anti-essentialism, the rejection of a universalising perspective and an insistent focus on the practices of the everyday (Hamington and Bardwell-Jones, 2012; Seigfried, 1996, 2002). Noting that "feminism incorporates what pragmatism initiates", Livingston (2001, 7) traces "an intellectual lineage that begins with William James and ends (for the time being) with Judith Butler". Seigfried discerns what she considers a feminist sensibility in pragmatism's commitments to metaphorical rather than deductive discourse, the experiential rather than universalising basis of theory, a focus on problematic situations rather than abstract formulations, a method of communal problem-solving rather than "rationally forced conclusions" and pragmatism's "valuing of inclusiveness and community over exaggerated claims of autonomy and detachment" (Seigfried, 1996, 32). Pragmatism and feminism both subscribe to the Deweyan idea that identity is not a given but an achievement (Dewey, 1920 [1957]; Bernstein, 1998), and both direct attention to uncovering the collective processes through which that achievement is accomplished.

Also in evidence are strong parallels and overlapping concerns between pragmatism and several intersecting strands of recent poststructuralist thought. Pragmatism (both classical and 'neo') articulated and anticipated several themes now at the centre of poststructuralist debate, including the abandonment of foundational thinking, an embrace of contingency and indeterminacy and attention to historicity, genealogy, process and practice in a world seen as emerging, unfolding and in flux, rather than already available for representation by a distanced or disinterested observer (Diggins, 1994). Both pragmatism and poststructuralism aim to avoid the perils of representation and highlight the performative power of ideas in producing the world, suggesting that research is potentially a tool for intervention rather than the disclosure of truth (Jones, 2008). Rorty's (1979 [2009]) pragmatist rejection of philosophy as the 'mirror of nature' was situated in Dewey's repudiation of the correspondence theory of truth and in what he (Rorty) termed the 'edifying philosophies' of Wittgenstein, Heidegger, Sellars and Quine. The shift from representation to enactment and a focus on "thought-in-action" (Anderson and Harrison, 2010, 9) characteristic of non-representational theory (NRT) in human geography owe an explicit debt to pragmatism's commitment to knowledge as certified in its consequences rather than in the accurate representation of an antecedent reality. Thrift's elucidation of NRT credits Peirce and Dewey for providing "pointers to subsequent work by … Deleuze, Castoriadis, and Joas, who … emphasise creativity (and) want to privilege the power of the imagination" (2008, 118–19).

In regard to Foucault's genealogical account of the ubiquity of power, Rorty famously asserted that "we should see Dewey as having already gone the route Foucault is traveling, and as having arrived at the point Foucault is still trying to reach" (Rorty, 1982, 207). When Latour (2005, 7) sought "to define the social not as a special domain, a specific realm, or a particular sort of thing, but only as a very peculiar movement of re-association and reassembling", he explicitly referenced Dewey's assertion, in *The public and its problems* (1927 [1954], 8), that "most concepts which are introduced by 'The,' (are) both too rigid and too tied up with controversies to be of ready use". Pragmatism's orientation to process, contingency and flux (Harney et al., 2016; Rogers, 2009) informed Latour's formulation of actor–network theory (ANT), in which "it all depends on the sort of action that is flowing from one to the other, hence the words 'net' and 'work' … It's the work, and the movement, and the flow, and the changes that should be stressed" (Latour, 2005, 143). The emphasis in ANT on interactions and relations (i.e. on the actor–network rather than on the isolated actors) reflects Dewey's claim that "[a] *distinctive* way of behaving in conjunction and *connection* with other distinctive ways of acting, not a self-enclosed way of acting, independent of everything else, is that toward which we are pointed" (1927 [1954], 188).[9]

Finally, pragmatism has been a growing influence in social science in France over the past twenty-five years. Scholars in what has been called 'the pragmatic sociology of critique' have sought to understand the forms and tenor of communication that develops in relation to disputed public concerns. This scholarship looks at the institutional, technical, legal and material supports deployed by people seeking justification for their particular views in relation to matters of (in)justice (Boltanski and Thévenot, 2006; Holden et al., 2013; Karsenti and Quéré, 2004). Like Dewey, this approach sees inquiry as arising in everyday life, as people contest decision-making and deploy various arguments to win others over to their point of view. Rather than using research to unmask power relations, as has been common in social-science research, or intervening to set up social inquiries as some pragmatists might suggest, the French pragmatists have developed "a framework for interpreting the actions of people as they argue with each other in the power-, and value-, and meaning-laden contexts that reproduce daily domination" (Holden et al., 2013, 4). Thus scholars have focused on the activities of what might be referred to as Dewey's publics and Mead's social interaction in order to understand 'the grammar of public disagreement' and its role in shaping a sense of the common good. They have highlighted the ways in which different forms of argumentation that include differentiated 'orders of worth' shape the outcomes of public debate. However, there is much less commitment to intervening in the trajectory of this debate than would be found in Dewey's or Rorty's approach. While the French scholarship highlights the importance of understanding the fraught emotional tenor of communication in the public realm, there is less of a sense in which social inquiry (or philosophy) can be a tool for telling new stories or a vehicle for engaging in public inquiry to find a way forward over a public concern. This approach has a less engaged focus without the pragmatic expectations that science and philosophy can – and should - contribute to the wider public good.

## The pragmatic approach to social research

The pragmatic approach to knowledge production represents a way of thinking that roots ideas in their geo-historical context, understands them in relation to their application and pays close attention to the collective communicative practices through which they are generated (Toulmin, 2001). Here we summarise what this means for the practice of doing pragmatic social research and point to some of the barriers to its implementation. We don't suggest that there is a pragmatic 'method' (Lake, 2014) but, rather, that we can develop a pragmatic orientation to inquiry and that this orientation, if taken seriously, has significant implications for the practice of academic scholarship and the kind of knowledge produced.

Relinquishing the certainty of foundational thinking poses sharp challenges for the practice of social inquiry. It is difficult to approach the task of research without *a priori* expectations based on experience and context, and it is all too easy to reinforce the circularity of existing thought. As Rorty put it in relation to philosophical research:

> To know what method to adopt, one must already have arrived at some metaphysical and some epistemological conclusions. If one attempts to defend these conclusions by the use of one's chosen method, one is open to the charge of circularity. If one does not so defend them, maintaining that given these conclusions, the need to adopt the chosen method follows, one is open to the charge that the chosen method is inadequate for it cannot be used to establish the crucial metaphysical and epistemological themes which are in dispute … every philosophical revolutionary is open to the charge of circularity or to the charge of having begged the question. (1967 [1992], 1–2)

Building on Dewey's approach to inquiry as collective experimentation, Rorty resolved this dilemma through a strong commitment to community and the rootedness of ideas in context rather than in 'reality' or 'truth'. He argued that "objectivity is not a matter of corresponding to objects but of getting together with other subjects" to identify concerns and work things out (Rorty, 1998b, 72). A pragmatic approach to research-in-community necessarily proceeds through a collective and collaborative process particular to specific social formations in time and space.

Thinking about the connection between social research and community offers at least two distinct avenues for delineating the community of inquiry within which one is engaged. On the one hand, it is possible to employ a prag-matist approach to examine how ideas are generated and mobilised within the community of academic scholarship. This is to treat one's academic community as the object of study, looking at the sources and implications of the practices being deployed and the ideas being produced. It is clear that one's choices of theoretical position, epistemological framework or research methodology pro-duce very different kinds of research 'data' and situate the researcher within particular camps with varying degrees of academic fashion and acceptability. Such choices, in turn, influence the chances of getting published, earning income and forging an academic career. Although chance events – having a good teacher, reading an exciting paper, having a prior personal interest or finding a fit between ideas and temperament – may influence one's trajectory, research practices are unavoidably constrained by the practical challenges of survival in the academic marketplace.

Under these conditions, the paradigm wars have a powerful effect in pro-pelling inquiry towards those *a priori* foundations prevalent within a particular epistemic community at a certain place and time. A pragmatist sensibility can help to deconstruct this process by tracing the genealogy of ideas at work within a given "disciplinary matrix" (Rorty, 1999, 178) as a first step in broad-ening the terms of inquiry and debate. The aim of such auto-critique is not to better align one's practices with prevailing norms of 'proper' research. Rather, as pragmatism is an idea about ideas and their role in social life, it is necessary to demonstrate that the adoption of a pragmatic orientation toward social inquiry produces useful outcomes for the kind of research that is done and the quality of the knowledge produced. In the phrase used by William James more than a hundred years ago, it is necessary to demonstrate pragmatism's 'cash value' to the community of inquirers and the institutionalised supports (funders, administrators, gatekeepers) that govern the practice of research. This is a mat-ter of changing ideas within our own community to attract a new generation of scholars to work outside the boundaries of conventional practice.

Second, and on the other hand, if pragmatism involves situated, collabora-tive engagement with a community of inquiry, then specifying the boundaries of the community is essential to the practice. For Jane Addams in Hull House, that community was her neighbours on Halstead Street in Chicago's West Side. For Dewey, the community of inquiry comprises the public that forms through recognition of a problematic situation. For Iris Marion Young (2000), the com-munity encompasses all those affected by any particular problem and associated deliberation. In all cases, establishing the boundaries of collaborative engage-ment is likely to involve interrelated questions of problem definition, geo-graphic scale and the absence of certainty in a contingent and mutable world.

Dewey has at times been criticised for a romantic attachment to face-to-face deliberation in the democratic community, but the challenge of geographic scale is inescapable within a relational ontology with no outside. Following the example of Addams and Hull House, pragmatists seek a lexicon of particularity by working with grounded publics in specific contexts to address local circumstances, conducting research that might speak to a wider audience but without guarantees. Experiments in university–community partnerships, for example, underway in several locations around the world, seek to develop methods of collaborative problem-solving based on mutual interests in teaching, research and civic activism within shared local spaces (Harney and Wills, 2017; Wills, 2016a, 2016b). In these instances, a strong pragmatist inclination to replace the distanced analytical gaze with a practice of neighbourly love (Zitcer and Lake, 2012) may encounter resistance from institutional pressures for visibility and presence. On the other hand, the practice of local specificity – of establishing boundaries around a local community of interest – instantiates the non-local as the 'other', thereby raising what Rorty (2010) describes as conflicting loyalties to particular groups. Rorty's solution is to use a collaborative agreement on a course of action as "the initial stage in expanding the circles of those whom each party to the agreement had previously taken to be 'people like ourselves'" so that "the opposition between rational argument and fellow-feeling thus begins to dissolve" (Rorty, 2010, 441). In every case, the establishment of spatial boundaries around the collaborative community is highly contingent, an initial foray rather than a conclusion and subject to continuing reassessment in light of the consequences of action under specific circumstances.

Working with (and within) a community of interest also requires deferral of the impulse to specify the scope and definition of the problematic situation in advance of the encounter. Here Nietzsche's frequently quoted aphorism is highly apropos: "Learning to see – habituating the eye to repose, to patience, to letting things come to it; learning to defer judgment, to investigate, to comprehend the individual case in all its aspects. This is the *first* preliminary schooling in spirituality" (Nietzsche, 1889 [1969], 6). The ability to bracket prior expectations in such a way, however, is counter-intuitive for academic researchers and runs counter to entrenched habits and established structures of knowledge production. Under conditions of 'normal science', being a social scientist assumes that there is an object of research, identified as social or intellectual 'problems' that can be formulated as research questions that sit outside, above or beyond any particular context. A would-be researcher applying for funding for a project must normally present a convincing 'problem statement', identify specific 'research questions' and detail a 'methodological approach', all in advance of initiating the inquiry. While researchers are rarely funded to forge relationships, pursue conversations and slowly develop a feeling for the issues affecting a community of inquiry, pragmatic research requires an investment in such relationships before any 'research' can begin.

And, finally, there remain the stubborn issues of contingency, fallibility and the futility of 'the quest for certainty' in delimiting the community of inquiry through the lens of pragmatism. The challenge of delimiting the community of inquiry is that all such delimitations are necessarily provisional and subject to change. In addition to the contingencies of problem definition and geographic scale is the provisionality of theoretical scaffolding and conceptual frameworks – the set of ideas used to frame a research project in advance of an inquiry. In an earlier period, terms such as 'class', 'capital', 'neoliberalism', 'the economy' or 'the state' were easily imported to guide analysis; more recently, work to map actor–networks or assemblages, efforts to prioritise embodied and emotional responses to the world or even the adoption of collaborative forms of research have all too easily been imposed on the world rather than responding to what a community brings to the inquiry. Despite the effort to avoid the quest for certainty and to produce knowledge that reflects local contingency, culture and the evolution of ideas in place, concepts such as the actor–network, affect or assemblage are moved from one place to another and used to frame analysis regardless of the particularities and contingencies of time and space, with a profound effect on the work that is done and the arguments made.

In many ways, little has changed since the early pragmatists denounced the prevailing correspondence model of knowledge production and its limits for understanding social life. As Dewey put it more than a hundred years ago: "The waste of energy due to conducting discussion of social affairs in terms of conceptual generalities is astonishing" (1920 [1957], 198). A pragmatic orientation to research provides no ontological certainty and no *a priori* commitment to a particular problem or set of problems or to work at a particular scale. It provides, instead, a justification for working within a particular community, however provisionally defined, to explore particular challenges as they are articulated by that community, and for allowing uncertainty to shape the production of thought. Such an approach, however, articulates an orientation to the project of knowledge production rather than a detailed set of research methodologies. In an essay titled 'Pragmatism without method', Rorty explicitly states that "[t]he advice to see if it might not pay to reweave your web of belief in the interests of a better ability to solve your problems is not the advice to formulate epistemic principles" (Rorty, 1991, 68). How, then, might pragmatist inquiry proceed?

At present, there is no clearly defined pragmatic 'method' of social inquiry, and, indeed, pragmatists have explicitly rejected the notion that pragmatism invokes a particular research method (Lake, 2014). In Rorty's view, as noted above, "The whole idea of ... choosing between 'methods'... seems to be misguided" (Rorty, 1982, 195), and Dewey, in *Reconstruction in philosophy* (1920 [1957], 72–3), held that "the release of philosophy from its burden of ... sterile epistemology ... would open a way to questions of the most perplexing and most significant sort". Nonetheless, a number of researchers have turned to Dewey's notion of 'inquiry' to develop a framework or approach for applying pragmatic ideas in the production of knowledge. In one such approach, David

Morgan (2014, 1047) has proposed a five-step 'model' for conducting pragmatic social inquiry that proceeds by: (1) recognising a situation as problematic; (2) considering the consequences of defining the problem one way or another; (3) developing a possible line of action as a response to the problem; (4) evaluating the potential actions in terms of their likely consequences; and (5) taking actions that are felt to be likely to address the problematic situation.

As suggested above, however, adopting the language of 'problems' requires caution in the practice of research. It easily links the social sciences – and the academy – to the project of technocratic expertise and problem-solving and neglects the extent to which social life involves so much more than 'problems' as they may be framed in conventional understandings of social problems and public policy. It also limits the scope for applying pragmatism to the broader contribution that can be made by thinking about ideas and their consequences, and the importance of the diversity of cultural practices for making meaning in the world. As Wolfe (2017, 126) recently put it in relation to the task of building solidarity across racial differences, there are dangers in assuming that "'problem-solving' accounts for enough of our doings to render all public-formation as primarily problem-solving activity". As Peirce recognised too, there is much of value in what he called 'conservative sentimentalism', by which he meant the beliefs that underpin our largely unthinking habits of love, loyalty and care that matter most in crafting a life well lived. A pragmatist method of inquiry, there-fore, seeks to identify social practices to be preserved as well as those to be altered; to identify beneficial practices that are vulnerable to eradication as well as practices that are normalised or naturalised that produce damaging effects; and, in every case, to identify social practices that advance the objectives of the community of inquiry.

Near the conclusion of *Reconstruction in philosophy,* Dewey offers several guidelines for inquiry conducive to his pragmatist ideal. "Inquiry is exacted," he says,

> [in] observation of the detailed makeup of the situation; analysis into its diverse factors; clarification of what is obscure; discounting of the more insistent and vivid traits; tracing the consequences of the various modes of action that suggest them-selves; regarding the decisions reached as hypothetical and tentative until the anticipated or supposed consequences which led to its adoption have been squared with actual consequences. This inquiry is intelligence. (Dewey, 1920 [1957], 94)

On this account, a pragmatic orientation to social inquiry might involve some of the following:

1 *Working with a particular community (at an indeterminate scale) in which it is possi-ble to understand the geo-historical context of the actors, institutions and cultures and appreciate the public debate and conversation that is already underway.* The com-munity is one in which the researcher is already embedded or can become

so to establish equal standing with other participants in the inquiry (Harney et al., 2016; Wills, 2016b).

2    *Listening to the diversity of truths that exist in the community in relation to the range of issues discussed.* Here Nietzsche's invocation to "habituating the eye to repose … to comprehend the individual case in all its aspects" is necessary to develop a feel for where people are coming from and the work their ideas are doing for them and their identified community. This situational awareness is what we do every day in safely navigating the world around us. Being pragmatic, however, requires a heightened sensitivity to the diversity of perspectives and the range of opinion that exists, even and perhaps especially to those that are not our own and with which we might otherwise not be attuned. This is similar to what anthropologists seek to do in 'thick description' (Geertz, 1973), but pragmatism explicitly focuses attention on the range of truths being articulated and their consequences for the community in question.

3    *If invited through conversations or relationships, to begin exploring the possibility of working on an issue identified as a matter of concern by the participants in the inquiry.* As distinct from conventional practices of induction or deduction, pragmatic research is associated with what has been called 'abduction', which "begins with a breakdown in our understanding of something and is oriented toward making the indeterminate more determinate in order to facilitate action" (Brinkmann, 2017, 91). For Peirce, this process started with doubt, and for Dewey, inquiry was triggered by encountering what he called 'forked-road situations' (Brinkmann, 2017, 100). In both cases, these are instances when it is not clear how to proceed, and research is needed to elucidate a range of options for action. As we already expect from a public inquiry or commission into a knotty public concern, evidence can be gathered, position statements collected and the commissioners advocate a particular course of action to address the problem at hand. Pragmatists advocate a similar role for social inquiry free of the conceptual, institutional and political constraints of conventional practice. This approach seeks to work within the traditions, norms, perspectives and values of the community, bracketing prior moral and political judgements about what is at stake, what is happening and what constitutes an appropriate course of action. In Dewey's words: "The evils in current social judgements of ends and policies arise … from importations of judgements of value from outside the inquiry. The evils spring from the fact that the values employed are not determined in and by the process of inquiry; for it is assumed that certain ends have an inherent value so unquestionable that they regulate and validate the means employed, instead of ends being determined on the basis of existing conditions as obstacles-resources" (Dewey, 1938 [1939], 503). Transcending the conventional dualism of ends and means, hypotheses regarding an appropriate course of action arise within the process of inquiry, in the context of the particular community involved, rather than being imposed from outside (Lake, 2016, 2017).

4    *Once an issue is identified in this way, engaging in some sort of inquiry through methods appropriate to the case.* Those methods might incorporate Morgan's five steps, as outlined above, but this is not a formula to be imposed without reference to the specificity and contingency of the case. First, the inquiry will need support in relation to its particular public(s), especially if it aims to facilitate the development of a solution through which to 'move on' over this issue. This is likely to be both more complicated but also more successful if the diversity and multiplicity of interests is included within the inquiry. Dewey recognised that administrators and managers tend to assume what the problem is and get on with trying to respond to it, often with little success. He argued that social inquiry could provide an opportunity to think more carefully about the "nature of the problem by means of methods that procure a wide range of data, that determine their pertinency as evidential, that ensure their accuracy by devices of measurement, and that arrange them in the order which past inquiry has shown most likely to indicate appropriate methods of procedure ... The futility of attempting to solve a problem whose conditions have not been determined is taken for granted" (Dewey, 1938 [1939], 494). In this model, inquiry is guided by the problematic situation and the need to resolve the problem at hand. Having a goal allows the inquiry to develop hypotheses about the possible outcome of different solutions that can then be tested.

Once an inquiry has developed a range of hypotheses for action, these can be tested in practice. As Dewey put it: "That which is observed, no matter how carefully and no matter how accurate the record, is capable of being *understood* only in terms of projected consequences of activities" (Dewey, 1938 [1939], 499, emphasis in the original). Dewey recognised the particular challenges of deciding what kind of data would be required, and how to acquire it, in the process of social inquiry. He aspired to such methods producing hypotheses that could be tested to resolve a problematic situation and, in so doing, to treat the development and application of ideas as experimental, always subject to future revision and improvement. He called this the "continuum of inquiry" that seeks "the determination of an indeterminate situation" (Dewey, 1938 [1939], iii). Given the importance of context and contingency in the generation of problematic situations and their potential solutions, there will never be an end to this process.

5    *Thus there is an imperative to continue the process in ongoing dialogue with the community and its interests.* If all universities had relationships with their local communities, this process of shared learning would be ongoing everywhere in the world. Researchers would exchange ideas and find common ground across space without presuming that the insights from one place can be simply applied in another. This would involve a new geography of social-research practice and new forms of locally sensitive internationalism.

The implications of pragmatism for the conduct of social research are profound. Pragmatic social inquiry incorporates the full gamut of relationship building, embedded engagement, public work and social organisation as integral elements of the research process. In sum, pragmatism is a clarion call to connect research to community. Its approach to understanding ideas and their consequences, in the context of a democratic ethos that seeks to foster inclusion, requires some kind of community through which to develop, test and consider ideas. As Bernstein (1989, 18) put it, pragmatism makes "the call to nurture the type of community and solidarity where there is an engaged fallibilistic pluralism – one that is based upon mutual respect, where we are willing to risk our own prejudgements, are open to listening and learning from others, and we respond to others with responsiveness and responsibility".

In an ideal world, our universities would nurture such communities around various interested publics, through which we could then conduct social research to foster reciprocal gain. However, all too often, our universities are poorly grounded in community. Encounters are imbalanced and self-interested, and the priority has been the international reputation of the institution and its scholars rather than investing in place. Academic institutions need to be encouraged to prioritise and support embedded relationship-building to underpin a pragmatic approach to social research. This would mean having research funders and academic journals that support pragmatic research. It would require recognition that the 'output' of pragmatic inquiry includes a range of activities, experiences and publications, with a more limited role for conventional academic publications that might materialise only when there is something of wider significance to report, such as a reflection on the ideas that circulate in the community and the work they are doing for people; or the creation of a new idea that has allowed some sort of resolution, however temporary, to a particular concern; or in relation to the impact of pragmatism on the process and outcomes of doing the work. Taking pragmatism seriously requires a commitment to particularity, to the illumination that comes from patient investment in relationships and to the sometimes small things that often matter the most.

## The potential pitfalls and limits to pragmatic research

The practice of engaged, pragmatic inquiry as described above faces substantial challenges, many of which have fuelled critiques of pragmatism since its inception. Here we consider, in particular, the pitfalls of expertise, the problem of meliorism and pragmatism's relation to progressive ideas.

The challenge of 'the epistemic division of labour' in society is a particular problem for pragmatic research and inquiry, not least because of the persistent Platonic divisions between thinking and doing that pragmatism has sought to overcome (Arendt, 1958, 1971; Bernstein, 1971). Dewey was acutely cognisant of this challenge, arguing in *The public and its problems* (1927 [1954], 364) that "[a] class of experts is inevitably so removed from common interests as to become a class with private interests and private knowledge, which in social matters is not knowledge at all." A few years earlier, in *Reconstruction in philosophy,* he observed that the specialisation of experts "can be trusted only when such persons are in unobstructed cooperation with other social occupations, sensitive to others' problems and transmitting results to them for wider applications in action. When this social relationship of persons particularly engaged in carrying on the enterprise of knowing is forgotten and the class becomes isolated, inquiry loses stimulus and purpose" (Dewey, 1920 [1957], 147). This dilemma has not only persisted but deepened with the ever-increasing technological complexity of contemporary problems. Drawing on the example of AIDS activists who organised to challenge the exclusivity of the medical establishment over information and research, Bohman (1999b) highlights the benefits of greater popular scrutiny of expertise, saying that "[c]hallenges by the public to expert credibility or to expert definitions of the epistemic enterprise do more than make experts accountable; they make the knowledge so gained genuinely social and shared, even if differentially distributed" (Bohman, 1999b, 602). While the rise of the internet and greater opportunities for civic engagement in political decision-making are providing ways to break down these divisions, universities, think tanks and the professions continue to champion elite-led models of problem-solving that serve to exclude a wider range of voices. The pragmatic orientation to research needs to work especially hard to break down these divisions, and, as outlined above, this can only be done through careful relationship-building over time.

Pragmatism has been frequently criticised for its meliorism and moderation. Pragmatists seek to appreciate the range of ideas in circulation at any one time, if there is to be some sort of inquiry over a pressing concern, pragmatic inquiry has to find some common ground, however provisionally, on which everyone in that community can stand. For some of its critics, this understates the need to take sides in the struggle for justice (Mills, 1943 [1964]; Mouffe, 1996; Mumford, 1926). All too often, the minority group are expected to sacrifice their interests for the wider public good, and there is always a danger that the common good can trump alternative ideas of the just (Allen, 2006). Brandom cites the example of democracy squeezing human rights in the North's response to the South after the American Civil War, whereby people of colour paid – and still pay – a great price. In Brandom's words: "We still have a lot of thinking to do about what is living and what is dead in pragmatism – both in philosophical theory and in political practice" (Brandom, 2009, 44–5).

C. Wright Mills also queried the extent to which pragmatic thinking can be applied to the dominant social formations in long-established and relatively institutionalised societies. He argued that the idea of inquiry could be most easily applied to social groups that are socially mobile and finding their way in the world. For Mills (1943 [1964]), pragmatism was less relevant for action associated with organised political parties, social movements and labour unions. He argued that pragmatism works for people "on the edge of social structures, such as frontier types of society that are edging out into places not hampered by social organization. It is predominantly outside the rationalized structures in which the actions of individuals face decisions, and almost by definition, decisions involving new factors that have come into the actor's horizon and path" (1943 [1964], 393). Writing in the middle years of the twentieth century, at the historic peak of the labour movement, Mills understandably emphasised the importance of mass movements and their struggle for power. This is much less pertinent today, and the break-up of strong workers' organisations has exposed the contingency of class experience and the necessity to act in non-standard ways, as required in context (Wills, 2008). However, he is right to highlight the importance of scrutinising the often taken-for-granted vested interests associated with established power relations, and pragmatic research needs to be rigorous about facing dominant power.

Interestingly, pragmatism has also been criticised from the perspective of conservative thought for its apparent affinity with the idea of 'progress' (Cahoone, 2002; Cavell, 1998; Lasch, 1991, 1995). Even though pragmatism seeks to understand ideas in relation to their consequences, which can be about maintaining established ways of life as much as anything else, this conservatism has often been lost in the application of pragmatism to wider debate. As we have seen, the use of pragmatism in relation to problem-solving through inquiry tends to imply activism, collective advance and even social cohesion around the process and the emergent ideas. Given that inquiry is argued to be triggered by experience which prompts doubt, uncertainty and inaction, the pragmatic approach tends to exclude an appreciation of established culture and practice.

Dewey, Rorty and others deployed pragmatism to make a contribution to the liberal and progressive political traditions of their times. In his related argument for 'prophetic pragmatism', Cornel West similarly endorsed the connection between the tradition and the need to foster a sense of collective hope for the future. He wrote that pragmatism "consists of a future-oriented instrumentalism that tries to deploy thought as a weapon to enable more effective action. Its basic impulse is a plebeian radicalism that fuels an anti-patrician rebelliousness for the moral aim of enriching individuals and expanding democracy" (West, 1989, 5). For some, this future-oriented approach smacks of utopian wishful thinking and is insufficiently realistic or sceptical about the notion of progress (Gray, 2007; Niebuhr, 1932, 1944). Stanley Cavell (1998) argued that we can understand Dewey pragmatically and that, like Rorty, he was making an intervention to create the world he wanted to see. Cavell argued that Dewey was making "a wager on democracy, a wager that is rational not because of the weight of evidence that his writing will prove effective, but because it is worthy of being listened to; because there is some reason to believe that it will be listened to; and because there is no other future worth wagering on and working to achieve" (Cavell, 1998, 79). As such, pragmatism comprises a political and performative argument as much as a philosophical or epistemological one, as recognised by many pragmatists who have defended Dewey's democratic position (Bernstein, 2010; Putnam, 1992; Rorty, 1989; Westbrook, 1991, 1998).

For critics like Diggins (1998) and Fish (1998), however, the goals of democracy often require forms of enforcement that are alien to the model of democracy advocated by Dewey and other pragmatists. As Fish suggests: "provisionality, openness, and toleration are not what the mechanisms of democracy generate, but what they enforce against the inclinations of citizens who remain as dogmatic, closed minded and bigoted as they were before democracy emerged" (Fish, 1998, 426). Rather than suggesting that democracy arises from the human spirit, Fish suggests that it arises only through Hobbesian forms of enforcement that suppress the sin of the people. While he is willing to accept the broad thrust of pragmatic thinking when it comes to the role of ideas and their connection to practice, he rejects any necessary association with democracy, public-formation and social improvement.

Thus there is nothing inherent in pragmatism to endorse a progressive approach, and pragmatism can be used to challenge ideologies of both the left and the right. Indeed, in his introduction to a later edition of *Reconstruction of philosophy*, Dewey sought to distance himself from any necessary association with reformers and progressives, arguing that his approach embraced the range of ideas generated in human society and declaring that while "[i]n a verbal sense reform and reconstruction are close together ... the reconstruction or reform here presented is strictly one of theory of the type that is so comprehensive in scope as to constitute philosophy" (Dewey, 1920 [1957], xli). Rorty spent much of his time exposing the limits of thought on the left and the need for a new form of patriotism that could appeal across society rather than being a point of polarisation (1998a).

A hundred years earlier, Peirce had pointed out that many beliefs and habituated practices do not need to be challenged, as they work perfectly well in getting things done. He self-identified as a 'conservative sentimentalist' while also highlighting the struggle involved in rethinking established ideas when they are no longer useful in making sense of the world. For Peirce, there was a time and place for rethinking ideas, and for making some sort of 'progress' in thinking, although this was about understanding the world and reflecting on the joy of human capacity to think as much as it was about material progress. As Cahoone (2002, 288) notes, "society is not a community of inquirers", and, most of the time, people live together despite their differences without needing to unpack their ideas. We need to think carefully about the time and place for pragmatic inquiry and the grounds on which interventions are made, and, in many cases, it may be best to listen and do nothing rather than rushing to act.

**The power of pragmatism: An introduction to the rest of the book**

In this introduction, we have sought to outline some of the key facets of pragmatism and to present an outline of what it means for social inquiry and knowledge production. At present, we see only glimmers of what pragmatic social research might look like, and the chapters that follow seek to advance that project. Divided into four further parts, the book begins with a section entitled 'Key thinkers, core ideas and their application to social research'. It then moves on to focus on the ways in which pragmatism inflects our understanding of university life, altering the ways in which we think about the academic community and its work. The four chapters in this middle section are grouped under the title '"Truth", epistemic injustice and academic practice'. The final group of four chapters then look at the significance of pragmatic approaches to knowledge production in relation to the ecological crisis, planning and development. Having set out the history of pragmatism and outlined some of the implications of this tradition for social science in this introduction, the following chapters spell out some of pragmatism's key ideas and their application in much more detail. We draw everything together in the final part of the book with a conclusion as well as a postscript written by Clive Barnett, a leading exponent of pragmatic ideas in social theory today.

The opening section includes four chapters that draw on the work of particular pragmatic philosophers, focus on one or more of their core ideas and explore the application of these ideas in social research. These include John Dewey's conceptualisation of 'habit' (Cutchin, Chapter 2) as well as his ideas about the situated nature of 'transaction' (Bridge, Chapter 3), George Herbert Mead's understanding of the 'social self' and its implications for understanding action (Fuller, Chapter 4) and Richard Rorty's advocacy of 're-description' as a way to advance new conversations in the process of changing the world (Barnes, Chapter 5). These chapters provide a powerful exploration of some of the ideas already developed within pragmatism and the as yet largely untapped application of these ideas.

Malcolm Cutchin's chapter provides a good introduction to the value of pragmatism for social scientists, not least because he starts by outlining the history of his own engagement with this tradition of thought as a graduate student. Cutchin then focuses on the Deweyan concept of 'habit' in order to emphasise the importance of entrenched habits of thought and action that necessarily limit and constrain the way that we think and act. As he suggests, "[a]s individuals co-develop … they unconsciously internalize predispositions (habits) inherent to intersecting places, cultures, and landscapes that in turn guide our thoughts, values and behaviours." Cutchin then explores Dewey's ideas about 'social inquiry' as a way to reconfigure such habituated ways of thinking and acting. By working with other people to respond to a problematic situation, identifying new ideas for action, it becomes possible to reconfigure deeply held ideas and expectations about what is possible, eventually remaking our habits. Cutchin's understanding of this process as being rooted in particular relationships in time and space sets up the rest of the book; this is a thread that runs through every chapter that follows. Cutchin provides the foundations, too, for understanding the way in which social inquiry can shift habit through developing new ideas that presage new ways of acting together (in what he calls 'social reconstruction'). In so doing, Cutchin ends his chapter by arguing for new kinds of research practice, elaborated in later parts of the book, particularly in the four chapters comprising Part III, which focus on the conditions in which ideas are produced.

Gary Bridge's chapter explores John Dewey's approach to the importance of time and space in the evolution of society. He alerts us to pragmatism's debt to Darwin and the ways in which Dewey adapted evolutionary analysis in order to understand the co-constitution of life, including human beings alongside our co-present others. Bridge focuses on Dewey's ideas about what he called the 'situation' and highlights the resonance of these ideas with contemporary debates about the need to fully appreciate the vitalism of the planet (ideas taken up later in the book in the chapters by Meg Holden and Owain Jones in Chapters 10 and 11 respectively). Bridge's chapter explores the idea of the 'problematic situation' that can trigger social inquiry and the potential recalibration of habits, as introduced in Cutchin's chapter. However, Bridge problematises the idea of the situation, developing a framework that can combine contemporary arguments about the importance of language and forms of rationality (that may translate across distances of time and space) along with his appreciation of vitalism. This chapter provides a thick account of what Dewey was trying to capture in his argument about problematic situations being a trigger to social inquiry, new conversations and action. Bridge highlights the scalar complexity of this argument and raises the challenges of using it as some sort of framework for academic scholarship. At the end of his contribution, he briefly explores the work of the Chicago School of Sociologists and the Hull House Settlement to illustrate the different ways in which time and place mediate the possibilities of every situation, shaping the divergent ways in which inquiry can develop.

The other two chapters in this opening section, by Christian Fuller and Trevor Barnes, look at the political insights generated by the particular pragmatic ideas they explore. Fuller's chapter picks up the theme of 'situation' by looking at the importance of social interaction (in various situations) for subjectivity, shared understanding and social change. He draws on the work of George Herbert Mead, outlining his analysis of the 'I' and 'me' of subjectivity and its implications for understanding urban politics today. In contrast to theoretically driven analysis that focuses on macro-economic processes, such as neoliberalism, or declares the advent of the 'post-political' city, Fuller uses Mead's approach to explore the particular decision-making of local politicians involved in the West Midlands Combined Authority, in the UK. He uses interview data to highlight the ways in which people justify their behaviour in relation to other people and their social situation; the 'I' of personal identity also comprises the 'me' that reflects wider social norms and expectations, and the two work in tandem. In this case, Mead's ideas help to explain why politicians are reluctant to challenge dominant narratives, and while other academics have explained this as being an example of the 'post-political', or 'post-democratic', Fuller develops an explanation based on a pragmatic analysis of political rationality, motivation and agency. He argues that people make decisions in particular contexts, or situations, in which the wider social community plays a key role in shaping understanding and analysis of the room for manoeuvre. In this vein of thinking, political behaviour can be explained in relation to the particular context rather than through the propositions developed in particular versions of theory that are then applied, regardless of context.

Trevor Barnes then turns to Richard Rorty's ideas about 'conversational philosophy' and the practice of 're-description' as a means to change the way people think and act in the world. Rather than being narrowly focused on 'social inquiry' as a response to 'problematic situations', as advocated by the early pragmatists, Rorty sought to work on a much bigger canvas, to change the national (and international) conversation through intervening in the terms and emotional dynamics of public debate. Rorty treated society as something akin to Dewey's problematic situation, arguing that creative new thinking, language and narratives were needed in order to mobilise and reorient the people. As such, there is an important public role for intellectuals, to work with their community through the arts of cultural politics, to create new stories that facilitate new ways of being. Barnes uses the maps produced by the geographer Bill Bunge (1928–2013) to illustrate this argument. The maps were Bunge's way of changing the conversation and trying to shift the story and the trajectory of life after the maps.

As it happens, the second set of maps, representing data collected through community-based research in the city of Detroit during the 1970s, were the product of social inquiry as advocated by Dewey. Bunge worked with a local community organisation in an area called Fitzgerald to organise students and residents to document the problematic situations encountered. The maps were a powerful means of facilitating new conversations and interventions to respond to local concerns such as rat-infested homes and deaths by dangerous driving. By deploying cartography as a weapon of 'truth', new worlds were seen and action facilitated. Bunge's later maps, designed to intervene in international debate about the dangers of nuclear weaponry, were based on his own analysis and efforts to re-describe the issues at stake. However, Bunge was still acting as part of a wider community of concern, responding to the existential threat of nuclear holocaust in dialogue with others. As Rorty himself suggested, we are always part of particular communities through which thought and action take place, and, as such, forms of inquiry into problematic situations can take place at a variety of spatial scales, deploying a range of media as weapons for change, as Barnes shows so well in this case.

If, as pragmatists, we seek to understand the power of habit, and recognise the difficulty of changing entrenched ways of thinking and acting (as outlined in Cutchin's chapter), we need to think carefully about what we are doing as academics: how we work, who we work with and the kinds of knowledge produced. As all our authors suggest, this means working in relationship with a wider community to both recognise the powerful influences shaping how we think (our 'habits' and Mead's distinction between the 'me, I and we', as elucidated by Fuller) and the collective challenges of finding a new language to re-describe and rethink the world and possible action. For Bridge (and for Owain Jones, in Chapter 11), this new language needs to recognise the plurality of agency to include the more-than-human, and to find ways of thinking and acting that include the wider ecosystem on which all life depends. As Barnes suggests, it also needs to engage a variety of creative interventions that re-describe the world, and these need to stretch beyond words.

The four chapters in the next section of the book, '"Truth", epistemic injustice and academic practice', all grapple with the implications of the pragmatic perspective for knowledge production. These chapters ask us to think about the truths we are producing, how we are producing them, whose interests are being represented and what they are seeking to do. The authors prompt us to query our own academic communities, the partnerships through which we work, the way we conduct research and the impact we have.

This section starts with a powerful chapter from Susan Saegert that focuses on the need to ensure that our academic communities are sufficiently inclusive to make sense of the world, and the dangers of epistemic injustice being experienced by those who are not recognised or heard in the pursuit of ideas. The chapter concentrates on the potential exclusions associated with 'race', but the lessons apply more widely as well. For Saegart, the pragmatic recognition of grounded and divergent 'truths' makes it imperative to think about the diversity of the academic communities in which we work. Despite being a 'community of inquirers', academic departments are not automatically open to everyone, nor do they do justice to all of their members. Saegart takes an honest look at these challenges and draws on the pragmatic tradition to find resources to promote greater democracy in her academic community and beyond. She explores the Deweyan democratic ideal in the light of ongoing injustice and seeks to chart a pragmatic route to shared inquiry, new ideas and action. Moreover, she argues that "the pragmatic tradition is in need of some enriching from the works of scholars of colour and in light of intersectionality", and the chapter provides important resources for doing this work.

The following contribution, by Klaus Geiselhart, extends this work to think more broadly about the situated 'truths' produced by social scientists and the basis on which we can make claims for them. Geiselhart goes back to

Dewey's understanding of social inquiry, and the formation of publics around problematic situations, in order to advocate that academics become better connected to a wider community that seeks truth for particular ends. As he puts it: "It is possible to make a distinction between well-founded and less well-founded theories by distinguishing between theories that are more or less useful." This pragmatic view of ideas, that judges their value in relation to their consequences, can be further augmented by academic efforts at public mediation in order to find mutual ground for new forms of action. Geiselhart argues that the academic should be considered as a mediator between situations and scholarship, finding truth through grounded encounters and the production of situated knowledge, rather than taking an *a priori* stance as critic, exposing the interests that operate 'behind' the backs of the people. Indeed, he calls on pragmatic academics to do more than echo wider concerns about fake news and 'post-truth', or to celebrate agonistic divisions and public critique, arguing that it is important to develop the arts of evaluation and judgement in relation to ideas and their context, a process he calls 'mediation' (see also Barnett, 2017, Chapter 15, this volume). As he puts it: "If academics situate their work as an intermediary between different social positions, they are no longer agents of (self-appointed) truth, opponents of hegemony, or proponents of specific academic discourses, but agents of mediation."

Geiselhart's bold intervention into debates about 'post-truth' and 'alternative facts' is particularly challenging for pragmatists, who have long pioneered a social-constructionist view of the world. However, he demonstrates that this doesn't mean that 'anything goes', and by rooting research and knowledge production in community, it is possible to highlight the diversity of truths that reflect the particular situation in hand. This role of academic as mediator is further illustrated in Chapter 8, where Alice Huff demonstrates the value of pragmatic research methods for understanding the social and political relationships shaping an existing community group in central Los Angeles. Having immersed herself in the conversations and relationships of the group, she illustrates the ways in which ideas develop in dialogue with people in context. She uses a pragmatic sensibility to reveal the delicate nature of human communities, the complicated development of ideas and the ways in which they change in response to experience (further illustrating Bridge's arguments about 'the situation'). In so doing, Huff is able to tell a very different story from those often reported in academic research. In contrast to the scholarship of Chantal Mouffe (2005, 2013), for example, who has argued for a perspective that prioritises agonistic conflict as the driver of change in democratic societies, Huff tells a more complicated and nuanced story about the nature of social organisation and change. Echoing Geiselhart's arguments about the potential power of the academic as mediator, she is able to see the complexities of the social dynamics involved in a way that would be masked by adopting *a priori* a preference for conflict and its attendant normative assumptions about what good politics looks like.

The chapter that follows, by Liam Harney and Jane Wills, takes this focus on community a step further by documenting their efforts to construct communities for the purposes of conducting pragmatic social research. Rather than studying or working with existing groups, as has been suggested in most forms of participatory action research, and as is described by Huff in her chapter, Harney and Wills describe the process of working with members of the local community living in a small part of east London as the starting point for collective inquiry. In the first phase of their project, the research involved people sharing stories about their own experiences and perspectives of the local area. In the second phase, the aim was to find problematic situations around which to share experiences, develop new ideas and take action for change. Taking a pragmatic sensibility towards the grounded nature of truth and its implications for action, the project sought to apply Dewey's ideas about the process of social inquiry to generate new ways of thinking and acting. In so doing, however, they exposed unspoken differences in the group that reflected cleavages in the wider society (echoing the challenges raised in Saegert's chapter, albeit in a very different context) and they also identified major barriers in realising change (not unlike the situation described by Huff in Los Angeles).

Harney and Wills develop an argument for a two-pronged approach to pragmatic research and knowledge production. The first prong focuses on the Deweyan approach to inquiry, in which people engage in research, thought and action around their concerns without prior assumptions about what those concerns would or should be. It is from this that we can understand the grounded truths that coexist in any society and their necessary connection to both experience and action. The second, however, involves a more Rortyan focus on changing the wider conversation in order to protect the social infrastructure on which our community and its very capacity for thought and action (and, indeed, democracy) depend. The east London experiment exposed the weakness of local social relationships and the depth of divisions between people. Without a national conversation to reflect and attend to these difficulties, it will prove difficult to sustain the democratic community to which people belong. As such, pragmatic knowledge production needs to be part of a wider narrative that supports a democratic community, working to undermine socio-political polarisation and political alienation.

The data and resources generated from the first type of action are needed to help create the stories that comprise the second, and both could work together to sustain the particular communities in which human beings can flourish. While Rorty himself made this case very powerfully, ahead of his time, in *Achieving our country: Leftist thought in twentieth-century America* (1998a), the argument is not necessarily attached to the 'left' and has as much to say in relation to conservatism as it does to progressive reform. Harney and Wills end their chapter by making this point in relation to both academia and the wider society in the UK.

The fourth section of the book, entitled 'Disciplinary applications in pragmatic research', is focused on the application of pragmatic thought and sensibility to particular research areas. The first two chapters, by Meg Holden and Owain Jones, explore the development of pragmatic responses to the ecological crisis; Ihnji Jon then considers pragmatic approaches to planning; and, in the final substantive chapter, Alireza Farahani and Azadeh Hadizadeh Esfahani look at the implications of pragmatism for development studies. Although speaking to different areas of scholarship, the overlaps between these chapters further illustrate the wider implications of pragmatism for research and knowledge production, providing concrete examples of some of the more abstract arguments made earlier in the book. In particular, these chapters highlight the ways in which pragmatism provides a mode of thinking, feeling and doing that can be applied to all areas of scholarship and inquiry. In every case, our authors advocate a pragmatic sensibility that means avoiding abstract generalisation in favour of rooting scholarship and inquiry in the particular situation, paying attention to the community in which publics are mobilised around a question or issue, listening to the diversity of opinion and mediating over the common good. They argue that this makes for more productive ways to respond to the ecological crisis and ensure good development practice and planning, but the same arguments can be more widely applied.

In her chapter, Meg Holden draws on the work of Hannah Arendt as well as the resources of the pragmatic tradition to develop a more adequate response to the ecological crisis today. Rather than embracing post-humanism, as many others have done, Holden advocates a more robust but pragmatic form of humanism. In so doing, she identifies a number of propositions that echo the arguments made in the rest of the book. In sum, she highlights the importance of the situation (see, in particular, Bridge, Chapter 3, this volume) and the institutions through which we organise and make decisions, as well as the need to engage a wider community in finding solutions to collective or public concerns. For Holden, this involves encouraging people to "dream, tell stories and imagine a different kind of future" as part of public debate.

Owain Jones then picks up on these arguments, highlighting the open, creative and experimental aspects of pragmatic thought that advocate the development of situated, co-created interventions that work with nature for positive change. Recognising the parallels with recent theoretical debate about non-representational theory (NRT), Jones argues that there is a danger such approaches neglect the importance of action; and, in contrast, pragmatism puts the need to act centre stage. Arguing that new ideas emerge through the drive to get something done, Jones advocates scholarship that focuses on action and doing rather than the misguided task of representation. Indeed, he goes beyond NRT to advocate for the development of anti-representational theory (ART), emphasising the value of engaging in community-based creative interventions in order to develop new ideas for action. For Jones, this means "you ask questions and you try things", just as Dewey advocated in his understanding of inquiry and Rorty in his notion of 're-description' (see also Barnes, Chapter 5).

These arguments are further illuminated in the final chapters of the book. In Chapter 12, Ihnji Jon outlines a pragmatic approach to planning theory and practice that embraces the insights of the dominant theories in the field. Her approach incorporates both communication and the potential for conflict, while locating policy and practice in what she calls 'the plurality of the social' and the need to recognise difference in democratic societies. Rather than opposing the role of communication and celebrating the inevitability of conflict, as is common in debate in this field, Jon argues that both comprise necessary aspects of the process of planning. Her use of pragmatism advances the field beyond its current impasse, and a similar contribution to development studies is made in the following chapter, where Alireza Farahani and Azadeh Esfahani chart a path beyond established and dominant discourses for and against development to reorient debate around a more pragmatic approach. Drawing on their experience in Iran, they argue that pragmatism can "transform [the] quest for transcendental, a-temporal and placeless models and frameworks towards socially-oriented, contingent, and community-based knowledgeability".

In sum, *The power of pragmatism* contains strong messages about the implications of pragmatism for social-science research practice and knowledge production. We highlight these broad implications in the conclusion to the book, in which we offer pragmatism as an orientation that skirts the twin challenges of rationalism and sentimentality. In the short postscript, Clive Barnett looks ahead to the ways in which the pressing concerns raised by pragmatism can be applied to academic research and knowledge production. It is now about 120 years since pragmatism first surfaced as a current of philosophical thought. While its fortunes have been mixed, it feels as though its time has now come; it brings powerful insights that can help us tackle the key intellectual, political-economic, social and environmental challenges we all face today.

In thinking about the title of this collection, it is striking that the question of power does not feature widely in the lexicon of pragmatism. The idea of pragmatism invoked in everyday usage – vulgar pragmatism, perhaps – evades considerations of power through an amoral surrender to sheer expediency and bare instrumentalism. The founding statements of philosophical pragmatism by Peirce, James and Dewey, and of neo-pragmatists such as Rorty, Bernstein and Hilary Putnam, rarely offer an explicit engagement with considerations of power. Indeed, a focus on 'power' as an abstraction preceding its materialisation in practice would violate the pragmatists' anti-foundational rejection of causal forces thought to exist before, behind or above the social practices through which they are formed. While Dewey, for example, devoted a lifetime to excoriating the pernicious effects of economic and political institutions, he did so by revealing their practice in the world and by not only avoiding but explicitly rejecting a merely theoretical discourse on power as an abstract mystical force posited to exist prior to its instantiation through practice (Misak, 2013; Ryan, 1995; Westbrook, 1991).

Yet, power is deeply implicated in pragmatism's commitment to practice understood as the ability to have an effect on the world. An abiding orientation to action – the 'power to' rather than 'power over' – constitutes pragmatism as an enabling philosophy insistently concerned with "what enables us to make a difference in the world" (Allen, 2008, 1614; see also Arendt, 1958). This book considers the power of pragmatism as an orientation towards the conduct of social research and as a way of understanding the role of ideas in making and remaking the world.

## Notes

1    Although Rorty took the world by surprise in 1979 when he published a glowing account of Dewey's contribution to ideas in his *Philosophy and the mirror of nature*, it is perhaps not surprising that Rorty had a counter-cultural view of the power of pragmatism. His mother, Winifred, had studied sociology at the University of Chicago during the heyday of its commitment to pragmatic social research. She was taught by George Herbert Mead, worked as a researcher for Robert Park and wrote a well-received biography of Park that was published in 1979, the same year as Rorty's *Philosophy and the mirror of nature* challenged the philosophical establishment. Her father, Walter Rauschenbusch, was a central figure in the social gospel movement, and he knew and was strongly influenced by William James and John Dewey. Thus Rorty grew up in a highly intellectual milieu in which pragmatism played a key role in both American political culture and his personal and family life (Voparil, 2010; Westbrook, 1991).

2    Christopher Lasch (1965) notes that "[i]t is difficult to say whether Dewey influenced Jane Addams or Jane Addams influenced Dewey. They influenced each other and generously acknowledged their mutual obligations" (quoted in Westbrook, 1991, 89). Dewey frequently lectured at Hull House both before and after arriving in Chicago; he served on its Board of Directors until Addams's death in 1935; and he named one of his daughters Jane in honour of Addams (Boronat, 2019; Deegan, 1990; Hamington, 2009; Ryan, 1995; Seigfried, 1996; Westbrook, 1991).

3    The University of Chicago was established in 1892, and John Dewey arrived two years later as chair of the philosophy department, having also secured a faculty appointment in philosophy for George Herbert Mead (1863–1931), who had previously taught with Dewey at the University of Michigan. Albion W. Small (1854–1926) was appointed head professor of the department of sociology in 1892 and was joined by W.I. Thomas (1863–1947) in 1895. By the 1920s, a 'second generation' of sociologists had established what became widely known as the Chicago School of Urban Sociology, primarily comprising Robert E. Park (1864–1944), Ellsworth Faris (1874–1953), Ernest W. Burgess (1886–1966), William Ogburn (1886–1959) and Louis Wirth (1897–1952) (Faris, 1970; Short, 1971).

4    Park and Burgess's *Introduction to the science of sociology* firmly asserted that sociology seeks "natural laws and generalizations in regard to human nature and society, irrespective of time and of place" (Park and Burgess, 1921, 11, quoted in Entrikin, 1980, 48). The 1924, second edition of the text complained that "[a] great deal of social information has been collected merely for the purpose of determining what

to do in a given case. Facts have not been collected to check social theories ... In very few instances have investigations been made disinterestedly" (Park and Burgess, 1924, 44). Robert Park's biographer, Winifred Rauschenbusch (1979), quotes Park as proclaiming that "In developing the techniques of sociology we must escape both *history* and *practical applications* ... The first thing you have to do with a student who enters sociology is to show him that he can make a contribution if he doesn't try to improve anybody" (quoted in Deegan, 1990, 152). Advocating for the importance of "a workable theory of urbanism", Louis Wirth insisted that

> only by means of some such theory will the sociologist escape the futile practice of voicing in the name of sociological science a variety of often unsupportable judgments concerning such problems as poverty, housing, city-planning, sanitation, municipal administration, policing, marketing, transportation, and other technical issues ... The prospects for doing this are brightest through a general, theoretical, rather than through an *ad hoc* approach. (1938, 24)

Short's account of the Chicago School after 1920 identifies the elevation of science as the pervasive ethos in the department. Of William Ogburn, Short (1971, xix) reports that "his scientific stance was based on the conviction that systematic and objective study of social change was more efficacious than was social reform as an approach to human problems". Robert Faris, Short (1971, xx) says, "describes the 'Chicago attitude' as essentially that of pure science", quoting Faris's (1970) opinion that "it is worthwhile to pursue many intellectual questions without reference either to their immediate service or to the question of what particular applications the knowledge may have ... the restrictions of scholarly attention to the search for immediate alleviation of present problems ... delays the development of the organized and tested knowledge which could be effective". However, there were differences within the group, and even in the ideas developed by individuals over time. Ernest Burgess, for example, played an important role with Clifford R. Shaw in the establishment of the Chicago Areas Project (CAP) in order to develop neighbourhood-scale collective capacity to improve social life. The CAP appointed Saul Alinsky to work in Back of the Yards in Chicago in 1931, and this spawned the tradition of community organising that remains a beacon of pragmatic politics in the USA and elsewhere today (Wills, 2016b).

5    A partial list of ethnographic field studies conducted by members of the Chicago School of urban sociology includes Thomas and Znaniecki (1918), Nels Anderson (1923), Louis Wirth (1928), Harvey Zorbaugh (1929), Clifford Shaw (1930) and Paul Cressey (1932) (for a descriptive overview, see Short, 1971). Several of these ethnographic accounts became highly popular bestsellers read as voyeuristic portraits of Chicago's forbidden urban worlds (Short, 1971).

6    The split between the Hull House Settlement and the Chicago School of Sociology was institutional as well as philosophical and practical. Addams formally rejected the university's bid to absorb Hull House within its administration, fearing a loss of autonomy and wishing to protect the Settlement's unique approach and mission. Writing to university president William Rainey Harper in December 1895, Addams held that such an affiliation "could not be other than an irreparable misfortune ... and most unfair" (quoted in Deegan, 1990, 38).

7    Entrikin's (1980) characterisation of Dewey's pragmatism as idealist emphasises the Hegelian influences on Dewey's early philosophical training, but Dewey moved decisively away from idealism in his later work (Bernstein, 1971; on pragmatism and realism in William James, see Putnam, 1998). Ryan credits Dewey's wife, Alice (Chapman), with having done "a great favour by making him focus on the

unsatisfactory, unjust, and thoroughly disorganized here and now, rather than the realm of the ideal" (Ryan, 1995, 82). Dewey's move beyond Hegelian idealism is evident in the concluding chapter of *Reconstruction in philosophy* (1920 [1957]), where he explicitly rejected the notion that philosophy involves "the purely rational application of the mind to problems and questions that have no real social genesis". Dewey instead professed a commitment to "practical idealism", in which the collective mind, as the realm of creative intelligence, offers imaginative solutions for problems encountered in experience of the world (Dewey, 1917 [1980]). As Diggins explains, "the mind for Dewey was not a looking glass reflecting the world nor a logical faculty for defining truth; instead it was a problem-solving tool for adjusting to an unstable environment" (Diggins, 1994, 229).

8    Anselm Strauss observes that "Robert Park and Ernest Burgess included none of Mead's writings in their 1921 reader-text that educated the Chicago graduate students for almost two decades" (Strauss, 1964, xi). Wirth's seventy-page 'Bibliography of the urban community', divided among eleven topical sections and fifty-three sub-sections ranging from "streets and sewers" to "the mentality of city life", contains no reference to Mead's work or ideas (Park et al., 1925 [1967], 161–228]. As if to affirm his pragmatist commitments, Mead concluded his 1938 essay on 'The nature of scientific knowledge' by asserting that "the experimental scientist, apart from some philosophical bias, is not a positivist. He has no inclination to build up a universe of such scientific data, which in their abstraction can be identified as parts of many different worlds. The reference of his data is always to the solution of problems in the world that is there about him, the world that tests the validity of his hypothetical reconstructions. Nothing would more completely squeeze the interest out of his world than the resolution of it into the data of observation" (Mead, 1938 [1964], 61).

9    For a detailed discussion of Dewey's influence on Latour, see Harman (2014, 161–78) and Marres (2005). In Rorty's anticipation of assemblage theory, he asserts that "[w]e antiessentialists ... suggest that you think of objects ... in the following respect: there is nothing to be known about them except an initially large, and forever expanding, web of relations to other objects ... There are, so to speak, relations all the way down, all the way up, and all the way out in every direction: you never reach something which is not just one more nexus of relations ... There is nothing to be known about anything save its relations to other things" (Rorty, 1999, 53–4).

## References

Abbott, A. (1999) *Department and discipline: Chicago sociology at one hundred*. Chicago, IL: University of Chicago Press.

Addams, J. (1902 [2005]) *Democracy and social action*. New York, NY: Macmillan.

Addams, J. (1910) 1961]) *Twenty years at Hull-House*. New York, NY: Penguin.

Allen, D.S. (2006) *Talking to strangers: Anxieties of citizenship since Brown v. Board of Education*. Paris: Éditions Hermann.

Allen, J. (2008) Pragmatism and power, or the power to make a difference in a radically contingent world. *Geoforum*, 39, 4, 1613–24.

Anderson, B. and Harrison, P. (2010) The power of non-representational theories, in B. Anderson and P. Harrison, eds, *Taking place: Non-representational theories in geography*. Farnham: Ashgate, 1–34.

Anderson, N. (1923) *The hobo: The sociology of the homeless man*. Chicago, IL: University of Chicago Press.

Ansell, C. (2011) *Pragmatist democracy: Evolutionary learning as public philosophy*. Oxford: Oxford University Press.

Arendt, H. (1958) *The human condition*. Chicago, IL: University of Chicago Press.

Arendt, H. (1971) *The life of the mind*. New York, NY: Harcourt.

Baert, P. (2005) *Philosophy of the social sciences: Towards pragmatism*. Cambridge: Polity Press.

Barnett, C. (2017) *The priority of injustice: Locating democracy in critical theory*. Athens: University of Georgia Press.

Bernstein, R. (1971) *Praxis and action: Contemporary philosophies of human activity*. Philadelphia, PA: University of Pennsylvania Press.

Bernstein, R. (1989) Pragmatism, pluralism and the healing of wounds. *Proceedings and Addresses of the American Philosophical Association*, 63, 3, 5–18.

Bernstein, R. (1992) *The new constellation: The ethical-political horizons of modernity/postmodernity*. Cambridge, MA: MIT Press.

Bernstein, R. (1998) Community in the pragmatic tradition, in M. Dickstein, ed., *The revival of pragmatism*. Durham, NC: Duke University Press, 141–56.

Bernstein, R. (2010) *The pragmatic turn*. Cambridge: Polity Press.

Biesta, G.J.J. (2015) *Beyond learning: Democratic education for a human future*. London: Routledge.

Blumer, H. (1969) *Social interactionism: Perspective and method*. Berkeley, CA: University of California Press.

Bohman, J. (1999a) Theories, practices and pluralism: A pragmatic interpretation of critical social science. *Philosophy of the Social Sciences*, 29, 459–80.

Bohman, J. (1999b) Democracy as inquiry, inquiry as democratic: Pragmatism, social science, and the cognitive division of labor. *American Journal of Political Science*, 43, 2, 590–607.

Bohman, J. (2002) How to make a social science practical: Pragmatism, critical social science and multi-perspectival theory. *Millennium: Journal of International Studies*, 31, 3, 499–524.

Boltanski, L. and Thévenot, L. (2006) *On justification: Economies of worth*. Translated by Catherine Porter. Princeton, NJ: Princeton University Press.

Boronat, N. (2019) Peace, bread, and ideas for a cosmopolitan world: Addams' unknown pragmatist legacy today, in K. Skowronski and S. Pihlstrom, eds, *Pragmatism, Kant, and Kantianism in the twenty-first century*. Nordic Studies in Pragmatism, vol. 4. Helsinki: Nordic Pragmatism Network.

Brandom, R. (2009) When pragmatism paints its blue on grey: Irony and the pragmatist enlightenment, in C. Kautzer and E. A. Mendieta, eds, *Pragmatism, nation, race*. Bloomington, IN: Indiana University Press, 31–45.

Bridge, G. (2005) *Reason in the city of difference: Pragmatism, communicative action and contemporary urbanism*. New York, NY: Routledge.

Brinkmann, S. (2017) *Philosophies of qualitative research*. Oxford: Oxford University Press.

Burgess, E.W. (1916) The social survey: A field for constructive service by departments of sociology. *American Journal of Sociology*, 21, 4, 492–500.

Burgess, E.W., ed. (1926) *The urban community*. Chicago, IL: University of Chicago Press.

Burgess, E.W. and Bogue, D.J., eds (1964) *Urban sociology*. Chicago, IL: University of Chicago Press.

Buxton, M. (1984) The influence of William James on John Dewey's early work. *Journal of the History of Ideas*, 45, 3, 451–63.

Cahoone, L.E. (2002) *Civil society: The conservative meaning of liberal politics*. Oxford: Blackwell.

Cavell, S. (1998) What's the use of calling Emerson a pragmatist?, in M. Dickstein, ed., *The revival of pragmatism: New essays on social thought, law, and culture*. Durham, NC: Duke University Press, 72–80.

Collins, P. (2012) Social inequality, power, and politics: Intersectionality and American pragmatism in dialogue. *Journal of Speculative Philosophy*, 26, 2, 442–57.

Commager, H. (1961) Foreword, in J. Addams, *Twenty years at Hull-House*. New York, NY: Penguin.

Cressey, P. (1932) *The taxi-dance hall: A sociological study in commericalized recreation and city life*. Chicago, IL: University of Chicago Press.

Deegan, M.J. (1990) *Jane Addams and the men of the Chicago School, 1892–1918*. New Brunswick, NJ and Oxford: Transaction Publishers.

Dewey, J (1916 [2004]) *Democracy and education*. Mineola, NY: Dover Publications Inc.

Dewey, J. (1917 [1980]) The need for a recovery of philosophy, in J.A. Boydston, ed., *The middle works, volume 10: 1916–1917*. Carbondale, IL: Southern Illinois University Press, 3–48.

Dewey, J. (1919 [1933]) Philosophy and democracy, in D. Morris and I. Shapiro, eds, *The political writings*. Indianapolis, IN: Hackett, 38–47.

Dewey, J. (1920 [1957]) *Reconstruction in philosophy (including a new Introduction: Reconstruction as seen twenty-five years later, v–xli)*. Boston, MA: Beacon Press.

Dewey, J. (1927 [1954]) *The public and its problems*. Athens, OH: Swallow Press, Ohio University Press.

Dewey, J. (1929 [1984]) The quest for certainty: A study of the relation of knowledge and action, in J.A. Boydston, ed., *The later works, 1925–1953, volume 4: 1929*. Carbondale, IL: Southern Illinois University Press, 1–178.

Dewey, J. (1938 [1988]) Freedom and culture, in J.A. Boydston, ed., *The later works, 1925–1953, volume 13: 1938–1939*. Carbondale, IL: Southern Illinois University Press, 63–79.

Dewey, J (1938 [1939]) *Logic: The theory of inquiry*. London: George Allen and Unwin.

Dickstein, M., ed. (1998) *The revival of pragmatism: New essays on social thought, law, and culture*. Durham, NC: Duke University Press.

Dieleman, S. (2014) Pragmatist tools for public administration. *Administration and Society*, 49, 2, 275–95.

Diggins, J.P. (1994) *The promise of pragmatism: Modernism and the crisis of knowledge and authority*. Chicago, IL: Chicago University Press.

Entrikin, J.N. (1980) Robert Park's human ecology and human geography. *Annals of the Association of American Geographers* 70, 1, 43–58.

Faris, E. (1937) The social psychology of George Herbert Mead. *American Journal of Sociology*, 43, 391–403.

Faris, R. (1970) *Chicago sociology 1920–1932*. Chicago, IL: University of Chicago Press.

Festenstein, M. (1997) *Pragmatism and political theory: From Dewey to Rorty*. Chicago, IL: University of Chicago Press.

Fischer, F. (2009) *Democracy and expertise: Reorienting policy inquiry*. Oxford: Oxford University Press.

Fish, S. (1998) Afterword: Truth and toilets: Pragmatism and the practices of life, in M. Dickstein, ed., *The revival of pragmatism: New essays on social thought, law, and culture*. Durham, NC: Duke University Press, 418–33.

Flyvbjerg, B. (1998) *Rationality and power: Democracy in practice*. Chicago, IL: Chicago University Press.

Flyvbjerg, B. (2001) *Making social science matter: Why social inquiry fails and how it can succeed again.* Cambridge: Cambridge University Press.

Fraser, N. (1998) Another pragmatism: Alain Locke, critical 'race' theory, and the politics of culture, in M. Dickstein, ed., *The revival of pragmatism: New essays on social thought, law, and culture.* Durham, NC: Duke University Press, 157–75.

Geertz, C. (1973) *The interpretation of cultures.* New York, NY: Basic Books.

Gieryn, T. (2006) City as truth-spot: Laboratories and field-sites in urban studies. *Social Studies of Science*, 36, 1, 5–38.

Gray, J. (2007) *Black mass: Apocalyptic religion and the death of utopia.* London: Macmillan.

Gross, M. (2009) Collaborative experiments: Jane Addams, Hull House and experimental social work. *Social Science Information*, 48,1, 81–95.

Hamington, M. (2009) *The social philosophy of Jane Addams.* Urbana, IL: University of Illinois Press.

Hamington, M. and Bardwell-Jones, C., eds (2012) *Contemporary feminist pragmatism.* New York, NY: Routledge.

Harman, G. (2014) *Bruno Latour: Reassembling the political.* London: Pluto Press.

Harney, L. and Wills, J. (2017) *Infrastructures for impact: Community–university partnerships in the USA and UK.* Queen Mary, University of London: Mile End Institute. http://mei.qmul.ac.uk/news-and-opinion/blog/items/194195.html.

Harney, L., McCurry, J., Scott, J. and Wills, J. (2016) Developing 'process pragmatism' to underpin engaged research in human geography. *Progress in Human Geography*, 40, 3, 316–33.

Healey, P. (2009) The pragmatic tradition in planning thought. *Journal of Planning Education and Research*, 28, 3, 277–92.

Hoch, C. (1984) Doing good and being right: The pragmatist connection in planning theory. *Journal of the American Planning Association*, 50, 3, 335–45.

Holden, M., Scerri, A. and Owens, C. (2013) More publics, more problems: The productive interface between the pragmatic sociology of critique and Deweyan pragmatism. *Contemporary Pragmatism*, 10, 2, 1–34.

Honneth, A. (1998) Democracy as reflexive cooperation. *Political Theory*, 26, 6, 763–83.

James, W. (2000 [1907]) *Pragmatism and other writings.* London: Penguin.

Jasanoff, S. (2012) *Science and public reason.* New York, NY: Routledge.

Joas, H. (1993) *Pragmatism and social theory.* Chicago, IL: University of Chicago Press.

Jones, O. (2008) Stepping from the wreckage: Geography, pragmatism and anti-representational theory. *Geoforum*, 39, 1600–12.

Karsenti, B. and Quéré, L. (2004) *La croyance et l'enquette: Auxsources du pragmatism* (Belief and inquiry: The sources of pragmatism). Paris: Editions de écoles en sciences sociales.

Kautzer, C. and Mendieta, E., eds (2009) *Pragmatism, nation, and race: Community in the age of Empire.* Bloomington, IN: Indiana University Press.

Kindon, S., Pain, R. and Kesby, M., eds (2007) *Participatory action research approaches and methods: Connecting people, participation and place.* London: Routledge.

Kloppenberg, J.T. (1998) Pragmatism: An old name for some new ways of thinking?, in M. Dickstein, ed., *The revival of pragmatism: New essays on social thought, law, and culture.* Durham, NC: Duke University Press, 83–127.

Lake, R. (2014) Methods and moral inquiry. *Urban Geography*, 35, 657–68.

Lake, R. (2016) Justice as subject and object of planning. *International Journal of Urban and Regional Research*, 40, 6, 1205–20.

Lake, R. (2017) On poetry, pragmatism and the urban possibility of creative democracy. *Urban Geography*, 38, 4, 479–94.

Lasch, C. (1991) *The true and only heaven: Progress and its critics.* New York, NY: W.W. Norton and Co.

Lasch, C. (1995) *The revolt of the elites and the betrayal of democracy.* New York, NY: W.W. Norton and Co.

Latour, B. (2005) *Reassembling the social: An introduction to actor–network-theory.* Oxford: Oxford University Press.

Lester, T. (2019) Replacing truth with social hope and progress with redescription: Can the pragmatist philosophy of Richard Rorty help reinvigorate planning? *Journal of Planning Education and Research,* doi: 10.1177/0739456X19827636.

Lippmann, W. (1922) *Public opinion.* New York, NY: Harcourt Brace.

Lippmann, W. (1927 [1933]) *The phantom public.* London: Transaction Publishers.

Livingston, J. (2001) *Pragmatism, feminism, and democracy.* New York, NY: Routledge.

MacGilvray, E. (2010) Dewey's publics. *Contemporary Pragmatism,* 7, 1, 31–47.

Malachowski, A. (2010) *The new pragmatism.* Durham: Acumen.

Marres, N. (2005) Issues spark a public into being: A key but forgotten point of the Lippmann–Dewey debate, in B. Latour and P. Weibel, eds, *Making things public.* Cambridge, MA: MIT Press.

Masumi, B. 2015. *The politics of affect.* Cambridge: Polity Press.

Mead, G. H. (1934 [2015]) *Mind, self, and society.* Chicago, IL: University of Chicago Press.

Menand, L. (1997) *Pragmatism: A reader.* New York, NY: Random House.

Menand, L. (2011) *The metaphysical club: A story of ideas in America.* New York, NY: Flamingo.

Mills, C. (1943 [1964]) *Sociology and pragmatism: The higher learning in America.* New York, NY: Oxford University Press.

Minnich, E. (2005). *Transforming knowledge,* 2nd edn. Philadelphia, PA: Temple University Press.

Minnich, E. (2017) *The evil of banality: On the life and death importance of thinking.* Lanham, MD: Rowman and Littlefield.

Misak, C. (2002). *Truth, politics, morality: Pragmatism and deliberation.* London and New York, NY: Routledge.

Misak, C. (2013) *The American pragmatists.* Oxford: Oxford University Press.

Mitchell, T. (2002) *Rule of experts: Egypt, techno-politics, modernity.* Berkeley, CA: University of California Press.

Mitchell, W.T. (1982) *Against theory: Literary studies and the new pragmatism.* Chicago, IL: University of Chicago Press.

Morgan, D. (2014) Pragmatism as a paradigm for social research. *Qualitative Inquiry,* 20, 8, 1045–53.

Morris, C. (1970) *The pragmatic movement in American philosophy.* New York, NY: Braziller.

Mouffe, C., ed. (1996) *Deconstruction and pragmatism: Simon Critchley, Jacques Derrida, Ernesto Laclau and Richard Rorty.* London: Routledge.

Mouffe, C. (2005) *On the political.* London: Routledge.

Mouffe, C. (2013) *Agonistics: Thinking the world politically.* New York, NY: Verso.

Mumford, L. (1926) *The golden day: A study in American experience and culture.* New York, NY: Horace Liveright.

Nelson J. A. (2003) Confronting the science/value split: Notes on feminist economics, institutionalism, pragmatism and process thought. *Cambridge Journal of Economics,* 27, 1, 49–64.

Niebuhr, R. (1932 [2013]) *Moral man and immoral society: A study in ethics and politics.* Louisville, KY: Westminster Press.

Niebuhr, R. (1944 [2011]) *The children of light and the children of darkness*. Chicago, IL: niversity of Chicago Press.

Nietzsche, F. (1889 [1969]) *Twilight of the idols*. Harmondsworth: Penguin.

Park, R.E. (1916) The city: Suggestions for the investigation of human behaviour in the urban environment. *American Journal of Sociology*, 20, 577–612.

Park, R.E. (1929) The city as social laboratory, in T. Smith and L. White, eds, *Chicago: An experiment in social science research*. Chicago, IL: University of Chicago Press, 1–19.

Park, R.E. and Burgess, E.W. (1921 [1924]) *Introduction to the science of sociology*. Chicago, IL: University of Chicago Press.

Park, R.E., Burgess, E.W., and MacKenzie, R.D., eds (1925 [1925]) *The city*. Chicago, IL: University of Chicago Press.

Pestoff, V., Brandsen, T. and Verschuere, B., eds (2012) *New public governance, the third sector, and co-production*. London: Routledge.

Polanyi, K. (1920 [2018]) Science and morality, in M. Brie and C. Thomasberger, eds, *Karl Polanyi's vision of a socialist transformation*. New York, NY: Black Rose Books, 269–86.

Polanyi, K. (1944 [2001]) *The great transformation: The political and economic origins of our time*. Boston, MA: Beacon Press.

Posner, R.A. (2003) *Law, pragmatism, and democracy*. Cambridge, MA: Harvard University Press.

Purcell, M. (2017) For John Dewey (and very much also for contemporary critical theory). *Urban Geography*, 38, 4, 495–501.

Putnam, H. (1992) A reconsideration of Deweyan democracy, in *Renewing Philosophy*. Cambridge, MA: Harvard University Press.

Putnam, H. (1998) Pragmatism and realism, in M. Dickstein, ed., *The revival of pragmatism*. Durham, NC: Duke University Press, 37–53.

Rauschenbusch, W. (1979) *Robert E. Park: Biography of a sociologist*. Durham, NC: Duke University Press.

Rogers, M.L. (2009) *The undiscovered Dewey: Religion, morality, and the ethos of democracy*. New York, NY: Columbia University Press.

Rorty, R., ed. (1967 [1992]) *The linguistic turn: Essays in philosophical method with two retrospective essays*. Chicago, IL: University of Chicago Press.

Rorty, R. (1979 [2009]) *Philosophy and the mirror of nature*. Princeton, NJ: Princeton University Press.

Rorty, R. (1980) Pragmatism, relativism, and irrationalism. *Proceedings and Addresses of the American Philosophical Association*, 53, 6, 710–38.

Rorty, R. (1982) *Consequences of pragmatism (Essays 1972–1980)*. Minneapolis, MN: University of Minnesota Press.

Rorty, R. (1989) *Contingency, irony, solidarity*. Cambridge: Cambridge University Press.

Rorty, R. (1991a) *Objectivity, relativism, and truth*. Cambridge: Cambridge University Press.

Rorty, R. (1991b) *Essays on Heidegger and others: Philosophical papers volume 2*. Cambridge: Cambridge University Press.

Rorty, R. (1996) Remarks on deconstruction and pragmatism, in C. Mouffe, ed., *Deconstruction and pragmatism*. New York, NY: Routledge, 13–18.

Rorty, R. (1997) Justice as a larger loyalty, in R. Bontekoe and M. Stepaniants, eds, *Justice and democracy: Cross-cultural perspectives*. Honolulu, HI: University of Hawaii Press, 9–22.

Rorty, R. (1998a) *Achieving our country: Leftist thought in twentieth-century America*. Cambridge, MA: Harvard University Press.

Rorty, R. (1998b) *Truth and progress: Philosophical papers volume 3.* Cambridge: Cambridge University Press.

Rorty, R. (1999) *Philosophy and social hope.* London: Penguin Books.

Rorty, R. (2010) Justice as a larger loyalty, in C. Voparil and R. Bernstein, eds, *The Rorty reader.* Oxford: Wiley-Blackwell, 433–43.

Ryan, A. (1995) *John Dewey and the high tide of American liberalism.* New York, NY: Norton.

Savage, M. (2010) *Identities and social change in Britain since 1940: The politics of method.* Oxford: Oxford University Press.

Shalin, D N. (1986) Pragmatism and social interactionism. *American Sociological Review,* 51, 1, 9–29.

Shaw, C.R. (1930) *A Jack-Roller: A delinquent boy's own story.* Chicago, IL: University of Chicago Press.

Shibutani, T. (2017) *Society and personality: Interactionist approach to social psychology.* London: Routledge.

Shields, P. (2003) The community of inquiry: Classical pragmatism and public administration. *Administration and Society,* 35, 3, 510–38.

Shields, P. (2008) Rediscovering the tap root: Is classical pragmatism the route to renew public administration? *Public Administration Review,* 68, 205–21.

Short, J., ed. (1971) *The social fabric of the metropolis: Contributions of the Chicago School of Urban Sociology.* Chicago, IL: University of Chicago Press.

Seigfried, C. (1996) *Pragmatism and feminism: Reweaving the social fabric.* Chicago, IL: University of Chicago Press.

Seigfried, C., ed. (2002) *Feminist interpretations of John Dewey.* University Park, PA: Penn State University Press.

Stears, M. (2010) *Demanding democracy: American radicals in search of a new politics.* Princeton, NJ: Princeton University Press.

Strauss, A., ed. (1964) *George Herbert Mead on social psychology.* Chicago, IL: University of Chicago Press.

Sullivan, S. (2009) Feminism, in J. Shook and J. Margolis, eds, *A companion to pragmatism.* Oxford: Wiley, 232–38.

Thomas, W.I. and Znaniecki, F. (1918 [1996]) *The Polish peasant in Europe and America.* Chicago, IL: University of Chicago Press.

Thrift, N. (2008) *Non-representational theory: Space, politics, affect.* London: Routledge.

Tolletsen, C. (2000) What would John Dewey do? The promises and perils of pragmatic bioethics. *Journal of Medicine and Philosophy,* 25, 1, 77–106.

Toulmin, S. (2001) *Cosmopolis: The hidden agenda of modernity.* Chicago, IL: University of Chicago Press.

Unger, R M. (2007) *The self awakened: Pragmatism unbound.* Cambridge, MA: Harvard University Press.

Voparil, C.J. (2010) General introduction, in C. Voparil and R. Bernstein, eds, *The Rorty reader.* Oxford: Wiley-Blackwell, 1–52.

West, C. (1989) *The American evasion of philosophy: A genealogy of pragmatism.* Basingstoke: Macmillan.

Westbrook, R. (1991) *John Dewey and American Democracy.* Ithaca, NY: Cornell University Press.

Westbrook, R. (1998) Pragmatism and democracy: Reconstructing the logic of John Dewey's faith, in M. Dickstein, ed., *The revival of pragmatism: New essays on social thought, law, and culture.* Durham, NC: Duke University Press, 128–40.

Westbrook, R. (2005) *Democratic hope: Pragmatism and the politics of truth.* Ithaca, NY: Cornell University Press.

Whyte, W.F.E. (1991) *Participatory action research*. London: Sage.

Wicks, A.C., and Freeman, R.E. (1998) Organization studies and the new pragmatism: Positivism, anti-positivism, and the search for ethics. *Organization Science*, 9, 2, 123–40.

Wills, J. (2008) Making class politics possible: Organising contract cleaners in London. *International Journal of Urban and Regional Research*, 32, 2, 305–24.

Wills, J. (2016a) (Re)Locating community in relationships: Questions for public policy. *Sociological Review*, 64, 639–56.

Wills, J. (2016b) *Locating localism: Statecraft, citizenship and democracy*. Bristol: Policy Press.

Wolfe, K. (2017) Pragmatism, racial solidarity and negotiating social practices: Evading the problem of 'problem-solving' talk. *Critical Philosophy of Race*, 5, 1, 114–30.

Wood, N. and Smith, S.J. (2008) Pragmatism and geography. *Geoforum*, 39, 1527–9.

Young, I.M. (2000) *Inclusion and democracy*. New York, NY: Oxford University Press.

Zitcer, A. and Lake, R. (2012) Love as a planning method. *Planning Theory and Practice*, 13, 606–9.

## Part II

# Key thinkers, core ideas and their application to social research

# Habits of social inquiry and reconstruction: A Deweyan vision of democracy and social research

*Malcolm P. Cutchin*

## Introduction

> The best we can accomplish for posterity is to transmit unimpaired and with some increment of meaning the environment that makes it possible to maintain the habits of decent and refined life. Our individual habits are links in forming the endless chain of humanity. Their significance depends upon the environment inherited from our forerunners, and it is enhanced as we foresee the fruits of our labors in the world in which our successors live. (Dewey, 1957, 23)

> The stuff of belief and proposition is not originated by us. It comes to us from others, by education, tradition and the suggestion of the environment. Our intelligence is bound up, so far as its materials are concerned, with the community life of which we are a part. We know what it communicates to us, and know according to the habits it forms in us. (Dewey, 1957, 287)

The argument that follows proposes a pragmatic orientation towards community-level inquiry, which entails a uniquely Deweyan sense of how we can participate in remaking our communities. The key points are that by better understanding our taken-for-granted socio-culturally formed habits, and what inquiry and democracy are (or can be) if conceptualised in pragmatist terms, we can have hope for the future, because we have a method for making it better. That method entails a role for ordinary citizens and for so-called experts who offer scholarly or scientific knowledge. I begin, however, with an introductory note about my journey to this argument, because I believe the backstory might be helpful to other social scientists who are utilising pragmatism, others who are approaching pragmatism for the first time or those who have previously entered the discourse only to find it confusing or lacking in some way. One of my beliefs is that persistence and patience are as necessary in the scholarship and practice of pragmatism as they are in other domains of life. Little comes easily to the scholar of Dewey (for example), but the rewards are, in my humble estimation, well worth the effort.

Twenty-five years ago, at the University of Kentucky, I was a graduate student in a hotbed of theoretical geography. With much native interest, and stimulated and guided by graduate student colleagues and faculty mentors, I read essential works in critical realism, Marxism, poststructuralism, postmodernism, etc. I took it for granted that theory and philosophy were important and helped me to view and think about the world in new and useful ways, and I fully expected that I would be using social theory in my own inquiries. At the same time, I had some gnawing reservations about the theorists we were reading; to wit, their arguments appeared to me as too detached from the active experience of everyday life and/or they said little beyond the critiques or descriptions they offered – they suggested little about development of a better future. Then, while studying qualitative methods in a sociology course, I discovered that Glaser and Strauss – the developers of grounded theory, an approach to the analysis of qualitative data based on openness to what the data suggest rather than using *a priori* theory – had been inspired and influenced by John Dewey (Strauss, 1987). My curiosity was piqued. Who was Dewey, and what was his philosophy about? The university library offered access to works about Dewey's philosophy and then some of Dewey's key ontological writings such as *Experience and nature* (1925). Dewey's thinking appeared to me as radical and critical of the Enlightenment project as any other theorist but, more importantly to me, he paid significant attention to the structure and action of life – for individuals and society – without discarding the importance of meaning, nature, change, ethics and values.

To my knowledge, then and now, only Dewey had developed such an integrative and critical perspective and, as I discovered, he continued it intently over the course of a very long career. Soon after, I began to wonder why we were not reading Dewey in our graduate programme and why he was not being read in other geography (or other social science) departments. The only reason I can determine is that Dewey was viewed as passé and therefore not as interesting or as sexy as the theorists in vogue at the time; and for some, I imagine, he was not perceived as a sufficiently critical theorist. And, I suppose, disciplines as much as the individuals that compose them are prone to be influenced or distracted by 'the new'. The result was, in my biased view, unfortunate for my discipline, because it delayed geography's significant encounter with pragmatism.

After a year or so of grappling with Dewey's and Deweyan scholars' publications, I concluded that he was the most significant of the pragmatists; I also realised that he published more scholarship on a wider set of issues than any scholar I had come across. I was compelled to make sense of his philosophy and its utility for social scholarship, yet the problem was this: which of his many works to read next, and how to find the necessary time to study them sufficiently? The obvious solution was to be selective and read what I needed to read at the time, and the unfortunate outcome was to miss many important dimensions of his thought – such as his political works and his writings on aesthetics – all of which are highly innovative and, at the same time, intricately woven into the fabric of his broader philosophy. What follows below is the result of some effort to address the gaps in my knowledge and to connect Dewey's political theory to his theory of social psychology and action. In my view, Dewey's political theory appears especially relevant in these times when democracy is under pressure and in question.

As I noted above, I assume that pragmatism will be foreign to most social scientists who read this volume. From my vantage point, a key issue to keep in mind when reading Dewey is this: his writings rarely provide direct answers to social problems. Although he did occasionally make suggestions about how to address democratic and economic problems, such as revolutionising education (Dewey, 1976) or granting workers cooperative control over the means of industrial production (Dewey, 1931), his main purpose as a philosopher was to provide critical conceptual and theoretical insights into human social life – as tools of inquiry available to all of us – so that we could cooperate to solve the problems of our own place and time. For me, even though Dewey's primary contribution leaves us with never-ending work to do, that is the most pragmatic gift possible.

As the other chapters in this book illustrate, advances in making use of that gift have taken place in the social sciences in recent years. For instance, several pragmatism-inspired scholars have, over the last decade, persuasively suggested the significance of Dewey's theories for central issues in political and urban theory and practice (e.g. Allen, 2008; Barnett and Bridge, 2013; Bridge, 2008, 2013; Cutchin, 2008; Lake, 2014). These authors have synthesised Deweyan conceptualisations of transaction, democracy, publics, inquiry and morality with geographic concerns of spatiality, power and social change. Those notable contributions have provided a basis for the additional development of a social science more fully shaped by Dewey's theories.

Yet Dewey's theory of habit is central to his philosophy and has been mostly overlooked by social scientists. To complement and contribute to the growth of social scientific scholarship in the pragmatic tradition, especially one concerned with democratic processes of social inquiry and social reconstruction, I attempt to flesh out some fundamental dimensions of Dewey's work on habit. I suggest that an understanding of the central role of habit in Dewey's body of work opens up the discourse to his associated ideas of embodiment, imagination and community – all of which are essential to his concept of democracy. In my view, the formation, implementation and modification of habits – whether viewed as individual-level, community-level or cultural-level – are fundamental to the problem of adept democratic activity and social functioning. To understand Dewey's theory of habit and these associated concepts allows us to see how social inquiry and social change are enabled and, importantly, situated in time, culture and place. In the closing section of the chapter, I turn to the applied side of the matter and sketch out potential implications of these ideas for doing social research and for social sciences as part of the university that engages in community life.

## A Deweyan theory of habit

John Dewey is one of the few theorists to take habit seriously as a foundation for understanding human action as well as for inquiry and social change. William James surely pointed Dewey in this direction. James's argument that habit is the 'fly-wheel of society' (James, 1890) is a good example. James's conceptualisation of habit was focused on its biophysical dimensions (Camic, 1986), although he argued that individual habits reproduced the social order. Dewey agreed, but he also deepened and expanded James's theorisation. Dewey's well-known definition of habit as "an acquired predisposition to *ways* or modes of response" comes from his 1922 book *Human nature and conduct* (Dewey, 1957, 40). In that work, Dewey provided an in-depth treatment of the ways in which social relations, institutions and customs shape human action through the acquisition of habits and their role in all types of behaviour (including thought).

Dewey argued ninety-seven years ago that habits are socially constructed and acquired through exposure to "integrated systems of activity" (1957, 58) and, more specifically, what he called social customs – local cultural practices and expectations. He wrote that "individuals form their personal habits under conditions set by prior customs" (1957, 58), or, as Dewey scholar Jim Garrison put it, Dewey was suggesting that "culture has us before we have it" (Garrison, 2002, 11S). As individuals co-develop with such systems, they unconsciously internalise predispositions (habits) inherent to intersecting places, cultures and landscape that in turn guide our thoughts, values and behaviours. Dewey argued that the 'environments' of everyday life – including language, traditions and institutions – shape thoughts, beliefs and desires to the effect that they, to a large extent, control goals and rewards (Fesmire, 2003). Dewey also suggested that the habit process is simultaneously bidirectional, because people unknowingly reproduce social customs through enacting acquired habits. In other terms, individual habits tend to reproduce social customs (Cutchin, 2007a). The most effective means of changing the transactional and mutually reinforcing relationship of social customs and individual habits, Dewey therefore argued, was by way of changing the social customs – and by those, the environmental conditions of habit development and reinforcement. For example, Dewey focused on education throughout his career because revolutionising the structure and process of schools was, in his view, the most powerful way to change a social custom and thereby develop 'active' habits of inquiry and collaboration among the next generation of citizens – habits of "thought, invention, and initiative in applying capacities to new aims" (Dewey, 1997, 52–3).

It is difficult to overstate how fundamental habit was for Dewey's social and political theory. Much more than behavioural automaticity, or a mechanism of conservation of human energy, Dewey argued that habit is "the mainspring of human action" (Dewey, 1927 [1954], 159). Dewey's view was that the most basic purpose of human action is to functionally coordinate with environments and that habits are the essential tools for doing so (Campbell, 1995; Garrison, 2002). Habits are therefore 'functions' that, while acquired from both natural and social dimensions of our habitats, provide the means to an end. They are social tools – sub-functions of their habitat – which are at the ready as potentialities and actualised through transactional coordination with a situation. In this last sense, Jim Garrison (2002) explains Dewey's multiple senses of habit, both as tools ready to use in ways used previously and as components of creative acts wherein habits are deployed in novel ways to adjust to changing situations. Such components include, for instance, the use of ideas or images from one's experience (and therefore, one's 'toolbox') that enable novel combinations with other habits in response to novel situations.

Dewey maintained that as individuals move through different environments, they adopt different habit configurations to enhance functional coordination based on the immediate surroundings (Kestenbaum, 1977). Given that most of us participate in numerous environments, each with potentially distinct traditions and institutions, it follows that different environments may engender particular sets of habit configurations and different ways of thinking. Accordingly, Dewey argued that "disposition is plural" (Dewey, 1957, 50). Taken together, we should understand Dewey as explaining a *habit process* – a part of the ongoing social transactions of people and their environments – as well as what habit is as a functional tool (Cutchin, 2007a).

In conclusion to this discussion of Dewey's theory of habit, I should comment on the place of habit in social thought and why Dewey's theory is important. Camic (1986) has provided a thorough exegesis of the demise of the concept of habit in the social sciences during the first half of the twentieth century, also making the suggestion that Dewey's thinking was (and remains) a fertile ground of opportunity for the concept's resurgence. In brief, Camic explains how Weber and Durkheim paid much attention to habit (habitus) in the early days of sociology but that Parsons effectively "wrote habit out of the whole history of modern social theory" (Camic, 1986, 1074). Parsons's purpose, among others, was to carve out autonomy for sociology, especially by distancing it from Watson's behaviourism and from the crude biophysical notion of habit that had come to dominate psychology during that time (Camic, 1986). Dewey's insights into the source and role of habit in social action are an important recovery. Although preceding Pierre Bourdieu's work by at least fifty years, Dewey's theory shares many of the traits of Bourdieu's theory of habitus (Cutchin et al., 2008). Moreover, Dewey's relational perspective on habit also presages the fluid and dynamic view of action set out by Latour's (2005) actor–network theory (ANT). Dewey's sense of the parity of individual and community in the habit process can be viewed as a form of flattening the social into the transactional relations that are continually and dynamically experienced in somewhat different ways – or, as Latour suggests, "a peculiar movement of re-association and reassembling" (2005, 7). Yet, Dewey stands alone in suggesting additional concepts that augment his theory of habit, and in his political works, he provides a case for why habit is essential to social reconstruction.

## Embodiment, imagination and inquiry

Individual habit development and use can be considered a *process of embodying* (Aldrich and Cutchin, 2013). In the Deweyan perspective, we are 'live creatures' who live *through* (and by virtue of) non-body aspects of the world (Campbell, 1995; Dewey, 1980; Kestenbaum, 1977). Dewey's theory of habit makes it clear that bodies are products of their environmental transactions from the beginning of life. The environments – i.e. places – with which a human body transacts have particularly powerful roles in the process of embodiment. In this view, communities inscribe bodies in particular ways, and habits are the manifestation and expression of that inscription. Those of us who share communities share habits, but we are individuals by the unique set of circumstances – and thus experiences – that shape our process of embodiment. In effect, we come to *embody our communities* through their physical, social and cultural influences (Aldrich and Cutchin, 2013; Cutchin, 2007a). In turn, we reproduce communities through our embodied practices (Wills, 2016). While we can focus on the negative effects that such inscription might cause, we also should recognise that such social and cultural inscription enables familiarity and understanding that, in turn, facilitate social interaction. At the same time, such familiarity is a habitual way of being that may restrain critical or imaginative thinking.

Dewey explained that our situations or situational relations inevitably evolve, shift or otherwise change and force us to deliberate upon them as well as upon the possible courses of action to take in response. Some trouble arises – some 'conflict' between action and some aspect of an environment or situation forces us to attend to it (Dewey, 1957). For Dewey, this was the initiation of *inquiry* – the human response to indeterminate situations. Per Dewey, inquiry is "the controlled or directed transformation of an indeterminate situation into one that is so determinate in its constituent distinctions and relations as to convert the elements of the original situation into a unified whole" (Dewey, 1960, 104–5). Understanding distinctions and relations via inquiry allows creative action to reconstruct the situation towards some envisioned end. It is relevant to emphasise that Dewey argued that the same structure of inquiry occurs in everyday life and in science. Knowledge gained from the process of inquiry is provisional and propositions about the distinctions and relations of a situation are best considered 'warranted assertions'. Moreover, all inquiry is a form of practice through which inquirers improve as new ideas, methods and data are employed in repeated use.

Creativity, and *imagination* in particular, were key to his theory of inquiry. Dewey framed imagination in inquiry as a process of 'dramatic rehearsal' (Cutchin et al., 2008; Fesmire, 2003). Everyday life has drama and tension that invoke emotion and feeling. An indeterminate situation has numerous potentialities or outcomes. Imagination is necessary in the rehearsal part of inquiry to (a) offer up images of potentialities and (b) deliberate about which of those foreseeable actions, and resulting new situations, is most desirable. Summarised differently, imagination is important because it generates a view of what is there, what is missing and what might become in a situation (Chambliss, 1991); but, of course, imagination is funded (or limited) by past experience and by the habits of thinking that have been embodied through that experience. For Dewey, imagination is dramatic because it is both utilised in the moment of construction of an unknown future and also occurs within the context of larger, shared narratives. As Fesmire eloquently put it, "[we] co-author a dramatic story with environing conditions in community with others" (2003, 78).

## Social reconstruction: Social inquiry as method (in need of habits)

Dewey the psychologist-philosopher was concerned with how people act and think in functional coordination with their environments. But much of his later career as a 'social pragmatist' was about developing a philosophy that would enhance the way communities could meet day-to-day challenges in the places where they faced them. Dewey the social pragmatist fully understood that the problems of communities are typically complex and deep-rooted and that actions to solve them are always provisional. Yet he believed that without a better understanding of community and processes of social reconstruction, failure would outweigh success in efforts to develop better community life. It is Dewey's spirit of meliorism and ideas from his social and political philosophy that are perhaps most notable for current pragmatism (Stuhr, 1998). Understanding the role of habits within that part of his philosophy provides us with greater power to enact it.

As we have seen in Dewey's theory of habits, place is intimately involved in shaping individuals and groups. Such individuals and groups are the basis of democracy; they are *publics* (Dewey, 1927 [1954]). In *The public and its problems* (1927 [1954]), Dewey's most extensive critique of political theory, he reconstructed the meaning of democracy – away from the state and elections towards the community-based, cooperative activity of publics. Recognising the failure of the US system to promote the participation of publics to address emergent problems that call publics to be organised, Dewey proposed that democracy be understood differently from the common conception of a political process of elections, law-making and governance. His concept of democracy was community life itself – that view being informed by his (melioristic) faith in the capacities of humans to cooperate, make intelligent judgements and act collectively to improve life under the proper circumstances (Campbell, 1998). The political context, in Dewey's time (and ours), was not amenable to this form of social democracy. Social institutions and the state had ossified and prevented publics from forming and acting in response to problematic situations. As Dewey put it, "the actual problem is one of reconstruction of the ways and forms in which men unite in associated activity" (Dewey, 1927 [1954], 192). In this view, cooperative inquiry in communities is the path to finding better values and customs, and the essential need is "the improvement of the methods and conditions of debate, discussion, and persuasion"; for Dewey, that need was "*the* problem of the public" (1927 [1954], 208). Such social reconstruction could only be done in beneficial ways through changing institutional forms and practices via a process of social inquiry. But what did Dewey mean by social reconstruction?

Deweyan scholar James Campbell has added great clarity in response to the question. What Campbell (1992, chapter 4) calls Dewey's "method of social reconstruction" was set out as a process of intellectual inquiry and deliberation followed by practical enactment of the consensus decisions and plan. In the first phase of reconstruction, a community's citizens work at naming and framing the problem as well as collecting information and explanations, clarifying the situation and developing possible options and consequences. Citizens need to find modes and materials to help them name and frame problems and imaginatively derive and deliberate possible solutions. Experts, such as social critics and scientists, may augment citizens' deliberative efforts through input of materials and ideas, but they should not drive those efforts; experts are best placed in a service role so as not to wield too much power and to engender other citizens' involvement. Dewey also thought it presumptuous not to trust people and communities to develop their own understanding of problems and of inquiry. Members of publics in communities should play the larger role as they "have the ability to judge of the bearing of the knowledge supplied by others upon common concerns" (Dewey, 1927 [1954], 209). This first phase of his method rests on a concept of democracy that is informed by a theory of inquiry that joins an understanding of scientific inquiry and common sense inquiry (Dewey, 1960) as well as a deep sense of the shared sociality of emplaced community life.

The second phase of social reconstruction is that of modifying social institutions (i.e. their makeup, functions or policies). At this second phase, there is the opportunity to experiment by way of modifying the conditions of social and political processes affecting a community. Dewey acknowledged that entrenched interests would always make social reconstruction difficult, especially at the level of institutional change. Yet the first phase is especially important because without it, we cannot, as citizens, effect changes in the second phase. Habits become an essential part of both understanding and enhancing the method and its potential. Since habits fund and enrich our ability to think and act, the greater the collection of such tools in our individual and collective toolbox, the greater the potential to name and frame problems and, especially, to imagine possible solutions. Dewey's work on education, with media and with public organisations was emblematic of his understanding of how an expansion of the habit toolbox at the individual and social level is essential to help such social reconstruction flourish. Dewey's educational reforms and experiments based on exposure to difficult but life-like problems for students, addressed with collaborative problem-solving exercises, were all about creating a well-skilled and well-funded citizenry prepared to enact the method of social reconstruction. His work with schools, as well as with various media outlets and organisations, were attempts to modify institutions in order to change social habits and individual habits of participation and engagement for such reconstruction.

Individuals need expanded experiences and habits to more fruitfully engage in discourse and help co-imagine possibilities for their communities' situations. Dewey suggested that the use of refined habits, in the sense of both imagination and intelligence, provides a community with the ability to see new connections among elements in a situation and informs better judgements about relative 'goods' and 'bads' of activity (Alexander, 1998; Campbell, 2011; Fesmire, 2003). Individuals also need to develop habits of engagement in deliberative practices – something that has become an unusual type of participation in modern Western societies. Those individual habits are part and parcel of social habits that are in need of reconstruction, both institutional as well as in Dewey's broader sense of customs. It has become common practice in many places to rely on elected officials or other 'leaders' to take charge and 'fix' community problems. The idea of citizens determining actions of social reconstruction has become uncustomary. The method of social reconstruction based in examination, deliberation and experimentation by the citizens of communities is needed. And while there are others who have suggested different perspectives, theories and approaches to deal with these matters, Dewey is unique in his vision and understanding of the dynamics that are central to change. Habermas, for one, has been suggested as Deweyan in approach via his theory of communicative action. Yet Dewey stands apart from Habermas in his philosophical underpinnings as well as in his regard for democracy as a radical project necessitating struggle and continuous change in institutions, often in small steps and in local contexts (Antonio and Kellner, 1992).

Habits of inquiry – especially social inquiry per Dewey – are so muted today that this Deweyan formulation seems odd at first consideration. Yet Dewey (1927 [1954]) argued that if our habit of such reconstruction had waned and been replaced by ossified and ineffective concepts and forms of the state, it did not mean that the method was not warranted and possible to put into effect. Of course, new social movements begin in such a way, and some eventually have some success in social reconstruction. But the primary point is that individual and social habits – as they exist today as practices and tools for imaginative social change – are inadequate for the significant social reconstruction needed in many communities and societies. Dewey was also committed to making practice intelligent and adaptable, which meant that a reconstruction of individual and social habits to address needs of communities would be necessary and ongoing (Stuhr, 1998). Such habits of inquiry are important, because democracy on these terms requires persistence, imagination and courage (Stuhr, 1998).

## Implications for social science and its practice

It is important to recognise that Dewey's concept of method is best understood as a framework for approaching and handling problems and not as a specific protocol for generating answers to particular problems (Campbell, 1995). As a framework, Dewey's conception of democracy as method includes the roles of social critics and scientists in the first, intellectual/deliberative level of reconstruction. The method emphasises social reconstruction through critical analysis of customs and habits, the work of publics engaged in democratic life and the assistance of experts in inquiry. This general approach requires a faith in human capacities together with an understanding that it also necessitates hard work and humility (Stuhr, 2010). What role is there for the social sciences in such a method, and what are the challenges and opportunities?

During this narrative, I have used the term 'communities' more often than I have used the term 'places'. Nonetheless, communities are entities that have meaning only in reference to their time and place; and by time, I mean to suggest that places or communities include their past and their envisioned future in their present. This view foregrounds customs (culture) as the main force that shapes individual habits and is in turn reinforced by the enactment of those habits. Individual and social habits persist until they are not supported by place, and places change and cause problems for habits. When the relation between habit and place becomes too incongruous, something must happen to reshape the situation. What Dewey argued is that rigorous and democratic forms of inquiry are the best approach to enhance the probability that change is positive (melioristic) for the future well-being of the community.

The social sciences have a potentially powerful role in the method of social reconstruction. Many problems of communities are problems of place that social scientists either understand or are well-prepared to study. But perhaps more importantly, Dewey emphasised that indeterminate situations – the problematic ones that need our communal attention via social inquiry – are always embedded in a particular time, place and culture. What was so maddening for Dewey's critics is that he preferred to focus on the method of social reconstruction as a generic process rather than give specific answers to worldly problems. Why was that his preferred response? Because the particularity of place, time and culture means those involved at the intersection of those domains would have to partake in inquiry and not rely on some pre-determined answers. Moreover, if communities practice using that method, it can be applied as circumstances change – and the community could become better at using the method (i.e. communal learning would happen). Social scientists are well suited to act as experts to support the process with data, inferences and suggestions. Yet we must work hand-in-hand with the public that is focused on the problem.

I have previously argued (Cutchin, 2007a, 2007b) that critical geographical work on cultural landscapes is a good match for this type of engagement. Geographer Richard Schein's critical interpretation of cultural landscapes as *discourse materialised* is important, because it provides a particularly good way to understand how place mediates the influence of social custom on habit (Schein, 1997). The cultural landscapes of places are the statements of collective habits that in many ways shape our individual habits, and they can be targets of our critical attention to inform the method of social reconstruction. As Dewey (1957, 23) stated it, "Our individual habits are links in forming the endless chain of humanity. Their significance depends upon the environment inherited from our forerunners." That inherited environment is the cultural landscape that communicates customs and values to us, shaping our habits.

For communities to employ Dewey's method of social reconstruction through social inquiry, social scientists also will need to help prepare and engage with communities in regular and supportive ways. The relatively new movement in the USA towards more community-engaged universities has potential in that it may allow more freedom and opportunities for social scientists to engage as such. An excellent model exists in the UK and has been well articulated by Harney et al.:

> the academic engages in socially-embedded inquiry on the basis that many potential problems exist, before proceeding to identify issues, ideas and potential solutions through participatory inquiry. Moreover, whereas scholar-activists will necessarily have to work with pre-existing publics that are already assembled around the pre-existing agendas that the academic is able and willing to endorse, process pragmatism seeks to use the process of research and knowledge production to construct new publics, new understandings and new capacity to act. Working in the spirit of pragmatism involves bringing together diverse groups of people with differing worldviews, to find common ground and to create new publics united around issues of common concern. Moreover, in a world of multiple truths, it may be valuable to work with as diverse a range of people as possible, facilitating projects that allow all participants to develop as effective, skilled citizens, even if their beliefs, traditions or politics clash with each other. (2016, 324)

This model of 'process pragmatism' is fully aligned with the argument I have presented here. What I would add, however, is that in addition to the various roles that students and social scientists can play in process pragmatism as organisers, educators, data collectors and so on, we can help focus a community's attention on the question of habits and customs. Habits are so often taken for granted that becoming aware of their origin and effect is a large part of the work in the democratic process of criticism and deliberation. Posing questions about habits would assist the process by opening up the imagination regarding possibilities. For example, what are the social habits in need of reconstruction? How can we encourage better habits through changing the conditions that will foster them? As Dewey (1957, 57) emphasised, the question of how people can "remake and redirect previously established customs is a deeply significant one".

This proposal, however, brings with it a set of interrelated challenges. First is the need for ongoing critical self-reflection upon our own habits of inquiry. Our disciplinary training and environments create habits of thought that may run counter to productive engagement in process pragmatism or other ventures. There are overlaying habits of social scientific inquiry, e.g. notions of methodological orthodoxy and associated expectations and rules that may be in need of reconstruction to provide necessary freedom for particular inquiries. There are other habits of practice and disciplinarity – language (jargon) being a common example – that prevent us from being good at collaboration and cooperation. And, without question, the habits of the academy and its institutional norms, from the guidelines and expectations for tenure and promotion to the continuance of disciplinary silos, should be targets of critical reflection, dialogue and reconstruction. These challenges are significant and must be part of the social reconstruction we engage in as part of our work as scholars and scientists.

In conclusion, I return to Dewey's statement introduced at the beginning of this chapter: "The best we can accomplish for posterity is to transmit unimpaired and with some increment of meaning the environment that makes it possible to maintain the habits of decent and refined life" (Dewey, 1957, 23). Social change taken on at the community level by citizens assisted by social scientists should mean taking up Dewey's ethical challenge. The process pragmatism model can do that, helped by additional attention to habit. We need to promote Dewey's method of social reconstruction with an eye towards the futures of places and people, including habits. This eye towards the intimate relationship of place, time, culture and habits gives us an additional means to amplify the effects of process pragmatism and have a positive effect on the future in communities.

## References

Aldrich, R.M. and Cutchin, M.P. (2013) Dewey's concepts of embodiment, growth, and occupation: Extended bases for a transactional perspective, in M.P. Cutchin and V.A. Dickie, eds, *Transactional perspectives on occupation*. Dordrecht: Springer, 13–23.

Alexander, T.M. (1998) The art of life: Dewey's aesthetics, in L.A. Hickman, ed., *Reading Dewey: Interpretations for a postmodern generation*, Bloomington, IN: Indiana University Press, 1–22.

Allen, J. (2008) Pragmatism and power, or the power to make a difference in a radically contingent world. *Geoforum*, 39, 4, 1613–24.

Antonio, R.J. and Kellner, D. (1992) Communication, modernity, and democracy in Habermas and Dewey. *Symbolic Interaction*, 15, 277–97.

Barnett, C. and Bridge, G. (2013) Geographies of radical democracy: Agonistic pragmatism and the formation of affected interests. *Annals of the Association of American Geographers*, 103, 1022–40.

Bridge, G. (2008) City senses: On the radical possibilities of pragmatism in geography. *Geoforum*, 39, 4, 1570–84.

Bridge, G. (2013) A transactional perspective on space. *International Planning Studies*, 18, 304–20.

Camic, C. (1986) The matter of habit. *American Journal of Sociology*, 91, 1039–87.

Campbell, J. (1992) *The community reconstructs: The meaning of pragmatic social thought*. Urbana, IL: University of Illinois Press.

Campbell, J. (1995) *Understanding John Dewey: Nature and cooperative intelligence*. Chicago, IL: Open Court.

Campbell, J. (1998) Dewey's conception of community, in L.A. Hickman, ed., *Reading Dewey: Interpretations for a postmodern generation*. Bloomington, IN: Indiana University Press, 23–42.

Campbell, J. (2011) Aesthetics as social philosophy, in L.A. Hickman, M.C., Flamm, K.P. Skowronski and J.A. Rea, eds, *The continuing relevance of John Dewey: Reflections on aesthetics, morality, science, and society*. New York, NY: Rodopi, 27–42.

Chambliss, J.J. (1991) John Dewey's idea of imagination in philosophy and education. *Journal of Aesthetic Education*, 25, 43–9.

Cutchin, M.P. (2007a). From society to self (and back) through place: Habit in transactional context. *OTJR: Occupation, Participation and Health*, 27, 50S–9S.

Cutchin, M.P. (2007b). The need for the "new health geography" in epidemiologic studies of environment and health. *Health and Place*, 13, 3, 725–42.

Cutchin, M.P. (2008). John Dewey's metaphysical ground-map and its implications for geographical inquiry. *Geoforum*, 39, 4, 1555–69.

Cutchin, M.P., Aldrich, R.M., Bailliard, A.L. and Coppola, S. (2008) Action theories for occupational science: The contributions of Dewey and Bourdieu. *Journal of Occupational Science*, 15, 3, 157–65.

Dewey, J. (1899 [1976]) The school and society, in J.A. Boydston, ed., *The middle works, 1899–1924, volume 1: 1899–1901*. Carbondale, IL: Southern Illinois University Press, 101–9.

Dewey, J. (1916 [1997]) *Democracy and education: An introduction to the philosophy of education*. New York, NY: The Free Press.

Dewey, J. (1922 [1957]) *Human nature and conduct: An introduction to social psychology*. New York, NY: The Modern Library.

Dewey, J. (1925) *Experience and nature*. La Salle, IL: Open Court.

Dewey, J. (1931) *Individualism old and new*. London: George Allen and Unwin.

Dewey, J. (1934 [1980]) *Art as experience*. New York, NY: Perigree Books.

Dewey, J. (1938 [1960]) *Logic: The theory of inquiry*. New York, NY: Holt, Rinehart and Winston.

Dewey, J. (1927 [1954]) *The public and its problems*. Athens, OH: Swallow Press/Ohio University Press.

Fesmire, S. (2003) *John Dewey and moral imagination: Pragmatism in ethics*. Bloomington, IN: Indiana University Press.

Garrison, J. (2002) Habits as social tools in context. *OTJR: Occupational Therapy Journal of Research*, 22, 11S–7S.

Harney, L., McCurry, J., Scott, J. and Wills, J. (2016) Developing "process pragmatism" to underpin engaged research in human geography. *Progress in Human Geography*, 40, 3, 316–33.

James, W. (1890) *Principles of psychology*. New York, NY: Holt. https://archive.org/details/principlespsych08jamegoog/page/n6/mode/2up (accessed 26 January 2020).

Kestenbaum, V. (1977) *The phenomenological sense of John Dewey: Habit and meaning*. Atlantic Highlands, NJ: Humanities Press.

Lake, R.W. (2014) Methods and moral inquiry. *Urban Geography*, 35, 5, 657–68.

Latour, B. (2005) *Reassembling the social: An introduction to actor–network-theory*. Oxford: Oxford University Press.

Schein, R.H. (1997) The place of landscape: a conceptual framework for interpreting an American scene. *Annals of the Association of American Geographers*, 87, 4, 660–80.

Strauss, A.L. (1987) *Qualitative analysis for social scientists*. Cambridge: Cambridge University Press.

Stuhr, J.J. (1998) Dewey's social and political philosophy, in L.A. Hickman, ed., *Reading Dewey: Interpretations for a postmodern generation*. Bloomington, IN: Indiana University Press, 82–99.

Stuhr, J.J. (2010) Looking toward last things: James's pragmatism beyond its first century, in J.J. Stuhr, ed., *100 years of pragmatism: William James's revolutionary philosophy*. Bloomington, IN: Indiana University Press, 194–207.

Wills, J. (2016) (Re)Locating community in relationships: questions for public policy. *Sociological Review*, 64, 639–56.

3

# Appreciating the situation: Dewey's pragmatism and its implications for the spatialisation of social science

*Gary Bridge*

## Introduction

A concern with temporality and change and its relationship to human experience has been a central contribution of pragmatic thought. In its widest register, this involves the full acknowledgement of Darwin's theory of evolution and the place of the human species within it. This form of naturalism means that humans are understood to be part of an ever-evolving natural environment. The relationship between human organisms and their environment is at the core of human experience for Dewey. This is a process philosophy in which substances, objects or human organisms, for example, are treated as events. They are part of a process and not made of permanent stuff. So, there are no rounded-out humans, nor objects, and what we should concentrate on is the relations between them, or what Dewey calls 'transactions' (Dewey, 1981; Dewey and Bentley, 1949 [1991]). Dewey is at pains to distinguish transaction from the idea of interaction, the latter being a relationship between solidly constituted things (for example, human tool bearers, objects that are utilised as tools). In transactions, the nature of objects and organisms is co-constitutive and not finished. The focus is on the 'nature' or 'character' of the transaction, subject to, and implicated in, evolutionary, historical and temporal changes. Flux, uncertainty and contingency are embedded in human experience. As William James put it, "life is in the transitions as much as it is in the terms connected: often it seems to be there more emphatically" (James, 1904, 568–9).

In this view, human experience consists of actions, thought (as a form of action), communication and habits (including cultural customs and artefacts).

The significance of evolution, history and temporality underlies the acknowledgement of the tension between stability and contingency that is embedded in pragmatist naturalism. Pragmatist philosophy offers an understanding of experience that acknowledges its temporality and contingency, but also one, I suggest, in which spatiality and temporality are both critical in shaping the relationship between human organisms and their environment.

What I argue in the rest of this chapter is that the tools to analyse the spatiality of experience exist in pragmatist philosophy. I look particularly to pragmatist philosopher John Dewey's work for the intellectual resources needed to address these concerns. Dewey's understanding of the space/time of human experience offers resources for interpreting (and beginning to address) contemporary problems. One example would be the conflicts between versions of globalism and localism in contemporary politics. In this case, Dewey was well aware, for example, of the effects of wider global forces on experience and the prospects for democracy, in his era associated with industrialisation, urbanisation and the growth of media in opening out communities to more diverse forces and influences, which made democratic coordination ever more difficult to achieve (Dewey, 2008).

Before embarking on an exploration of the spatialities of Dewey's philosophy, it is important to emphasise the point that this does not aim to elevate an idea of space and spatiality over and above time and temporality, nor indeed to suggest a separate realm of the spatial. This would be against the grain of Dewey's philosophy and its emphasis on process, interconnection and co-development through transaction (primarily between organisms and their environment). Dewey's anti-Cartesian outlook would indeed shun a separation of time and space as separate coordinates of existence. The priority given to space in experience here is purely analytical and a way of compensating for the prior emphasis on time and temporality in pragmatist philosophy (Margolis, 1986; Stuhr, 1997; and especially Koopman, 2009). Nevertheless, there is always the risk that this one-sided approach can end up reifying the separateness of the focus of analysis, and I hope to provide sufficient correctives throughout the discussion to avoid this possibility. One other preliminary is that this discussion focuses on the *human* experience of space. This is not uncontroversial, given current discussions of more-than-human environments, distributed agency and flat ontologies of human–non–human–object assemblages (DaLanda, 2006; Deleuze and Guatarri, 1987). In the course of the discussion, I suggest how the exclusive focus on human experience and action can be justified in terms of the focus on space and spatial relations.

## Pragmatism's view of human experience

Human relations with the environment are just that – a series of mutual relations in which the environment itself is as active as the organisms. This is the strain of pragmatism that has in part inspired contemporary vitalist pragmatics, in which human organisms and their agency are embedded in a live environment of effects or a series of assemblages or actor networks (DaLanda, 2006; Latour, 2007). But a second strain of pragmatist thinking has been more centrally concerned with human action, either in terms of an idea of human experience or language use (see Koopman, 2009). These strains explore the relationship between knowledge and action, both what Dewey (1983) called 'known' knowledge and forms of implicit or 'had' knowledge and what Peirce (1897 [1931]) distinguished as 'firstness' (quality of feeling), 'secondness' (relations; brute facts) and 'thirdness' (representation). This approach helped shift understandings of human knowledge from Cartesian cognitive apperception to practical forms of action.

These streams of thinking (vitalist and rationalist; experience-oriented and rational), although issuing from a similar source, may now seem to be far apart in the social sciences: one strand dealing with human agency, understood to be distributed, diffused and flattened into networks of human, non-human and environmental actants, and the other concerned exclusively with human experience or human reasoning and deliberation as a form of privileged action (and especially realised in linguistic coordination and action). The first approach seeks to locate human action within a diverse set of effects, in assemblages where non-human actants and objects have equivalent effects. The other seeks to emphasise the distinctiveness of human organic action, especially in human capacities for linguistic communication and the commitments and responsibilities (in action) that come from credibility in language use (Brandom, 1998).

A focus on time-space transitions in human activity and experience has the capacity, I argue, to reduce this apparent division between distributed action in assemblies on one side and humanly concerted and concentrated forms of action involving human experience or forms of judgement and reason on the other. It starts to connect these separating streams of pragmatist thought: vitalist pragmatism and experience pragmatism, and experience pragmatism and linguistic (or rationalist) pragmatism. In what follows, I examine time-space transitions through Dewey's idea of 'situation', which links the immediacy of time-space in what he called problematic situations with a wider fund of experience (both individual and shared), including habits, which relate to wider networks of time and space. The distinctiveness of human experience is that problematic situations collapse time-and-space relations into a single situation with selective emphasis depending on the exigencies of the immediate circumstances, including the human organisms, objects and non-human actants that comprise it. This is mostly achieved non-cognitively through habit, but it is sometimes pushed into the cognitive realm, involving forms of reasoning and justification. This latter aspect is exemplified in the linguistic competences of human organisms and the orchestration of public life.

## Space, experience and situation

For Dewey, human experience is continuous with nature and is itself in flux:

> experience is *of* as well as *in* nature. It is not experience that is experienced, but nature – stones, plants, animals, diseases, health, temperature, electricity and so on. Things interacting in certain ways *are* experience; they are what is experienced. Linked in certain other ways with another natural object – the human organism-they are *how* things are experienced as well. Experience thus reaches down into nature; it has depth. It also has breadth and to an infinitely elastic extent. It stretches. (1981, 12–13, emphasis in the original)

Thus human experience is a part of, and continuous with, nature, though it is in fact only a small part. The natural conditions that allow for human experience are specialised and limited, both in terms of evolutionary history (humans were late on the scene) and in terms of all the other forces in nature alongside which human experience and human action exist. These forces can act indifferently to human activities and purposes, as well as to those activities and purposes being implicated within them, creating "the sense of our slight inability even with our best intelligence and effort to command events: a sense of our dependence on forces that go their own way without our wish or plan" (Dewey 1983, 200). Thus human organic experience is a highly specialised and vulnerable activity with limited occurrence. Nevertheless, where it does occur, it tends to have ramifying effects. As Dewey (1981, 12) argues, "when experience does occur, no matter at what limited portion of time and space, it enters into possession of some portion of nature and in such a manner as to render other of its precincts accessible".

Other of nature's precincts are made accessible through the sustained organisation of organic human energies through inquiry. This sustained organisation is achieved as a result of the character of human experience in which nature is experienced in two different ways: first, as an immediate qualitative experience that, Dewey argues, has a completeness and finality to it; and second, it is experienced as a situation in which qualities of nature require a human experiencer. These qualities are not confined to the experiencing human organism: they are distributed in the wider situation (or transaction). If this experience becomes unsettled or unclear, it can become a 'problematic situation' (Dewey, 1986), prompting a process of inquiry to clarify or resettle the situation. This process involves, to different degrees depending on the situation, non-cognitive and cognitive action and non-discursive and discursive communication, and it implicates time and space in several ways. The problem-solving activity results in a transition from one situation (uncertain, uncanny, etc.) to another (more certain, less threatening). The attempt to define the difficulty and re-establish continuity means that there is a reaching out to wider experience and other spaces and times. This takes place as a form of inquiry involving practical reason. As such, Dewey's understanding of inquiry sits on top of arguments about time, space, experience and reason that are worth exploring in more depth.

## Space, time and situation

Dewey points out how time and space are imbricated in the behaviour of mobile higher organisms:

> A sessile organism requires no premonitions of what is to occur, nor cumulative embodiments of what has occurred. An organism with locomotion is as vitally connected with the remote as well as with the nearby; when locomotor organs are accompanied by distance-receptors, response to the distant in space becomes increasingly prepotent and equivalent in effect to response in the future in time. A response to what is distant is in effect an expectation or prediction of later contact. (1981, 197)

Dewey argues that mobility of this kind is not confined to the actions of the organism itself but is a characteristic of the wider environment. Thus prey fleeing the hunter and finding refuge is also an environmental change in that it changes the ability of the environment to act. There are continuities in these responses: watchfulness and alertness in a higher animal is on a continuum with anticipation in humans. Just as time and space are harbingers of change and potential uncertainty, they are also resources that are marshalled by higher animals in dealing with change.

Indeed, the bank of previous experiences of times and spaces is deployed as an ongoing mode of response. As Dewey argues:

> In contrast with lower organisms, the more complex forms have distance receptors and a structure in which activators and effectors are allied to distance even more than to contact receptors. What is done in response to things nearby is so tied to what is done in response to what is far away, that a higher organism acts with reference to a spread-out environment as a single situation. We find also in all these higher organisms that what is done is conditioned by consequences of past activities: we find the act of learning or habit-formation. In consequence, an organism acts with reference to a time-spread, a serial order of events, as a unit, just as it does in reference to a unified spatial variety. (1981, 213)

Thus spatio-temporal experience exists in habits as enduring, and sometimes extensive, dispositions towards the world. The integration of organic environmental connections is evident in habits in which the environment "has its say" (Dewey, 1986, 15). Thus organic environmental connections are *in* habits. These are selectively drawn on by the demands of more immediate situations where the smooth functioning of such dispositions is interrupted or ceases to function properly, leading to an experience of uncertainty or indeterminacy. That experience (and the feelings they initiate) are situational rather than individual: "it is the situation that is, for example, apprehensive" (Dewey, 1981, xi). If problematic situations challenge habits, then it is habits that are the first step in attempting to resolve the situation. Habitual action is the first step in the problem-solution. Initial attempts at resolution might thus be action-orientated but with low cognitive engagement – more about reorganisation of the exigencies of ongoing action, more about re-arrangement of immediate spatio-temporal relations through manipulating the elements of the situation.

If objections or difficulties persist in the environment, then responses are pushed into a subsequent phase of action that is more cognitive and reflexive. In human organisms, the resources that can be drawn on in this more selective phase of action are much wider than the immediate situation. As Dewey argues,

> It may be a mystery that there should be thinking but it is no mystery that if there is thinking it should contain in a 'present' phase, affairs remote in space and time, even to geologic ages, future eclipses and far away stellar systems. It is only a question of how far what is 'in' its actual experience is extricated and becomes focal. (1981, 213).

This gives us two aspects of situation in relation to space and time. There are "extensive and enduring" situations of what Dewey elsewhere calls "togetherness" (Dewey, 2012, 340). These are what we might call dispositional fields, which frame modes of response in the ways that objects 'call out' to human organisms and how they are 'taken' (in the sense of understood as well as physically grasped) by humans: "That which is 'given' in the strict sense of the word 'given', is the total field or situation" (Dewey, 1986, 127). This frames the existentially given situation:

> This larger and inclusive subject-matter is what is meant by the term 'situation' … the situation as such is not and cannot be stated or made explicit. It is taken for granted, 'understood' or implicit in all propositional symbolization … [and] the situation controls the terms of thought. (Dewey, 1984, 247)

The second understanding of situation concerns the selective use by individuals, or, more likely, by groups of communicating individuals, of the resources of extensive and enduring situations as they are applied to problematic immediate situations. Dewey argued that there is continuity between immediate time-space action and experience and the more extensive time-space 'situations' that are part of the 'reach' as well as depth of the connections of human experience in nature. This is continuous, to differing degrees, across species (the watchfulness of the higher mammals is continuous with planning and anticipation in humans, for instance). It is also continuous from immediate to more extensive situations. As we have seen, in immediate experience, spatial distance is a form of pre-potency. Communication is here often gestural and non-discursive, involving visual clues, atmospheres and spatial positions of organisms or objects. What is significant for the present argument is that, in forms of shared communication, the repertoires of communicative performance that inform immediate situations are continuous with more discursive repertories in extensive problematic situations. Thus non-discursive pre-potency becomes an "anticipatory share in the communication of a transaction in which (both communicators) participate" (Dewey, 1981, 142).

Dewey's pragmatism emphasises the continuities and interactive relationship between tacit and explicit knowledge and its consequences for communicative action (see especially Brandom, 1998). I have explored elsewhere the significance of implicit, non-discursive forms of communication in performances for setting the tone or providing a platform for more discursive action in spatial arenas, particularly in urban public space, where these non-discursive routines can be established (Bridge, 2005). This can be traced through the work of the ethnomethodologists and dramaturgical sociologists (Garfinkel, 1967; Goffman, 1955). Roberto Frega (2015), though less concerned with the spatialities of these processes, highlights the significance of these forms of communication, even for moral problems in what he calls 'the normative structure of the ordinary'.

Frega emphasises the significance of everyday interactions as being absolutely crucial in maintaining social order and ongoing life, given their fragility and uncertainty. These are "the ongoing accomplishments of the concerted activities of daily life" (Garfinkel, 1967, vii; cited in Frega, 2015). This involves adjustments and reconfirmations of the normative structure of action "that only seldom take the shape of explicit and discursive acts" (Frega, 2015, 4). Ethnomethodology points to the significance of the exigencies of the situation in making normative judgements, both in making judgements and construing meanings and also in the binding together of participants in communication as a hedge against uncertainties and ambiguities. This relates to a view of normative work as a shared endeavour in which participants take responsibility for, in particular, the minor infringements and misdemeanours of other participants in order to maintain 'face'. This is an understanding of normativity that is derived from efforts at maintenance, repair and pardons for social slips or infelicities, rather than explicit assertion, justification or critique of those social transgressions.

Referring to Dewey, Frega argues that "the structure of our normative commitments is irreducibly transactional ... It is not only rooted in the social context which constitutes the action-situation but it is also constituted through face-to-face interaction and the transactional relationship integrating the organismic agent and their social and natural environment" (Frega, 2015, 14). What we see here is how more immediate situations are instrumental in the reproduction and regulation of much wider normative social structures. To adapt Frega's idea of the 'normative structure of the ordinary', normative structures are as much situational as they are structural. Actions taken in the immediate situation may be carried into other situations just as much as the selective use of the more enduring and extensive situation can help overcome obstructed action in the immediate, problematic situation. There is no eliminating the situation and its contingencies – there are no ultimate certainties on which to base action – but there are holding operations that can facilitate action for the time being (I have elsewhere referred to reasoning as a perch for action; Bridge, 2005).

## Space, language and situation

The spatio-temporal understanding of situation and modalities of experience also implicates linguistic communication, in terms of providing a context of language use in the immediate situation as well as the connectivity of meaning into the more extensive and enduring situation to which linguistic meaning can apply (through human experience). Complex discursive communication and the functioning of language are, of course, distinctive features of human organisms. Again, though, there is a relation between immediacy and mobility. In a Deweyan framework, meaning is produced through a transaction between human activities and varied objects and purposes: "The flower is the thing which it immediately is, and it is also a means to a conclusion. All of this is directly involved in the existence of intelligible speech" (Dewey, 1981, 143).

Language makes objects mobile and, in this sense, dispositional – able to be applied in different contexts in extensive and enduring situations of experience and modes of response. But language is also indexical and about specific context in its meaning. To adapt Wittgenstein (1953 [2009]), 'meaning is use', and use is always contextual (indexical) and related to situations. This idea of indexicality (deriving meaning by pointing to objects in context) is derived from Charles Peirce's semiotics and is the basis of linguistic pragmatics (Peirce, 1897 [1932]; see also Austin, 1962). The significance of indexicality for the present discussion of space, time and situation is that it emphasises the significance of context and the particular constellations of elements in fixing meaning. In the problematic situation, the particular assemblage of human actants, non-human actants and objects and materials is important in how human actors select the elements to start reasoning (the institution of the problem) if ongoing habits fail to resolve the indeterminate situation. A second important feature of indexicality is that it needn't be solely discursive. Non-discursive and gestural actions can be indexical (like pointing an index finger), and this emphasises the continuities between non-discursive and discursive action – in this case, in the constitution of linguistic action. Furthermore, in the context of the contingencies, indeterminacies and ambiguities that characterise problematic situations are where the indexical functions of language that capture the nuance and context – such that the meaning can be construed – are crucial. The spatio-temporal relations of the situation are part of the context and part of the constitution of meaning. In the case of the human communicators, the significance of indexicality (ambiguity) increases the attention and commitment of the participants, out of which judgements emerge.

As well as having contextual, or situational, elements, language is at the same time, for Dewey, a release from the constraints of the immediate environment and a continuation of animal/organic responses beyond the local environmental constraints (which dominate the activities of other higher mammals). Language makes the immediate potentiality of the situation portable: "the flower means portability instead of being simply portable" (Dewey, 1981, 142). Thus linguistic meaning has two spatio-temporal effects: it can transport meaning or extend the problematic situation to draw on other spaces and times in the more extensive and enduring situation that reflects experience, but it is also what I would call 'funded' (i.e. informed, filled-in) by the immediate situation. Some of these characteristics are also captured in contemporary topological thinking (Allen, 2016, for example). Given the way that language can transport events (objects) that are filled with meaning to expanded fields of 'togetherness', the immediate situation need not be a co-present one. Contemporary socio-cultural environments are highly mediatised, involving a multiplicity of digitised forms of personal communication, as well as different forms of media and communication more widely. These present a myriad of potentially 'immediate' situations (not involving co-presence). However, there is also a sense in which co-presence retains its communicative power as a source of 'funding' meaning.

Within language use, there is a relationship between implicit, indexically funded situations and more extensive and enduring situations. Again, in a related vein, Roberto Frega (2015) points to the work of Robert Brandom as conducting a parallel exercise in extending the interactional repertoires involving implicit forms of communication (discussed with reference to ethnomethodology) into language use. Brandom's (1998) inferential semantics posit that meaning in language is established in terms not of representational accuracy but of how explicit statements in language result from implicit social interactions, which are freighted with normative obligations. To make a statement is to make a commitment, which comes with obligations and entitlements in how it logically implies other terms and meanings, which are mutually recognised in social interaction (Brandom, 1998). Thus social normativity is inherent in the basic structure of language and discourse (Frega, 2015). In taking a normative stance, agents commit themselves inferentially to a set of assumptions, the validity of which can be argued in what Wilfred Sellers (2007) called 'the space of reasons'.

There are strong parallels between the performative and non-discursive aspects of interaction that we have discussed and the linguistic/discursive forms of communication and meaning that Brandom identifies in his inferential semantics. Both rely on certain implicit structures of convention and commitment and strategic rationality that are at the same time highly reliant on context and indexicality for the ongoing fixing of the context/meaning/ normative situation. More enduring norms or meanings are refunded in contextual situations.

## Space, time and aesthetic experience

For Dewey, the forms of aesthetic communication have the greatest potential to combine the qualitative wholeness of immediate experience with more extensive and enduring situations of 'togetherness'. Aesthetic practice has the greatest scope for creative re-arrangement or re-ordering or, indeed, the creation of novel spatio-temporal experience. But again, for Dewey, aesthetic practice is communicative, and it is not restricted to the work of any individual artist or art object (Shusterman, 2000). These contextual wholes of aesthetic communication (situations) are "events of mutual participation [with] particular potentialities for shaping space and time" (Langsdorf, 2002, 151). It is the transactional, communicative qualities of art (rather than individual creativity or the art object) that are important for Dewey and that give art a transformative democratic potential. Aesthetic experience is par excellence a combination of qualitative immediate experience and consummation with more extensive and enduring situations in which the art object is filled with meaning and the effects of its communication are experienced as a transaction between the art object and observer or listener. Moreover, aesthetics are part of everyday life – not as they are rendered at present, spatially separated as art in the gallery or as artefacts in the museum – they are the "clarified and intensified development of traits that belong to every normally complete experience" (Dewey, 1986, 52–3).

Aesthetic communication points to the constitutive nature of communicative experience that can

> direct participants toward the unsayable: to what cannot be transmitted because there is no antecedent to transmit. It requires calling upon the enduring presence of non-discursive, somatic experience to expand our discursive parameters, and so relies upon Dewey's thesis that somatic experience – which is 'had' but not known (1981 198) – continues its efficacy throughout all modes of communication. (Langsdorf, 2002, 152)

This experience comes out of the "ways in which people (and animals) somatically develop their interaction with their environments (e.g. chronemics, haptics, kinesics, proxemics, and vocalics) in ways that cannot be represented but must be performed by communicating bodies" (Langsdorf, 2002, 147). Aesthetic experience combines the immediate situation of qualitative wholeness and consummation with more enduring and extensive communicative paths. It combines the integrative qualities of space with space as extension and distanciation: a breathing in and out of space through practice.

This is partly about the way that co-presence opens up channels of communication (both discursive and non-discursive) to the extent that the spatial co-presence of bodies and their arrangements (proxemics, vocalics), as well as atmospheres and affect, can have communicative effects. Feminist pragmatist philosopher Shannon Sullivan (2001, 61; for a further discussion, see Bridge, 2005, 22–4) has used Dewey's idea of 'body-mind' as a continuity of communication and response, and she points to the importance of 'situational excess', such that the "discursivity of bodies be acknowledged and that room be made for discussion of the concrete 'had' experiences of lived bodies". As such, bodies are part of a wider social discursivity (Butler, 1993, 1997) or habitus dispositions (Bourdieu, 1984). But in problematic situations, where the dispositional qualities of habits are disrupted, novel communicative 'reads' are more possibly changing meaning through use (Butler, 1997, points to miscues, mistakes and slips, for instance).

We have seen in this section how micro-spatial settings and relations and non-discursive forms of communication can fund, transgress or even begin to transform more explicit communicative commitments that have more extensive (spatial) and enduring (temporal) reach. Equally more extensive situations are brought to bear selectively in more immediate problematic situations. In the following section, I consider experience in settings that pose multiple problematic situations, specifically the problem of coping as a new immigrant or migrant in a growing city. The first example is the Chicago School of Urban Ecology, which utilised pragmatist philosophy to inform the study of immigrant communities in early-twentieth-century Chicago. The second, related example – in the same city and in the same era – is the Hull House settlement, which provides an example of problem-solving through action and experimentation rather than the more abstract approach of the Chicago School.

## Experiencing space

The Chicago School of Urban Ecology represented the first systematic investigation and analysis of the modern industrial city. Chicago School sociologists focused on the conditions of immigrant neighbourhoods and the adjustments made by the community to a new and challenging environment. In this analysis, spatial registers were especially significant. Dewey had collaborated extensively with Chicago School sociologist George Herbert Mead. The journalist, later turned Chicago School academic, Robert Park also collaborated with John Dewey on *The Thought News*, a periodical/newssheet aimed at broadcasting the findings of social science to the wider public of Chicago. It was Robert Park alongside other Chicago sociologists who investigated the immigrant neighbourhoods and the ways in which residents coped with and adapted to life in a rapidly growing city. That spatial analysis, particularly the identification of certain spatial patternings of social dynamics and the impact of spatial segregation of communities, was taken up in subsequent studies in urban social geography (Jackson and Smith, 1984; Peach, 1975). Measurement of the spatial segregation of different immigrant communities became an indicator of social isolation, the processes of discrimination and resultant social problems. But Park's original essay was also concerned with the city as "a spatial pattern and moral order" (Park, 1926). That moral order referred to the social norms that immigrant communities brought from their 'home' countries and how those norms were challenged, changed or adapted through the experience of life in a growing, multicultural, North American industrial metropolis.

The Chicago School sociologists investigated these changing norms through extensive ethnographic work. In this, they were investigating how normative structures were reconstituted in 'ordinary' situations of everyday life. They investigated how uncertain situations of interaction were constituted and negotiated (and, as we have seen, this was later taken up by dramaturgical sociology and ethnomethodology). It was argued that non-discursive as well as linguistic forms of communication constituted space in certain ways. The Chicago ethnographers recorded transactions that were space-shaping, including the practices associated with relations between communicator and audience, significant object and background, received statements and the background hum of activity. Space was also understood as being constituted 'on the go' in the more conventional micro-spatial setting or stage. They also addressed abrupt spaces: situations come upon in everyday activity, which had to be construed – what Chicago sociologist W.I. Thomas (1923) referred to as the 'definition of the situation'. These were situations that acted back on communication and in which early non-discursive cues and adjustments could be critical. The Chicago urban ecologists' ethnographic approach immersed them in the situations of social and spatial experience, but primarily from the point of view of analytical observers concerned with representational accuracy. This is very much the territory of established social science, even though the framing of the analysis was pioneering in many ways. However, contemporaneously with the work of the Chicago ecologists, and in the same city, there were very different spatial practices being developed by those involved in the Hull House settlement in Chicago.

Hull House practices illustrate the combining of the immediate space-time situation with more extensive regimes. In this regard, I turn to Shannon Jackson's (2001) analysis of the settlement, in which she captures what she calls the 'interspatiality' of Hull House and the dual notions of 'settlement' that attached to it (settlement as place-making and agreement across division and difference). The house was purchased and occupied by middle-class philanthropists (led by Jane Addams), who gave their professional expertise and personal contacts in service to a poor Italian-American neighbourhood in Chicago in the late nineteenth and early twentieth century. Hull House was led by Jane Addams and her friends and colleagues, but it also involved John Dewey as a member of the

Hull House Board of Trustees, a regular visitor and lecturer, and as someone who acknowledged the influence of Jane Addams's ideas (Jackson, 2001, 14–17). Hull House has been discussed in a number of different ways, but Jackson focuses on what she calls the process of 'settling' in Hull House. By this, she refers to the sense of coming to occupy and belong in the house and settling conflicts, disputes and differences in ways that combined experiential and linguistic pragmatisms. Hull House itself afforded certain interactions, activities and atmospheres. The open qualities of the space allowed for a flexible mix of activities as well as the degree to which it acted as a public or domestic space to include a mix of bodies, objects and class practices. Hull House resident Dorothea Moore, having described all the rooms of the property, found it difficult to define something that, as she wrote, was "essentially plastic" (Moore, 1897, 635; cited in Jackson, 2001, 24). Jackson portrays how repeated performances and somatic practices created the domesticity of the house but also the idea that current enactments were instilled with historic performances. Recursive as well as transgressive practices were always in play.

In her *Twenty years at Hull House,* Jane Addams (1919 [1968]) recalled an interactive moment in which she picked up on the minutiae of body and face work as some of the neighbourhood families reacted to coming into the sitting room and seeing the objects there, such as candlesticks and heavy brocade curtains. Their somatic reaction and the resultant atmosphere of unease, along with Addams's cognition of that situation and her reaction to it, all combined to produce a transformative moment. She realised that for the working-class immigrant incomers, the objects conveyed bourgeois comfort and taste: the objects became filled with meaning – a communicatively significant non-discursive interaction. This was a problematic situation prompted by an immediate, qualitative experience of unease on all sides (the residents' unease in the room and Addams's reaction to their awkwardness was displayed in their bodily movements). The ornaments were subsequently removed and the curtains replaced. As Jackson comments, long before Pierre Bourdieu's analysis, Jane Addams was registering the communicative import of habitus, class division and taste, which, to her at that time, were obstacles to the wider purposes of Hull House, which sought to collaboratively overcome some of the social problems that the surrounding low-income neighbourhood suffered, by mingling middle-class settlers and working-class residents. As Jackson (2001, 23) explains, "In the process of facilitating new kinds of performances, the settlement also experimented with alternative styles of living and created various kinds of transformative spaces for middle-class reformers, late Victorian women, unnaturalised immigrants, adolescent girls and incorrigible boys". And again:

> the legacies of various spaces intersected and overlaid themselves on its walls, in the
> practices its occupants performed, in the writing Hull House reformers produced,
> in the curriculum its classes offered, in the physical and environmental reforms

> Progressives sought, in the ruptures and failures of particular experiments, in the architecture of the new buildings it erected. To theorize the semiotic hybridity of interpreted spaces, the term *interspatiality* gestures to a 'space as text' paradigm. Like a complex text that contains illusions, suggestions, parodies and quotations from other texts, strains of many spaces may permeate selected spaces. (Jackson, 2001, 24, emphasis in the original)

This same transposition of space was evident in the House overall, which was at various times through the day a crèche, a school, a night school, a dance floor and a dining room. It also pertained to the wider civic politics of Hull House, as the domestic space of an immigrant apartment in which the curtains were filthy became a public campaign for local communal washhouses and a clean-air act to limit the pollution from the local factory, which was making the curtains dirty in the first place. The transposition of public and private space was instilled in Addams's notion of 'civic housekeeping' (Addams, 1968).

Hull House privileged embedded experience, which was subsequently translated into practices that sought to change the situation, in contrast to the priority given to the representation of situations by the Chicago School sociologists. In the illustration above, Jane Addams picked up on the discomfort of the visitors, which prompted an action – removal of the offending objects – which in turn changed the situation. In contrast, the Chicago ethnographers' task, first and foremost, was to represent the situations they encountered (with a more arm's-length approach to intervention in the situation). This relates to Brandom's (1998) arguments (discussed earlier) of pragmatism favouring experiential engagement over representational accuracy. This pragmatist approach has numerous implications for methods in social science, some of which are explored in other chapters in this book. However, the main point to be made at this juncture is that privileging experiential engagement is not to wholly fold the analysis of the social scientist into the experiential situation. The distinction to be made between social scientist and 'subject' is itself situational. When applied to social science methodology, it is possible to use the problematic situation in a dialogical sense in order to analytically connect the social scientist's 'extensive and enduring situation' of social science knowledge and practice, which is then brought to bear on 'a single situation' (as Dewey would put it) from which the dialogical reconstruction of the problem situation will selectively draw. In this sense, the combination of Chicago School sociology and Hull House experimentalism continues to offer a powerful model for social science methods, and one that fully integrates the experience of space.

## Conclusion

Situations, and the relationships between implicit and explicit action, have spatial qualities (see also Bridge, 2005). The emergence of problematic situations is a form of 'closeness' involving the selection of other, more extensive times and spaces of experience of the various participants in the situation. In this way, the overall situation brings the selective emphases (from habits through to reflection, depending on the nature of the problematic situation) from the diverse extensive situations of participants into engagement in the immediate problematic situation. This experience of space has certain qualities that I have characterised elsewhere as 'transactional thickness' (Bridge, 2013). Transitions into situations can be gradual or abrupt. Certain spatial arrangements can themselves be the shock of transition (abrupt space, if you like). Thus there are a number of ways in which spatial transitions feature in the relationship between problematic situations and more extensive and enduring situations.

The combining of selective emphases from diverse extensive and enduring situations involves non-discursive as well as discursive action, but if the situation is sufficiently problematic, it forces these engagements more and more into that phase of action that is thinking, and ultimately into the realms of reason and justification. I have argued elsewhere (Bridge, 2005, 2008) that the combinations of participants' non-discursive actions can constitute a platform or perch from which more discursive action and reason can operate. I also suggest that certain urban spaces themselves can be seen as more conducive to this constitutive platform in the way that they allow non-discursive engagements to unfold. In a related approach, Lussault and Stock (2010) take the idea of pragmatics as a research area in which practice is the focus to understand the relationships between practice and space. They characterise this as 'doing with space' rather than 'being in space' (Lussault and Stock, 2010). This is the idea of space produced through practice, or what I have called elsewhere, adapting Dewey, 'transactional space' (Bridge, 2005, 2013). This is neither Cartesian space as a container of activity, nor relational space (relations between objects with no fixed location). Rather, as Lussualt and Stock argue, space is emergent and woven into practices. Following Werlen (1992), they rightly associate 'doing with space' with *situations*, rather than appealing to any fixed notion of space (Lussault and Stock, 2010).

I concur with this. Dewey talks more about situations than about space. Language use has the capacity to extend the reach of participants from the problematic situation into more enduring/extensive situations by putting agreed meanings (as part of wider instrumentalities of action) in motion. In this processual view of life, discursive communication has the capacity to put things, as potentialities, into motion and actualisation. It stretches space. But space is also a fund, a resource (though one that is socially differentiated). Lussault and Stock (2010) here bring in the idea of spatial capital discussed in French sociology. Like Bourdieu's ideas of social and cultural capital, spatial capital is the differentiated ability to cope with, manage or dominate social life (or, in the case of spatial capital, spatial problems). It is developed out of different acquired competences from the experience of space/other spaces. This reinforces the point they make about situations being open to other influences (rather than, as they see it, a closed idea of situation in traditional dramaturgical sociology). Differentiated capacities in the situation illuminate this point; the immediate experience of space is differentially funded but also potentially transformative by being constantly refunded.

In problematic situations, we can see how 'had' knowledge, somatic communication and implicit rationalities are often the first phase of recognition of the problem (and rely initially on established habits to move forward). But we have also seen how the fragility and contingency of transactions mean that the characteristics of the situation itself (the collection of constituent elements, both human and non-human) play a part in the direction of change. Space is transitional and transactional, involving transactional immediacy in the problematic phase and distanciation and distribution in its outward, ongoing phase.

I have started to suggest some ways in which space is implicated in this inward/outward motion and in opening up other 'precincts' of nature. Through human organisms, this implicates the 'how' as well as the 'what' of organic experience, and the 'how' is the way in which nature comes to consciousness and re-appraises itself.

## References

Addams, J. (1919 [196]) *Twenty years at Hull House*. New York, NY: Macmillan.
Allen, J. (2016) *Topologies of power: Beyond territory and networks*. London: Routledge.
Austin, J.L. (1962) *How to do things with words*. Oxford: Clarendon Press.
Bourdieu, P. (1984) *Distinction: A social critique of the judgement of taste*. London: Routledge and Kegan Paul.
Brandom, R. (1998) *Making it explicit: Reasoning, representing, and discursive commitment*. Cambridge, MA: Harvard University Press.
Bridge, G. (2005) *Reason in the city of difference: Pragmatism communicative action and contemporary urbanism*. London: Routledge.
Bridge, G. (2008) City senses: On the radical possibilities of pragmatism in geography. *Geoforum*, 39, 4, 1570–84.
Bridge, G. (2013) 'A transactional approach to space' in special issue 'epistemologies of space: seeking spatial quality'. *International Planning Studies*, 18, 3/4, 304–20.
Butler, J. (1993) *Bodies that matter*. London: Routledge.
Butler, J. (1997) *Excitable speech: A politics of the performative*. London: Routledge.
DaLanda, M. (2006) *Assemblage theory*. Edinburgh: Edinburgh University Press.
Deleuze, G. and Guattari, F. (1987) *Thousand plateaus: Capitalism and schizophrenia*. London: Athlone.
Dewey, J. (1981) *The later works, 1925–1953, volume 1: 1925*, J.A. Boydston, ed. Carbondale, IL: Southern Illinois University Press.
Dewey, J. (1983) *The middle works, 1899–1924, volume 14: 1922*, J.A. Boydston, ed. Carbondale, IL: Southern Illinois University Press.
Dewey, J. (1984) *The later works, 1925–1953, volume 5: 1925–1930*, J.A. Boydston, ed. Carbondale, IL: Southern Illinois University Press.
Dewey, J. (1986a) *The later works, 1925–1953, volume 10: 1934*, J.A. Boydston, ed. Carbondale, IL: Southern Illinois University Press.

Dewey, J. (1986b) *The later works, 1925–1953, volume 12: 1938*, J.A. Boydston, ed. Carbondale, IL: Southern Illinois University Press.

Dewey, J. (2008) *The later works, 1925–1953, volume 2: 1925–1927*, J.A. Boydston, ed. Carbondale, IL: Southern Illinois University Press.

Dewey, J. (2012) *Unmodern philosophy and modern philosophy*, P. Dean, ed. Carbondale, IL: Southern Illinois University Press.

Dewey, J. and Bentley, A. (1949 [1991]) Knowing and the known, in J.A. Boydston, ed., *The later works, volume 16: 1949–1952*. Carbondale, IL: Southern Illinois University Press.

Frega, R. (2015) The normative structure of the ordinary. *European Journal of Pragmatism and American Philosophy*, 7, 1, 1–22.

Garfinkel, H. (1967) *Studies in ethnomethodology*. Englewood Cliffs, NJ: Prentice Hall.

Goffman, E. (1955) On face work. *Psychiatry*, 18, 213–31

Jackson, P. and Smith, S.J. (1984) *Exploring social geography*. London: Allen and Unwin.

Jackson, S. (2001) *Lines of activity: Performance, historiography and hull-house domesticity*. Ann Arbor, MI: University of Michigan Press.

James, W. (1904) A world of pure experience. *Journal of Philosophy, Psychology and Scientific Methods*, 1, 21, 561–70.

Koopman, C. (2009) *Pragmatism as transition*. New York, NY: Columbia University Press.

Langsdorf, L. (2002) Reconstructing the fourth dimension: A Deweyan critique of Habermas's conception of communicative action, in M. Aboulafia, M. Bookman and C. Kemp, eds, *Habermas and pragmatism*. London: Routledge, 141–64.

Latour, B. (2007) *Reassembling the social*. Oxford: Oxford University Press.

Lussault, M. and Stock, M. (2010) "Doing with space": Towards a pragmatics of space. *Social Geography*, 5, 11–9.

Margolis, J. (1986) *Pragmatism without foundations*. Oxford: Blackwell.

Moore, D. (1897) A day at Hull House. *American Journal of Sociology*, 2, 5, 629–42.

Park, R. (1926) The urban community as a spatial pattern and moral order, in E.W. Burgess, ed., *The urban community*. Chicago, IL: University of Chicago Press.

Peach, C. (ed.) (1975) *Urban social segregation*. London: Longman.

Peirce, C.S. (1897 [1932]) *Collected papers*. Cambridge, MA: Harvard University Press.

Sellers, W. (2007) *In the space of reasons*, K. Sharp and R. Brandom, eds. Cambridge, MA: Harvard University Press.

Shusterman, R. (2000) *Pragmatist aesthetics: Living beauty, rethinking art*, 2nd edn. Oxford: Rowman & Littlefield.

Stuhr, J. (1997) *Genealogical pragmatism*. Albany, NY: SUNY Press.

Sullivan, S. (2001) *Living across and through skins: Transactional bodies, pragmatism and feminism*. Bloomington, IN: Indiana University Press.

Thomas, W.I. (1923) *The unadjusted girl*. Boston, MA: Little, Brown and Co.

Wittgenstein, L. (1953 [2009]) *Philosophical investigations*, translated by G.E.M. Anscombe, P.M.S. Hacker and J. Schulte. Oxford: Wiley-Blackwell.

Werlen, B. (1992) *Society, action and space: An alternative human geography*. London: Routledge.

# 4

# Mead, subjectivity and urban politics

## Crispian Fuller

### Introduction

This chapter examines the contribution that G.H. Mead's conception of the self can make to understanding political subjectivity, and it deploys this approach in a case study of urban politics in the UK. Mead was a key figure in the development of pragmatist psychology and philosophy. He powerfully argued that there can be no self, consciousness of self or communication separate from society (Mead, 1934). His work has profound implications for thinking about human agency, and in this chapter I explore the potential impact of his ideas on thinking about the (urban) political subject.

The chapter elucidates a Meadian understanding of the political subject as a socially determined entity, constantly constructed through social (political) relations. Utilising a pragmatist approach allows us to place social interactions and the construction of the social at the forefront of analysis of political agency and politics. The chapter critically engages Mead's conception of 'me' and 'I' as interrelated dimensions of political subjectivity and explores Markell's (2007) argument for a return to Mead's (1913) early focus on the 'social self', which emphasised the interdependence of these aspects of identity and subjectivity. This is followed by a review of the under-theorisation of the political self in urban studies. From this position, the chapter then applies a pragmatic approach to political subjectivity and agency in explicating a short case study of the politicised rescaling of state responsibilities in a city-region in England, illustrating the importance of taking account of how human actors are produced as political subjects through social relations.

## Mead, subjectivity and political agency

Mead's conception of the intersubjective self provides a broad framework through which to examine the development of human agency. Building on Dewey (1958) and James (1907), Mead (1913; 1934) argued that agents continually construct and reconstruct meanings of both self and situations through social interaction. The self is constituted by both the 'I', as the unpredictable self, and the 'me', which forms through interaction with and adoption of social conventions. For Mead (1913; 1934), the construction of the self through interaction between the self and situations informs both 'habitual' and 'creative' thought and action (Joas, 1997a). This builds on the belief that human agents have the ability to anticipate the intentions of other actors through the development of language as a means to describe the intricacies of reality, allowing complex forms of social interaction and negotiation. Mead (1934) argues that meaning derives from social action, which comprises what he terms a 'conversation of gestures', in which one gesture elicits a response from another actor. This takes the form of the actor defining him/herself by way of understanding and taking the roles of others through iterative and cognitive processes. Practices not only produce meaning and social order but also encompass the reconfiguring, destruction, disruption and manipulation of meaning, sometimes causing social disorder (Carreira da Silva, 2007). This takes place through transactions of meaning exchanged between interconnected actors within social environments (Bridge, 2008).

In Mead's (1934) thinking, the 'me' relates to the role of previous situations in which social transactions have produced common understandings of how to act. The organised values, norms, beliefs and attitudes of other actors inform the 'habitual', communicatively transmitted through the 'generalised other' and significant symbols that are recognised by both the conveyer and responder, such as in the recognition between actors of the critical values and related actions associated with a particular political party (see also Cutchin, this volume). They reflect common understandings among a group of social actors, although such processes are also dynamic in nature and subject to change through ongoing transactions, including the development of misunderstandings and new understandings (Farr, 1996). Significant symbols facilitate the production of the social order, since such processes create expectations and legitimacy between actors, shaping the forms of behaviour deemed appropriate for social situations (Joas, 1997b). Mead (1934) referred to such arrangements within organised systems as the 'generalised other', encompassing common and habitual forms of understanding and behaviour between groups of social actors (Farr, 1996).

Human agents become conscious of themselves when they can understand and interpret themselves from the perspective of the generalised other through significant symbols (Gillespie, 2005). When actors assume the behaviour they think is expected of them through social interactions with other actors, they are adopting the perspective of the generalised other (Gross, 2009). Such processes are reflected in a configuration of significant symbols that are representative of the values, norms, beliefs and subsequent discourses of particular social groups and, as such, they are subject to constant change through transaction. Importantly, 'generalised others' are numerous in nature, reflecting the diversity of social values and beliefs in operation at any one time in a given situation.

At the same time, these generalisable values and beliefs are critical to understanding human agency, as actors either conform to the generalised other or seek to move beyond it, and this is where the impulsiveness of the 'I' becomes salient in explaining social action and social change. Mead argued that 'creative' thought and action arises through an internal 'conversation of gestures' between the 'me' and the 'I'. The 'me' constitutes the dominant thought and expected actions of human actors in response to the habitual behaviours that are fostered through the generalised other and significant symbols (Crossley, 1996). Following James (1890), however, the 'I' is the manifestation of an individual's subjective disposition, and there can be incongruence and conflict between the 'I''s emotions and the wider social norms (or generalised other) of the 'me.' More expansive understandings of this relation include the 'I' encompassing drives such as the will for freedom or the response to injustice (Roberts, 2006). It is here that there is the possibility for divergence between the individual and the broader social norms and beliefs shaping the social order (Farr, 1996). The 'I' can produce values and beliefs that diverge from or conflict with social norms, creating ambiguity, internal deliberation and, potentially, societal change (Barbalet, 2009). More specifically, the individual response to a stimulus takes a particular course of action: (1) impulse (immediate responses to the need to take action); (2) perception (use of senses and mental images to satisfy impulses by perceived objects); (3) manipulation (to take action); and (4) consummation (the act to satisfy the impulse) (Mead, 1934). This process will involve each individual ('I') deciding how to respond and, potentially, to act in a particular social context in which the 'me' comes into play to reinforce or challenge the decisions being made.

There have been notable critiques of Mead's conception of the self, although for the purposes of this chapter I focus only on two issues. First, the concept of the 'me' and 'I' has been subject to critique in relation to its dualistic approach. In later Mead (1934), and approaches that have incorporated his thinking, such as symbolic interactionism (Blumer, 1969), the 'I' of the individual is insulated from society (as not yet realised potential), while society is an external regulator and enforcer of social conformism (Markell, 2007). Correspondingly, the 'potentialities' of the 'I' are only realised (or actualised) once they are recognised through the intersubjective 'me', but this limits the possibility for creativity, since any such action would have to conform to broader social conceptions and practices. This conformity is critical, as statements and actions seeking social change have to be understood by other actors for them to be able to influence and enact change. Such critiques raise the issue of whether the 'me' and 'I' should be as distinct as they are presented in Mead's later work, and the extent to which individual creativity is possible in complex societies.

Second, for Barbalet (2009), Mead tends to overemphasise the role of the creative cognitive capacities of agency and to downplay the importance of conflicting values and beliefs that can produce ambiguity, provoke internal deliberation and stimulate action. Barbalet (2009) argues that James (1890) is better able to conceptualise such processes by emphasising the important role of emotion in the self, particularly in terms of actors considering the future consequences of action and non-action through emotions, which are subsequently elaborated in generative processes of action or non-action. James (1890) argues that the 'me' comprises three main elements that make the self complex and beyond rational thought: first, the 'material self', comprising the body (gender, as well as elements such as the maintenance, comfort and welfare of others); second, the 'social self', constituted through the recognition acquired from others; and, finally, the 'subjective self', produced through the accumulation of an individual's subjective disposition, involving aspects such as personal values and norms. Consideration of emotions and the reactive qualities of agency is therefore required within Mead's conceptualisation of the self. While emotion is not the central concern of this chapter, what this discussion highlights is the need for sensitivity towards the intricacies of the self in Mead's conceptualisation of the intersubjective constitution of human actors.

For Markell (2007), one way forward is to return to Mead's original intentions. This involves developing an understanding of the interdependence of the self and community via conceptualising a constant conversation between the 'I' and 'me'. The 'I' is not simply a response to participation and recognition in the community but, rather, it is constantly converted into the 'me' and vice versa. In this conceptualisation, the relation between the 'I' and the stimulus conditions producing the 'me' are dynamic and indeterminate, and stimulus conditions (relating to the views of others) are also open and uncertain. The reaction of the 'I' is actualised in relation to the memory and remembrance of an individual actor and through recognition and responses by other actors as part of the generalised other. This means that we must understand the 'I' and 'me' as interwoven and not distinct, as emphasised in many perspectives and accounts (e.g. Blumer, 1969; Honneth, 1994).

The potentialities of human actors to act and change intersubjective relations and the perceptual and discursive construction of objects are not fully enclosed within an 'I' that can only be released through intersubjective recognition (Markell, 2007). Potentialities are embedded within ongoing actions taking place through intersubjective relations ('me'), and, as such, the wider social collective remains key to understanding the action of individual subjects. The individuality and agency of subjects are formed as they choose specific attitudes and responses to symbols. For Etzrodt (2008), action and creativity are related to the actor's need to generate desired 'reactions' by other actors, since actors have to adhere to a common meaning structure in order for their actions to be understood. However, this does not fully explain how individual action and creativity produce and influence significant symbols. Stronger forms of creativity are possible in relation to change that seeks to reconfigure attitudes, involving the recombination of old symbols to create new symbols and attitudes that rely, at least to some extent, on common meanings that are already understood. This understanding exposes the way in which social change comes about through routine cooperation deploying existing attitudes to create incremental change. However, in the absence of substantive societal and institutional change (e.g. revolution), this reflects the dominance of incremental and evolutionary change in society (see, e.g., Jessop, 2002).

To summarise, Mead presents a powerful framework through which to understand the intersubjective construction of the self. Applied to the creation of the political subject, one must treat the 'I' and 'me' as co-constituted, rather than the 'I' being a potential that simply has to be realised. It is with such issues in mind that this chapter now moves on to apply this theoretical framework to the analysis of political subjectivity in contemporary forms of urban politics.

## Urban governance and post-politics

While Mead's (1934) conceptual framework elucidates how human agency is produced by various social interactions, it raises questions relating to why and how 'political' awareness, attitudes/values, behaviours and actions are produced in relation to both broader societal significant symbols and the impulsiveness of the 'I' (Häkli and Kallio, 2014). Such issues will be analysed here in relation to the examination of particular political subjectivities in the case-study analysis, but it is important to first examine contemporary perspectives on urban politics and governance, and their particular and limited theorisation of political agency. I then contrast this with a more pragmatic approach.

Within urban geography in particular, the contemporary political landscape of cities is often considered to be a space of heterogeneous, relationally configured agents, encompassing state, market and civil-society actors, working through broadly defined governance arrangements (Cochrane, 2018). These urban governance arrangements comprise multi-scalar networks, with change arising from nation-state-led rescaling since the 1980s in response to inherent crisis tendencies within capitalism (Peck et al., 2013), mainly in relation to the retreat of social welfare provision and the rise of pro-market and private-sector economic-growth priorities (Jessop, 2002). The role of political agency in such processes has tended to be viewed in the context of meso-level analysis of organisational and governing change, rather than developing analysis of the intricacies of individual political agents and the formation of political subjects.

However, such perspectives have faced increasing criticism, not least because actors, strategies and practices are all assumed to be working through an over-riding neoliberal strategic framework. In such literatures, neoliberalism is described in terms of the growing role of the private sector and market priorities and values in urban governance, the declining role of the state and the privatisa-tion and marketisation of public services (Jessop, 2002; Storper, 2016). As vari-ous scholars have argued, these accounts tend to see neoliberalism as having a global 'operational logic', whereas, in practice, contingent local conditions pro-duce a degree of variation (Ong, 2006; Springer, 2012). Many studies ignore the importance of alternative values, norms and practices beyond neoliberalism, and the diverse 'subjectivities' that these alternatives imply (Storper, 2016). The complexities of the human 'self' and the role of individual agency in producing, performing and resisting neoliberal political economy are rarely critically inter-rogated or examined in the mainstream literature (Furlong et al., 2017).

Alongside the focus on neoliberalism, there has been growing concern with the extent to which 'post-political' arrangements now characterise the growing fragmentation and complexities of urban governance (Davidson and Iveson, 2015; Swyngedouw, 2011). Building upon Rancière (2001, 2006), this approach argues that 'politics' increasingly involves the institutionalisation of a particular 'common sense', based on a conceptualisation of a homogeneous population (and shared political subjectivity) (Swyngedouw, 2011). Within political arenas and decision-making, this generally involves efforts at the production of consensus between a limited number of 'expert' actors, and a homogenisation of assump-tions about interests and beliefs. Correspondingly, particular social groups, such as the private sector, have biased decision-making arenas and practices (Davidson and Iveson, 2015). The purpose of this is to marginalise and subordinate alterna-tive political viewpoints from those of mainstream thinking, reduce political contestation and resistance to such views and legitimise the distribution of resources and rights through institutions (what Rancière refers to as the 'police order') in ways that favour particular policy priorities and social groups.

While this 'post-political' perspective has had a significant influence on urban studies, accounts of urban post-politics underplay the nature and role of human agency. More specifically, Rancière (2001) views the political subject in terms of its constitution through political struggle. However, given that a polit-ical 'act' of contestation seeks to disrupt in visible and performative terms the construction of political actors, there is a need for greater consideration of the actual human agency of the political subject. Rancière also recognises the fail-ure of a police order to fully control people because it can never take account of all the complexities of social life and human actors. As such, human agency is more than simply constituted and constructed through political struggle, since it exists in the everyday social world, and it comprises both the 'me' and the 'I'. Thus we must take account of the multidimensional character of human actors beyond Rancière's particular view of the political.

Mead's framework, discussed above, examining the continuous intersubjective production of the 'I' and 'me', provides a way forward for considering the subjectivity and agency of actors in the post-political moment. At issue is the creativity of actors in transforming their social (spatial) relations in ways that impact on the practices in urban governance, particularly around the extent to which there is constant interaction between 'I' and 'me' and whether actors have to adhere to common understandings, which limits their creativity. As previously discussed, Mead's analysis is good at illuminating relatively weak forms of creativity where incremental change takes place, rather than major moments of political action and resistance, which are the exception. Utilising Mead's understanding of the intersubjective construction of the political subject, or 'me', as being constituted by broader social relations, and that of the 'I' as the impulsiveness of the self as the individual interprets, reacts, changes and seeks to produce broader societal practices, provides a valuable way to enhance our understanding of politics in general, and we can apply it to the political life of cities and regions, as outlined in a case study below.

## Using Mead to understand urban governance: A case study

This section deploys Mead's approach, as elucidated by Markell (2007), in an examination of the construction of new city-region governance spaces in England, focusing on one particular local council. The purpose of the analysis is to examine how the political subjectivity of the politician in this particular city is constructed through a new combined-authority governing arrangement, and how it is possible, or not, to contest and change the developing city-region governance regime. This city-region governance space stems from the creation of city-regional 'deals', enacted by then Chancellor George Osborne through HM Treasury, largely as a means to ensure city-region areas adopt central-government priorities but forming part of a new government emphasis on tackling deficits in productivity while also recognising the potentialities of cities as sites of economic growth (Cabinet Office, 2011; Marlow, 2012). City-region deals have been arranged with central government around devolved powers for particular activities. These devolved powers typically relate to spatially focused issues and agendas in city-regions, such as powers for transport and housing, in exchange for agreeing to an elected mayor for the city-region in question. This involves the creation of a new enlarged authority called a combined authority, which has to be led by an elected mayor, but which has responsibility only for particular policy areas and no control over the member local authorities involved (O'Brien and Pike, 2015).

One of the largest city-region deals involves the new West Midlands Combined Authority (WMCA), encompassing the established metropolitan local governments of Birmingham, Coventry, Dudley, Sandwell, Solihull, Walsall and Wolverhampton (Figure 4.1; Table 4.1). There is a long history of tension

**West Midlands boroughs**

1  Birmingham
2  Coventry
3  Dud ey
4  Sandwell
5  Solihull
6  Walsall
7  Wolverhampton

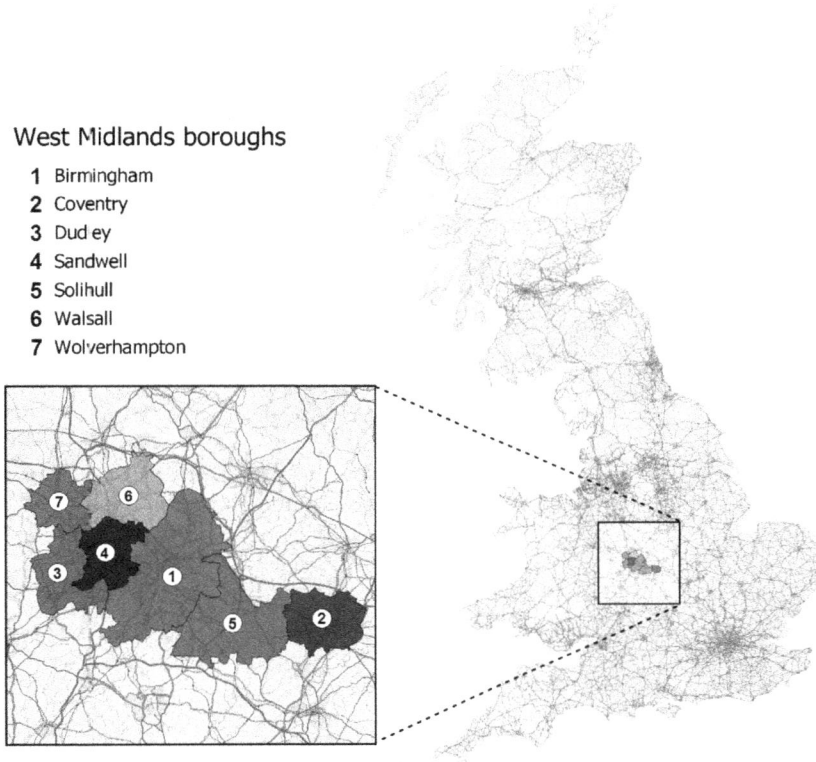

*Figure 4.1*   West Midlands Combined Authority constituent local-authority partners

between Birmingham and the other local authorities, as well as tensions between the different councils of Dudley, Sandwell, Solihull, Walsall and Wolverhampton. The onset of austerity and a major retrenchment of local-government spending, combined with rising social-care service demands, prompted a major change in the attitudes of local politicians who promoted greater collaboration. The WMCA city-region deal was agreed with central government in November 2015 and formally approved by the constituent local authorities in 2016. It involves the devolution of powers in the areas of transport, housing, regeneration and economic development, as well as associated funding streams, working to different timescales but in the context of a thirty-year plan. The Conservative Andy Street was elected as mayor in 2017 on a turnout of just over 26 per cent.

Rather than examine WMCA as a whole, this brief analysis concentrates on the dynamics taking place in one constituent partner, Coventry City Council.[1] Before city-region deals were introduced, central government had a policy of encouraging the election of 'city' mayors. Coventry held a referendum in 2012

*Table 4.1* Main attributes of the West Midlands Combined Authority area

| Attributes | |
| --- | --- |
| *Population* | 4.6m (2015) |
| *Members* | 18 local authorities and four Local Enterprise Partnerships |
| *Political representation (main constituent members)* | 7 members |
| | (5 Labour and 3 Conservative – leaders of Birmingham, Coventry, Dudley, Sandwell, Solihull, Walsall and Wolverhampton councils) |
| | Mayor (Conservative) |
| *Political representation (non-constituent members)* | Staffordshire Cannock Chase District Council |
| | Warwickshire North Warwickshire Borough Council |
| | Warwickshire Nuneaton and Bedworth Borough Council |
| | Worcestershire Redditch Borough Council |
| | Warwickshire Rugby Borough Council |
| | Shropshire Council |
| | Warwickshire Stratford-on-Avon District Council |
| | Staffordshire Tamworth Borough Council |
| | Shropshire Telford and Wrekin Council |
| | Warwickshire County Council |
| *Local Enterprise Partnerships (LEPs)*[1] | Black Country LEP |
| | Coventry and Warwickshire LEP |
| | Greater Birmingham and Solihull LEP |
| *WMCA number of employees* | 269 (2017)[2] |
| *WMCA budget - Operational budget* | £2m |
| *WMCA budget – Transport budget* | £121.54m |
| *WMCA budget – Capital investment* | £8bn budget for thirty years, from various sources, agreed, agreed in principle and some dependent upon third parties This includes an annual £36.5m devolution grant |

*Notes*: [1]LEPs are the main subnational bodies with responsibility for promoting economic development. They are managed through voluntary partnerships between local authorities and the private sector. [2]The vast majority of employees come from the incorporation of the West Midlands transport authority, Centro.

for the establishment of such a city mayor, but this was comprehensively rejected by the public. Nonetheless, when the subsequent city-region deal was being constructed with the other West Midlands authorities, the Labour administration's ruling cabinet and leader successfully argued against another referendum within the city to decide whether to join WMCA. One could argue that this represents depoliticisation within the Labour Party, the 'me' reciprocating significant symbols embedded within nation-state policy discourses, pushed down from central government in terms of the policy priority of having a mayor. A critical aspect of this has been the Labour cabinet justifying the city-region deal and mayor and, in so doing, seeking to construct significant symbols that are able to produce the 'me' of local politicians but also ensure that emergent forms of the 'I', as the impulsive and emotive aspects of political life, are congruent with the dominant city-region agenda. An aspect of this is to ensure that any political resistance and resulting changes are limited to weaker 'same reactions' by contesting politicians, thus guiding the potential within the 'I' to be not too dissimilar to the city-region significant symbols being fostered and framing significant symbols around two key Labour Party council administration discourses: 'critical challenges' and 'opportunities'.

In relation to the first discourse, politicians use the term 'critical challenges' to relate to the dominant issues that concern them in a period of substantive austerity. These issues, such as an ageing population placing huge demands on adult social-care services, are argued to be impossible to address through a single administrative area, requiring inter-city collaboration, representing the rescaling of the issue and solution. As stated by the previous leader of Coventry City Council: "Across the region we face some critical challenges; skills, transport infrastructure, productivity, land use and public service reform" (Cllr Lucas, previous council leader, quoted in WMCA, 2015). In so doing, we see these politicians internalise national political debates about the ability to maintain public-service levels and satisfy demand through efficiency measures while reducing overall budgets as part of the drive to reducing nation-state debt levels (Davies and Blanco, 2017). What is not evident in any of the leadership's discourses to justify the city-region deal is a critique of the actual austerity being devolved down to the council, which has culminated in a net expenditure budget reduction between 2010–11 and 2017–18 of £147 million in Coventry. Rather, the council leader and cabinet narrated the city-region deal in terms of a necessary response to austerity and as an opportunity to address local issues. In effect, this represents the 'I' of these politicians echoing a 'generalised other' that has largely accepted austerity as a necessity (Stanley, 2014). This has led to a situation where the potentialities of the 'I' are congruent with the 'me' in focusing on the 'means' of implementing austerity through which services are to be reduced or abolished.

A critical element of this involves discursively constructing the benefits of reorganisation and collaboration between neighbouring authorities. This conveys a belief that greater partnership working and the rescaling up of governing to the wider sub-region can assist in mitigating austerity in the city. Such thinking builds on long-held attitudes in which adhering to central-government policies facilitates the devolution of powers and an increase in local autonomy, which, in turn, expands the scope in which to address local issues. As the council leader at the time publicly stated: "By working together we can move powers from Whitehall to the West Midlands and start building a Midlands engine in the heart of the country" (Cllr Lucas, previous council leader, quoted in WMCA, 2015). It has also been important for the Labour Party council administration to construct significant symbols that convey a new world of

collaboration, and to embed these within the context of a history of past working relations, thus recombining old symbols to produce particular 'attitudes' in
the present. As the leader of the council argued: "Since the general election in
May there has been unprecedented collaboration ... Our aim is to consult and
work with more partners across the private, public and third sector so that we
can establish our combined authority" (Cllr Lucas, previous council leader,
quoted in Morris, 2015). However, as one Labour politician noted, the basis of
this partnership is not quite what is presented, as relationships had previously
been about sharing ideas with their Labour party colleagues in other boroughs,
not sharing budgets nor crossing party lines. As such, the construction of a
political subject's 'me' is not completely guided by the efforts of the Labour
council administration, since they are able to recognise that past collaboration
was party political, and it is still possible for the 'I' to utilise past alternative
significant symbols to contest the discourse of the WMCA.

Efforts to construct a new 'me' that seeks to shape the 'I' of Labour politicians to ensure their continual political support rely upon generating and
engaging common tropes and discourses that produce desired reactions based
on common understandings (Etzrodt, 2008). In some cases, this involves combining past efforts around partnership working and acquiescence to austerity
embedded within the 'I'. For instance, one politician noted that they have not
contested nation-state-led austerity as much as they should have, producing
feelings of guilt as they see the effect on particular constituents in marginalised
spaces in the city. This guilt has meant they have found it hard to contest the
'scalar' initiative of the WMCA, with its intentions of improving social and
economic conditions through new forms of public-service governance and
delivery. Such efforts by the leadership have therefore been successful, with one
opposition politician noting that debate has essentially been taken away from
this issue, largely because the leadership was able to convince the majority of
Labour politicians of the necessity of acting in this way. Ironically, this has
relied on an intersubjective construction of the 'me' based on the adoption of
Conservative national-government attitudes and a belief that it is possible to
maintain service levels with fewer resources.

The second aspect in negotiating the 'I'–'me' relationship in Coventry
involves the framing of 'opportunities'. There has been a general discourse
about devolved responsibility presenting an opportunity for WMCA to fulfil
desires and objectives that have previously been impossible to achieve. As one
councillor put it: "This is an opportunity for devolved powers. This is an
opportunity for Coventry to get the kind of resources and investment that the
city council could not possibly get otherwise" (Cllr Lucas, previous council
leader, quoted in Gilbert, 2016a). In essence, there is an appeal to politicians
that their support for the deal will produce more autonomy and the ability to
influence change. This represents a disjuncture with their present and past
experience and builds upon long-held desires, beliefs and attitudes among

local-government politicians for greater autonomy from central government (Allen, 2016). Despite the congruence of attitudes that produces the 'me' of local politicians, such efforts at generating new pro-WMCA attitudes are dependent upon eroding the space for the 'I' to resist. As one politician noted: "it certainly did give the initial appeal of greater freedoms, but we saw this under New Labour, the promises that we all bought into that never arrived. It leaves you feeling a bit disheartened; I've felt wary of anything mentioning devolution since" (anonymised author's interview).

Nonetheless, the political power of a discourse of autonomy and, with it, an acceptance of the national government's approach has helped to foster particular subjectivities and thus influenced the 'I', serving to depoliticise the agenda. As the leader of a neighbouring authority noted: "We recognise there is a sixteen billion pounds output gap between the West Midlands and the national average … Last year the Chancellor spoke about the need to rebalance the UK economy and now, collectively, we are responding in our own terms, through the creation of the West Midlands combined authority" (Cllr Sleigh, Leader Solihull Council, quoted in Morris, 2015). The WMCA represents the potential for change but within an already defined symbolic landscape that aims to produce the same reactions and attitudes in the 'I' rather than moving beyond it.

We must not, however, reduce urban politics to the simple adoption of national priorities and direction. As highlighted by Fuller (2017) and Davies and Blanco (2017), local-government responses to austerity and devolution have been 'pragmatic', characterised by reluctant acceptance, circumvention, internal everyday resistance and manipulation. There were major political deliberations around the mayor and city-region deal, but since the decision was agreed there has been public acquiescence to the new arrangements. For local politicians, the new deal represents devolved powers and a greater potential for influence in that the "WMCA is closer than Whitehall", satisfying their internal desire for influence (anonymised author's interview). Local leaders remain apprehensive about their level of impact, however, because any realised influence has to adhere to the government priorities set for WMCA, and political actions have to conform to established ideas (anonymised author's interview). Acquiescence to post-political tendencies through the 'I' has occurred in this landscape, and the 'me' is seeking to frame the 'I' as rational and city-region-focused (rather than purely concerned with the 'place' of their constituents). This has served to align the 'I' to the broader city-region societal agenda being set up the combined authority. As the present leader explained:

> Sometimes in politics you have to be pragmatic. Nobody opposed an elected mayor harder than I did. But sometimes you have to accept that to go forward, you may at times compromise. (Cllr Duggins, Coventry City Council Leader, quoted in Gilbert, 2016a)

The political landscape nonetheless remains complex. Within and beyond party politics, politicians are responding to WMCA in relation to the kinds of attributes we see characterising the 'I' as they move beyond the 'me'. One particular aspect of this is the relationship between the 'I' of local politicians and the perceived threat to the city's identity. This threat relates to the belief that WMCA will be dominated by Birmingham and a perception of WMCA as 'Greater Birmingham'. Politicians opposed to the proposal believe it also represents a loss of their own identity, not just as a representative of the city but because their sense of political purpose and self is heavily constituted by the past, present and future identity of the city, namely as a unique, independent and important Midlands city, particularly in relation to Coventry's historical significance as the home of automotive manufacturing in the UK.

Opposition is largely in relation to the recombination of existing significant symbols, namely the democratic and bureaucratic legitimacy of the local state, and with the purpose of creating new attitudes among local citizens and other politicians that were in favour of the combined authority. As one anonymous politician noted: "This is central government's view of regions which doesn't take account of cities. Cities like Coventry have and can look after their own affairs; these can't simply be bundled together with issues affecting Dudley and the like. They are unique to us" (anonymised author's interview). A further aspect of this was for local politicians to emphasise present and past symbols which rely upon particular spatial relations and similar attitudes. The city's population and politicians have long held concerns over the potential domination of the West Midlands area, and therefore Coventry, by the close and far larger city of Birmingham. What this represents is the actualisation of the 'I' of politicians, based on their fear of domination, through the recombination of these significant symbols within the city based on their fear of its much larger neighbour. As the opposition leader argued: "It is absolutely blindingly obvious that the WMCA is, to all intents and purposes, Greater Birmingham. That will not change until the geographical shape of the combined authority is changed dramatically" (Cllr Blundell, opposition leader, Coventry City Council, quoted in Gilbert, 2016b).

## Conclusion

Through examination of the early works of Mead (1934), it is clear that explication of the relationship between intersubjective relations and the self is critical in understanding everyday politics. For Mead (1934), the self is constructed through 'social acts' where there is a dyadic relationship between the 'I' and the 'me', since the self develops through adopting the attitudes of others, which they reflect upon through social relations. Important in this are significant symbols, such as similar attitudes to the positive benefits of inter-local-authority collaboration, which relay particular gestures and attitudes within social relations, and which come to direct the 'me' through certain ways of thinking and acting. Within Mead's later work and the approaches that he inspired, such as symbolic interactionism, the 'I' and the 'me' have been demarcated as separate, and from this position the 'I' has been viewed as a 'potential' that is only realised through social relations of the 'actual'. This has therefore subordinated the role of the 'I', as various forms of psychological disposition (e.g. emotions), to the 'me'. However, Markell (2007) argues against a separation of the 'me' and the 'I'. This approach highlights the dynamic potential for either confirmation of the 'me' through the self, or the creativity of the 'I' to emerge within and beyond the role of significant symbols and the influence of the 'generalised other'. Because the 'I' is the everyday site where it is possible to disrupt significant symbols and the generalised other, the examination of the political self, and its dynamic relationship with the 'me', is critical in the post-political moment.

Contemporary accounts of urban governing largely reduce the role of the political self to acquiescence to broader capitalist processes (e.g. political-economy perspectives) or as being produced through broader societal power relations (e.g. Foucauldian accounts). Radical democratic theories view the self as being constructed through the actions of the masses as they develop common desires for equality. In contrast, a Meadian view places the self at the centre of analysis, but a self that is produced through intersubjective relations and which is complex and uneven, forged within the dynamics of different attitudes, values and conventions of social groups and the individuality of the constantly emergent 'I'. Such a perspective can advance our understanding of why and how political action comes about through the political self (e.g. as conforming to or contesting the generalised other) and how political acts are often far more incongruent and uneven than is often presented. This approach builds upon the understanding that political actors need to produce similar 'reactions' and 'attitudes' when seeking to influence other actors because of the need for common understanding. This also means that forms of incremental change, which involve existing attitudes, are very common within the realm of governance (Crouch, 2005). However, there is always the potential for the 'I' to accompany the transformation of the 'me', and new significant symbols and a generalised other can reshape psychological disposition and human agency. As I hope to have shown in this chapter, this approach to the 'self' can contribute a great deal to both theoretical and empirical analysis in political studies.

## Note

1   The empirical material for this chapter comes from a broader study of urban entrepreneurialism in an age of austerity, which involved the case study presented here. During the course of this study, ten interviews were conducted with local politicians, divided equally between the Labour and Conservative parties. Participants have been anonymised because of the politically sensitive nature of the data, except where publicly available and published quotes have been used, as cited.

## References

Allen, J. (2016) *Topologies of power*. Oxford and New York, NY: Routledge.

Barbalet, J. (2009) Pragmatism and symbolic interactionism, in B.S. Turner, ed., *The new Blackwell companion to social theory*. Chichester: Wiley-Blackwell, 199–217.

Blumer H (1969) *Symbolic interactionism: Perspective and method*. Berkeley, CA: University of California Press.

Bridge, G. (2008) City senses: On the radical possibilities of pragmatism for geography. *Geoforum*, 39, 4, 1570–84.

Carreira da Silva, F. (2007) *G.H. Mead: A critical introduction*. Cambridge: Polity Press.

Cochrane, A. (2018) Here, there and everywhere: Rethinking the urban of urban politics, in K. Ward, A. Jonas, B. Millar and D. Wilson, eds, *The Routledge handbook on spaces of urban politics*. Abingdon and New York, NY: Routledge.

Crossley, N. (1996) *Intersubjectivity: The fabric of social becoming*. London: Sage.

Crouch, C. (2005) *Capitalist diversity and change: Recombinant governance and institutional entrepreneurs*. Oxford: Oxford University Press.

Davidson, M. and Iveson, K. (2015). Recovering the politics of the city. *Progress in Human Geography*, 39, 5, 543–59.

Davies, J. and Blanco, I. (2017) Austerity urbanism: Patterns of neo-liberalisation and resistance in six cities of Spain and the UK. *Environment and Planning A*, 49, 7, 1517–36.

Dewey, J. (1958) *Experience and nature*. New York, NY: Dover Publications.

Etzrodt, C. (2008) The foundation of an interpretative sociology: A critical review of the attempts of George H. Mead and Alfred Schutz. *Human Studies*, 31, 157–77.

Farr, R.M. (1996) *The roots of modern social psychology, 1872–1954*. Oxford: Blackwell Publishers.

Fuller, C. (2017) City government in an age of austerity: Discursive institutions and critique. *Environment and Planning A*, 49, 745–66.

Furlong, K., Carré, M.N. and Acevedo Guerrero, T. (2017) Urban service provision: Insights from pragmatism and ethics. *Environment and Planning A*, 49, 12, 2800–12.

Gilbert, S. (2016a) Coventry agrees to West Midlands mayor and devolution deal. *Coventry Telegraph*, 31 May. www.coventrytelegraph.net/news/coventry-news/coventry-agrees-west-midlands-mayor-11410042 (accessed 27 February 2018).

Gilbert, S. (2016b) West Midlands Combined Authority online survey branded a 'propaganda exercise'. *Coventry Telegraph*, 20 January. www.coventrytelegraph.net/news/coventry-news/west-midlands-combined-authority-online-10761693 (accessed 27 February 2018).

Gillespie, A. (2005) G.H. Mead: Theorist of the social act. *Journal for the Theory of Social Behaviour*, 35, 1, 19–39.

Gross, N. (2009) A pragmatist theory of social mechanisms. *American Sociological Review*, 74m 358–79.

Häkli, J. and Kallio, K. (2014) Subject, action and polis: Theorising political agency. *Progress in Human Geography*, 38, 2, 181–200.

Honneth, A. (1995) *The struggle for recognition: The moral grammar of social conflicts*. Cambridge: Polity Press.

James, W. (1890) *The principles of psychology*. New York, NY: Holt.

James, W. (1907) *Pragmatism: A new name for some old ways of thinking*. Indianapolis, IN: Hackett Publishing.

Jessop, B. (2002) *The future of the capitalist state*. Cambridge: Polity Press.

Joas, H. (1997a) *The creativity of action*. Chicago, IL: University of Chicago Press.

Joas, H. (1997b) *G.H. Mead: A contemporary re-examination of his thought.* Cambridge, MA: MIT Press.

Markell, P. (2007) The potential and the actual: Mead, Honneth, and the "I", in B. Van Den Brink and D. Owen, eds, *Recognition and power.* Oxford: Oxford University Press, 100–31.

Marlow, D. (2012) *City deals – Implications for enhanced devolution and local economic growth.* London: LGIU.

Mead. G.H. (1913) The social self. *Journal of Philosophy, Psychology and Scientific Methods,* 10, 374–80.

Mead, G.H. (1934) *Mind, self, and society.* Chicago, IL: University of Chicago.

Morris, S. (2015) West Midlands 'economic powerhouse' plan unveiled. *Guardian,* 6 July. www.theguardian.com/society/2015/jul/06/west-midlands-economic-power-house-leaders-councils-combined-authority (accessed 27 February 2018).

O'Brien, P. and Pike, A. (2015) City deals, decentralisation and the governance of local infrastructure funding and financing in the UK. *National Institute Economic Review,* 233, 1, 14–26.

Ong, A. (2006) *Neoliberalism as exception: Mutations in citizenship and sovereignty.* Durham, NC: Duke University Press.

Peck, J., Theodore, N. and Brenner, N. (2013) Neoliberal urbanism redux? *International Journal of Urban and Regional Research,* 37, 3, 1091–9.

Rancière, J. (2001) Ten theses on politics. *Theory & Event,* 5, 3.

Rancière, J. (2006) *The politics of aesthetics: The distribution of the sensible.* London: Continuum International Publishing Group.

Roberts, B. (2006) *Micro social theory.* Basingstoke: Palgrave Macmillan.

Springer, S. (2012) Neoliberalism as discourse: between Foucauldian political economy and Marxian poststructuralism. *Critical Discourse Studies,* 9, 2, 133–47.

Stanley, L. (2014) 'We're reaping what we sowed': Everyday crisis narratives and acquiescence to the age of austerity. *New Political Economy,* 19, 6, 895–917.

Stationery Office (2011) *Unlocking growth in cities.* London: HM Stationary Office.

Storper, M. (2016) The neo-liberal city as idea and reality. *Territory, Politics, Governance,* 4, 2, 241–63.

Swyngedouw, E. (2011) Interrogating post-democratisation: Reclaiming egalitarian political spaces. *Political Geography,* 30, 7, 370–80.

WMCA (2015) *Growing the UK economy through a Midlands engine.* www.wmca.org.uk/news/growing-the-uk-economy-through-a-midlands-engine/ (accessed 27 February 2018)

# 5

# Rorty, conversation and the power of maps

## Trevor Barnes

### Introduction

In the late American writer Raymond Carver's (1981) celebrated short story 'What we talk about when we talk about love', there is both conversation and experiment – maybe even pragmatist conversation and experiment. Carver's story is set during one early evening in suburban Albuquerque, where two increasingly drunken couples – two bottles of gin are consumed before dinner – talk across a kitchen table about what counts as love. Each of the four offer different stories. One of the women, Terri, says the man that she lived with previously "loved her so much he tried to kill her" (Carver 1981, 170). Mel, an ER cardiologist and Terri's current partner, says, "My God, don't be silly. That's not love" (Carver 1981, 171). Instead, he offers a different story. It is of an elderly couple who are horribly injured in a freeway accident but who survive following all-night surgery in which Mel participates. After two weeks, they are taken out of the ICU, but both remain swaddled, as Mel puts it, in "casts and bandages, from head to foot … Little eye holes and nose holes and mouth holes" (Carver 1981, 183). The elderly man is incredibly sad, but not about the traffic accident. His "heart was breaking", says Mel, "because he couldn't turn his goddamn head and *see* his goddamn wife". "'Do you see what I'm saying?' Mel said" (Carver 1981, 183). That's love.

The conversation that Carver imagines in his short story represents an example of the kind of larger practice that the American pragmatist philosopher Richard Rorty (2007) believes should be a model for philosophy. It is philosophy of conversation and experiment (Rorty 2007, chapter 8). Engaging in dialogue – telling and listening to compelling stories such as those told by the two sets of couples in Carver's story, experimenting with new vocabularies and points of view – allows us to think of both ourselves and the world in which we live in new ways. In turn, that makes possible acts never undertaken before, never conceived before. In Rorty's view, the point of philosophy is not to describe what the world is "really" like but rather to enlarge our cultural repertoire, to experiment by making up new self-descriptions that are richer and more complex than previously, to unblock past impasses, to let us realise new achievements that were not imagined before. That is going on between the two couples across that kitchen table in Albuquerque. The stories they tell one another widen their cultural inventory, provide potential grounds for new ways to think and to talk – in this case about love – and to act in the name of love in hitherto unimagined ways. Not that those in the conversation always agree: "My God, don't be silly," Mel says. But that is part of conversation and experimentation too.

Rorty pursued the goal of 'conversational philosophy', beginning with his publication of *Philosophy and the mirror of nature* (1979). Earlier, he was an analytical philosopher concerned with epistemology, scrupulous in his desire to identify the logical foundations of true knowledge. That was overturned in *Philosophy and the mirror of nature*, where he declared the project of epistemology bankrupt, the search for Truth hopeless. Instead, he drew on American pragmatism, especially the work of John Dewey, along with a variety of philosophers from Continental Europe, to pursue a philosophy without epistemology, based instead on conversation and experiment.

The new Rorty argued that there are no foundations such as neutral facts, or rationality, or Platonic essences that could ever provide an unassailable backstop for epistemology, for providing an iron-clad warrant for true knowledge. Consequently, there is no rationale for epistemology as a philosophical undertaking. Instead, following American pragmatism, Rorty avers that knowledge arises only from contingent social practices, from trying out vocabularies that allow humans within a given context to cope with their world, to navigate their way around and in it. That's why pragmatism is called pragmatism. It treats knowledge like a knife or a fork, an implement to accomplish a specific task. If a particular piece of knowledge no longer helps to get things done, if it is no longer pragmatic, then it isn't knowledge. It needs to be dropped and different knowledge found. Pragmatism is a philosophy of practical achievement, not of transcendental truth. As William James (1902 [2012], 24), one of the early American pragmatists, famously put it, knowledges and ideas are to be judged "by their fruits ... and not by their roots".

For Rorty and other pragmatists, there is no special method for producing knowledge, for achieving practical ends – no set of foolproof rules to follow. That kind of thinking is found only within epistemology. Under pragmatism, the best we can do, the only thing we can do, is to "cast about for a vocabulary that will help" (Rorty, 1979, 321): that is, to experiment by using novel and creative forms of language, including narrative, metaphor and irony, along with other tropes and techniques to re-describe the world. By inventing new words, telling new stories and putting those words and stories into motion, it is sometimes possible to break through old stand-offs and logjams where earlier conversation has lagged or stalled or was abandoned. The new words and stories become potential sparks for reigniting the conversation, permitting us to do things that we have never accomplished before. "Philosophy should be transformational rather than foundational," as Richard Shusterman (1997, 157) puts it.

Key to that process is experimentation, a willingness to take a risk. Not that all or even most of those experiments will succeed. Thomas Edison said about his unsuccessful experiments in trying to make a working lightbulb: "I haven't failed. I've just found 10,000 ways that won't work." Failure is built into experimentation, but that doesn't mean we shouldn't try. After 10,000 failures, Edison finally succeeded and in doing so transformed the world, creating a new reality: radiant night-time city streets, brightly lit homes after dark and illuminated factory spaces enabling round-the-clock production.

Experimentation is necessary. But because of low frequency of success, the more experimentation the better. This was the view of one of the early pragmatist philosophers (and US Supreme Court justice), Oliver Wendell Holmes, who said, "all life is an experiment" with "our salvation ... [necessarily] based on imperfect knowledge" (quoted in Menand, 2001, 430). We therefore need as many different people providing experiments as possible, even, as Holmes said, those whose "opinions we loathe" (quoted in Menand, 2001, 430). Rorty makes the same point, contending that experimentation should be open to everyone, even to people whom we might think of as cranks or who are marginal or with whom we disagree. Diversity of experimenters is crucial, increasing the likelihood of experimental diversity and, in turn, producing better conversations, livelier forms of what Rorty (1979, 390) calls *kibitzing*, richer re-descriptions, and more profound forms of edification. Edification means here, as Rorty (1979, 360) put it, the "project of finding new, better, more interesting, more fruitful ways of speaking". That quest never ends. To suppose that it does is to fall into the trap of epistemology. For pragmatists, in contrast, the point is always to continue the conversation, "a conversation which presupposes no disciplinary matrix which unites the speakers, but where the hope of agreement is never lost so long as the conversation lasts" (Rorty 1979, 318). That happens even across that kitchen table in Albuquerque. The couples offer different ways of speaking about love: that is, they engage in different experiments; and while they disagree, they continue talking, at least until dinner time, with the hope of agreement never extinguished.

My purpose in this chapter, then, is to take Rorty's pragmatist model of philosophy as conversation, with its associated emphasis on experimentation, and to think through how it might apply to social inquiry. I use as my case study the work of the maverick American geographer Bill Bunge (1928–2013).

At various times during his life, Bunge was deemed by his mainstream detractors as a crank, marginal to geography, a contrarian, a person with whom nearly everyone disagreed (Bergmann and Morrill, 2018, 291). Following Rorty, I suggest that Bunge and his experiments are best interpreted within the pragmatist frame of philosophy as conversation and experimentation. Throughout his career, much of which was completed outside the formal academy, Bunge carried out novel experiments, mobilising new spatial vocabularies to realise geographical edification.

Those innovative spatial vocabularies often took the form of maps and cartographic techniques. Maps for him were, in effect, geography's language, geography's talk, geography's conversation – the basis of any geographical story. As Bunge wrote in his doctoral thesis, "the reason geography has always paid such respect to maps is that they have been the logical framework upon which geographers have constructed geographic theory" (quoted in Wilson, 2017, 54). For Bunge, however, the form taken by maps was not inviolable, not fixed in character, nor rooted in any essential cartographic Truth. Rather, the vocabulary of maps was sufficiently flexible that, in pragmatist fashion, it could be creatively bent and reshaped to cope with specific needs that required solution, to cope with the world. Cartography offered fruits, not roots: novel map talk could be transformational. By carrying out original cartographic re-description, Bunge aimed in his work to break through the existing crust of cartographic convention, to create something brand new, to change the world for the better, to revolutionise it. To illustrate this argument, I work through three different phases of Bunge's pragmatist cartographic re-description: his early work within spatial science on formal map transformations; his later work in black inner-city Detroit to produce community-based maps to effect political change; and his last substantive work on a nuclear-war atlas that warned against the ultimate catastrophe, atomic Armageddon, the end of human life as we know it.

## Bill Bunge, spatial science and map transformations

Bunge's first exposure to formal geographical talk was in 1951. Conscripted for the Korean War, serving in the American Fifth Army, deployed at the Chemical, Biological and Radiological Wartime School at Camp McCoy, Wisconsin, Bunge (1988, xi) taught there what he later called 'atomic war'. It was also while he was enlisted in the US military that he enrolled in his first class in geography. It was given by the then doyen of American geography, Richard Hartshorne, author of what he thought of as the definitive book on the subject, *The nature of geography* (1939). Hartshorne was professor at the University of Wisconsin's main campus in Madison, but he also lectured in the university's Extension Division, teaching at campuses across the state, which is how Bunge first met him. Their relationship began well but increasingly soured as Hartshorne indulged his habit of meticulous correction (Barnes, 2016). Hartshorne's definition of geographical study was ideographic regionalism, the idea that the purpose of geography was the scrupulous empirical description of unique regions. Maps, within this view, were mirror representations of the singular regions they represented. In turn, mimesis was secured by demonstrating a one-to-one correspondence between the objective unique empirical entities constituting the region and their depiction on the map.

While Bunge may not have always agreed with Hartshorne (indeed, they were often in violent dispute: Barnes, 2016), the extension classes nevertheless sparked in Bunge a lifelong obsession with geography. Bunge later said that obsession produced a tortuous but deeply satisfying life. As he put it in 1968, "I must say I have not found it easy. It is an agony but a marvellous agony ... geography is wonderful" (Bunge, 1968a).

The agony part was quick in coming. As a result of that extension class, Bunge completed a Master's degree with Hartshorne in 1956 (Bergmann and Morrill, 2018, 291), staying on to do a PhD. That is when the first trouble began. Bunge failed his doctoral comprehensive exams, in part because of a negative vote by Hartshorne (Barnes, 2016), and was asked to leave Wisconsin. In 1958, he moved to the University of Washington at Seattle.

It was a much better place for him to be. There was a group of graduate students and faculty at Washington who were questioning Hartshorne's ideo-graphic regionalism, offering instead a nomothetic view set within the methods and philosophy of physical science, aspiring to scientific generalisation and ulti-mately the discovery of geographical laws. One of the Washington graduate stu-dents, Richard Morrill, later said, "Richard Hartshorne, whose work we studied in detail, was what we struggled against" (1984, 59). From a Rortyan perspective, for the Washington group, the dialogue in human geography around Hartshor-nean regionalism had reached gridlock and come to a halt. It was the moment to try out new vocabularies, attempt a revolutionary re-description. The geograph-ical conversation needed to be reignited by a blaze of novel vocabularies and re-descriptions. This was already happening in Seattle when Bunge arrived. The region remained the focus, but it was re-described, put into a new conver-sation with the methods and philosophy of physical science, joined to a general conception of spatial relations expressed mathematically and explained by sys-tematic theory exactingly tested.

Bunge's PhD thesis, completed in 1960, represented the foremost fulfilment of that new form of re-description. Bunge was going to call his dissertation *Fun-damental geography*. It might have made a better title than the one he eventually chose, *Theoretical geography*. The former pointed to the root-and-branch character of the kind of change he envisioned and wanted to put into practice. In Bunge's case, he brought together in conversation, in effect as an experiment, the region and a mathematical – and particularly a geometrical – vocabulary of space. There had not been anything quite like it before. It was his attempt to break what the University of Washington group saw as the impasse in geography.

Key to his project was cartography. He was adding to the geographical conversation primarily a new cartographic vocabulary, a fundamental re-description
of maps. Of course, it had long been an article of faith within geography that
maps were central to the discipline. Carl Sauer famously said: "Show me a
geographer who does not need [maps] constantly and want them about him
[sic], and I shall have my doubts as to whether he [sic] has made the right choice
of life" (1963, 391). Maps were crucial. For ideographic regional geography,
maps were the mirror representation of the object of investigation. These were
maps of the 'map thumpers', as Bunge (1968b, 2) called them: that is, the maps
of older regional geographers who upheld the ideographic definition of the
discipline, like Hartshorne. It was the "view from nowhere" approach to cartography, as O'Sullivan et al. (2018, 130) label it.

In his essay on 'The philosophy of maps', Bunge (1968b, 2) argued that the
geometric principles, "the mathematical functionals", as he called them, underlying such maps needed to be made explicit. They were Euclidean, he con-
tended, which, in turn, produced an absolute (Newtonian) conception of space
(O'Sullivan et al., 2018, 10). To move the conversation forward beyond
ideographic regionalism and its associated mirror-like, Euclidean "view from
nowhere", Bunge instead pushed for a new cartography that would realise a
"more-than-Euclidean, non-absolute spatial representation" (O'Sullivan et al.,
2018, 110). While Bunge never worked through the formal derivations (Michael
Goodchild, 1978, 12, says "there is precious little mathematics in the book"),
*Theoretical geography* is strewn with original cartographic depictions. They were
produced by applying map transformations. This was Bunge's means to create
novel maps, his version of creative re-description, showing what could be
achieved by advancing beyond the impasse of ideographic geography and its
concomitant cartography.

Map transformations is a complicated topic, but the gist is that by transforming the measurement of distance or area on a map from the conventional
metric of kilometres or miles to another metric, like time or cost or, famously
in the case of one of Bunge's (1988, 79) later maps, dead bodies, cartographic
space is radically altered. The geometry of the map frequently becomes non-
Euclidean. It is no longer absolute but relational space. This is seen in Figure 5.1,
taken from *Theoretical geography,* of travel time from Seattle's CBD to outlying
city points. Figure 5.1a is of the untransformed travel times, with distance measured in miles, with the map of Seattle retaining its conventional Euclidean
form. Figure 5.1b is after the transformation: distance is converted to travel
times, producing a non-Euclidean map, with the cartographic spaces of Seattle
shrunk or stretched. These spaces are now drawn relationally, illustrating, as
Bergmann and Morrill put it, "the nonlinearities, the foldings, and the social
production of space" (2018, 292).

The broader point, following Rortyan pragmatism, is Bunge's deployment
of a novel geographical vocabulary to represent spatial relationships, moving

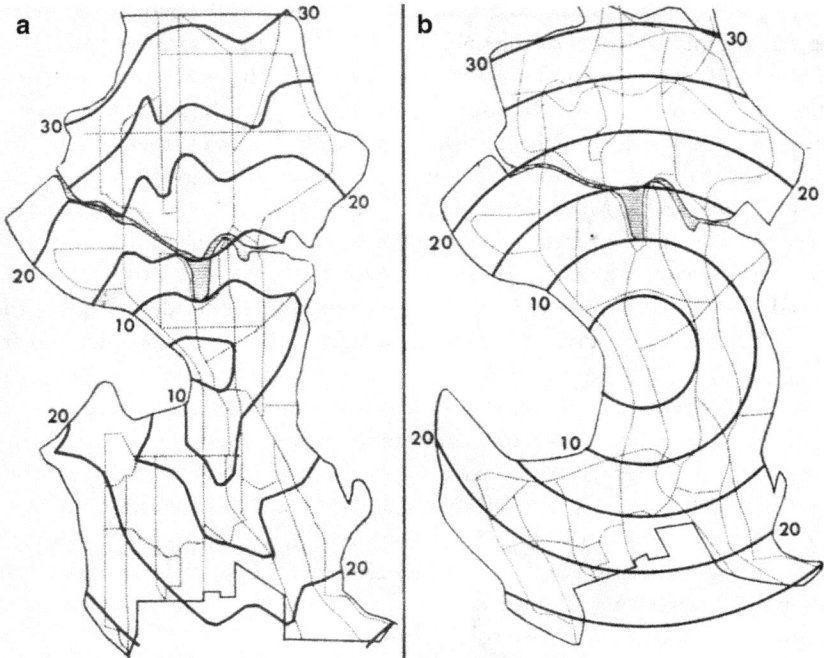

*Figure 5.1a–b* 'Peak hour travel times from Seattle's CBD in five-minute increments' (Bunge, 1966, 55)

geography beyond the old ideographic blockage. Not that Bunge achieved this single-handedly. He drew explicitly on the work of other so-called 'space-cadets' at the University of Washington at the time, especially Waldo Tobler and the Professor of Cartography, John Sherman. The year after Bunge submitted his doctoral thesis, 1960, Tobler (1961) completed his own *Map transformations of geographic space*, under Sherman's supervision. Furthermore, Alan Werritty (2010) has argued that both Tobler's and Bunge's works were based on prior ideas, which both acknowledged, by the early-twentieth-century Scottish biologist D'Arcy Thompson in his book *On growth and form*. Whatever the exact complicated genealogy, Bunge's and Tobler's use of the idea of map transformation represented an experiment – in this case in cartographic re-description – to reawaken what they took as a dormant geographical conversation.

That experiment did not go entirely smoothly. From Bunge especially there was some bluster, things said that were not entirely true, an awkward moment or two. But that is so for most conversations. Perhaps more significantly, Bunge did not foresee where his work might lead when linked to computerisation. In the 1966 'Introduction to second edition' of *Theoretical geography*, published in Sweden, Bunge was clearly a bit rattled by what the computer might do: "To see region construction, one of the last preserves of the non or anti-mathematical geographers, crumble away before the ever-growing appetite of the computing machine is a little unnerving even for a hard-case quantifier" (1966, xiv). He was not sure what he had let out of the bag. But that is also a consequence of initiating a new conversation. They take on a life of their own, are hard to control. That was the case for Bunge. On the one hand, the innovations in his *Theoretical geography* contributed to "revolutionizing post-war cartography", as Barney (2015, 13) writes, preparing it for the "automation and digitization that would power military surveillance and mapping applications". On the other hand, it also helped produce tools and trajectory for critical GIS and its application, as found in works such as Dorling (2012) and Wilson (2017).

## The cartography of urban revolution

From the mid-1960s, Bunge began experimenting with a different kind of cartographic re-description. It derived from his work in the one-square-mile, predominantly black inner-city neighbourhood of Fitzgerald in Detroit, where he also resided, and about which he later wrote his eponymously titled book (Bunge, 1971). He had taken a job at Wayne State University in 1961, initially continuing to offer his mathematical cartography. His living in Fitzgerald, in combination with a series of turbulent political and social events that just kept piling up in 1960s America around war, poverty, racism, civil rights, urban riots and political assassination, made him rethink that project. The trigger, Bunge once said, was looking out of his Wayne State office window at the mainly African-American inner-city of Detroit and realising that his cartographic geometries alone were never fully going to explain the world he saw, the processes propelling it, or change it. It was an acute case of the need for a new experiment in geographical re-description.

He found it by going on to the street, going into his own increasingly black neighbourhood of Fitzgerald, becoming involved and engaged, undertaking new forms of cartography and raising questions about both the kinds of people who could draw maps and the kinds of things that maps could represent. His new style of mapping began almost immediately after Bunge took up his post at Wayne State in autumn 1961. In his first class, he took "the students out to do field mapping" in Detroit's inner city (Bunge, 1969, 9). By 1964, the students were surveying the poorest inner-city districts on Detroit's east side, as well as shadowing "new poverty program workers" in the same neighbourhoods (Bunge, 1969, 9–10). In 1966, he had the first germ of the idea for *Fitzgerald*, although he imagined it initially as simply a "background study for Federal aid in the Great Society 'boomlet'" (Bunge, 1969, 10). The Detroit riots (or "rebellion", as Bunge called it), which lasted over five days – 23–28 July, 1967 – and resulted in forty-three deaths, with a thousand injuries, more than 7,000 arrests and close to 3,000 buildings burnt down, changed all that. The following year, 1968, he along with an eighteen-year-old black woman,

Gwendolyn Warren, already a community activist in Fitzgerald, conceived at a meeting in Bunge's living room the Detroit Geographical Expedition and Institute (DGEI).[1] In part it came about as a response to Warren's rebuke to Bunge that he had not yet given back anything to the community, and in part because Bunge was fired from Wayne State the same year, ostensibly for swearing in class. The DGEI took on both education and research, both of which bore on cartography.

First, in 1969, with Bunge acting as a go-between, DGEI set up free university courses for Detroit inner-city residents, initially from the University of Michigan (held at Wayne State) for 40 students and then, in 1970, at Michigan State University for 400 students (Horvath, 1971). The courses included subjects like urban planning and design, along with cartography, which would enable, in this case, Fitzgerald residents to use academic knowledge for their own purposes. For Heyman (2017, 2), this represented a "radical move" in pedagogy, away from academics as distant experts to academics as civic educators "who help people become better equipped to organize and take control over their communities".

Second, research would be carried out by community members for community members, using, in part, research techniques learned in university classes. As Knudson puts it, Fitzgerald's "residents [became] contributors to knowledge rather than sources of knowledge to be appropriated" (2017, 3). That research would take different forms, but it would always involve being there, "talking, listening, arguing, befriending, and [even] making enemies", as Bunge (1969, 6) wrote. The result could be community flyers, advocacy reports, position papers, submissions to the city council or maps. Especially maps. But not maps as "a god's eye view of the world ... as austere and authentic" (Thatcher, 2017, 3) but instead representations of the "lived, daily experience of a community ... made legible through mapping". Those maps would be, as Phil Cohen (2017, 1) labelled them, "life maps, maps that tell stories in a way that brings data to human life".

The maps that were produced are found in Bunge's (1971) *Fitzgerald* and in the four sets of *Field notes* that functioned as annual reports for the DGEI generated by Fitzgerald community members and especially Gwendolyn Warren.[2] In Rorty's terms, these maps were radical geographical re-descriptions. The maps expanded the cultural repertoire available to Fitzgerald's residents, providing potential means to make possible achievements not realised before, including neighbourhood change. That cartography based on lived experience and a charged political impulse "both subtended and expanded the possibility of map making" (Morris and Voyce, 2015). They were "oughtness maps", bearing a visual critique of existing social relationships, starkly revealing the many structural forms of injustice and inequity that bore on Fitzgerald's community members as they lived out their lives, while at the same time pointing to potential changes that would make those lives better (Bergmann and Morrill, 2018, 294).

WHERE COMMUTERS RUN OVER BLACK
CHILDREN ON THE POINTES-DOWNTOWN TRACK

*Figure 5.2* 'Where commuters run over black children on the Pointes-downtown track' (Detroit Geographical Expedition, 1971, 17–18)

A striking example is the map 'Where commuters run over black children on the Pointes-downtown track', which that appeared in *Field notes no. 3*, "The geography of the children of Detroit" (Detroit Geographical Expedition, 1971) (Figure 5 2). At its most basic, the map tells a story of the everyday experiences of black children in Fitzgerald as they try to cross the road during rush hours as white drivers commute from their eastern suburban homes (the 'Pointes') to downtown. At one corner alone, six black children are run over and killed. The extreme subject makes a powerful oughtness map, both exposing the social relations that produce such a tragic outcome and demonstrating what must be changed to prevent what is portrayed. Dee Morris and Stephen Voyce (2015) call the map "a radical cartography of murder sites", laying bare the social facts that lay behind it, such as "pedestrian paths, commuter traffic, and race relations". Denis Wood (2010, 115) is blunter: "It is a map of racist infanticide, a racial child murder map."

Bunge's cartographic experiment here is not technical, as were his maps in *Theoretical geography*. But it is just as experimental, transformational and revolutionary, likely much more so. By intervening into the cartographic conversation by changing who can make maps, and about what kinds of things can be mapped, Bunge makes us think about the world in new and different ways, including ways to change it. He wants his map to provoke us, to become geographically edified, to produce a world in which no black children are ever run over in Detroit by white commuters.

## The cartography of apocalypse

The third case of Bunge using cartography as novel geographical re-description was perhaps the most difficult, certainly the most haunting and chilling. The aim of Bunge's (1988) *Nuclear war atlas* was to re-describe the geography of nothing: the world after the bomb. The bomb was a menacing presence from early on in Bunge's adult life. He was seventeen when Enola Gay dropped Little Boy on Hiroshima and twenty-two when he taught 'nuclear war' at Camp McCoy. From then on, he experienced the continual existential threat of Cold War nuclear annihilation that included the 1962 Cuban crisis; numerous close calls because of faulty radar equipment, flying flocks of geese and solar flares; and, from 1983, President Reagan's Star Wars plans, which had US nuclear missiles orbiting earth ready to destroy any weapon launched by the Soviets. Bunge believed nuclear war was not survivable. It would not only be the end of human civilisation as we knew it, it would be the end of humans. That was geographically demonstrated, he believed, by his nuclear war atlas.

Bunge conceived and produced the atlas in Canada. After he was fired from Wayne State in 1968, he initially remained in Detroit, writing *Fitzgerald* and directing the research carried out by the DGEI. He moved permanently to Canada in 1972, initially to Ontario, later to Quebec, founding the Society of Human Exploration (Bergmann and Morrill, 2018, 296). In 1982, the Society put out a pamphlet of twenty-eight maps called the *Nuclear war atlas*, which in 1988 was expanded to the full-length book with fifty-seven maps. It is not for the faint of heart. Fraser McDonald (2006, 58) writes, "Bunge's *Atlas* maps out a post-apocalyptic terrain, without any attempt to 'soften the theme of unremitting and sense-numbing disaster.' Few geographers have offered their readers such a bleak cartography."

The bleakness had a purpose, though – in fact, the same purpose as the maps that were in *Fitzgerald* and the *Field notes*. All those maps, as Bergman and Morrill (2018, 292) write, are "motivated by an urgency to have geography analyse and respond to human crises of the times, responses that relied on analysis with creative spatial methods". That creativity is found, for example, in the map titled 'The closest neighbour ever – the Soviet Union and the United States' (Figure 5.3).

It is an attempt to intervene creatively in the conversation, in this case about nuclear war, by drawing on a geographical vocabulary. It is also an experiment. It is not how world maps should be, with seemingly missing land blocks (in this case, the Soviet Union and the USA), but which in fact are there; indeed, they are now everywhere as the legend and red-hash markings that cover the entire map make clear.

The point of Bunge's experiment in mapmaking, as Timothy Barney (2015, 200) suggests, is to show how nuclear armed inter-continental ballistic missiles (ICBMs) have produced a world of "radical proximity", where the entire

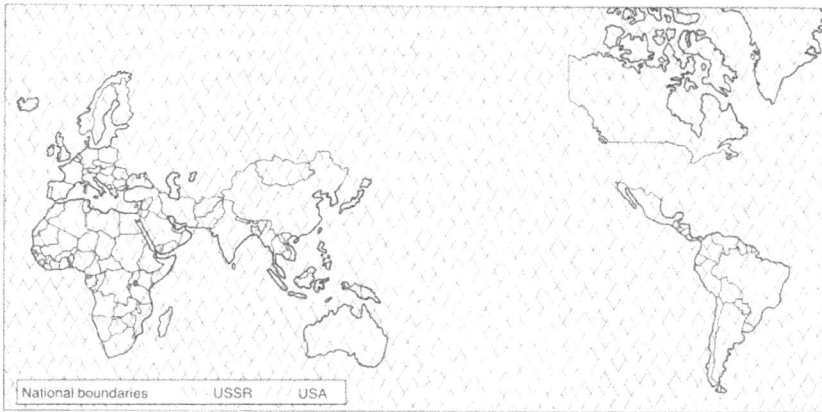

*Figure 5.3* 'The closest neighbour ever – the Soviet Union and the United States' (Bunge, 1988, 93)

surface of the globe – everywhere – shares the same nuclear apocalyptic space. There is no hiding, no escaping outside – no outside. Consequently, political space and boundaries are radically reconfigured. Bergmann and Morrill, writing about this map, say it is:

> A cartographic and geometric vision of a "topological space collapse" of the political spatiality that had preceded the advent of the intercontinental ballistic missile after which superpowers could suddenly reach all points on the planet with maximal force nearly instantaneously, eliminating the interior, transforming the topological nature of superpower borders, and reordering the very connectivity of space. The new border was not south or north but "up". (2018, 292)

Bunge's contribution to the conversation about nuclear war is to say that to be fully understood it needs to be represented through maps. But not as conventional cartography, based on Euclidean principles, which only freezes space and naturalises points and lines. Nuclear war under a regime of ICBMs is dynamic, changing the very topology of space. Far becomes near, fixed points are no longer fixed, planes fold, curl and collide. Bunge's cartographical re-description in Figure 5.3 enlarges the existing repertoire for talking about the consequences of nuclear war, but it is so horrific that he hopes it will prevent those very consequences.

## Conclusion

The purpose of this chapter was to show how thinking from a pragmatist perspective might be useful in understanding work carried out in social science. My exemplar was the human geographer William Bunge and the maps he produced at three different points in his career – that is, insofar as he had a career. Pragmatism cannot be used to determine the validity of Bunge's claims embedded in his maps. It is not a philosophy like positivism or realism, or even Marxism, which provide criteria to evaluate truth claims. Rather, as Menand (2001, xi) puts it, pragmatism is "an idea about ideas", a means to think about thinking. I used pragmatism to think about geographical thinking, but there is every reason to suppose that pragmatism can be used also to think about the thinking of any social science.

Following Rorty's pragmatism, I suggested we should conceive of thinking as experiments in an ongoing conversation about how to cope with the world. That pair of couples in a suburban Albuquerque kitchen did it by telling one another stories about love. William Bunge did it by drawing different kinds of maps. What you do to cope, and how you cope, will be contextual and contingent. Further, there are no guarantees. Whether an experiment is deemed to work is established only consequently by its fruits. On this criterion, Bunge's experiments with mapping have remained enormously fertile and productive more than sixty years after he first began conceiving them at the University of Washington. His ideas around moving away from Euclidean geometries of mapping and absolute space, treating the community studied as partners and participants in research rather than objects of research, being open-minded about what can be mapped and how it can be portrayed, and thinking of maps as critical political artefacts to make progressive social arguments about justice, fairness and equality – these ideas continue to hold sway. Bunge may now be a historical figure, but his work is not yet history. He is still part of the conversation, still enjoined within the pragmatic task we all face of coping with the world.

## Notes

1    Warren provides another link to pragmatism, although it is not with the Rortyian kind but the version produced at the University of Chicago, where John Dewey was initially Professor of Philosophy (1894–1904). He, in turn, influenced especially the early-twentieth-century Chicago urban sociologists Robert Park and Earnest Burgess (Wills, 2016, 170–6). During the interwar period, one of the students attending the University of Chicago urban sociology programme was Saul Alinsky, who later became the most renowned politically progressive American urban community organiser during the early postwar period (Wills, 2016, 74–5). Alinsky drew on pragmatist ideas (Engel, 2002). Harney et al. (2016) label his approach 'process pragmatism', which involved engaging with community organisations before determining the object of research; promoting leaders within the community and letting them guide and fully participate in the research process (thus undermining any idea of an outside expert); and, through democratic participatory inquiry, identifying potential solutions and strategies for their realisation. Alinsky's process pragmatism was taken up from 1961 by the Fitzgerald Community Council (FCC), an alliance of different local community organisations within

Detroit's Fitzgerald neighbourhood (the FCC is recognised and celebrated by Bunge, 1971,76–86). The FCC was, as Harney et al. (2016, 325) put it, "DGEI's sister organisation". It was also one in which Gwendolyn Warren participated, connecting her to the Rortyan variant of pragmatism.

2  The four sets of Field Notes produced between 1969 and 1972 are available as pdfs at https://antipodefoundation.org/2017/02/23/dgei-field-notes/ (accessed 23 June 2018).

# References

Barnes, T. J. (2016) The odd couple: Richard Hartshorne and William Bunge. *The Canadian Geographer*, 60, 4, 459–65.

Barney, T. (2015) *Mapping the Cold War: Cartography and the framing of America's international power.* Chapel Hill, NC: UNC Press.

Bergmann, L. and Morrill, R. (2018) William Wheeler Bunge: Radical geographer (1928–2013). *Annals of the Association of American Geographers*, 108, 1, 291–300.

Bunge, W. (1966) *Theoretical geography*, 2nd edn. Lund: Gleerup.

Bunge, W. (1968a) Letter to Richard Hartshorne, no date (but likely late October), Box 194, Hartshorne correspondence – William Bunge, File F, Richard Hartshorne Papers, American Geographical Society Library, University of Wisconsin, Milwaukee, WI.

Bunge, W. (1968b) The philosophy of maps, in W. Bunge, ed., *Michigan Inter-University Community of Mathematical Geographers discussion paper number 12, The philosophy of maps.* www-personal.umich.edu/~copyrght/image/micmog.html (accessed 19 June 2018).

Bunge, W. (1969) The first years of the Detroit Geographical Expedition Institute: A personal report, R. J. Horvath and E. J. Vander Velde, eds, *Field notes, the Detroit geography expedition, a series dedicated to the human exploration of our planet, discussion paper no. 1, The Detroit Geographical Expedition Institute.* East Lansing, MI: Michigan State University, 1–30.

Bunge, W. (1971) *Fitzgerald: Geography of a revolution.* Cambridge, MA: Schenkman.

Bunge, W. (1988) *Nuclear war atlas.* Oxford: Basil Blackwell.

Carver, R. (1981) *What we talk about when we talk about love.* New York, NY: Alfred Knopf.

Cohen, P. (2017) William Bunge: Expeditionary geography: A commentary on six iconic maps for 'Fitzgeralds's geography of a revolution'. *Mapworks* # 2, Spring, 1–5. http://livingmaps.review/journal/index.php/LMR/article/download/59/99 (accessed 23 June 2018).

Detroit Geographical Expedition (1971) The geography of the children of Detroit. *Field notes: A series dedicated to the human exploration of our planet, discussion paper no. 3.* Detroit, MI: Detroit Geographical Expedition and Institute.

Dorling, D. (2012) *The visualization of social spatial structure.* Chichester: John Wiley.

Engel, L.J. (2002) Saul D. Alinsky and the Chicago School. *The Journal of Speculative Philosophy*, 16, 1, 50–66.

Goodchild, M. (1978) William Bunge's *Theoretical geography*, in P. Hubbard, R. Kitchen and G. Valentine, eds, *Key texts in human geography.* London: Sage, 9–16.

Harney, L., McCurry, J., Scott, J. and Wills, J. (2016) Developing 'process pragmatism' to underpin engaged research in human geography. *Progress in Human Geography*, 40, 3, 316–33.

Hartshorne, R. (1939) *The nature of geography: A critical survey of current thought in the light of the past.* Lancaster, PA: Association of American Geographers.

Heyman, R. (2017) Knowledge production, political action and pedagogy in Trumbull, Antipode Foundation Symposium. https://radicalantipode.files.wordpress.com/2017/02/dgei-field-notes_rich-heyman.pdf (accessed 23 June 2018).

Horvath, R. J. (1971) The 'Detroit Geographical Expedition and Institute' experience. *Antipode*, 3 1, 73–85.

James, W. (1902 [2012]) *Varieties of religious experience*. Oxford: Oxford University Press.

Knudson, C. (2017) Detroit, geography, expedition, institute: Unpacking the history and structure of the DGEI. Antipode Foundation Symposium. https://radicalantipode.files.wordpress.com/2017/02/dgei-field-notes_chris-knudson.pdf (accessed 23 June 2018).

MacDonald, F. (2006) Geopolitics and 'the vision thing': Regarding Britain and America's first nuclear missile. *Transactions of the Institute of British Geographers*, 31, 53–71.

Menand, L. (2001) *The metaphysical club: A story of ideas in America*. New York, NY: Farrar, Straus and Giroux.

Morrill, R.L. (1984) Recollections of the quantitative revolution's early years: The University of Washington, 1955–65, in M. Billinge, D. Gregory, and R. Martin, eds, *Recollections of a revolution: Geography as spatial science*. London: MacMillan, 57–72.

Morris, D. and Voyce, S. (2015) William Bunge, the DGEI, and radical cartography. 2 Jacket: Counter map collection. https://jacket2.org/commentary/william-bunge-dgei-radical-cartography (accessed 23 June 2018).

O'Sullivan, D., Bergmann, L. and Thatcher, J. (2018) Spatiality, maps and mathematics in critical human geography: Towards a repetition with difference. *The Professional Geographer*, 70, 1, 29–39.

Rorty, R. (1979) *Philosophy and the mirror of nature*. Princeton, NJ: Princeton University Press.

Rorty, R. (2007) *Philosophy as cultural politics. Philosophical papers, volume 4*. Cambridge: Cambridge University Press.

Sauer, C. (1963) *Land and life: A selection from the writings of Carl Ortwin Sauer*, J. Leighly, ed. Berkeley, CA: University of California Press.

Shusterman. R. (1997) *Practicing philosophy: Pragmatism and the philosophical life*. New York and London: Routledge.

Thatcher, J. (2017) Looking back to Detroit for a (counter-mapping) path forward. Antipode Foundation Symposium. https://radicalantipode.files.wordpress.com/2017/02/dgei-field-notes_jim-thatcher.pdf (accessed 23 June 2018).

Tobler, W, (1961) *Map transformations of geographic space*. Unpublished PhD thesis, Department of Geography, University of Washington. https://digital.lib.washington.edu/researchworks/handle/1773/5629 (accessed 21 June 2018).

Werritty, A. (2010) D'Arcy Thompson's *On growth and form* and the rediscovery of geometry within the geographical tradition. *Scottish Geographical Journal*, 126, 4, 231–57.

Wills, J. (2016) *Locating localism: Statecraft, citizenship and democracy*. Bristol: Policy Press.

Wilson, M. (2017) *New lines: Critical GIS and the trouble of the map*. Minneapolis, MN: University of Minnesota Press.

Wood, D. (2010) *Rethinking the power of maps*. New York, NY: Guilford.

# Part III

# 'Truth', epistemic injustice and academic practice

# 6

# Embodied ignorances: A pragmatist responds to epistemic and other kinds of frictions in the academy

## Susan Saegert

### Introduction

A specific incident a few years ago sharpened for me the distinction between individual ignorance that can be corrected by learning in community and ignorance as a product of certain ways of knowing in certain communities. Students of colour (SOC) in the PhD programme where I teach organised an intervention around how the practices and conditions of their education actively ignored their experiences. Similar events were occurring in other universities, colleagues told me. Following a year of discussion within the SOC group about the experience of being a person of colour in the programme, the group called a community meeting and presented an analysis of unequal treatment and the university's failure to meet their educational needs. They pointed to the scarcity of scholars of colour on the faculty and in the curriculum and they spoke of micro aggressions that made them feel excluded and demeaned.

The intervention was deeply disturbing to many in the audience. This PhD programme accepts, funds and graduates a higher proportion of students of colour than most other programmes in our discipline. Many of the faculty have spent their careers studying and exposing the psychosocial, material, political, cultural and economic processes and histories of inequalities related to race and gender. It was itself a sign of progress that there were enough students of colour to stage the intervention and that a setting was available that allowed the confrontation to occur. For these and other reasons, the students' charges were experienced by some as really painful, a point that needs pondering as it eludes most academic discourse, fuels problems arising from difference and can block progress moving forward. For faculty members, the intervention posed challenges to our obligations as educators and scholars. I joined many in the audience in feeling hurt, misunderstood and misrepresented, mirroring, to a certain extent, the feelings expressed by the students of colour. Yet when it came to my curriculum, they were not wrong; some of my syllabi predominantly include readings by white men and, in some areas, I showed little knowledge of the contributions of authors of colour. In addition, while I study problems affecting people of colour, especially women of colour, and often quote their voices, I write as if I wasn't part of the social history creating the problematic situations that the students described. Because I value diverse perspectives and accept the situated and interest-driven nature of the pursuit of knowledge, the students' charges were matters of concern to me as a person, teacher, scholar and pragmatist.

The students' intervention created a situation of *"epistemic friction"* (Medina, 2013, 158–9, italics in the original) in which the heterogeneities and discontinuities in the "experiential space" of people of colour and white people (Mills, 1998, 27) are brought to the surface by acts of resistance by those who experience injustice in the dominant, everyday ways of understanding the world. Much earlier, DuBois used the term "double consciousness" to describe the disconnect between how a person of colour is perceived, treated and expected to act and the actual lived experience of being a person of colour (DuBois, 1897, 1903 [1994]). Mills (1997) analysed the causes of this double consciousness for people of colour as residing in the 'racial contract' in which the privileges of white people depend on white people ignoring the experiences of people of colour and people of colour being unable to speak and be heard. Whiteness, then, exemplifies a form of embodied ignorance both through observable skin colour (socially interpreted) and the habits of body non-dualistically understood as including habits of mind.

The embodied condition of ignorance connotes that, on the one hand, we are each contained in a unique body that occupies particular times and places and, on the other hand, that our bodies elicit particular interpretations and treatments from others. Whiteness alone can powerfully exemplify a category of embodied ignorance. Yet bodies come with many other traits – gender, 'ableness', place of origin – that bring with them epistemological and material consequences at the intersection of different oppressions and forms of privilege (Collins, 2011, 2012; Medina, 2013). Those occupying specific intersections of categories or sources of oppression are often blind to the experiential worlds of others as well as to the ways they habitually erase others' experiences from their perceptions and thoughts and benefit, unconsciously and consciously, from ignoring those worlds. This kind of ignorance, which Medina calls "meta-blindness", resists change through experience and learning because of its utility in maintaining privilege. Thus it contrasts with individual ignorance as described by Peirce (1869 [1992]), which arises from the physical, mental, temporal and spatial limitations of being just one person.

The students' intervention brought to the fore their experience of the embodied ignorances of white students and faculty. Informed by Mills's (1997) framing of the racial contract, they lodged their analysis in a charge of white epistemological ignorance that included several distinct elements: (1) white people's ignoring of how the lives of students of colour are marked by race; (2) white people's lack of awareness of the effects of white behaviours and habits on students of colour; (3) the inadequacy of texts written by white scholars for advancing knowledge that is faithful to their experience and would aid in meeting their goals of a larger, freer life, including a life of scholarship; and (4) that faculty members of colour would better understand them and advance their goals. They argued, further, that a fuller recognition of the bodily, epistemological and moral harms done to people of colour requires a form of academic reparation that privileges people of colour in order to redress the weight of historical oppression. These include changes in admissions and fellowships; a greater commitment by teachers to work with the differential academic knowledge base of students of colour; and hiring, promoting and tenuring faculty of colour. Motivating and justifying these claims was the proposition that if, as Mills postulates, white people and people of colour live by implicit rules that prevent white people from seeing, feeling and understanding the worlds of people of colour, then people of colour are prevented by white people from joining the community that informs collective norms and actions. Given the failure to rectify such epistemic ignorance, the democratic aspiration of an ever-expanding community cannot be realised.

In the rest of this chapter, I attempt to analyse the different kinds of embodied ignorances that converged to create the sense of injustice expressed by the students. First, I distinguish between the harm done by personal ignorance and the use of that ignorance to undergird privilege. Some of these harms limit individual and collective possibilities of knowing, while others reinforce distributive inequality. The chapter identifies forms of epistemic injustice and possible remedies and then examines the social and political conditions that make this injustice enforceable. I then turn to the pragmatist tradition as a resource for going forward towards a more inclusive community of inquirers and establishing the conditions that would support equality and democracy. The contributions of women pragmatists and pragmatists of colour expand our resources and suggest that moving our inquiries outside the academy will do much to achieve these goals. I end with a story about how moving struggles for epistemic and material justice outside the academy contributes to a more inclusive community of inquirers and produces conditions more conducive to the equality necessary for a democratic way of life.

## Hot stoves and epistemological injustice

A child hears it said that the stove is hot. But it is not, he says; and, indeed, that central body is not touching it, and only what he touches is hot or cold. But he becomes aware of ignorance, and it is necessary to suppose a *self* in which this ignorance can inhere. (C.S. Peirce, 1869 [1992], 20, emphasis in the original)

What happens to you doesn't belong to you, only half concerns you. It's not yours. Not yours alone. (Claudia Rankin, 2014, 141)

The real, then, is that which, sooner or later, information and reasoning would finally result in, and which is therefore independent of the vagaries of me and you. Thus, the very origin of the conception of reality shows that this conception essentially involves the notion of a COMMUNITY, without definite limits, and capable of an indefinite increase of knowledge. (C.S. Peirce, 1868 [1992], 52, emphasis in the original)

Touching a hot stove and being ignored or abused by others – the two experiences described in the introductory quotations above – hurt in different ways. The child who touches a hot stove and learns that such an action results in pain represents a kind of universal embodied ignorance inherent in the limitations of individual experience situated at a particular time and place. When Claudia Rankin expresses her alienation from what happens to her ("What happens to you … only half concerns you"), she recounts the experience of being acted upon because of her perceived social body category. She is the object of ignorance rather than the ignorant subject. As a poet, she speaks eloquently to readers occupying bodies categorically subject to oppressions while still seeking an ever-expanding community of inquirers into multiple realities. The students of colour acted, I believe, from much the same impulse to be heard and seen. Along with Rankin, they echoed DuBois's concept of "double vision" that encompasses both the lived experience of a black person and awareness of the erasure and distortion of that experience in the actions of white people. Rankin and the students of colour follow DuBois (1897) in their hopes when he observed that "The history of the American Negro is the history of this strife – this longing to attain a self-conscious manhood, to merge his double self into a better and truer self. In this merging he wishes neither of the older selves to be lost" (DuBois, 1897, 1903 [1994]). Leaving aside his universalising of "manhood", DuBois achieved in his writing the desire to participate "as a co-worker in the kingdom of culture". The intervention by the students of colour acted towards a similar goal.

The concept of epistemological injustice (Fricker, 2007) illuminates the students' sense of being wronged by the failure of the dominant white society to recognise and understand their experiences and by the exclusion of scholarship by people of colour from course readings and from the ranks of the faculty. Epistemological injustice has two components: testimonial injustice, which occurs when prejudice causes the listener to deny the credibility of the speaker; and hermeneutical injustice, which refers to the listener's lack of interpretive resources needed to understand situations and utterances. Both dimensions of injustice can shape the friction that arises when scholars within the academy practise the canons and standards of truth characteristic of their discipline or school of thought. Dieleman, for example, describes presenting the concept of epistemological injustice and its remedies to audiences of philosophers. Her listeners often responded by arguing that philosophers "prize clear articulation and precise argumentation" and it is their job to correct those they deem "in-credible or in-competent" according to the "canons" of their discipline (Dieleman, 2015, 795). If the world as described by an "in-credible" or "in-competent" speaker did not make sense to legitimate philosophers, it failed to meet the test of clear articulation and precise argumentation. Such judgements were not seen as inviting deeper inquiry into what the "in-credible" speaker was saying but merited exclusion from conversation on the grounds of failing to meet accepted disciplinary standards. Dieleman (2015) concluded that attempting to correct epistemological injustices might not be the charge of philosophers *qua* philosophers but rather was a public political project necessary for democracy.

For pragmatists, inviting in excluded experience is central to an increase in valid, moral and useful ways of knowing. Dewey challenged empiricists and rationalists to include the moral and social consequences of ways of knowing as intrinsic to the goals of empirical inquiry (cf. Putnam, 2017). As a remedy for testimonial injustice, Fricker (2007) prescribed virtuous hearing and perception rooted in efforts towards accuracy and sincerity in interactions, reflection and representation. Righting hermeneutical injustice stemming from lack of interpretive resources requires rigorous critical scholarship to develop better cultural resources for understanding oppression. Congruent with pragmatist thinking, these virtues have instrumental and intrinsic ethical value. Pragmatists seek useful truths, as James and Dewey elaborated, that make a difference for choices of courses of action and their consequences (Dewey, 1929 [2008]; James, 1907 [2004]). Dewey argued that what is good is different from what is dictated by social norms or is personally satisfying. The conditions of enjoyment or achievement of what is good must also be taken into account. There can be no fixed idea of what is good but rather constructions of good must be experientially tested and analysed to determine what has value. By these criteria, the conditions that produce and continue discriminatory practices against people of colour, women, the disabled and other categories of disadvantaged people should call into question the value of epistemic and other practices of exclusion.

In addition to embracing inclusive epistemological practices, it is incumbent on scholars to recognise and rectify their own lack of hermeneutical resources arising from insufficient attention to the scholarship of oppressed groups. Many academic practices narrow our hermeneutical resources. Ghettoising and marginalising scholarship by members of oppressed groups under labels such as black studies, queer theory, feminist theory, etc. frees those not 'specialising' in those 'topics' from needing to know the scholarship. It also fixes our understandings of oppressions unidimensionally and denies the complexity of experience. It allows editors, reviewers and teachers to demand the citation of canonical (and not so canonical) sources that exclude scholars of colour and other non-dominant groups. Epistemological ignorance, in short, reflects both the absence of virtuous hearing and perception and the persistence of exclusionary habits and in-group norms.

There are real stakes for the oppressors in losing privilege if epistemological injustices were to be overcome, producing what Medina (2013) called the problem of meta-blindness:

> the inability to recognise and acknowledge one's limitations and blind spots …. the kind of active ignorance that protects itself and becomes a durable obstacle for responsibility, the kind of ignorance that has the tendency to persist across the individual's lifetime and to perpetuate itself across generations, the recalcitrant ignorance that has deep roots in cognitive and affective structures and requires a whole battery of critical interventions and structural transformation to be uprooted. (Medina, 2013, 149–50)

### Forms of embodied ignorance

The students' intervention focused on one form of embodied ignorance arising from structural oppressions that produce different life experiences, resources and privileges conveyed in ingrained habits and through inheritances of property, wealth, health and legal standing (Alcoff, 2007). But their presentation obscured other forms of embodied ignorance. These include (1) individual ignorance that inescapably accompanies being only one biological and biographical person and a singular occupant of time and space; and (2) the conditionally embodied ignorance related to each person's sociological position as student, teacher or administrator in the academy. Individual embodied ignorance is of the sort described by Peirce, as noted above, that arises from the limits of an individual's experience. Membership in an expansive, democratic community of inquirers can ameliorate individual ignorance by making visible a variety of perspectives and experiences. Aspects of the structurally determined ignorance of those who are privileged by historical and existing practices of discrimination might also be ameliorated by full membership in such a community, at least to some extent. A distinct type of embodied ignorance stems from differences in role-related knowledge and the expertise of faculty and students. In the context of the highly racially and gender-stratified encounters of power differences in the academy, the distinct kinds of ignorance tend to blend together and limit the potential of the academy as a place of critical inquiry (Alcoff, 2007; Kelley, 2016).

Dewey wrote extensively about the importance of educational institutions as sites for the development of the capacity for autonomous thought within collaborative inquiry, both essential for democratic ways of life (cf. Dewey, 1916 [2008]). In his public life, he and Alice Dewey established the well-known

Laboratory School at the University of Chicago and inspired others. These same principles of learning and democracy were evident in the educational aspects of the Hull House founded by Jane Addams who influenced and was influenced by Dewey (Westbrook, 1991). Yet the intervention by the students of colour and the persistence of racial, gender and other forms of discrimination challenge us to find new ways to achieve Dewey's vision.

## Social power and identity in the academy

The capacity to exercise power undergirds the maintenance of all forms of embodied ignorance. Thus it is important to understand the relationship between the often unacknowledged power of embodied identities and the more identifiable forms of social power that produce direct consequences for the partners to an interaction. Different forms of embodied ignorance are maintained through different exercises of power. Only individual ignorance carries no implicit guarantee of the power to maintain itself unless it is embedded in a privileged identity or is maintained through the exercise of social power.

The students of colour created epistemic friction by resisting both kinds of power. Identity power is dependent on both parties sharing an imaginative conception of an identity category specifying dominance and submission, while social power is "a practically socially situated capacity to control others' actions, where the capacity may be exercised (actively and passively) by particular social agents, or alternatively, it may operate purely structurally" (Fricker, 2007, 13). Ambiguity inheres in identity power because all people belong to multiple categories of identity, each occupying a different power position. In the situation experienced by students of colour, race, gender, personal characteristics and academic status were confounded. The students of colour focused their intervention on race, recognising that the categories of "people of colour" and "white people" have a long history of white control of the bodies, living conditions, legal standing and life chances of people of colour.

In a graduate school with a primarily white faculty, the identity power of race mingles with social power as faculty exert power over students through their status and role expectations. These powers include admitting students into the programme, awarding fellowships, setting course requirements, deciding course content, writing letters of reference, supporting student projects and providing feedback on limitations and inaccuracies in their work (remarked on as far back as 1972 by renowned sociologist Robert Merton). The structure and practices of higher education encourage the maintenance of pernicious ignorance when it is confounded with structural forms of embodied ignorance. The deference expected of students towards faculty members confounds identity power when there are few people of colour, women and other non-dominant groups at the higher-status levels of university teaching and administration. As a result, then, both identity power and social power deriving from faculty and administrative roles enhance the capacity of higher-status academics to ignore lower-status people. The students of colour made the claim that this is especially true when students occupying socially lower positions of power are also people of colour. Thus the role of faculty and administrators in facilitating student learning can be compromised through practices of epistemological injustice as well as other forms of discrimination. Further, students in graduate study are charged not only with learning but also with creating new knowledge that might be stymied or stifled if the student's perspective is discounted or silenced. The goal of building a community of inquirers inheres in a university department tasked with defining, representing and teaching the core concerns of the field and methods of inquiry and debate. Departments thus present reasonable sites of contestation about these matters by future members of the discipline and students have a legitimate interest in the disciplinary content and composition of the community of inquiry. Faculty members must find a useful space in which instruction in content and ways of knowing does not exclude or silence others.

A basic tenet of pragmatism is that people will make the best (i.e. most useful and morally sound) contributions to shared understandings and lives when able to speak from their whole selves, including their ability to express their own experience of difference. Both a willingness and a capacity to engage in difficult individual and group interactions are likely to be required for this to happen. Achieving this space may be difficult given differences in social power based in social structural positions and role identities and the process is likely to be understood and navigated differently by different parties to the interaction. These tensions will not be resolved solely within the university as the distribution of social power is also established in part by forces outside the limited community of the university including discipline-wide tenets and practices, external funding priorities, political winds, and ideological stances of those with social and economic power, among other factors.

## Remembering affirmative action

That the students of colour situated their intervention in struggles over the nature of the university made salient my membership in the category 'woman' (Pateman, 1998). As I worked my way through writing this chapter, I was reminded that I had benefited from a kind of reparations for past racial and sexual oppressions. My life as a would-be professor began by entering graduate school in 1969 with the first class in social psychology at the University of Michigan to be half black and half female (overlapping categories, obviously). Previously, few black people had been admitted or hired; women graduate students were few; and women were rarely appointed to the faculty even when it was widely acknowledged that women contributed significantly to their faculty husbands' published work and grant proposals. Political pressures within and outside the university partially determined the composition of my entering class.

Activists in the Students for a Democratic Society, the Black Action Movement and other national and international groups protested, made demands and organised a student strike at the beginning of my first term on campus. Many of the social psychology department faculty were sympathetic to the left-activist politics of the time. External pressure appeared when federally funded grants to the university were threatened because of discrimination against African Americans and women. The legal case for including previously discriminated-against groups rested on equal protection and equal rights. Moreover, feminists and people of colour asserted that our voices would broaden and deepen understanding of the world by including the experiences, values and perspectives coming from the social position of women and people of colour.

The inclusion of more diverse contributions to what DuBois called the "kingdom of culture", however, resulted not only from legal sanctions and arguments about grasping reality. In going from admitting almost no people of colour and women to an entering class comprising fifty per cent of each, the white male faculty acted on their understanding of social–psychological group dynamics and their concern for social justice. They believed that including equal numbers of previously excluded groups would mitigate the power dynamics of previous discrimination (and this conjecture continues to be empirically supported, as documented in a recent report (Parker, 2018)). Some faculty members unthinkingly treated some women and black students like inferior or dangerous beings and, for women at least, as sexual conquest material. But due to the cultivated climate of mutual respect in the programme, we were met with unflagging efforts at intellectual fairness. The faculty accepted the 'fact' of the history of racial and sexual oppression and exclusion and acted institutionally to correct it.

The social psychology faculty hired a dynamic young black faculty member, James Jackson, who attracted more students of colour. Together with white faculty members, they began a decades-long research programme on the factors that support and undermine racial equality. More faculty of colour and women were hired and Jackson became director of the internationally important Institute for Social Research at the University of Michigan. Thus despite some recalcitrant racist and sexist attitudes, habits and impulses, the Michigan social psychology faculty and the university administration acted institutionally to broaden knowledge about the social psychology of race and worked to increase black and female membership and power within the academy.

But these correctives have been difficult to sustain. Lawsuits challenged the University of Michigan's affirmative action efforts throughout the early 2000s. In 2006, a majority of Michigan voters supported Proposal 2 amending the state constitution to ban preferential treatment based on race, gender, colour, ethnicity or national origin in public education, public employment or public contracting (State Constitution of Michigan, Section 26). A US Supreme Court ruling in 2014 allowed the amendment to the state constitution to stand.

Supreme Court Justice Sonia Sotomayor, who went to Harvard through a door that affirmative action opened, wrote an outraged dissent (Litak, 2014). The Equal Rights Amendment to the US Constitution, although ratified by thirty-seven of a required thirty-eight states, is technically dead (Haag, 2018). The Black Lives Matter movement, the recent high profile of 'white supremacists', the emergence of movements challenging the ways men use power over women (cf. the '#MeToo' movement), and counter-movements defending masculine prerogatives (cf. the 'Incels') demonstrate that the issues of racism and sexism are far from dead in the broader culture. The sense that we as students felt in 1969 that racism and sexism were in inevitable decline is long gone. The concept of gender has become more fluid in popular and academic discourse while that of race seems to have hardened. Both race and gender remain the basis of legal and illegal (but tolerated) discrimination. While I and many of my cohort personally flourished in the decades after 1969, the hopes for a university that welcomes and supports people of colour and women remain to be realised and need continuing effort.

As part of the history of efforts at improving inclusion and valuing people of colour and women in the production of knowledge in the academy, the intervention by students of colour placed me in a position of real doubt. In contrast to the hypothetical doubt of philosophical scepticism, real doubt does not refer to the existence of a reality apart from our thoughts but springs from experiences that do not yield to our analyses and actions in practice. Real doubt is specific and context dependent (Peirce, 1877 [1992]). It brings us up short in our engagement with the world. Acts of resistance that bring into question received epistemologies aim to provoke real doubt. Both doubt and belief prompt us to engage with a wider community in inquiring into how to bring about successful action. The conversation I seek with a broader community is motivated by several objectives: a growth of knowledge; a better grounding in embodied facts experienced differently by people of colour and white people, and along other fault lines; and actions for changing conditions of injustice that are political, cultural, institutional, intellectual and personal.

## Pragmatism revisited

Peirce (1868 [1992], 1869 [1992]) asserted that ignorance inheres in the limits of being an individual person and can be overcome only through engaging in an ever-expanding community of inquirers. Such a community gets closer to an encompassing way of perceiving, discussing and acting in reality that offers more forms of knowing and satisfactions in living. Dewey likewise encouraged individuals to bring their experiences into a collective practice of tolerant and inclusive democratic inquiry. He expanded pragmatism to a brief for a way of life that is open to the experiences of others, especially when those experiences differ from one's own (Dewey, 1929 [2008], 1939 [2008]). This line of thought committed American pragmatism to experimental, democratic and open-ended inquiry within an ever-expanding community of inquirers and actors as a means of finding serviceable truths. Such provisional, tentative truths prove good bets on how to bring about successful actions in a specific context, producing a more satisfactory set of conditions for the actors involved.

In 1939, with the outcome of World War II far from clear, Dewey, at the age of 80, published an essay on 'Creative democracy'. His tone reflected his sense that many people found him incredible and naïve and that his side may not then or ever win. Still, he insisted that:

> Democracy is a way of life controlled by a working faith in the possibility of human nature … That belief is without a basis or significance save as it means faith in the potentialities of human nature as that nature is exhibited in every human being irrespective of race, colour, sex, birth and family, of material or cultural wealth. This faith may be enacted in statutes, but it is only on paper unless it is put into force in the attitudes which humans display to one another in all the incidents of daily life … a belief that brings with it the need for providing conditions which will enable these capacities to reach fulfilment. (Dewey, 1939 [2008], 226)

Here is the rub. Legally, socially and economically, we seem to be moving ever further from this Deweyan attitude as a unifying scheme, away from tolerance on "display in incidents of daily life", and away from the conditions needed to assure the fulfilment of human potentialities regardless of race, sex and wealth. Democratic practices and institutions depend on subjects capable of tolerant and attentive engagement with others while, circularly, social practices and institutions must enable such subjects. Dewey explicitly implicated educational institutions in contributing to a democratic way of life (Dewey, 1916 [2008], 1929 [2008], 1939 [2008]) and education in the Deweyan tradition seeks to overcome embodied ignorances through democratic processes that require fundamental respect for the inherent value of others.

I have been forced to ask myself if attaining the Deweyan democratic ideal is possible given the obduracy of social inequality. Does the persistence of embodied structural inequalities allow the continuing pursuit of educational projects and social inquiry inspired by Dewey's faith in democracy and education without succumbing to a utopian blindness to structural injustices that do not appear to be going away? The problem of epistemological injustice that cannot be overcome is a challenge to the Deweyan perspective. Yet, as Ruth Anna Putnam wrote in questioning what pragmatism might mean today:

> To take your problems – where you stand as a representative of humanity – seriously, I must take it for granted that the toe I would step on, were I not to take care, is the toe in which you would feel pain …. So to take pragmatism seriously is to take oneself to be living in a world that one shares with others, others with whom one cooperates in inquiry, others with whom one may compete for scarce resources or

with whom one may cooperate in seeking to achieve common goals. (Putnam, 2017, 15–17)

Not all pragmatist views of embodied ignorance require convergent realities, however, and Medina (2013, 282–3) has explicated three different views on epistemic difference among pragmatists. Medina ascribes to the classical pragmatists such as Peirce and Mead the idea of a "converging pluralism" that values difference while preserving the goal of eventual resolution through a unified perspective. In William James, Medina finds a "melioristic pluralism" that understands epistemic difference to be inevitable but constrained for the purposes of cooperation and amelioration of a situation. Third, Medina attributes "guerrilla pluralism" to Foucault, in which pluralism provokes epistemic frictions through the mobilisation of counter memories that activate resistance and support "differently constituted and positioned subjectivities and their discursive practices" (Medina, 2013, 284). Both James and Foucault, in Medina's view, apply a genealogical perspective to how truths are made, with the difference that Jamesian genealogies work with differing epistemologies to see what they can still accomplish, while Foucauldian genealogies seek to articulate truths that are incompatible with existing discourses and dominant epistemologies. For Foucault, Medina argues, the plurality of "centers of experience and agency … function as centers of *resistance and contestability*" (Medina, 2013, 288, italics in the original). He concludes that we can engage intersections of historically situated oppressions without reducing them to each other. Guerrilla pluralism is useful for deconstruction; melioristic pluralism for reconstruction. Medina's categories lead us to ask: were the students of colour engaging in guerrilla pluralism or meliorative pluralism? How do their demands for a different kind of learning environment relate to the Deweyan tradition of increased mutual understanding and more supportive conditions for mutual growth?

Working in a long tradition of feminist inquiry, Medina recommends listening for silences. That, I think, has largely been the response to the students' intervention. Many courses, invited lectures and informal reading groups give space to voices of people of colour and other non-dominant groups. Faculty, students and alumni produce research and publications expanding the representations of diverse realities and advocating for excluded groups (cf. Fine, 2018; Lee, 2018; Payne and Bryant, 2018; Torre and Ayala, 2009; Saegert, 2018). But these efforts are not entirely new and the listening and inquiring needs to go deeper.

The affect expressed and aroused by students of colour suggests an emotional rawness that is held at a distance by the foregoing discourse on epistemological resistance and epistemological virtues. The students' indictment was a starker claim to embodied damage: as Ruth Anna Putnam (2017) insisted, the toes on their feet were the ones I stepped on because of my inherited privileges gained in the long history of harm done by white people to people of colour. Their intervention was not only an effort to make the audience aware of their experiences but also an effort to change power relations and the conditions of life perpetuated in and through our embodied differences. The students demanded recognition and acknowledgement but also the actual redress of hurts and inequalities they have inherited and continue to live. Ignorance of these pains among white faculty was thus not only an instance of epistemological injustice. As Mills pointed out, the oppressors' ignorance of the cause of pain is a more fundamental injustice meant to assure that the oppressed continue to be subject to real material loss and pain. The students' intervention aimed not only to have their stories and voices heard but also to make sure that the toes they stepped on hurt. It seems doubtful that practising epistemic virtue alone would be a sufficient response and, beyond the goal of changing the balance of power, the students wanted the actual conditions of their education to change through concrete practices such as hiring initiatives and redistribution of resources. Those demands would be very hard to realise, however, given the austerity practices and institutional reorganisations taking place within the university and the legal turn against affirmative action emerging at the national level.

## Moving epistemic and other frictions outside the academy

The pragmatist tradition of seeing educational institutions as a critical arena for developing democratic ways of life continues. Shusterman (1994) argued that even if there has been little space in the world of neoliberal educational institutions for the kind of deep democratic institutions Dewey envisioned, some good comes of working as academics to try to more fully achieve Dewey's vision of inclusive tolerant education as necessary for making democratic ways of lives and citizens, and for personal growth. But this line of argument has been severely challenged by African American scholars (cf. Baldwin, 1963 [2008]; Coates, 2015; DuBois, 1897, 1903 [1994]). The common thread among African American authors is that education is essential and freeing but the way African Americans are educated in the USA obscures their true histories and represents an effort at brain washing them into shame and subservience. This suggests the need to extend these efforts beyond the establishment of departments and curricula to include fighting the kind of battles the students of colour asked for about hiring, about admissions, about funding. Boxhill (2018) raised the significance of active efforts to change historically accrued injustices even when, as he believes, racism will outlast our lives. By doing so, we will learn to understand racism better and improve strategies and tactics for change.

Moving into the community and the *polis* beyond the university provides greater exposure to the workings of the structural constraints on equality and challenges the epistemological ignorances fostered by the lack of epistemological and embodied pluralism within the academy. Inquiry rooted in places and people and informed by a perspective of intersectionality offers resources (and constraints) for confronting threats to the body, to livelihood and to rights.

Intelligent inquiry in service of advancing those goals provides an arena of practice, experience and multiple, if transient, solidarities that may be able to change unjust conditions. This may not fully succeed but it sharpens the wits and tactics of those struggling for greater justice; it allows inquiry into what possible justice might be; it provides room for individual growth and satisfaction in associated life; and it improves the public record by putting the knowledge process in closer touch with the parts of life and places erased by exclusion and the meta-blindness (Medina, 2013) attendant on privilege. For the larger community of social inquiry to use their disciplinary strengths and discover the limitations of these strengths, and to grow in our collective and personal selves, we must enter spaces outside of books, classrooms and academic offices. But harms can also come to oppressed communities by contact with the more privileged (Lipsitz, 2011; Sullivan, 2014). Finding common cause is a delicate business that requires a great deal of caution.

For oppressed communities, entering off-limits spaces requires effective means of challenging exclusion and discrimination. Active engagement can be a corrective to meta-blindness by bringing differently privileged and discriminated-against groups into interaction (Medina, 2013, 7, 222). For those suffering discrimination, a kind of epistemological enlightenment and personal/collective transformation can occur when resources are pooled and experiences and imaginations are shared, compared and contrasted in both practical and epistemological modes with the goal of perfecting both our practices and *"our sensibilities"* (Medina, 2013, 7, italics in the original). By engaging with others suffering similar injustices, the conditions are formed for what Medina (2013) calls *"chained action"*. First, *"epistemic heroes"* arise from brave actions in circumstances that bring them into the consciousness of others and make their actions *"echoable"*, giving rise to *"collective action"* (Medina, 2013, 225, all italics in the original). Focusing on representation, Medina (2013) then brings us back to Deweyan democracy: "At the level of language and communication, a social network becomes an organized social group or movement – a *public* as Dewey would say – when and because its members engage in communication with one another and make their problems, interests, and goals explicit, developing their own discursive resources and distinctive ways of talking about themselves and their experiences" (2013, 226, italics in the original).

But focusing on representation and communication alone does not account for the deep overlays of selective attention and habit that continue to reinforce discriminatory epistemologies and conditions. To have an effect, epistemological friction must be felt by the privileged through conflictual or at least unexpected and challenging encounters with actual others (Alcoff, 2006; Sullivan, 2006). While such encounters can result in the attainment of a sort of double consciousness among the privileged (Alcoff, 2006), it can also do harm. For example, well-meaning white people may engage black people in ways they think will improve equality but actually make conditions worse for black people while making some white people feel better (Sullivan, 2014). As with the plight of affirmative action, when discriminated-against groups engage in sustained interaction fraught with "*lived disruptions*" (Sullivan, 2006) and epistemic friction, privileged groups may use their power to try to constrain or eliminate the conditions of these friction-filled disruptions.

## Multiple pragmatisms

Moving the arena for contesting epistemic justice beyond the academy broadens available hermeneutic resources and connects political struggles for equality to the production of new ways of knowing, new solidarities and new conditions of life. This move opens the way for more creative and democratic communities of inquirers but one in which the encounter among divergent life situations and ways of knowing poses new or greater challenges. African American scholars have drawn on the heritage of American pragmatism by rooting the history of black people in the USA in the same conditions and aspirations that constituted the milieu that produced Peirce, James, Dewey and, later, Rorty (Holden, this volume; Molesworth, 2012; Pascal, 1971; West, 1989, 1999, 2001). These scholars were drawn to the work of James and Dewey especially because of their non-unitary conception of truth as something that happens to an idea and because of their democratic aspirations. They also constantly critiqued the glaring obstacles to pragmatic ideals posed by race relations in the USA. In doing so, they broadened the hermeneutic resources of pragmatism. Analysing the plight of the "American Negro", they developed economic critiques of capitalism. DuBois, for example, championed a form of cooperative economics within a socialist framework and used Marxism to complicate his analysis of racism (Nembhard, 2014; West, 1999, 2001).

These black male writers, however, did not usually complicate their analysis with other embodied inequalities such as gender, but more recent authors have embraced intersectionality as a necessary concern of pragmatic inquiry into inequality (Collins, 2011, 2012; Medina, 2013). Pragmatism prefigures an intersectional analysis in its concept of identities as mutable, relational and multiple (Sullivan, 2001). As a black feminist scholar, Collins (2011) has argued that the writings and political work of nineteenth-century African American women who were intellectuals, writers and political activists should also be considered part of the pragmatist tradition. From their location as women among black male activists and theorists and as black people among white women and men, they inserted a gender analysis into debates about race and class in social and political thought. They sought new practices and epistemologies that made multiple the understandings of identities. These black women activists were concerned with using intelligence to address real and obdurate problems through collective inquiry and action in order to change the oppressive and discriminatory conditions of life reinforcing the embodied ignorances addressed above.

By joining an intersectional analysis with American pragmatism around the concepts of experience, complex social inequalities and social action, multiple embodied ignorances can be better understood. American pragmatism is a useful resource because of its ideas about the complex, multiply emergent and relational social self and the political potential of social groups (Collins, 2011; Fuller, this volume). Dewey especially brought the structural issue of class under pragmatic scrutiny (Dewey, 1932 [2008]; 1936 [2008]). However, the classical pragmatists' inattention to race and, often, gender, means that the pragmatist tradition is in need of some enriching from the works of scholars of colour and in light of intersectionality. When academic discourses of pragmatism regain a social movement focus on race, class, gender and sexuality, they bring the confluence of multiple embodied ignorances and conditions of disadvantage and privilege into the world of collective action. The scholarship and actions of nineteenth-century black women in a slave-owning nation in which women were denied full legal status exemplify the epistemic and practical resources such ignored voices can bring to the discussion. One's position in the fray matters to experience, both discursively and conditionally. Dewey paid this kind of attention to class and Collins suggests we pay the same kind of attention to race and gender.[1]

Once we recognise the multiple and divergent positions of privilege and domination and the ways that the world looks different from these differently situated positions, the ideal of democratic consensus can give way to the goal of limited and provisional improvement. "Situated freedoms" (Collins, 2011, 107) can be achieved by changing conditions in ways that may be understood differently by differently situated actors. The pragmatist understanding of social action and social order would thus more fully encompass understandings of the power dynamics that structure groups, communities, polities and society. Black women's visionary pragmatism augments the pragmatic method of open-ended, action-oriented social inquiry by invoking principled commitments to particular social outcomes. It embraces and works with the "creative tension between the desirable, the possible, the probable and the practical" (Collins, 2011, 108). Like Sullivan (2014), Collins (2011, 2012) invites an open-ended critical scrutiny of ideas, actions and their consequences. Rather than focus on the cultivation of critique and self-examination, Collins turns to a reinvigoration of the concept of community as socially expansive and collective action as multi-faceted and arising from different visions.

A less unitary, more mobile and multiple concept of community derived from fusing the insights from pragmatism and intersectionality might develop a construct of community that "provides a template for describing the actual power relations as people live them and conceptualize them", thus anchoring the "universal of community as a construct that is always understood through an emerging set of particulars that attend to intersecting power relations" (Collins, 2012, 445–6). Community arouses conflicting emotions and meanings that can be experienced and worked with in the practical living of community life and in discourses expressing commitments and motivating action.

Pragmatists link participatory democratic processes with the emergence of community and the construction of relational selves (Dewey, 1939 [2008]). Community supplies a transactional idea and the social and geographic space that mobilises multiple social identities, relations and contradictions (Collins, 2010, 2011, 2012). Within community understood as a field of intersecting structural vectors of power, differently situated groups and individuals can seek possible situated freedoms. The emotionality, symbolic resonance and power-saturated dynamics performed within the continually emerging conceptual and lived field of community can be mobilised around both egalitarianism and difference. They can open space and language for creative action. "In this sense, participating in building a community is simultaneously political, for negotiating power differences within a group, dynamic for negotiating individual and collective goals, and aspirational" (Collins, 2012, 448).

Between Dewey's Great Community (1927 [1954]) but going beyond Shusterman's (1994) limited aspirations for a university community lies Collins's realistic version of a diverse community that includes power differentials and inequality but that can be mobilised for more just and democratic purposes. Perhaps social inquiry rooted in both the quest for and questioning of claims to social justice can begin to fill the spaces excluded from but lying within the polity. Our communities of inquiry and our personal selves will have to change in this process.

## Making academic and political communities

Situating ourselves as scholars, citizens and individuals within diverse communities both inside and outside the academy makes us work with multiple oppressions, privileges and ignorances. Since we are invested as scholars in the validity of our knowledge, our personal and community identities are challenged when we recognise our ignorances. We then imperfectly and divergently strive for epistemological justice as a community of inquirers in search of moral and intellectual growth and as we work in our fractured and fractious collective actions towards conditions that support greater and more diverse situated freedoms. Working as scholars and activists, we need to understand, heal and support others in acknowledging the deep resistances and hurt occasioned by the oppressions we live with and in which we participate. The methods of our research include the particular ways we live with these struggles (Fine, 2018).

At a recent doctoral dissertation defence in my university, the author, a Korean-American, reported the findings of empirical research conducted on and with immigrant delivery cyclists caught in a multitude of oppressions in New York City (Lee, 2018). Summarising the most valuable lessons he had learned in the course of research, he observed that (1) doing this work is painful and changes you more than you can foresee; and (2) both the changing and the work itself can only be done in a community. Among those attending the dissertation defence were the students of colour who had staged the intervention described at the outset of this chapter, as well as many of the faculty and white students who had been in the audience at that event. Also attending the defence were delivery cyclists and Asian American political activists who worked with the cyclists and the researcher to improve working conditions in the city. The applause and emotional response to his presentation felt like our different but shared appreciations of his struggles and successes were in some way also our own.

## Note

1    Early pragmatists were rather silent on the topic. For example, the index to the Complete Works of John Dewey reveals eleven entries regarding race. Only one three-page letter actually discusses in any detail wrongs done to people of colour in the US. The majority concern discussions of race in Germany and Japan, criticising racial claims in those countries and worrying that claims of race discrimination in the US. undermine support for democracy. There are a few passing references to unfair treatment of Negroes, Jews and Catholics as an impediment to democracy in the US. Dewey wrote one letter to the editor pleading with the Supreme Court to hear a challenge to the death penalty on behalf of a black sharecropper who killed his white farmer employer. The letter repeatedly states that failing to do so alienates poor people, and especially poor whites, from democratic processes in the US. Failing that, he suggested commuting the death sentence in recognition that both the white farmer and the black sharecropper were disadvantaged in the US. economic system. In contrast, the Complete Works contain 24 entries related to social class, including essays on class warfare and class consciousness and development of a consistent anti-capitalist position (for example, Dewey 1929/2008 b). Mentions of women are in the middle in frequency, at nineteen, and are less well developed theoretically.

## References

Alcoff, L.M. (2006) *Race, gender and the self.* Oxford: Oxford University Press.

Alcoff, L.M. (2007) Epistemologies of ignorance: Three types, in S. Sullivan and N. Tuana, eds, *Race and epistemologies of ignorance.* Albany, NY: State University of New York Press, 39–57.

Baldwin, J. (1963 [2008]) A talk to teachers. http://p9003-sfx.cuny.edu.ezproxy.gc.cuny. edu/sfx_local?sid=google&auinit=J&aulast=Baldwin&atitle=A+talk+to+teachers& id=doi:10.1111/j.1744-7984.2008.00154.x&title=The+forty-first+yearbook+of+ the+National+Society+for+the+Study+of+Education:+Part+II,+The+psychology+of+ learning&volume=107&issue=2&date=2008&spage=15 (accessed 12 March 2018).

Boxhill, B. (2018) Race and equality. Paper presented at Race Inequity conference, the Graduate Center of the City University of New York, New York, NY, 9 March.

Coates, T-N. (2015) *Between the world and me.* New York, NY: Spiegel and Grau.

Collins, P.H. (2010) The new politics of community. *American Sociological Review,* 75, 1, 1–70.

Collins, P.H. (2011) Piecing together a genealogical puzzle: Intersectionality and American pragmatism. *European Journal of Pragmatism and American Philosophy,* 3, 2, 88–112.

Collins, P.H. (2012) Social inequality, power and politics: Intersectionality and American pragmatism in dialogue. *Journal of Speculative Philosophy,* 26, 12, 441–57.

Dewey, J. (1916 [2008]) *Democracy and education: An introduction to the philosophy of education.* New York, NY: Macmillan Company. www.gutenberg.org/files/852/852-h/852-h.htm (accessed 16 March 2018).

Dewey, J. (1927 [1954]) *The public and its problems.* Chicago, IL: Swallow Press.

Dewey, J. (1929 [2008]) The quest for certainty: A study of the relationship of knowledge and action, in J.A. Boydston, ed., *The later works 1925–1953, volume 4: 1929.* Carbondale, IL: Southern Illinois University Press, 3–250.

Dewey, J. (1932 [2008]) Ethics: Part III: The world of action, in J.A. Boydston, ed., *The later works 1925–1953, volume 7: 1932.* Carbondale, IL: Southern Illinois University Press. 311–462.

Dewey, J. (1936 [2008]) Liberalism and social action and social frontier: Class struggle and the democratic way, in J.A. Boydston, ed., *The later works 1925–1953, volume 9: 1933–1934.* Carbondale, IL: Southern Illinois University Press, 1–69; 382–6.

Dewey, J. (1939 [2008]) Creative democracy: The task before us, in J.A. Boydston, ed., *The later works 1925–1953, volume 14: 1939–1941.* Carbondale, IL: Southern Illinois University Press, 224–30.

Dieleman, S. (2015) Epistemic justice and democratic legitimacy. *Hypatia,* 10, 4, 794–310.

DuBois, W.E.B. (1897) The strivings of the Negro people. *The Atlantic,* August. www.theatlantic.com/magazine/archive/1897/08/strivings-of-the-negro-people/305446/ (accessed 1 February 2020).

DuBois, W.E.B. (1903 [1994]) *The souls of black folks.* Mineola, NY: Dover Publications, Inc.

Fine, M. (2018) *Just research: Widening the methodological imagination in contentious times.* New York, NY: Teachers College.

Fricker, M. (2007) *Epistemic injustice: Power and the ethics of knowing.* Oxford: Oxford University Press.

Haag, M. (2018) The Equal Rights Amendment was just ratified by Illinois: What does that mean? www.nytimes.com/2018/05/31/us/equal-rights-amendment-illinois.html (accessed 24 July 2018).

James, W. (1907 [2004]) Pragmatism: A new name for some old ways of thinking. The Gutenberg Project e-book 5116. www.gutenberg.org/files/5116/5116-h/5116-h.htm (accessed 26 November 2018).

Kelley, R. (2016) Black study, Black struggle. *Boston Review,* 7 March. http://bostonreview.net/forum/robin-d-g-kelley-black-study-black-struggle (accessed 11 March 2018).

Lee, D.J. (2018) *Delivering justice: Food cyclists in New York City.* A dissertation granted in partial fulfilment of PhD, The Graduate Center of the City University of New York.

Lipsitz, G. (2011) *How racism takes place.* Philadelphia, PA: Temple University Press.

Litak, A. (2014) Court backs Michigan on Affirmative Action. www.nytimes.com/2014/04/23/us/supreme-court-michigan-affirmative-action-ban.html (accessed 24 July 2018).

Medina, J. (2013) *The epistemology of resistance: Gender and racial oppression, epistemic injustice, and the resistant imaginations.* New York, NY: Oxford University Press.

Merton, R.K. (1972) Insiders and outsiders: A chapter in the sociology of knowledge. *American Journal of Sociology,* 78, 1, 9–47.

Mills, C.W. (1997) *The racial contract.* Ithaca, NY: Cornell University Press.

Mills, C.W. (1998) *Blackness visible: Essays on philosophy and race.* Ithaca, NY: Cornell University Press.

Molesworth, C. (ed.) (2012) *The works of Alain Locke.* Oxford University Press.

Nembhard, J.G. (2014) *Collective courage: A history of African American cooperative economic thought and practice.* University Park, PA: Penn State Press.

Parker, K. (2018) Women in majority-male workplaces report higher rates of discrimination. Pew Research Center Reports, 8 March. www.pewresearch.org/fact-tank/2018/03/07/women-in-majority-male-workplaces-report-higher-rates-of-gender-discrimination/ (accessed 11 March 2018).

Pascal, A. (ed.) (1971) *W.E.B. DuBois: A reader.* New York, NY: Macmillan Publishing Company.

Pateman, C. (1988) *The sexual contract*. Palo Alto, CA: Stanford University Press.

Payne, Y.A. and Bryant, A. (2018) Street participatory action research in prison: A methodology to challenge privilege and power in correctional facilities. *The Prison Journal*, 98, 4, 449–69.

Peirce, C.S. (1867–1913 [1992]) *The essential Peirce*. Volumes I and II, N. Houser and C. Kloesel, eds. Bloomington, IN: Indiana University Press.

Putnam, R.A. with a reply by H. Putnam (2017) Taking pragmatism seriously, in H. Putnam and R.A. Putnam, edited by D. Macarthur, *Pragmatism as a way of life*. Cambridge, MA: Belknap Press of Harvard University Press, 13–20.

Rankin, C. (2014) *Citizen, an American lyric*. Minneapolis, MN: Graywolf Press.

Saegert, S. (2018) Invited focus articles comment: Opening up housing theory: Who speaks, who listens, and to what end? *Housing Theory and Society*, 35, 2, 238–41.

Shusterman, R. (1994) Pragmatism and liberalism between Dewey and Rorty. *Political Theory*, 22, 391–413.

State Constitution of Michigan, Section 26 (2006) www.legislature.mi.gov/(S(uvf-cvgrfj5qgbrrisrtq3b34))/mileg.aspx?page=GetObject&objectname=mcl-Article-I-26 (accessed 24 July 2018).

Sullivan, S. (2001) *Living across and through skins: Transactional bodies, pragmatism, and feminism*. Bloomington, IN: Indiana University Press.

Sullivan, S. (2006) *Revealing whiteness*. Bloomington, IN: Indiana University Press.

Sullivan, S. (2014) *Good white people: The problem with middle-class white anti-racism*. Albany, NY: State University of New York Press.

Torre, M.E. and Ayala, J. (2009) Envisioning participatory action research. *Entremundos. Feminism and Psychology*, 19, 3, 387–93.

West, C. (1989) *The American evasion of philosophy: A genealogy of pragmatism*. Madison, WI: University of Wisconsin Press.

West, C. (1999) *The Cornel West reader*. New York, NY: Basic Books.

West, C. (2001) *Race matters*. New York, NY: Vintage Books.

Westbrook, R.B. (1991) *John Dewey and American democracy*. Ithaca, NY: Cornell University Press.

# 7

# Truth and academia in times of fake news, alternative facts and filter bubbles: A pragmatist notion of critique as mediation

*Klaus Geiselhart*

## Introduction

The talk-show host Stephen Colbert satirically introduced the term 'truthiness' in 2005, referring to his observation of political rhetoric whereby the belief in what you feel to be true is privileged over what the facts support. 'Post-truth' became the Oxford Dictionary's word of the year in 2016, defined as "relating to or denoting circumstances in which objective facts are less influential in shaping public opinion than appeals to emotion and personal belief" (Oxford Dictionaries, 2016). Both terms were discussed in connection with the rise of right-wing populists such as Marine Le Pen in France and Geert Wilders in the Netherlands, and they continued to gain popularity during the 2016 presidential elections in the USA. That election was distinguished by the use of dubious information and questioning of established truths, and Donald Trump has become *the* populist par excellence (Oliver and Rahn, 2016).

It is widely believed that these rightist populists and their respective parties deliberately use misleading or insufficient information in order to influence public opinion. Populists seed mistrust in the expertise of media organisations (Oliver and Rahn, 2016) by terming media reports 'fake news', which has its German equivalent in the term 'Lügenpresse'. Such designations are intended to provide space for the populist interpretation of reality. When Trump's spokesperson Kellyanne Conway was accused of spreading misinformation, she explained that she had merely given 'alternative facts' in the case. Despite the fact that most false information can easily be refuted, such assertions nonetheless enter public discourse and thus have effects. Furthermore, the extensive use of internet search engines and social network services produces 'filter bubbles' in which users get pre-selected information with which they already agree. Algorithmic pre-selection and social bots are seen as endangering independent opinion, making and producing 'echo chambers' where people are surrounded by likeminded others. Members of such enclosed communities mutually amplify the radicality of their opinions. Furthermore, the internet forums of minority groups are often targeted by individuals who post derogatory or threatening comments. By starting quarrels, such 'trolls' destroy the quality of discussion in social media platforms (Herring et al., 2002).

Fake news, alternative facts and filter bubbles are thus the means and the effects of rightist populists endangering basic democratic values (Cooke, 2017; Schweiger, 2017). As populists profit from social disunion they impede the public, discursive and rational negotiation of political issues. Populist political styles create emotional effects to win votes. Interestingly, the new right seem to have internalised the antagonistic spirit that poststructuralist theory considers crucial for democracy (Mouffe, 2005). They also make use of corresponding patterns of critique by staging themselves as counterhegemonic fighters opposing the establishment elite holding positions of power in society.

Against these developments, pragmatism can play two of its strengths. First, according to pragmatic epistemology, truths cannot be denied their validity simply by referring to the contingency of all truths. Despite its consistent truth relativism, pragmatism offers guidelines by means of which it is possible to make a reasonable distinction between well-founded and less well-founded ideas and theories. Pragmatist social science can provide important advice for collective, democratic decision-making based on its ability to assist in discerning and assessing the consequences of actions as well as reflecting the validity and relevance of scientific statements.

Second, convictions and political positions must be seen as constantly in the making. Since political actors often trigger each other in ways that harden and polarise opinions, good mediation can help to establish mutual understanding and respectful interaction. Mediation is not only about intervening between conflicting parties but also explicates the implications of each party's position to opposing parties and the wider public and can improve the formation of public opinion. Mediation is not aimed at achieving consensus but rather attempts to open up a way forward by improving the chance that viable proposals are developed. For social science to participate in this process requires an understanding of critique as mediation.

In the discussion that follows, I summarise current academic approaches to criticism and their misuse and I explain how critique has become a project of opposition while gradually losing its mediating character. The chapter highlights the role of poststructuralist thinking in this regard, arguing that it has had pernicious effects on the role of academics in public life. A look at the poststructuralist restriction of democracy to the principle of agonism reveals the shortcomings of this perspective and helps to identify how pragmatism can contribute to a more positive approach to problem-solving. Then, a discussion of pragmatist notions of learning, opinion-formation and democracy shows how pragmatism's combination of epistemology and praxis-orientation supports the reformulation of critique through mediation. Finally, the chapter outlines how such critique can make a valuable contribution in addressing current social conditions.

## The trustworthiness of truths and academic critique

Natural scientists and their supporters in the USA reacted to the Trump administration's bending of truths with a march for science on 22 April 2017 (March for Science, 2017). Their effort to rehabilitate truth used the distinction between bullshit and lies (Marmot, 2017), or mis- and dis-information (Cooke, 2017) as criteria to evaluate statements and assertions. Bullshit or misinformation is considered to be unsound, misleading or otherwise unintentionally corrupted belief, while lies or disinformation designate deliberately produced false truths. Such debate about the trustworthiness of information aims at rehabilitating 'truth' as a criterion for asserting the validity or reliability of scientific findings (Horton, 2017; Marmot, 2017). With a grounding in the possibility of 'real' or pre-existing truth, natural scientists are particularly perturbed when scientific findings are deliberately undermined by falsehoods. A terrifying example is the so-called 'tobacco strategy' through which a particular group of scientists deliberately destroyed the reputation of scientific findings in subject areas as varied as tobacco smoking, acid rain, DDT, global warming and the hole in the ozone layer. This strategy was never substantive in terms of providing new evidence or contradictory findings but was always purely defamatory and served the economic and political interests of particular groups (Oreskes and Conway, 2010).

While scientists fear that truth may lose its prestige, social scientists and humanities scholars are increasingly alarmed that their emphasis on the contingency of truth is now being used by groups lobbying for specific interests (Horton, 2017) and by right-wing populists to advance their political agendas. Latour (2004, 227, 230) reports being worried about the wider implications of his research as he always highlighted "'the lack of scientific certainty' inherent in the construction of facts". He is concerned about the way his ideas have been used "like weapons smuggled through a fuzzy border to the wrong party".

In the course of the cultural turn, authors sought to deconstruct established categories of thought, such as gender, race or ethnicity, and showed how the use of language is permeated by relations of power (e.g. Butler, 1999; Said, 1978). Accordingly, a belief in the relativity of truth is common among left intellectuals and is deployed in the fight against hegemonic social conditions. Such an understanding has long been a basis for the self-definition of poststructuralist academics and much critique in the social sciences is associated with the pursuit of social justice and the empowerment of minorities. It can now be observed that the new right is increasingly using similar means to assert their claims. Right populists addressing the 'man on the street' have done exactly what Laclau (2005) describes as an essential feature of populism, which is to selectively challenge established norms while claiming to advocate for the underdog.

In this spirit, right-wing female politicians such as Marine Le Pen, her niece Marion Maréchal Le Pen, and the Belgian senator Anke Van Dermeersch represent a modernised image of conservative women which "is open to women's economic independence and their rights to a professional career" (Mayer, 2015, 399). They focus on family policy and the right of women to self-determination. They target immigration or Islam in the name of democratic values and women's rights as prototypically reflected in Dermeersch's campaign 'Freedom or Islam?' (Vrijheid of Islam?) in which she showed a picture of herself wearing a mini skirt. On her naked legs, she had marked the reactions and consequences that women in Islamic countries would have to face if they wore skirts of this length (Delfin, 2016). Questions of women's rights and the security of women against assault are used as arguments to justify anti-multiculturalism. Beyond that, the right-wing women Lana Lokteff, a supporter of the American alt-rights, and Alina von Rauheneck, a German supporter of the identitarian movement, present themselves as part of a misunderstood counterculture that upholds traditional values such as family in the name of the nation. They consider feminism as a hegemonic attempt to forbid them to live their lives according to their natural femininity. They claim to represent a new kind of patriotic feminism in which the classical gender arguments of self-determination and oppression are reinterpreted in nationalist terms (Darby, 2017; Miller, 2017).

This attitude is strangely reflective of the poststructuralist position of counter-hegemonic criticism. Admittedly, the term poststructuralism is difficult to use here, since its use is usually an ascription and less often a self-portrayal. Definitions vary. Finkelde (2013) sees the roots of poststructuralism in structural linguistics and anthropology, while Harrison (2006) defines poststructuralism in distinction to analytical philosophy. In contrast to logical positivism, whereby statements need to be empirically verifiable in order to be scientific, poststructuralism emphasises contexts, conditions of possibility, historicity and the textuality of truth. In this respect, poststructuralism focuses on the production of meaning and the 'social construction' of reality and it looks at "how social relations of power fix the meaning and significance of social practices, objects, and events" (Woodward et al., 2009, 396).

Foucault's (1993) concept of discourse, which describes the historical contextuality of truths, is particularly influential in the development of poststructuralist thought. In this perspective, discourse is understood not only as argumentation or social debate but as reflecting the dominant order of society, shaping behaviour and defining what is expected and accepted by society. The concept has found its way into critical gender and post-colonial studies where, for example, Butler (1999) and Said (1978) describe how dualistic social categories (men–women, Orient–West) are mutually dependent, with one usually dominating the other. Since such categories are embodied in everyday routines and attitudes, one can only counteract them by breaking the established practices of their everyday reproduction. Foucault (2007) conceptualises critique as a means of clarifying the powers that preceding politics of truth have inscribed into discourse. Accordingly, counter-hegemonic thinking seems to be the only way to be political. In similar ways, other academic critique opposes ideologies, formal policies, inequalities, injustice, power-permeated societal conditions and the naturalisation of certain discourses or practices.

Critique as opposition sees humanity as being unrealised in actual praxis. In this vein, opposition is best when it reveals abuses and injustices in confrontational language. Horkheimer (1937 [1975], 2016) once argued for the critical academic to employ "an aggressive critique not only against the conscious defenders of the status quo but also against distracting, conformist, or Utopian tendencies within his own household". In poststructural readings this opposing approach was even elevated to a central characteristic of all democratic politics. According to Mouffe (2005), political positioning functions only by means of distinctions, at best agonistic, at worst antagonistic. She sees consensus-oriented politics as an illusion, which in the end can only ever reproduce established inequities. Such an account of democracy is based on an overemphasised difference-theoretical paradigm and concludes that "the end of populism coincides with the end of politics" (Laclau, 2005, 48). In their conception of radical democracy, Laclau and Mouffe (2001) propose establishing a leftist hegemony capable of taming the infinite production of difference and dissent in order to restrict oppressive power relations and right-wing populist strategies. However, the emancipatory impetus of critique is no longer exclusively a left-wing undertaking. Right-wing populist strategies aim at countering what they claim to be a current leftist hegemony, echoing the common pattern of academic critics on the left who have opposed power relations underlying social conditions (Butler, 2002; Foucault, 2007; Horkheimer, 1937 [1975]).

Furthermore, right-wing and left-wing thinking converge in the fact that they both criticise liberalism and egalitarianism. The right criticises multiculturalism as a promotion of individual freedom at the expense of nationalistic solidarity and community. The left, on the other hand, criticises liberalism as propelling the untamed dynamics of capitalism (Nassehi, 2015). The right wing argues against abstract equality that favours minorities who do not represent the majority of the population. Leftists claim to protect minorities and argue that *de jure* equality does not make disparities disappear. In Europe, Euroscepticism is also common among left- and right-wing positions (Elsas et al., 2016). While the left is dissatisfied with the functioning of the EU, the right firmly opposes further European integration.

In this confluence of critical accounts, it is not clear whether poststructuralists are analysts or unintentionally agents of the new right-wing populism; it seems that academic strategies of critique have turned against their inventors.

## How pragmatism can contribute to reformulating critique

On any number of issues, current politics gives reason to rethink the role of academic critique as being preoccupied with outright opposition to established ways of thinking. In the last chapter of *Experience and nature,* Dewey (1929, 394–437) outlines the societal role of philosophy and introduces a mediating attitude into the notion of critique. In political discourse, people do not always succeed in making themselves understood and people are often not aware of how deep their convictions are rooted in their own experience. As Dewey (1929, 410) put it: "Philosophy as a critical organ becomes in effect a messenger, a liaison officer, making reciprocally intelligible voices speaking provincial tongues, and thereby enlarging as well as rectifying the meanings with which they are charged". Even if today 'critique' is normally understood differently, Dewey's formulation aligns with a longstanding tradition. The term 'critique' derives from the Greek expression for the *art of judgement.* Aristotle, for example, associated it with judicial decisions that create order in disputes (Röttgers, 1975). With Kant, too, 'critique' comprised clarifying scientific issues by investigating the quarrelling parties' respective use of reason. Critique understood as opposition, in contrast, is arguably a rather new, abbreviated development in the concept of critique.

To summarise the current situation, if a populist attitude misuses oppositional critique to undermine the reliability of truth and thereby consciously creates disorientation, pragmatism can contribute to addressing this dilemma in two ways. The first concerns an epistemological question about the role of social research in society and the second concerns democratic theory, highlighting that democracy is more than agonistic struggle and calling on academics to adopt a mediating attitude. Regarding the role of social research, pragmatism, in agreement with poststructuralism, deploys an understanding of truth in relation to context. But moving beyond critique as opposition, pragmatism also establishes the value of social science in determining productive insights that are worth believing (Dewey, 1938). Scientific findings, even if they are contingent, are by no means arbitrary and social science has a double task: to make visible the contingency of perceptions and constructions of reality while simultaneously taking account of the actual processes involved on the basis of well-established experimental methods (Morgan, 2014). The separation of these perspectives is, according to Dewey (1938), a product of the modern dichotomy between *subject* and *object,* a dualism that he sought to transcend. Positivism, on this account, seeks to determine the *objective* dimension of empirical phenomena. Some immediate aspects preceding our human reflection cannot be ignored in all awareness of the constructivism of human perception. Positivism is an attempt to define the limits of human influence. Constructivism, in contrast, tries to make us aware of what is *subjective* in our beliefs – that is, to identify those parts of our truths that derive from social imprints. These parts, for constructivists, represent path dependencies of our collective past which restrict us to certain conventions and thus contribute to the constriction of our creative potential. Both perspectives, according to Dewey, are equally useful in providing helpful insights into social realities in which phenomena should be understood as constructed and real at the same time. Accordingly, academics should remain close to observable praxis when developing theories and should focus attention on the particular circumstances of the respective praxis or practices they address rather than exercising criticism across the board.

The keyword 'praxis' leads directly to the consequences of pragmatist thinking for democratic theory. Pragmatism argues that there will always be different ways of seeing things in problematic situations. There is a key role for deliberation across difference in democratic life and Dewey returned to this time and again. However, it is commonly neglected that "deliberation in this strand of democratic theory is not necessarily understood as a medium of rational consensus formation" (Barnett and Bridge, 2013, 1024). Pragmatism does not assume that there will be unanimous consensus at the end of the negotiations, nor that negotiations will mainly be rational, a point overemphasised by the discourse ethics of the later Frankfurt School. Politics is emotional, for better or for worse. Emotions can create democratic majorities but they can also divide societies. It may be true that institutionalised orders can only be challenged antagonistically and that a certain amount of populism is indispensable for this to occur. However, Laclau (2005) himself states that populist rhetoric becomes inoperative in the daily business of governmental praxis. Populism's fixation on over-emotionalised categories, its binary logic of otherness and its confrontational impetus generate antagonism and resentment rather than a willingness to cooperate and find compromises. Politics cannot be built on an agonistic momentum alone: it also needs a mediating momentum that makes decisions possible and generates confidence that these decisions will be respected by all parties.

Pragmatism allows us to "move beyond the stylized contrast of poststructuralist agonism and liberal consensualism" (Barnett and Bridge, 2013, 1022). According to the concept of *transaction* (Dewey and Bentley, 1949), political actors constitute each other in their subjectivity, in contrast to *interaction* that assumes pre-existing fixed entities. Democratic space is characterised not only by different political opinions referring to each other but also by the fact that politicians as *whole persons* influence each other inter-humanly. They develop emotionally charged relationships (Saunders, 2005) and, ultimately, they have to coexist in their self-created space of mutual co-constitution. Politics takes place in a transactional space in which the actors have co-produced their respective subjectivities in differentiation from one another. Moreover, these actors act in a site and situation that they co-inhabit and are thus responsible for a solution with which everyone can live.

It can become critical in this context that "if one is seen to give up a belief, 'face' and credibility may be lost" (Dryzek, 2004, 73) and this concerns not only the relations between politicians but also the relations of political representatives to their electorate. Politicians generally see their public image as part of their personal identity and are therefore not only professional representatives but also must be recognised as being personally affected. Governance can therefore be understood as an emotionally charged nexus of communication and action in which experts, interest groups and lay people contribute to problem-solving. Pragmatism puts trust in the dynamics of such multi-perspectivity and sees a decentred deliberative democracy as a resource for problem-solving (Bohman, 2004). Regarding politics "as an ecology of communicative spaces (both agonistic and accommodative) might enable us to rethink and redo the democratic process" (Bridge, 2008, 1581).

In Dewey's (1927) transactional account of the political, the state is not conceived as a fixed entity determined by a constitutional setting. Democracy as a political system does not derive from formal institutions but unintentionally from the manifold processes of establishing and adjusting regulations. The ongoing adjustments of political structures are ideally the result of negotiations flanked by public discussions and debates. Public debates emerge because "human acts have consequences upon others, that some of these consequences are perceived, and that their perception leads to subsequent effort to control action so as to secure some consequences and avoid others" (Dewey, 1927, 12). Publics form as a result of people's shared interest in a controversial topic. The ways in which discussions and opinion-formation in such public spheres take place, whether these publics are inclusive or exclusive, for instance with regard to underprivileged actors, and whether ideas developed in these publics are allowed to gain influence in political decision-making processes, ultimately characterise a democratic culture.

Democracy, according to Dewey, cannot be formally established but is an ongoing process. Democracy is less a system of government than an ideal that can never be fully achieved and remains an aspiration. "Democracy is not an alternative to other principles of associated life. It is the idea of community itself" (Dewey, 1927, 148). Democracy thus means aspiring to community: "Associated or joint activity is a condition of the creation of a community. But association itself is physical and organic, while communal life is moral, that is emotionally, intellectually, consciously sustained" (Dewey, 1927, 151). Communal life thus involves full body–mind citizens and is full of striving, promising, enforcing, retreating, concealing, causing suffering and enjoyment, etc. Communal life is always heterogeneous whereby dissent prevails not only along major lines of differentiation but also in multiple details between a multitude of individuals participating in the transactional dynamics of public formation (Barnett and Bridge, 2013). This is why communal life survives dissent better if it is not solely confrontational but also reconciliatory.

## Becoming subjects

Dewey's notion of experience describes the way individuals become subjects embedded in communal life. Individuals become experienced within society when they learn how to act skilfully and with social competence. They develop a sense of what they can expect from others if they themselves stick to common behavioural norms, which they constantly seek to fathom. However, people make their experiences in unique ways. They experience themselves as both a part of and an exception to their community, as both a common member and simultaneously a singularity. Dewey (1929, 244) explains this as a *dialectic of the self*, which each and every person experiences as tension between conformity and self-assertion. People adopt conventionalised positions according to their social identity, e.g. as children, adults, pupils, teachers, fathers, mothers, professionals or religious persons, but they give these subject positions an individual face.

From a pragmatist point of view, three aspects are interesting about the way subjectivity emerges within the continuous, unending process of transactional social life. First, the term 'subject' specifies the individual in its social functioning. While the term 'individual' comprises a countable, isolated, unconnected unit, 'subject' in contrast describes the individual in its social significance. Individuals *become* subjects only when socially related and this means that one only becomes a subject in social relationships. To become a subject means to become socially affected, to be socially addressed, to be activated and, in turn, to activate others through one's reactions. It means not only taking on a social position but also being emotionally involved and developing an attitude. In contrast to *identity*, which derives largely from intellectual reflection on one's own *self*, subjectivity is achieved practically. *Identity building* requires thinking about oneself, trying to clarify the essence of one's own self, but *being a subject* means being socially involved and requires reactive behaviour. It is standing one's ground in actual situations. It means experiencing that one's own behaviour is not always controllable and by no means always rational. Situational behaviour depends on the current mood, the presence or absence of emotional triggers, practical obstacles, and unconscious needs, wants and desires. In the process of situationally becoming a subject, individuals appear as living humans. New situations can trigger habitual dispositions in unique ways, depending on their singular conditions, such that occasionally an individual can appear as a completely different person. Individuals are always in the process of becoming subjects.

Second, the fact that people *transact* means that they are dynamically interconnected. As they trigger each other and thus make each other into subjects, they establish *relationships* that can only exist with and between them (Saunders, 2005). The character of these relationships depends on the interplay between the people involved, not only on the sociological functions, positions and roles that they represent but also on their individual personalities. Gordon All-port's (1961) pragmatist-inspired transactional approach to personality psychology explains that personality is influenced by the environment, while at the same time people influence their environment. In addition, personality, as it is the basis for a person's characteristic behaviour and thinking, is open to growth. Democratic processes are particularly demanding on the personalities of the persons involved. Personal traits can conflict, making politics not always rational, often unpredictable and prone to develop in locally unique ways depending on the given situation and constellation of personalities. This is why it is particularly important that people reflect on their personal traits and develop their interpersonal competences and can be criticised for their interpersonal behaviour.

Third, Dewey's distinction between 'individuals with minds' and 'individual minds' is essential for framing human agency. Individuals normally proceed in everyday thinking based on "a system of beliefs, recognitions, and ignorances, of acceptances and rejections, of expectancies and appraisals of meanings which have been instituted under influence of custom and tradition" (Dewey, 1929, 219). Individuals equipped with minds thus master their everyday life to a large extent by following their 'common sense'. In this mode, they merely reproduce intellectual conventions or habits (see Cutchin, this volume). Common sense is what is not normally spoken about (Salaverría, 2007). It is what we unconsciously base our actions on. It is the context of our thoughts, but it is not explicit. We normally do not become aware of this context as long as it does not become fragile or problematic, e.g. when dealings do not proceed as usual or established skills do not work. In such situations, individuals might start thinking and at least potentially have the chance to individuate their minds and to change what they think and do.

The fact that subjectivity depends on common sense, on the situational conditions of social encounters, on the personalities of the persons involved and on mental reflections of the individuals has an impact on thinking about democratic processes. People usually derive their convictions from the context in an unreflected way but pragmatism places trust in people's ability and desire to qualify their opinions. In principle, people are able to evade their own imprints and individualise their thinking when they engage in a process of *having an experience* (Dewey, 1980, 35ff). This means to seriously inquire into the issue at hand and to engage in discussions, while perceiving contradictions emotionally, reflecting on arguments intellectually and experimenting practically with possible solutions. People might thus come up with qualified context-specific opinions. People need to learn to be affected (Barnett and Bridge, 2013), which means that they have to understand whether or not and how they are affected by an issue. Ideally, public debate individualises the minds of all participants and contributes to their individual personality development as well as to collective change.

## Populism and the blindness of common sense

Looking at the way people are embedded in their life-worlds and seeing how they produce both their selves and an affirmation of society is important for rendering a notion of critique as a practice of mediation. Making visible the blindness of common sense helps us understand how right-wing identitarian politics gains its convincing power, and why populist rhetoric is able to provoke such a high degree of aggression and conflict among those involved in actual debates.

Individuals usually experience themselves as self-efficacious and intellectually powerful. Psychology has shown that a pronounced sense of self-efficacy is conducive to ensuring that people do not give up at an early stage but take on their tasks and challenges (Bandura, 2001). However, it has also been shown that self-efficacy is based less on true agency than on positive self-image and practical experience of success. Since the allure of the Enlightenment and the beginning of modernity, people began to overestimate their ability to act freely and to underestimate the mutual co-conditionality of social positions. Common sense tends to be rather blind to processes of transaction and individuals are usually unaware of how the co-presence of others makes them social subjects. Situational sensations and feelings can directly influence attitudes and opinions, and populists are very effective in appealing to people's emotions. Convictions and attitudes are not permanent but are constantly being recreated in real-life situations. Populists do not use this human constitution in a mediating manner but, on the contrary, are socially divisive, charge social divisions with emotions and exacerbate antagonism, which in turn is compounded by another blindness of common sense.

Common sense, in Dewey's view, is "innocent of any rigid demarcation between knowledge on one side and belief, conduct and aesthetic appreciation on the other. It is guiltless of the division between objective reality and subjective events" (Dewey, 1929, 426). Accordingly, common sense "fails to recognise that deliberate and systematised science is a precondition of adequate judgments and hence of adequate striving and adequate choice" (Dewey, 1929, 426) and populists' manipulation strategies take advantage of this fact. For example, the economic development of recent decades has had a disproportionately negative impact on middle- and low-skilled workers, which makes this segment of the population particularly susceptible to right-wing populism (Gest et al., 2017, 3). Populism refers to such negative experiences and thereby implicitly promises relief. Establishing emotional connections between lived experiences and simplified truths has potential to transform these truths into uncircumventable realities.

Moreover, it is an everyday experience "that some things sweet in the having are bitter in after-taste and in what they lead to" (Dewey, 1929, 398). This experience causes a fear that one could suffer long-term harm, such as addiction or financial debt, if one does not restrain one's behaviour. It is a widespread conviction that if you do not tame your desires, you run the risk of ending up in miserable conditions. But what is the right balance between *joie de vivre* and puritanical discipline or between individual freedom and communal responsibility? Such balance is encoded in a specific way in traditions, customs and norms. But letting oneself be guided by the experiences of previous generations, as identitarian thinking suggests, will never completely resolve this tension. Instead, it depends on the individual person's ability to accept themselves and others in a certain perplexity in the face of the future's openness and as bearers of conflicting desires, needs or opinions. Such *tolerance of ambiguity* is regarded as an important personal resource in psychology (Müller-Christ and Weßling, 2007) and each person must develop such tolerance in the face of multiple sources of difference.

Right-wing populist rhetoric, however, offers a shortcut by portraying community as a homogeneous 'we' with established common values and customs. It creates the illusion that inner emotional tension can be resolved if one would only have discipline in adhering to binding values. People are especially receptive to such politics of identity if they fail to recognise that real communities will always include dissent about values and customs. If people fail to see that mutual respect and acceptance are required, they also miss that democracy is not secured by an institutional setting but that it is itself a value of inclusiveness that needs to be cultivated. To not succumb to identitarian rhetoric, individuals must have reflected about such aspects of community and democracy.

## Critique through mediation

Pragmatists believe that most people, when properly addressed, tend to be open to learning and to qualifying their ideas or opinions. In organisational development, it has been shown that greater success can be achieved by means of an appreciative inquiry instead of a critical approach (Cooperrider and Srivastva, 1987). Inquiry should examine the innovative potential within an organisation rather than focusing on failures, problems and unmet responsibilities. Organisational leadership should pursue appreciative capacity-seeking rather than evaluative control. If a positive impulse can be activated, then organisational development schemes can be productively transformative (Bushe and Kassam, 2005). By analogy, it can be assumed that an appreciative form of critique can better support political processes.

Understanding critique as mediation involves investigating actual constellations of actors and real-life political situations, as intended by the sociology of critique, by analysing different patterns of justification (Boltanski and Thévenot, 1991 [2006]). Ultimately, however, Boltanski (2011) assigns his sociology of critique a social role similar to that played by critique in the Frankfurt School. In so doing, he unfortunately abandoned the pragmatist empirical–experimental character of his earlier work (Bogusz, 2010; Peter, 2011). Moving beyond that, critique as mediation adopts a perspective on whole body politics situated in relationships among contending parties in a given situation (Saunders, 2005). The voices that arise in political discourse do not always rationally justify their opinions but rather speak directly from experience. The unspoken values hidden behind seemingly rational proposals or, conversely, the good reasons behind emotional expressions often go unattended. To make these voices intelligible, it is necessary to trace them through at least three dimensions of experience. First, the *intellectual foundation* of the positions in relation to each other must be examined. Second, the *practical qualities* of the measures that are used politically or proposed for problem-solving must be evaluated. Are the actors aware of how their practices affect their social counterparts and do they deal responsibly? And third, the *emotional charge* of the relationships must be characterised. Reasons for dissent and misunderstandings can be situated at any or all of these levels of experience. The involved parties produce and reproduce each other as subjects and have developed a path dependency that determines the character of their actual relationships. Mediation can help to make these relationships more productive.

Mediation is critique when it reveals the different values underpinning political positions. Most likely, it will be found that some positions are more powerful than others and that there is inequality within the constellation of actors involved. It is tendentially the dominant members of a majority or an otherwise privileged group who lack openness to other positions. They easily take for granted the ubiquitous self-evidence of their position, either because they experience superiority or because they rarely experience their views being challenged in everyday situations. Marginalised people, on the other hand, often experience the subordination or silencing of their positions and are therefore forced to reflect on the attitudes of the privileged. However, this cannot be unconditionally assumed but requires examination in the case in question. Both dominant and subordinate positions must be critically assessed to expose their respective blindnesses to the other party.

Critique as mediation is convinced that community life will never exist without a certain degree of inequality. *De jure* equality alone can never produce justice, but it is also the case that the alleged homogeneities of identitarian politics are only illusions. Power relations will always develop in society and can have productive effects. Boltanski (2011), for example, points to the stabilising function of institutions. It would similarly be counterproductive not to entrust persons with good leadership skills with managerial responsibilities and they will only be able to fulfil these roles if they are given certain authority. So it cannot be the goal to abolish power, an apocryphal goal in any case. Rather, power must be exposed and evaluated in actual relationships, to ask whether power relations are productive of desirable outcomes or unbearable injustices. By considering all positions, the superior and the inferior, governing and the ruled, critique as mediation creates the basis to regulate power if necessary.

Critique as mediation looks particularly closely at situations where practices are used in a targeted manner to undermine mediation, where, for example, disinformation policy is pursued, interest groups are deliberately played off against one another, or discord is sown among previously amicable people. It opposes such practices, makes these practices transparent and conveys a message about the inappropriateness of such practices to a democratic public. Conveying and imparting are the values to which mediation is committed. Communication is at the heart of democracy and thus also marks the boundary of mediation. Positions that do not engage in any attempt at mutual understanding or even subvert deliberation can ultimately only be met with opposition.

Politics can be understood as the sphere of democratic experimentation in which innovative institutional designs can be developed and tested (Barnett and Bridge, 2013). Mediation is a means of promoting and facilitating democratic publics and a democratic culture. Critique as mediation makes the foundations of different perspectives visible. It shows how opinions are based on transactions, how subjects constitute each other and whether knowledge, values, personal experiences and mindful reflections are utilised in forming opinions and taking political positions. Good mediation ensures that all camps participate in the process and deal with the critique. Mediation does not have its own position on the content of the debate but merely supports better communication among the parties involved. Mediators do not develop their own solutions to the problems at hand but can propose concepts that are capable of bridging the gap between opposing positions. Mediators do not strive for a general consensus but help to choose a way forward when parties disagree.

## Conclusion: Epistemology and mediation

'The only statistics you can trust are those you falsified yourself.' This proverb reflects the widespread acceptance of truth relativism in contemporary societies. Accordingly, it is possible to invoke the contingency of truth when it is desirable to do so, for example when scientific knowledge is contrary to one's own interests, as for example in the case of the tobacco strategy. However, in different circumstances, the same person might not have any problem using scientific knowledge if it helps to support their claims (Latour, 1993). Pragmatism helps to understand how and why such an arbitrary dualism of constructivism and positivism arises in social praxis and why right-wing populism is the consequence of an over-simplified and deliberately abused constructivism.

A pragmatist approach to counter current social tendencies begins with epistemology and extends central insights into the practical procedures of democratic politics. This chapter has explored how pragmatism offers an epistemology in which constructivism and realism do not contradict each other. In addition to *media literacy*, meaning the ability to identify which reports and media organs are trustworthy (Cooke, 2017), a kind of *science literacy* should also be promoted. People should be educated that scientific findings cannot only be true or false, but that they can be judged in their appropriateness, reliability and relevance. This implies an awareness that research results are connected to the conditions, methods, assumptions, measurement accuracy or naturalisation of categories of the underlying study. Democratisation of such competencies changes the social role of experts. Pragmatism establishes the humanities and social sciences in an advisory role. In micromodels of deliberative democracy such as citizens' juries, planning cells or National Issues Forums (Dryzek, 2004; McAffee, 2004), experts have no exclusive prerogative for interpretation but are used as facilitators and mediators. They do not simply present their often highly specialised works but are available for questions and discussions throughout the process. Ideally, democracy itself is a form of cooperative research on the conditions and possibilities of current social problems (Bohman, 2004, 24).

Academics are often called upon to provide general theoretical insights rather than to participate directly in democratic decision-making processes. Accordingly, academic criticism often prioritises opposition both to social conditions and to individuals who reproduce these social conditions (Butler, 2002; Foucault, 2007; Horkheimer, 1937 [1975]). Accordingly, it often advocates for only one party, the party of those who are suppressed, deprived or ruled, or it opposes societal conditions in general by negative dialectics. Pragmatist criticism, in contrast, focuses on the ways in which different societal camps are transactionally constituting each other and thus promotes a concrete dialectics in critical thinking. Political processes span a *transactional accommodating space* that all involved persons *co-inhabit*.

Understanding critique as mediation aims to analyse the character of given social divisions and develop concepts that have the potential to generate respect and mutual understanding between contending camps. In inter-cultural hermeneutics, for example, the pure representation of emic concepts (i.e. the view from inside) is not the best way of bringing outsiders closer to foreign cultures. This requires epistemic bridges. If academics situate their work as an intermediary between different social positions, they are no longer agents of (self-appointed) truth, opponents of hegemony, or proponents of specific academic discourses, but agents of mediation.

In addition, pragmatism can also contribute to strategies for dealing with populist rhetoric, the new right, the identitarian movement and the escalating violence of populism's adherents. If populists are confronted with critical questions, they usually employ a charade. They claim to represent majority opinion and argue that the current situation is once again typical of these opinions being suppressed by the prevailing hegemony. Mediation skills are necessary to challenge the populist rhetoric in a way that exposes its manipulative character. The way in which critique is expressed can determine where those who are so far undecided will turn.

For example, experience with hate speech in social media has shown that angry answers lead the hate-filled blogger to even more hateful comments. However, the strategy of 'not feeding the trolls' does not silence them. Their statements remain on the internet without being challenged and internet users who tend towards radical ideas can find their opinions unchallenged and thus implicitly confirmed. 'Counter-speaking' was developed to prevent trolls from completely 'eating up' the culture of discussion in social media. It is a narrow margin to question the trolls' statements without provoking the beasts. Counter-speakers neutralise the antagonism that populists try to establish. They oppose the hateful speakers by exposing the inadequacy of their positions to a wider public. Even if the original hateful writers resist changing their attitudes, manners or argumentation, counter-speaking is successful if the discourse behaviour in the forum is positively influenced and the conversation is sustained in a civil manner (Benesch et al., 2016).

In a similar way, academic critique as mediation aims to decipher conflict-ridden social constellations. Rather than criticising one side in a conflict, mediation reflects different perspectives regarding the way in which they are founded and how they co-constitute each other in current politics. Mediation requires an appreciative impetus to promote the willingness to participate in the mediation process. "The essential need, in other words, is the improvement of the methods and conditions of debate, discussion and persuasion. That is *the* problem of the public" (Dewey, 1927, 208).

## References

Allport, G.W. (1961) *Pattern and growth in personality.* New York, NY: Holt, Rinehart and Winston.

Bandura, A. (2001) Social Cognitive Theory: An agentic perspective. *Educational Psychologist*, 28, 2, 117–48.

Barisione, M. and Mayer, N. (2015) The transformation of the Radical Right Gender Gap: The case of the 2014 EP Election. Paper presented at the 4th European Conference on Politics and Gender.

Barnett, C. and Bridge, G. (2013) Geographies of radical democracy: Agonistic pragmatism and the formation of affected interests. *Annals of the Association of American Geographers*, 103, 4, 1022–40.

Benesch, S., Ruths, D., Dillon, K.P., Saleem, H.M. and Wright, L. (2016) Considerations for successful counterspeech. https://dangerousspeech.org/wp-content/uploads/2016/10/Considerations-for-Successful-Counterspeech.pdf (accessed 26 January 2020).

Bogusz, T. (2010) *Zur Aktualität von Luc Boltanski.* Wiesbaden: VS Verlag.

Bohman, J. (2004) Realizing deliberative democracy as a mode of inquiry: Pragmatism, social facts, and normative theory. *The Journal of Speculative Philosophy*, 18, 1, 23–43.

Boltanski, L. (2011) *On critique. A sociology of emancipation.* Cambridge: Polity Press.

Boltanski, L. and Thévenot, L. (1991 [2006]) *On justification. The economies of worth.* Princeton, NJ: Princeton University Press.

Bridge, G. (2008) City senses: On the radical possibilities of pragmatism in geography. *Geoforum*, 39, 1570–84.

Bushe, G.R. and Kassam, A.F. (2005) When is appreciative inquiry transformational? A meta-case analysis. *Journal of Applied Behavioral Science*, 41, 2, 161–81.

Butler, J. (1999) *Gender trouble. Feminism and the subversion of identity*. New York, NY: Routledge.

Butler, J. (2002) What is critique? An essay on Foucault's Virtue, in D. Ingram, ed., *The political: Readings in continental philosophy*. London: Basil Blackwell: 212–28.

Cooke, N A. (2017) Posttruth, truthiness, and alternative facts: Information behavior and critical information consumption for a new age. *Library Quarterly: Information, Community, Policy*, 87, 3, 211–21.

Cooperrider, D.L. and Srivastva, S. (1987) Appreciative inquiry in organizational life, in R.W. Woodman and W.A. Pasmore, eds, *Research in organizational change and development*, Vol. 1. Stamford, CT: JAI Press, 129–69.

Darby, S. (2017) The rise of the Valkyries. In the alt-right, women are the future, and the problem. *Harper's Magazine*, 29, September. https://harpers.org/archive/2017/09/the-rise-of-the-valkyries/ (accessed 26 January 2020).

Delfin, R. (2016) Former Miss Belgium Anke Van Dermeersch: Islam threatens women's rights and Muslim immigration must be stopped. *Critical Beauty*, 24 May. www.criticalbeauty.com/2016/05/former-miss-belgium-anke-van-dermeersch.html (accessed 26 January 2020).

Dewey, J. (1927) *The public and its problems*. Denver, CO: Alan Swallow.

Dewey, J. (1929) *Experience and nature*. London: George Allen and Unwin.

Dewey, J. (1938) *Logic. The theory of inquiry*. New York, NY: Henry Hold.

Dewey, J. (1980) *Art as experience*. New York, NY: Perigee Books.

Dewey, J. and Bentley, A.F. (1949) *Knowing and the known*. Boston, MA: Beacon.

Dryzek, J.S. (2004) Pragmatism and democracy: In search of deliberative publics. *The Journal of Speculative Philosophy*, 18, 1, 72–9.

Elsas, E.J. Van, Hakhverdian, A. and van der Brug, W. (2016) United against a common foe? The nature and origins of Euroscepticism among left-wing and right-wing citizens. *West European Politics*, 39, 6, 1181–204.

Finkelde, D. (2013) Post-structuralism, in R.L. Fastiggi, ed., *New Catholic Encyclopedia Supplement 2012–13: Ethics and philosophy*. Detroit, MI: Gale, 1245–8.

Foucault, M. (1993) *Die Ordnung des Diskurses*. Frankfurt: Fischer.

Foucault, M. (2007) *The politics of truth*. Los Angeles, CA: Semiotext(e).

Gest, J., Reny, T. and Mayer, J. (2017) Roots of the radical right: Nostalgic deprivation in the United States and Britain. *Comparative Political Studies*. doi: 10.1177/0010414017720705.

Harrison, P. (2006) Poststructuralist theories, in S. Aitken and G. Valentine, eds, *Approaches to human geography*. London: SAGE, 122–35.

Herring, S., Job-Sluder, K., Scheckle, R. and Barab, S. (2002) Searching for safety online: Managing 'trolling' in a feminist forum. *The Information Society*, 18, 371–84.

Horkheimer, M. (1937 [1975]) *Critical theory: Selected essays*. Continuum International Publishing Group, 188–243.

Horton, R. (2017) Offline: Difficult truths about a post-truth world. *The Lancet*, 389, 10075, 1282.

Laclau, E. (2005) Populism: What's in a name?, in F. Panizza, ed., *Populism and the mirror of democracy*. London and New York, NY: Verso, 32–49.

Laclau, E. and Mouffe, C. (2001) *Hegemony and socialist strategy. Towards a radical democratic politics*. London: Verso.

Latour, B. (1993) *We have never been modern*. Cambridge, MA: Harvard University Press.

Latour, B. (2004) Why has critique run out of steam? From matters of fact to matters of concern. *Critical Inquiry*, 30, 225–48.

Legrand, D. (2007) Pre-reflective self-as-subject from experiential and empirical perspectives. *Consciousness and Cognition*, 16, 3, 583–99.

Mayer, N. (2015) The closing of the radical right gender gap in France? *French Politics*, 13, 4, 391–414.

McAffee, N. (2004) Three models of democratic deliberation. *The Journal of Speculative Philosophy*, 18, 1, 44–59.

March for Science (2017) https://marchforscience.org/ (accessed 31 May 2017).

Marmot, M. (2017): The art of medicine. Post-truth and science. *The Lancet*, 389(10068), 497–498.

Miller, S. (2017) Lipstick fascism. On Lana Lokteff, the women of the alt-right, and the feminization of fascism. *Jacobin*, 4 April. www.jacobinmag.com/2017/04/alt-right-lana-lokteff-racism-misogyny-women-feminism/ (accessed 26 January 2020).

Morgan, D.L. (2014) Pragmatism as a paradigm for social research. *Qualitative Inquiry*, 20, 8, 1045–53.

Mouffe, C. (2005) *On the political*. London and New York, NY: Routledge.

Müller-Christ, G. and Weßling, G. (2007) Widerspruchsbewältigung, Ambivalenz- und Ambiguitätstoleranz. Eine modellhafte Verknüpfung, in G. Müller-Christ, L. Arndt and I. Ehnert, eds, *Nachhaltigkeit und Widersprüche*. Münster: LIT, 180–97.

Nassehi, A. (2015) *Die letzte Stunde der Wahrheit*. Hamburg: Murmann.

Oliver, J.E. and Rahn, W.M. (2016) Rise of the Trumpenvolk: Populism in the 2016 election. *The Annals of the American Academy of Political and Social Science*, 667, 1, 189–206.

Oreskes, N. and Conway, E.M. (2010) *Merchants of doubt. How a handful of scientists obscured the truth on issues from tobacco smoke to global warming*. New York, Berlin, London: Bloomsbury Press.

Oxford Dictionaries (2016) Word of the year – post-truth. https://en.oxforddictionaries.com/word-of-the-year/word-of-the-year-2016 (accessed 26 January 2020).

Peter, L. (2011) Soziologie der Kritik oder Sozialkritik? Zum Werk Luc Boltanskis und dessen deutscher Rezeption. *Lendemains*, 36, 73–89. www.periodicals.narr.de/index.php/Lendemains/article/download/203/187 (accessed 26 January 2020).

Röttgers, K. (1975) *Kritik und Praxis. Zur Geschichte des Kritikbegriffs von Kant bis Marx*. Berlin and New York, NY: Walter de Gruyter.

Said, E. (1978) *Orientalism*. New York, NY: Pantheon Books.

Salaverría, H. (2007) *Spielräume des Selbst. Pragmatismus und kreatives Handeln*. Berlin: Akademie Verlag.

Saunders, H.H. (2005) *Politics is about relationship*. New York, NY: Palgrave.

Schweiger, W. (2017) *Der (des)informierte Bürger im Netz. Wie soziale Medien die Meinungsbildung verändern*. Stuttgart: Springer.

Woodward, K, Dixon, D.P. and Jones III, J.P. (2009) Poststructuralism/poststructuralist geographies, in R. Kitchin and N. Thrift, eds, *International Encyclopedia of Human Geography 2009*. London: Elsevier Science, 396–407.

# 8

# Learning from experience: Pragmatism and politics in place

*Alice E. Huff*

## Introduction

The negotiation of difference is a central concern of democratic politics. In wrestling with empirical and normative questions of difference, scholars have drawn on agonistic democratic theory to illuminate problematic ways of managing pluralism and advocate for adversarial conflict as a check against neoliberal governance strategies (Derickson and MacKinnon, 2015; Featherstone, 2008; Purcell, 2008; Swyngedouw, 2009). Without discounting these important interventions, I argue that Deweyan pragmatism's emphasis on contextualism, fallibilism and experiential learning provides a necessary counterpoint to agonistic theory, pointing scholars towards more generative ways of thinking about difference in democratic life. For Dewey, engagement across difference is important because it provides experiences that help people to test and revise their assumptions about the world; people learn from the experience of negotiating conflicting ideas and values and this in turn produces new political opportunities. A scholarly focus on contextualised experience surfaces concerns that preoccupy political participants, but which are often ignored in theorisations of democratic politics. Coupled with an openness to perspectives that challenge our assumptions, this orientation expands the scope of academic inquiry, makes our theories more accountable to lived realities and reworks relationships between researchers and the communities we write about. Learning is at the heart of this work; centralising the role of learning (in political and in academic practice) allows scholars to better recognise and support transformative political practices.

This argument is developed in several stages. First, I describe key intersections and disjunctures between Chantal Mouffe's agonism and John Dewey's engaged pluralism. Having laid out the contours of these two models, I apply both to the analysis of an empirical case involving conflict within a New Orleans neighbourhood group, highlighting the unique insights into the negotiation of difference that a Deweyan lens provides. I conclude with a discussion of the benefits of integrating a Deweyan sensibility into social research practices and the process of knowledge production.

## Agonistic pluralism versus engaged pluralism

While Dewey and Mouffe are rarely brought into conversation with one another, their democratic visions share crucial features. Both thinkers are anti-foundationalists. They reject appeals to fundamental truths and proceed from the assumption that the world is always in the making. In addition, both thinkers understand democracy as an embodied, active, never-completed project rather than a set of formal institutional mechanisms or an ideal end-state. These shared features make both strands of thought useful for researchers interested in the politics of democracy. But looking at the implications of their divergences is also helpful and here I consider differences in relation to identity formation and conflict.

For Mouffe (2013), political identity is formed by constructing ourselves in opposition to others. There is no 'us' without a 'them', no possibility of a unified social body. The threat of antagonism is ever-present. While Mouffe does not imagine identity as fixed, the us/them dynamic she describes engenders strong, relatively stable commitments to one's own political group and the values that such groups are built around. People can and do 'switch sides', but this identity construction is not, in Mouffe's view, a product of deliberative interaction, nor is it situational. For Mouffe, "to accept the view of the adversary is to undergo a radical change in political identity. It is more a sort of conversion than a process of rational persuasion" (2000, 102).

From this point of view, conflict is not only inevitable but desirable. Unlike other theorisations of democracy that emphasise the value of consensus, Mouffe's agonistic democracy embraces the recognition of difference as a prerequisite for hegemonic struggle between groups advocating different interpretations of democratic values (2005b). Because Mouffe sees conflict as constitutive of the political, governance strategies that make it difficult to discern and contest political difference are suspect, as are modes of interaction that seek to suture division and diffuse tension.

Despite her rejection of that which masks difference, however, Mouffe is mindful of the threat to democratic arrangements that difference poses when it is defined in moral, essentialist terms. In order to mitigate this threat, agonistic pluralism calls for treating political opponents as adversaries whose ideas must be contested rather than enemies to be destroyed (Mouffe, 2000, 2005a, 2005b, 2013). This adversarial stance entails acting on what Mouffe calls "conflictual consensus" – that is, "consensus about the ethico-political values of liberty and equality for all, [but] dissent about their interpretations" (Mouffe, 2005b, 120). It requires vigorously advancing one's own political commitments and opposing incompatible positions, while still acknowledging the right of opponents to do the same.

In contrast to Mouffe's conception of democracy as hegemonic struggle, American pragmatist John Dewey describes democracy as a mode of associational living guided by social inquiry and action (Dewey, 2008b, 2: 329; Barnett, 2014; Lake, 2014; Pappas, 2008). As we shape and reshape the conditions of our lives, we recognise new problems and devise new methods for addressing them. Democracy *is* this always-ongoing process of collectively experimenting with ways to reconstruct problematic situations so that we might create environments that better support human flourishing and facilitate even more fruitful opportunities for learning (Dewey, 2008a, 9: 93). This, rather than any specific end-point, is for Dewey the purpose and substance of democratic practice.

Although Dewey forwards hypotheses regarding the role of particular habits (such as openness and courage) that facilitate democratic work, the experimental character and contingent nature of democratic practice preclude adherence to fixed principles and *a priori* goals (Pappas, 1996). As he puts it: "All ends and values that are cut off from the ongoing process become arrests, fixations. They strive to fixate what has been gained instead of using it to open the road and point the way to new and better experiences" (Dewey, 2008b, 14: 229). Instead, Dewey insists that contextual experience furnishes sufficient means for identifying problematic situations, generating ideas for possible transformative actions, and evaluating the results (Dewey, 2008a, 14: 195, 2008b, 14: 229).

This conception of democracy entails a particular orientation towards pluralism and conflict. Because people may belong to many different publics and hold many different values, experimenting with better ways to manage our lives together is necessarily fraught with tension. Dewey does not deny the existence of irreconcilable differences (Dewey, 2008b, 2: 362). What sets Dewey's attitude towards pluralism apart from Mouffe's is the possibility he sees for learning from conflicts over values, ideas and orientations to action. While agonistic democracy prescribes an adversarial stance that restricts consideration of opponents' positions, for Dewey, "Every way of life that fails in its democracy limits the contacts, the exchanges, the communications, the interactions by which experience is steadied while it is also enlarged and enriched" (Dewey, 2008b, 14: 229–30). Individual experience is limited and limiting. Dewey believes that experimentation is made more reliable through collective inquiry, and especially by engaging difference with a sense of fallibilism that accepts a willingness to acknowledge that our best thinking may be misguided. Such interactions may prompt the reconsideration of settled understandings, and are therefore crucial for democracy understood as ongoing inquiry (Dewey, 2008b, 6: 21).

From a pragmatist's point of view, political identity is not bound by us/them distinctions. Like Mouffe, Dewey understands identity as constructed and subject to change. His understanding of how identity changes, however, bears little resemblance to Mouffe's description of switching sides. Dewey points out that people are members of multiple publics, hold multiple allegiances and see themselves as part of multiple groups (Glaude, 2007, 131). Not only is identity multi-faceted in ways that complicate us/them distinctions, but it is also more fluid than Mouffe's model allows. Dewey sees democracy and its associated political activity as an experimental project and, as such, identity (along with everything else) must be open to change through experience, encounter and reflection.

While Dewey concedes that some situations might require adversarial (or even antagonistic) responses, he does not assume that interactions across difference *must* be adversarial in nature. Dewey's engaged pluralism encourages people to negotiate difference, even across power differentials, in the understanding that communicative experience might allow people to come to new and beneficial understandings. The point of Deweyan democracy is to mandate neither consensus nor conflict but, rather, to encourage people to bring their collective experiences to the negotiation of problematic situations as they arise (Dewey, 2008a, 5: 288).

For Dewey, determining political responses to difference in advance of particular situations is undesirable not only because the world is too complex and dynamic for such prescriptions but also because working with others to figure out what we should do is the crux of democratic life. Dewey argues that people learn democracy by practising it, and practise democracy by learning. This means that democracy cannot be given in advance of its practice in a particular context (Dewey, 2008b, 7: 347). It depends upon experiences that foster inquiry, through which democracy is made and remade (2008b, 14: 367).

Some critics have suggested that this Deweyan approach to pluralism reflects a lack of concern for dimensions of struggle and rupture that radical change requires (Koopman, 2017). From this point of view, engaged pluralism risks bolstering existing uneven power relations and plays into the hands of those who seek to mask the irreconcilable, deeply political, tensions between social groups espousing different value systems (Purcell, 2008). The openness that Deweyan democracy demands may undercut efforts to identify and challenge injustice, and put those with fewer resources in positions where they may be silenced, denigrated or co-opted (Grattan, 2016). A commitment to contextualism may make it particularly difficult to address systemic problems. And Deweyan pragmatism asks a lot from participants in the democratic process. Perhaps it is too time consuming, uncertain and ethically strenuous a project – especially given the pressing, uneven nature of social problems. For social researchers there is a concern that inattention to these risks might lead to analyses that deny persistent divisions of power.

Without discounting these critiques, I argue that there are also important benefits associated with a Deweyan perspective. In particular, emphasising the experimental character of democratic practice helps to ensure that our hypotheses about how to handle democratic problems are accountable to people's actual experience and are open to revision. To explore how using a Deweyan lens can illuminate the dynamics of democracy in a particular place, in the next two sections of this chapter I draw on ethnographic data collected through work with a New Orleans neighbourhood-based action group, the Pullman Neighbourhood School Initiative (PNSI) from 2013–14. Data presented here are drawn from participant observation of weekly PNSI meetings, ad hoc gatherings, public events related to the struggle, meeting of the New Orleans School Board, public events sponsored by PNSI and informal gatherings that occurred from April to September of 2014. The names of the neighbourhood, school, initiative and participants described in this chapter are pseudonyms. To protect the anonymity of group members, some identifying details have been changed.

## New Orleans schooling struggles and PNSI

The struggle I discuss in this chapter occurred in the context of the most sweeping attempt to marketise public schooling in US history. Following black-led efforts to desegregate New Orleans schools in the 1960s, government-sponsored white abandonment of urban spaces led to under-resourced public schools primarily used and run by black New Orleanians. In the wake of Hurricane Katrina in 2005, proponents of market-based school reform (most of whom were white) gained control of the New Orleans public school system. The reforms they enacted abolished New Orleans's neighbourhood schooling model, disempowered the locally elected school board and led to the mass firing of all public school employees. The resulting city-wide charter school market was largely unaccountable to public oversight. Under this system, children were no longer guaranteed a place in a neighbourhood school. Instead, they competed for places in schools across the city, which opened and closed under market pressure.

While the city's schools had not always been able to adequately serve the neighbourhood residents who depended on them, they were deeply embedded in geographic communities. In addition to providing unionised jobs and furnishing academic and social services, schools were a source of neighbourhood identity, they provided public meeting space within the community and they memorialised the achievements of black-led social movements. Given the pivotal role schools played in community life, school closure catalysed heated contestation (Huff, 2013, 2015).

One such struggle focused on Pullman school – an imposing three-storey brick building on a shaded city block in the gentrifying but still majority poor and black Pullman neighbourhood. Despite being shuttered in an earlier round of school closures pre-Katrina, Pullman remained in many ways the heart of the community. Neighbourhood groups had pushed to reopen the school for years but, after Katrina, the school board listed Pullman School as 'surplus property'. As a result of this designation, Pullman officially ceased to be a neighbourhood school and could be bought as property by charter school management organisations or, if none of these were interested, by private developers.

In the summer of 2014, a charter school management organisation attempted to buy Pullman School. Because the organisation represented a selective-admission charter, the sale meant that the majority of neighbourhood residents would not be able to use the school. In response, neighbours formed the Pullman Neighbourhood School Initiative – PNSI – with the goal of advocating for neighbourhood influence over the fate of Pullman School.

PNSI consisted of about a dozen core members but ten times as many attended PNSI events. The initiative was fairly diverse in terms of race, ethnicity, age, socio-economic status and gender. It was almost evenly split between black and non-black members and between women and men. Most participants were long-time neighbourhood residents; about a quarter had moved in post-Katrina. The oldest member was in her late eighties, the youngest was in her early twenties. A few considered themselves politically active but most had never been involved in any kind of political initiative before.

Ultimately, PNSI was not able to stop the sale of the school. This is not, then, the story of a grassroots David able to slay the neoliberal Goliath (Chatterton and Pickerill, 2010, 486). Nevertheless, I suggest that the negotiation of conflict described below can be instructive for social researchers interested in democracy and the politics in and of place, especially when viewed through a Deweyan lens.

## PNSI and the negotiation of difference

Like many neighbourhood groups involved in place-based politics, PNSI's members were not united by an allegiance to any particular ideology. Participants came together not to challenge the neoliberal underpinnings of post-Katrina reforms but to address immediate concerns regarding school closure in their neighbourhood. This shared interest brought people with very different values, experiences and identities into the same political community.

Differences among the members of PNSI were especially evident when the group discussed the use of confrontational tactics. Some members thought PNSI should aggressively call those in power to account, disrupt the flow of business in school board meetings and occupy school grounds. Other members were interested not in challenging existing political structures but in navigating them more effectively and demonstrating the group's willingness to "play ball".

In arguments about whether to protest school closure by occupying the Pullman School yard, Jess, a young woman who identified as white and Native American, described the need to call the Orleans Parish School

Board (OPSB) to account by reclaiming space in the predominantly black neighbourhood:

> Our big moral juncture with the Orleans Parish School Board is that they have created an environment [where] public property, and access to public property, has become a crime. And it has created a culture of crime. [We're occupying the school so] that the neighbourhood can have a sense of belonging, they can feel like the space that their tax dollars have publicly funded does belong to them. Although the school board has jurisdiction over what happens to that [school], we're calling negligence! (Field notes, PNSI meeting, 6 August 2014)

For Jess and others, the Pullman School closure was inextricably linked to other forms of spatialised social and economic violence. These sentiments were expressed in a PNSI-authored neighbourhood newspaper article:

> Our history is dirtied with genocide, slavery, segregation, oppression, violence, and injustice. We have to show the people in power that our neighbourhood is not for sale. That we are not for sale.
>   We are here for justice. We are here because we believe that it is criminal to sell off public property to private developers that do not care about who we are, what we need, or what we've built up here over generations. (PNSI open letter to Orleans Parish officials, 26 June 2014)

Yet not all PNSI members wanted to highlight these issues. A reluctance to publicly link the fight for Pullman school with broader efforts to combat racialised violence was evident in conversations about how to present the PNSI cause to the OPSB, which was then majority pro-charter. In a closed PNSI meeting, one white PNSI member, Lee, argued that referring to racial injustice would hurt the cause, "We can talk about that stuff in here. But we're going to turn people off if we go in the race direction [at the school board meeting]." Another white member, Tom, agreed. "We can allude to it, maybe…but it shouldn't be the main focus. The focus is Pullman." Reluctance to address racial issues was tied to broader disagreement about the role of conflict and disruption in effecting political change. Early in the struggle, for instance, a black pastor who was one of the founding PNSI members argued for minimising conflictual relations with the school board. He shared this observation:

> I have noticed that when you go to these, uh, meetings at the school boards, or any other meeting, I've noticed that the people who get the results, or get what they want from the School Board, are those who go before the School Board with a meek, you know, humble, uh, grateful, you know…disposition. (Field notes, PNSI meeting, 23 July 2014)

Aubry, a young black developer who joined PNSI late in their struggle went one step further. He ridiculed the desire to contest schooling injustices at all, calling it "a joke". Instead of disruptive politics, he wanted to recruit funders and pitch a business plan to the board outlining a process for "returning the property to commerce".

> The bottom line is that if you don't have $360,000, you can't have Pullman. If you don't at least have this, you're wasting everybody's time right now. Including the School Board. Including your neighbourhood.
>
> [...] Right now the plan is to rabble-rouse [...] That's the plan. And that's a bad plan. Because nobody wants the obstructionist. (Field notes, PNSI meeting, 6 August 2014)

At the outset of the Pullman struggle, Ian, a young single father with Filipino roots and a business in the neighbourhood, was also interested in "playing ball" with those in power. Ian agreed with Aubry that PNSI should stop being antagonistic and start behaving more professionally in order to "trigger" a positive response from the board.

> In my opinion, in every situation there's a certain way to go about things. You know, when you step into somebody's office in City Hall, there's a different trigger than [for] somebody on the corner. [And it's that trigger] that's gonna activate them to get behind the case, you know? [...] And so I think in every situation it's like a [...] true, like, moral reason [behind what you do]. But you're doing it the way [the person you're talking to] is going to react to. You're just doing it the way that makes them react, you know. And I think there's nothing wrong with that, you know what I'm saying? (Field notes, PNSI meeting, 13 August 2014)

Marcus, a middle-aged black Pullman alum, challenged Ian and others who thought that working in a deferential manner with the board was likely to yield positive results. Marcus believed that those in power would denigrate neighbourhood residents no matter how respectfully residents communicated. He responded to Ian:

> At the same time, those people [on the school board] are conditioned already. You can stand up there on your toes, and being polite, and they will slam you after they listen to all that. (Field notes, PNSI meeting, 13 August 2014)

The two went back and forth until, finally, Ian agreed that if they experienced disrespect from the board, then they would call for a more adversarial response.

> Then that's when you go off, then. If you approach them in the right way and it doesn't work, then that's when you approach them from the other way, the way that you know how to basically make noise. (Field notes, PNSI meeting, 13 August 2014)

In fact, Ian and other PNSI members did become more open to adversarial tactics as a result of experience in the Pullman School struggle. After trying unsuccessfully to be heard in public meetings and listening to the stories of other neighbourhood groups fighting school closure, the pastor who had advocated for maintaining a "meek" and "grateful" attitude later spoke quite differently about the obligations associated with citizenship:

> [The school board] have plans for tomorrow. They have plans to filibuster and to draw things out so we can't speak. But [...] we have to demand: "No, you're going to hear our voice". (Field notes, PNSI meeting, 13 August 2014)

These disagreements sprang from real ethico-political differences between group members. Rather than strive for internal coherence, however, the group tried to accommodate multiple (sometimes conflicting) values. Along the way, many PNSI members were tempted to either leave the group or force non-likeminded others out. But for the most part, the group remained committed to working together in difference. Individual members held strong convictions but when decisions had to be made regarding the group's mission and tactics, they tried to remain open enough for all voices to be heard and divergent options considered. Ms. Ida was an elder in the black community, and she argued forcefully for inclusivity:

> I'll tell you like this: it comes to P-Town, I don't see nothing wrong with community. Why everybody don't just come together and work together with new ideas? You know? Because it should be open to everybody. (Field notes, PSNI ad hoc meeting, 29 July 14)

Susan, a white retiree who had worked for years to reopen Pullman, agreed, emphasising the fact that neighbourhood organising necessarily throws people with different viewpoints together:

> We are going to have people in our neighbourhood, that I'm gonna sit there and go, "Oh my God. Do I really got to sit in the room with this person and deal with them?" But yes I do! Because if we're gonna make this work, we all got to learn... how to deal with... [each other]. (Field notes, PSNI ad hoc meeting, 29 July 14)

Marcus was also adamant that the group needed to be able to engage with different ideas. He had faith in his own ability (and that of the group) to evaluate alternative viewpoints, even those of Aubry the developer, who seemed so dismissive of the group's efforts to amplify community voices. Speaking to another member, John, Marcus explained:

> You can tell me anything. I can... I can funnel it. I can adjust to it, or I can just leave it alone. I... I heard harsh stuff all my life. So to me, it was nothing threatening about what Aubry was saying, because he can't even weigh in on anything if it's a collective... if it's a collective thing that we have going on. He can talk all all all day. He can say whatever, you know? In the end, [we could say] 'Okay, yeah, we gonna x that out and move forward to this way"... If you hold it in and we don't hear it – we don't know what's your feelings... if you say what you got to say then

we can weigh like – "Well, John has some key points and I... I... think this out-weighs what Aubry is saying'. (Field notes, PSNI ad hoc meeting, 29 July 14)

Marcus's support for learning across difference was echoed by Jess, one of the strongest advocates for centralising racial (in)justice in the narrative and action developed by the PNSI:

I feel like we [those who agreed with her framing] almost need a declaration of truths, where we say, If you're uncomfortable talking about this, and you don't see the big picture, then you just hang tight, because we know why we're here. And you'll have your own time to figure it out. This is going to be a learning process. (Field notes, 18 August 2014)

In creating this space for learning, PNSI members forged bonds that became sustaining beyond the confines of the Pullman struggle. Many of the members saw the experience as personally transformative. Tonya, a deeply religious middle-aged black Pullman alumna whose sister had been shot dead a block from the school, described the impact of her participation in PNSI to several other women in the group. Of the time before she joined PNSI, Tonya said:

I was a ghost... I was a prisoner in that big house. I never went nowhere but to church and back. Because I didn't trust people in the neighbourhood... But I found trust in y'all. (Field notes, 25 August 2014)

The willingness to entertain differing viewpoints came at a cost, however. Providing space to discuss conflicting views meant that PNSI members often felt uncomfortable, angry and impatient with co-participants. The absence of a cohesive, shared set of values and the imperative to engage across difference slowed organising momentum, sapping energy that was already in short supply. Members were frustrated by the iterative nature of their decision-making processes and by having to delay action until all voices could be heard. This kind of engagement also opened PNSI up to co-optation by more experienced actors like Aubry, the developer who hoped to profit from reopening Pullman. And then there is the fact that PNSI was ultimately unable to stop the sale of the school. While any neighbourhood group would have had difficulty challenging the policy regime in place at the time, openness to difference may have further hindered PNSI's ability to achieve its goals.

## Dewey and geographies of political experience

### What matters?

As many scholars have pointed out, neoliberalisation is characterised by inter-locking dynamics that stifle possibilities for political action. These include the privatisation of public spaces and institutions, the transfer of authority from elected government to entities that are not publicly accountable, the privileging of technocratic expertise, the deployment of strategies designed to divert attention from the causes of problems to their symptoms and the orchestration of fora that legitimate non-democratic decision-making by maintaining the appearance (but not the substance) of democratic participation in governance (Allmendinger and Haughton, 2012; Gill et al., 2012; Swyngedouw, 2009, 2014). PNSI's efforts to publicly frame New Orleans school closure as a political issue were made more difficult by each of these manoeuvres.

Agonism provides a solid theoretical base from which to challenge such depoliticisation strategies. Mouffe's theorisations help scholars to better understand the relationship between these dynamics and the suppression of opportunities for adversarial conflict essential to democracy. In outlining this relationship, Mouffe also provides academics with a definition of radical democratic work as that which operates within the values framework of liberal democracy to unsettle existing hegemonic orders and instantiate less hierarchical and unequal ones. This definition becomes a guideline for identifying and evaluating the transformative potential of contemporary political practices.

While compelling, this formulation of democracy excludes many actually existing forms of grassroots organising and ignores many of the concerns that occupy the attention of political participants. Certainly PNSI does not fit easily into Mouffe's model of hegemonic struggle between clearly defined adversaries with clearly defined political commitments. PNSI's members held multiple and conflicting values that blurred us/them distinctions. Members' understandings shifted in response to their interactions. Groups like PNSI may not be likely to produce the kinds of changes Mouffe is interested in but they do comprise a relatively common form of actually existing collective action. Given the impediments to political work that Mouffe and others describe, dismissing them altogether may be a mistake. Doing so cuts off opportunities to investigate that which moves people to engage politically, even under adverse circumstances, in ethically complicated situations.

In addition to marginalising certain kinds of organisation and mobilisation, agonistic theory tends to ignore the *dilemmas* that occupy the attention of people practising politics. At issue for Mouffe is the problem of preserving and foregrounding difference without devolving into antagonism (or bloodshed). PNSI members were similarly concerned with how to live together in difference but, for them, this involved negotiating questions regarding their mission and tactics, as well as practical issues regarding the future of their effort to reopen the school if they splintered into disparate likeminded subgroups. By providing a solution for pluralism in advance of particular situations, Mouffe ignores the fact that how to deal with difference remains an open question for many groups and she obscures the difficult political work that such groups do as they go about addressing it. In the case of PNSI, dealing with difference was intrinsic to maintaining the campaign. Their struggle illuminates the challenges of agonism in practice and the reasons why people may choose to augment adversarial interactions with other kinds of engagement across difference. From a Mouffean perspective, however, the inability to deal agonistically with values difference is simply a failure of democratic practice. PNSI is of little interest except as a cautionary tale illustrating the futility and danger of attempting to deliberate across ideological difference rather than confronting proponents of marketised schooling.

In contrast, a Deweyan lens provides insight into PNSI and similar cases, highlighting the importance of context, experience and learning in politics in plural societies. Dewey would say we cannot know what is required of us, ethically and politically, apart from particular situations (Pappas, 2008). From this perspective, our work as researchers is not to hold initiatives to a pre-determined standard for 'properly political' behaviour, but to examine how participants embedded in the particularities of political situations understand their work and make the decisions they do. Working from the inside out, we can then begin to trace the systemic relationships that shape the work of particular groups in particular places (and vice versa). As researchers, we necessarily enter this process with ideas and experiences of our own. A Deweyan outlook does not imply that we discount such knowledge but it does ask us to seek out experiences that might unsettle it, and be willing to alter our positions in light of new interactions.

Seen from a Deweyan perspective, PNSI is an interesting case even though (or perhaps because) its members engaged in practices that seem unsuited to contesting neoliberal urban reform. The tensions raised within PNSI indicate that participants were aware of dynamics that concern many scholars but they negotiated them in ways we might not expect. For example, while many PNSI members were interested in addressing felt injustice through the Pullman struggle, not all of them envisioned the fight in this way and some, indeed, preferred not to fight at all. Further, some participants were far more concerned with combating injustices rooted in historical forms of racial violence than those associated with the marketisation of public education per se. If we do not assume that radical politics must always focus on contesting neoliberalisation, and if we abandon the notion that such politics must be enacted in particular ways, then we become more able to discern how people who are actually engaged in grassroots movements think about their work and the connections between their experiences and broader social, political and economic dynamics.

For this reason, a Deweyan lens helps researchers to more fully engage with practices that include but also exceed adversarial conflict. When democracy is framed as an ongoing attempt to collectively identify and act upon problematic situations, accommodation of difference might be seen as an effort to create the conditions for democracy rather than its negation. PNSI participants often operated in an adversarial mode, especially with representatives of the state. They also deliberated across values differences. Neither posture came naturally:

PNSI struggled to figure out how to deal with difference and participants learned as they went along. But they knew they would have to continue living together after the Pullman struggle ended and they saw benefits in treating each other as more than adversaries. From a Deweyan perspective, the decisions that PNSI made are on their face neither bad not good – instead they become the focus of analysis and the material from which to learn more about the way that democracy works.

Paying attention to how groups like PNSI understand their own work allows social scientists to see and appreciate different kinds of struggles, but this does not invalidate the benefits (both for scholars and political participants) of articulating connections between grassroots initiatives and broader social movements. A concern for contextual experience does not relegate researchers to descriptive accounts of isolated cases. The context of contemporary political work will necessarily be interconnected, global and local, and dynamic. Utilising a Deweyan lens encourages scholars to draw out these connections without ignoring how people decide how to work together and against each other, how people themselves reshape their circumstances (or find themselves unable to do so) and how they are changed in the process. This perspective fosters a more robust understanding of how people engage in political life, which is necessary if we concede that every political project must be carried out in actual places by actual people who are shaped by a lifetime of experiences.

## A radical pragmatist's view of political subjectivity

Beyond an expansion of academic inquiry, a Deweyan lens encourages a view of political subjectivity that is both radical and markedly different from Mouffe's. For Mouffe, the threat of antagonism cannot be eradicated. Agonism merely channels antagonistic impulses into forms of interaction that are more compatible with democratic pluralism. The model is designed to compensate for people's presumed inability to otherwise work across difference without violence or the coercive suppression of difference.

By comparison, Dewey's notion of engaged pluralism is notable for its profound faith in the ability of diverse groups to identify problems (including those associated with pluralism) and to experiment with methods for addressing them. Dewey's approach relies on a willingness to operate in spaces of discomfort, to reflect on personal limitations and to alter deeply held beliefs in response to new experiences. In its assertion that everyday people can do this work and its focus on how they do it, a Deweyan perspective challenges notions of defective political subjectivity that can colour theory across the political spectrum.

A Deweyan outlook does not require scholars to support the understandings and choices of those most directly affected by particular problems, however. One might disagree with those PNSI members, for instance, who argued that maintaining space for all voices was more important than building momentum around a unified set of values. Engagement across difference does not carry with it the obligation to take on the views of others or to forgo judgement. But a Deweyan sensibility does guard against moving from disagreement to derision. A sense of fallibilism and respect for lived experience, combined with a faith in the capacity to self-govern, might make social scientists less inclined to imagine political participants as dupes or chess pieces lined up on either side of a clearly defined winner-takes-all battle for change. If democracy involves people managing for themselves the conditions of their own lives, this starting place is important for scholars studying the politics of place and supporting democratic solutions to pressing problems.

Dewey's assumptions regarding people's willingness and capacity to do the work he describes can seem idealistic; some pragmatists have been rightly criticised for insufficient attention to systemic constraints on action (especially those associated with race, class and patriarchy) and to power and antagonism more generally (Talisse, 2017). I suggest, however, that the issue lies more with how pragmatic conceptions of democracy have been mobilised (including, at times, by Dewey himself) rather than an inherent flaw in the model. As Dewey argued in *The public and its problems* (1988 [1927]), democratic practice must "counteract the forces that have so largely determined the possession of rule by accidental and irrelevant factors, and in the second place an effort to counteract the tendency to employ political power to serve private instead of public ends" (Dewey, 2008b, 2: 287). In order to do so, we are obligated to militate against dynamics that produce uneven participation and efficacy in democratic life. A Deweyan focus on experience helps scholars to address this issue directly, but crucially, it does so in a way that surfaces democratic barriers *and* provides an important bulwark against inattention to the life-sustaining practices and experience-based understandings of those most directly harmed by social, spatial and economic violence. As Katherine McKittrick has argued regarding portrayals of black geographies, too many critics of such violence depict the implicated people and places as always dead and dying, in effect naturalising the very dynamics they condemn (2013, 9). If pragmatists have not always been sufficiently attuned to what Cornel West (2005) calls the "night side" of American democracy, pragmatism's emphasis on people as active shapers of circumstance does provide a way out of the trap McKittrick describes.

Returning to the PNSI case, we can see how the loss of Pullman School might be used to anchor narratives of neoliberal dominance and place annihilation. Doing so, however, may negate the work, even the humanity, of residents who continue to shape their geographies. Taking a pre-determined approach to political analysis can obscure potentially transformative practices that persist in even the most prohibitive circumstances, such as the interactions that made Tonya feel visible and connected to her neighbourhood for the first time since her sister was killed, or the ways in which experience of working on a shared problem allowed PNSI members like Ian and Marcus to be generous with each other, to consider different perspectives, to learn from their experiences and to use these understandings in other political contexts. A Deweyan view of political subjectivity challenges the sense of deterministic inevitability that is sometimes present in structural narratives. It resists the implication that the logic of neoliberalism supersedes all others, and refutes the notion that communities targeted by punitive policies are only acted upon.

This orientation has profound implications for research practice. By centralising people's experience as active (if constrained) decision- and meaning-makers, Dewey helps to illuminate the limits of expertise as it is currently defined and the need to change scholarly practices that fail to acknowledge these limits. Because knowledge springs from experience, those closest to particular problems have expertise for which there is no substitute. Acknowledgement of this fact requires more from researchers than simply analysing the experiences of people who might otherwise be ignored; it requires engaging with how people understand their own activity and its significance to them. It insists on the role of political participants as meaning-makers and, in so doing, lays the groundwork for unsettling power relations between researchers and the people involved in the worlds we write about.

## Learning

Dewey's emphasis on experience and inquiry, even his formulation of engaged pluralism, is tied to the role of learning in democracy. Learning in a Deweyan sense does not signify the acquisition of skills or information that would allow people to come closer to a predetermined political ideal (Dewey, 2008a, 9: 46). Instead it is self-directed; it is what happens as people work across difference to experiment with better ways of living together, reflect on the results, revise subsequent actions and thereby change their ideas.

Experiential learning of this kind often leads to significant changes in political attitude and action. At the beginning of their struggle, for instance, many PNSI members seemed to be abetting a neoliberal agenda through an unwillingness to engage in disruptive politics and a desire to fit themselves into a technocratic, market-based governance structure. The pastor urged members to be meek and grateful before the school board, Aubry berated the group for not developing a business plan for the school property and Ian advocated "playing ball" with officials. Many members worried about appearing unprofessional, angry or irrational, and about making others who disagreed with them uncomfortable. Not all interaction across difference led to more radical position-taking. Nevertheless, members' values and their interpretation of ethical political behaviour shifted over the course of their interactions with different others and through their efforts to reopen the school. The pastor became far more confrontational in his interactions with officials. For Ian and Marcus, sustained interaction with different others provided a check on beliefs formed out of each man's inevitably limited experience.

The group became less inclusive as a result of their experiences working with Aubry, who appeared to be focused on his own profit-oriented agenda.

A Deweyan lens enables researchers to see such changes and to view them as learning through experience over time – as democratic practice – rather than as a measure of their commitment to a particular set of principles. This reorientation leads scholars to develop analyses that acknowledge and examine dynamism in identity and values formation. Such formulations admittedly complicate us/them narratives in ways that might make it more difficult to identify and fight adversaries and this is a concern that Deweyans must address, but studying the process of learning provides opportunities for empirically investigating the mechanics of transformation.

By centralising learning, a Deweyan perspective highlights the fact that individual and collective change is possible. As the PNSI case demonstrates, people do not believe just one thing; they do not adhere to just one set of practices, forever. This insight may seem out of step with a world where views appear increasingly rigid and where the possibilities for transformation seem distant and small. But perhaps this narrowing of democratic hope makes a Deweyan perspective on political learning even more necessary and valuable.

Admittedly, a focus on learning requires scholars to examine practices that are in and of themselves unequal to the task of profound transformation. The shifts PNSI members experienced, for instance, might seem trivial and particular, especially against the immediate need for sweeping change. They do not constitute proof that engaged pluralism will lead to more effective and/or radical political action. But through an emphasis on experiential learning, Dewey helps us to think about how PNSI members' work might extend beyond the boundaries of the specific struggle described in this chapter. Regardless of outcome, people learn from their political experiences, potentially building capacity for more fruitful inquiry in the future. Learning in this Deweyan sense is both portable and generative – albeit unpredictable and sometimes slow. If radical democracy must be both ongoing and practised by people in the world, however, factors affecting participation and the experience of it become more important. The tension at the heart of transformational democratic change is that it must necessarily be enacted by imperfect people under sometimes crushingly imperfect circumstances. Learning is one mechanism by which people create change. It is a kind of change that does not happen once, in a revolutionary clearing of the decks but it enables further transformation, engendering more and different possibilities.

## Conclusion

The testimony recounted in this chapter indicates how PNSI members learned from their engagements across difference. However, they did not win. And that matters – to the people involved and in terms of broader democratic projects.

Why then should we pay attention to the messy work of learning from internal conflict, especially within failed political projects, especially when that failure may be due in part to practising engaged pluralism? Dewey's model suggests that we do so because this work – as messy and prone to failure as it is – constitutes democracy and, as such, we need to understand and support it through scholarship as well as political practice.

Democratisation requires broad-based participation. We will better understand how people become activated if we seek out the problematic situations that move people to become engaged in political activities, even (or especially) when those activities do not seem congruent with our own ideological positions and commitment. Struggles over public schooling are illustrative of this dynamic, making them an important context for research.

However, even in contexts where people are negotiating difference, political learning is not always easy for an outside observer to identify. As others have demonstrated (Arenas, 2015; Chatterton and Pickerill, 2010; Hankins, 2017; Martin, 2013, 85; Routledge and Derickson, 2015; Sziarto and Leitner, 2010), there is a need for scholarship that examines political work from the inside out. This orientation allows insight into how participants themselves understand their work, how these understandings shift in response to their experiences and how outcomes are translated into further action. Crucially, we need to acknowledge that political participants have a role to play as co-creators of meaning that evolves in real time and space.

Dewey provides us with a useful lens for paying attention to these understandings and to how people are changed through their political work. The PNSI case demonstrates that individuals hold multiple and sometimes conflicting values that shift in response to the demands of particular situations. As neoliberalisation and racialised discourses of political, cultural and spatial change shape how people understand struggle and space, they also create dissonance within individuals and among members of political organisations. Dewey's model of experiential inquiry provides a rationale for examining these conflicts as potential opportunities for learning across difference and for inquiring into the dynamics that hinder learning. It gives us a way to inquire into the structural impediments to engagement, providing new avenues for analysing how people work within the world that presently exists, in order to change it.

A Deweyan perspective offers no shortcuts and no guarantees of success, however. People are flawed and so are the places in which we act. We have a tendency not only to mark difference but to demonise it. We can be hateful and selfish and careless and hungry for power. We are systemically positioned in ways that make it more or less difficult to shape political, economic and social contexts. In other words, we operate in environments that often stymie the kinds of inquiry Dewey imagines.

In spite of all this, however, a Deweyan willingness to bet on people's capacity to engage across difference in useful ways is important because any other solution ultimately works against self-governance. Arrangements that purport to save people from themselves are anti-democratic in effect if not intent, if only because such arrangements do not provide the kinds of experiences that would allow people to decide for themselves how to handle the demands of living in difference and to respond in real time to a changing world. If we learn through experience, political work can be a means to achieve a more democratic society only if those means are themselves democratic, meaning, unless they involve experiences that in and of themselves help all of us to participate more fully in social inquiry and action – not at some future date when the world is different, or when people are different, but right now.

## References

Allmendinger, P. and Haughton, G. (2012) Post-political spatial planning in England: A crisis of consensus? *Transactions of the Institute of British Geographers*, 37, 1, 89–103.

Arenas, I. (2015) The mobile politics of emotions and social movement in Oaxaca, Mexico. *Antipode*, 47, 1121–40.

Barnett, C. (2014) What do cities have to do with democracy? *International Journal of Urban and Regional Research*, 38, 5, 1625–43.

Chatterton, P. and Pickerill, J. (2010) Everyday activism and transitions towards post-capitalist worlds. *Transactions of the Institute of British Geographers*, 35, 475–90.

Derickson, K.D. and MacKinnon, D. (2015) Toward an interim politics of resourcefulness for the Anthropocene. *Annals of the Association of American Geographers*, 105, 2, 304–12.

Dewey, J. (1988 [1927]) The public and its problems, in J.A. Boydston, ed., *The later works of John Dewey, volume 2: 1925–1927*. Carbondale, IL: Southern Illinois University Press, 235–372.

Dewey, J. (2008a) *The middle works, 1899–1924, volume 6: 1910–1911*. J.A. Boydston, ed. Carbondale, IL: SIU Press.

Dewey, J. (2008b) *The later works, 1925–1953, volume 7: 1932*. J.A. Boydston, ed. Carbondale, IL: SIU Press.

Featherstone, D. (2008) *Resistance, space and political identities: The making of counter-global networks* (Vol. 103). Hoboken, NJ: Wiley-Blackwell.

Gill, N., Johnstone, P. and Williams, A. (2012) Towards a geography of tolerance: Post-politics and political forms of toleration. *Political Geography*, 31, 8, 509–18.

Glaude, E.S. (2007) *In a shade of blue: Pragmatism and the politics of Black America*. Chicago, IL: University of Chicago Press.

Grattan, L. (2016) *Populism's power: Radical grassroots democracy in America*. Oxford: Oxford University Press.

Hankins, K. (2017) Creative democracy and the quiet politics of the everyday. *Urban Geography*, 38, 4, 502–6.

Huff, A. (2013) Reforming the city: Neoliberal school reform and democratic contestation in New Orleans. *The Canadian Geographer/Le Géographe Canadien*, 57, 3, 311–77.

Huff, A. (2015) Re-forming the post-political city?, in L. Miron, B. Beabout and J. Boselovic, eds, *Only in New Orleans: Public education in New Orleans ten years after Katrina*. Rotterdam: Sense Publishers, 87–102.

Koopman, C. (2017) Contesting injustice: Why pragmatist political thought needs DuBois, in S. Dielman, D. Rondel and C. Voparil, eds, *Pragmatism and justice*. New York, NY: Oxford University Press, 179–96.

Lake, R.W. (2014) Methods and moral inquiry. *Urban Geography*, 35, 5, 657–68.

Martin, D.G. (2013) Place frames: Analysing practice and production of place in contentious politics, in W. Nicholls, J. Beaumont and B. Miller, eds, *Spaces of contention: Spatialities and social movements*. Farnham: Ashgate, 85–102.

McKittrick, K. (2013) Plantation futures. *Small Axe*, *17*, 3(42), 1–15.

Mouffe, C. (2000) *The democratic paradox*. Brooklyn, NY: Verso.

Mouffe, C. (2005a) For an agonistic public sphere, in L. Tønder and L. Thomassen, eds, *Radical democracy: Politics between abundance and lack*. Manchester: Manchester University Press, 191–205.

Mouffe, C. (2005b) *On the political*. London: Routledge.

Mouffe, C. (2013) *Agonistics: Thinking the world politically*. Brooklyn: Verso.

Pappas, G.F. (1996) Open-mindedness and courage: Complementary virtues of pragmatism. *Transactions of the Charles S. Peirce Society*, 32, 2, 316–35.

Pappas, G.F. (2008) *John Dewey's ethics: Democracy as experience*. Bloomington, IN: Indiana University Press.

Purcell, M. (2008) *Recapturing democracy: Neoliberalization and the struggle for alternative urban futures*. New York, NY: Routledge.

Routledge, P. and Derickson, K.D. (2015) Situated solidarities and the practice of scholar-activism. *Environment and Planning D: Society and Space*, 33, 3, 391–407.

Swyngedouw, E. (2009) The antinomies of the postpolitical city: In search of a democratic politics of environmental production. *International Journal of Urban and Regional Research*, 33, 3, 601–20.

Swyngedouw, E. (2014) Where is the political? Insurgent mobilisations and the incipient "return of the political". *Space and Polity*, 18, 2, 122–36.

Sziarto, K.M. and Leitner, H. (2010) Immigrants riding for justice: Space-time and emotions in the construction of a counterpublic. *Political Geography*, 29, 7, 381–91.

Talisse, R. (2017) Pragmatism, democracy, and the need for a theory of justice, in S. Dieleman, D. Rondel and C. Voparil, eds, *Pragmatism and justice*. New York, NY: Oxford University Press, 281–94.

West, C. (2005) *Democracy matters: Winning the fight against imperialism*. New York, NY: Penguin.

# 9

# Reflections on an experiment in pragmatic social research and knowledge production

*Liam Harney and Jane Wills*

## Introduction

This chapter describes an experiment in pragmatic social research that took place in east London, UK, lasting for 14 months from January 2015. The experiment, called the 'E14 expedition' after the postcode covering the area of Poplar and the Isle of Dogs, involved recruiting volunteers who were interested in joining a new community initiative to foster local relationships and identify shared interests and issues around which to campaign. Conducted in two phases, the first focused on thinking about the local community and its history, and the second was designed to develop solutions to pressing concerns. In the event, two different groups of people were involved; twenty-four people took part in phase one and nineteen in phase two. However limited in scale and depth, the E14 expedition provided a mechanism to think about what pragmatic social science might look like. The research was focused on understanding the infrastructure needed to allow people to engage in community-based relationships created for research, knowledge production and action. It highlighted questions about the role to be played by academics and the implications for epistemological practice. While the expedition was designed to have significant benefits for those taking part, providing training, new opportunities and the chance to learn new skills, it also provided an opportunity for careful thought and learning about the processes, challenges and potential benefits involved in conducting pragmatic social research through the establishment of communities of inquiry.

In many ways this project built directly on the work of earlier generations of pragmatic social scientists such as Robert Park, Ernest Burgess, George Herbert Mead and Herbert Blumer, and their work is outlined in the opening chapter of this book. Being located in the discipline of human geography, how-ever, the E14 expedition also sought to follow in the footsteps of Bill Bunge who similarly tried to bridge the gap between the university and its local com-munity in Detroit during the late 1960s. In his Geographical Expedition, Bunge deployed university resources (staff, students and research expertise) to work with a broad-based community organisation and its leadership to expose the pressing needs of a local community (see Barnes, Chapter 5, this volume; Bunge, 1969, 1971; Heynen and Barnes, 2011). Building on the traditions already established in human geography in particular, and social science more generally, the E14 expedition sought to operationalise and test this existing 'model' of pragmatic social research. As outlined in the opening chapter of this book, this involves a number of key principles including: (1) starting from the provocations of the field and the community living there rather than basing research on the interests of the academy or the particular academic; (2) working with a particular community to identify the issues of pressing concern from their point of view and then co-producing possible solutions; (3) conducting research and creating new knowledge as part of this process; and (4) building the capacity of participants and strengthening the democratic voice and power of the community to act and resolve these concerns.

Pragmatists advocate that the processes of research and knowledge produc-tion are always embedded in a particular community (Rorty's (1991) 'ethnocen-trism') as part of ongoing efforts to solve collective concerns and find ways of living together. The pragmatic approach to research and knowledge production re-orientates the focus of academic inquiry away from the campus, international conference circuits and publishing houses towards the society in which the aca-demic is already embedded. It directs academics away from lone scholarship and a refinement of expertise towards active partnership and collective endeavour in the process of producing new ideas. Perhaps most troublingly for many, it also advocates that the work is forward-looking and creative (Gergen, 2015; and for a critique see Wolfe, 1989). Moving beyond the dominant focus of academic scholarship on realism and critique, pragmatists advocate an epistemology that is proudly political with a small p; in the spirit of post-representational thought, their work is focused on generating ideas that can reconfigure the world.

In this vein, the expedition was an attempt to facilitate the formation of publics comprising diverse groups of people focused around issues of common concern. The expedition was based on the pragmatic notion of multiple truths existing in the world, the validity of which are determined not by appeal to an *a priori* moral compass or external reality, but by the strength of belief and the action they enable. As such, the expedition sought to explore how the pluralism of the citizenry and its knowledge could be adequately respected in pragmatic social research.

The approach taken to this experiment was inspired by the model of broad-based community organising developed by Saul Alinsky, in which people from a range of backgrounds, but inhabiting a shared geographic area, put aside their differences in order to pursue the common good (Alinsky, 1971; Schutz and Miller, 2015). In this model, major differences of outlook and values are effectively 'parked' and left at the front door of the public realm in which areas of common concern and interest can be identified and acted upon (Wills, 2012).

In developing this work in E14, Harney intended his role as an academic to be a facilitator of relationship-building and dialogue among a community of inquirers. He did not choose the issues for inquiry, or the social identity of the inquirers before the study, but cast the net wide to gather a group of people from various communities and social worlds and allow shared issues to emerge through conversation among them. Place, rather than other forms of social identification, such as class, sexuality, gender, ethnicity or religion, was deployed as a relatively neutral lens through which to gather citizens and form a community of inquiry, ensuring that the academic had minimal control over which citizens' knowledges were articulated through the project and whose interests it potentially served. As Lake (2014) argues, all inquiries are 'moral inquiries', filtered through *a priori* ontological outlooks that shape the framing of issues, ideas and action. In the interests of pluralism, the expedition was designed to minimise the ability of the academic and academic interests to shape the moral nature of inquiry in E14.

The expedition was designed as an alternative to much participatory action research (PAR) that is conducted within the social sciences in which specific moral framings are employed by academics prior to processes of collective inquiry (see Harney et al., 2016 for a fuller discussion). The expedition was about testing whether, and if so, how, universities could work with a range of citizens to address public problems, instead of selecting and prioritising the experiences, knowledge and interests of certain groups of people who are given moral priority by mainstream social science (such as women, LGBT people and ethnic and racial minorities). The expedition was based on an understanding that, whilst valuable and well-meaning, approaches to engaged research and action with citizens that focus primarily on these social categorisations are limited in scope and potential, serving to ignore and exclude a large range of other people, experiences, ideas and beliefs. The first part of this chapter explores questions of pluralism in pragmatic social research. We then look at the challenges encountered in regard to the pragmatic focus on action.

## Building a diverse community of inquiry

Harney recruited participants to the project through an application process based in local schools, community centres, churches and mosques. The project was pitched as an opportunity to build relationships between residents in the area, to explore people's experience of living there and to identify pressing local concerns that would form the focus for research and action. Following the processes of application, twenty women and four men engaged in the project that ran from late January until the end of May 2015. These individuals ranged in age from sixteen to sixty-nine and included atheists alongside active Christians, Jews and Muslims, established residents from the white and Bengali-British populations, and immigrants from America, Brazil, Lithuania, Italy, Nigeria and South Africa (with eleven different nationalities included in total). The early training sessions focused on the power of story-telling to build relationships and rethink possible futures. Participants were asked to talk to their friends and neighbours and listen to their stories of living in E14, recording them for a book.[1] Rather than telling one story, the expedition explicitly sought to capture the diversity of local experience, holding a session for collective deliberation about the range of stories collected, trying to ensure that everyone was able to speak. The narratives were then compiled into a book with pictures of many of the sixty people interviewed, published as *E14 our stories*, and launched at a local school on 30 May 2015 (Agugu et al., 2015).

Participants in the expedition were subsequently interviewed to explore their experiences of the project and to enable Harney to reflect on the way that this phase of the expedition impacted on local relationships and community-building and the wider lessons for pragmatic research. These interviews raised important issues and questions about pluralism, and although most participants reported that they valued having the space to talk about their experiences of diversity. one respondent stood out as she felt unable to articulate her concerns and we consider her experiences further below.

In the group discussions, participants seemed able to express their feelings about living in an area marked by the co-presence of many different kinds of people. As an example, one Jewish participant reported feeling worried about putting a Mezuzah on her door, saying "I want to hide from people, I don't want my neighbours to know." While she welcomed the chance to talk to Muslim participants involved in the expedition, saying "I want this conversation to continue", she had concerns as a Jew living in a largely Muslim area. Similarly, two members of the group shared that they had suffered for being gay, one from homophobic verbal abuse and another by family rejection, and the group expressed their support for these individuals, albeit within a rather unrealistic space where those involved were largely willing to leave their prejudices at the door in order to take part.

Indeed, it was the individual interviews with participants that revealed the potentially surface-level nature of these group conversations, as the experience of Barbara highlights. In her interview she told Harney that she felt the project was dominated by a "left-wing point of view" that she felt was at odds with her own politics, which she described as "Conservative with a capital C".

Barbara felt that the stories and conversations shared by the group were based on assumptions that she did not share or agree with. In particular, the assumption that the settlement of the Bangladeshi population in E14 has been positive for the area was something she felt unable to argue against. Given the balance of opinion in the group she reported that "there were many times when I just kept my mouth shut", saying: "I was totally outnumbered. There wouldn't have been a person who agreed with me. Why would I put myself in that position? It's like putting the Christians into the Coliseum with the lions, you know? I was not going to be a Christian, OK?"

Barbara appeared to be engaging fully in the project; she took part in the conversations and shaped the debate about the story of E14, but she clearly felt silenced by the group dynamic. Her experience raises difficult questions about how to respect the principle of pluralism in pragmatic research, particularly when it takes place against the backdrop of profound divisions in the wider community and society at large.

It could be argued that this situation could be remedied by effective facilitation skills on the part of the academic, working to ensure that all voices are given an equal hearing in the conversation (Cahill, 2007). Yet we feel that this problem reflected wider forces than were at play within the group and the project. Barbara felt outnumbered in the group; she felt herself to be in a minority in regard to her conservative views in a room that she perceived to have 'left-wing' leanings. Arguably, Barbara's predicament was reflective of a situation in wider society in the UK, in which conservative views and values have been culturally and politically marginalised in favour of more progressive worldviews.

David Goodhart (2017) provides a convincing account of this, analysing two broad 'value clusters' that now exist within UK society. He suggests that the citizenry can be split, broadly, into those who possess an 'anywhere' worldview and those who can be classified as 'somewheres'. The former value independence, mobility, multiculturalism and cosmopolitanism, whilst the latter place higher value on stability, tradition and familiarity. Goodhart argues that 'anywheres', whilst fewer in number than 'somewheres' (for Goodhart, the ratio is about 30:70), disproportionately make up the ranks of the political and cultural elite in the UK. This is due to their possession of university degrees and their entrance to middle-class networks that give them access to jobs in the professions, politics, the media and government. For this reason, those with 'anywhere' worldviews are culturally and politically dominant, asserting their worldview and values over 'somewheres'.

Goodhart's controversial analysis of UK society has highlighted the crucial role that universities play in maintaining this cultural split by nurturing an anywhere worldview among graduates through the lived experience of mobility and change associated with studying at a residential university. He argues that being uprooted from social networks at home and being surrounded by new people from across the country and wider world inculcates a more 'progressive' worldview. In contrast, 'somewheres', less likely to have been to university, tend to have stayed in close proximity to the people and places they grew up around, promoting more conservative outlooks. This is also reinforced by the ideas that students are exposed to in their classes. Within the social sciences, these ideas and values tend to be mainly those associated with a left-wing or 'progressive' worldview, stemming from the radical politics and ideas that became dominant in the academy from the 1960s onwards (Williams, 2016).

Given that university graduates disproportionately make up the ranks of political and cultural professions, this has implications for democracy, with the 'anywhere' worldview having disproportionate influence over public decision-making processes, public discourse and political power. As such, universities play a major role in reproducing the gap between large numbers of ordinary citizens and a smaller political elite.

For some conservative thinkers the dominance of 'anywhere' or progressive worldviews in universities, politics and the media has created a climate in which large numbers of ordinary citizens feel un-represented or ignored by mainstream politics and culture (Lasch, 1991; Slater, 2016; Williams, 2016). This feeling of having been ignored over the past few decades partly explains the vote for Brexit in the United Kingdom and the election of Donald Trump in America. These votes shocked the political and cultural establishment as they asserted 'somewhere' or conservative values in the interests of citizens who felt they had lost out because of the policies of 'anywhere' elites (Chwalisz, 2015; Goodhart, 2017; Inglehart and Norris, 2016).

Going back to the expedition, Barbara's experience reflected her perception of the dominance of more progressive values in the group. Whether or not the other participants held such views was unclear, but Barbara's sense of being a minority for holding more conservative views was probably symptomatic of the cultural dominance of more 'progressive' values in society at large. In the local context, east London's party politics has also been shaped by a contest between 'anywhere' and 'somewhere' worldviews that began in the late 1970s. The East End has been a Labour party stronghold for decades with the party having its roots in the trade unionism of the docks at the turn of the twentieth century. However, Dench et al. (2006) explain how, in the late 1970s, the party became divided between activists and members who espoused and sought to advance more conservative values, and those with more progressive ideas. This divide was centred on matters of social housing allocation at a time of large-scale immigration of Bangladeshi people to the area. The conservatives were pushing for council tenancies to be reserved for the 'sons and daughters' of the established population, whilst the progressives sided with the growing Bangladeshi community and their perceived right to housing as homeless, over-crowded, migrant families.

This struggle played out over years, provoking a period of instability in local politics, including the election of a Liberal Democrat council for the first time and the rise in popularity of the British National Party, both of which attempted to represent the interests of the white working class against an increasingly influential Bangladeshi population (Dench et al., 2006; Foster,

2011; Pile, 1995; Torode, 1994). However, with support from new housing legislation, the progressives won out and homeless migrant families were given statutory rights to council housing above the children of existing tenants. From the 1990s onwards, a progressive worldview and set of values has shaped the local Labour party in Tower Hamlets, facilitated by a (somewhat tumultuous) alliance between left-wing, progressive activists and the highly organised Bangladeshi community (Dench et al., 2006).

Given this history, Barbara deemed her conservativism to be a minority, or taboo, stance among the other participants, and indeed, the wider community too. Regardless of whether one shares Barbara's view, this reflects a democratic culture in which certain people do not feel comfortable articulating their opinions and ideas as they clash with the perceived mainstream view. And this is not just a case of an extreme minority view; the E14 area is home to many people who, like Barbara, feel that change in their community associated with large-scale migration of people from different cultures has been negative for them. From a pragmatist perspective, the dominant culture within politics and academia shows little respect for the truths of people like Barbara and this is something that needs to be addressed.

Although it was conceived as a way of overcoming the dangers of hard-and-fast ideologically driven beliefs in the wake of the violence of the American Civil War (Menand, 2011), pragmatism has often been accused of silencing difference and power relations in the quest for the middle ground (see Saegert, Chapter 6, this volume). However, this argument is usually made in relation to the experiences and views of oppressed groups of people with whom progressives usually align themselves (Brandom, 2009; Fraser, 1989, 1990) rather than those with conservative views. Moreover, despite such differences, pragmatism would also urge a 'forward-looking' response. In a fast-changing community of diverse interests like east London, text-book pragmatists might argue that there is little practical benefit in revisiting battles that have been and gone rather than looking ahead. As a tradition that urges us to focus on the consequences rather than the antecedents of our ideas (Brandom, 2009), pragmatist thought would advocate finding areas of common ground around which to work despite deep-felt difference. In this regard, the focus of the E14 expedition, particularly of phase two, was to move on to find areas of shared interest around which participants could develop new ideas about working together. The whole point of the project was to find new ways of going forward together.

However, as Barbara's case shows, certain differences are too significant to be pushed to the side (and she chose not to participate in phase two of the expedition). Her conservative views were shaped by her experiences of living in east London during a period of widespread social change and must not be dismissed as wrong or misguided. Given the sharp – and widening – divisions in national political culture, and the lack of acceptance of conservative views in mainstream political discourse, it proved very difficult to do justice to the pluralism of opinion via pragmatic research. Moreover, these divisions have arisen in part because there is little willingness to listen to and respect the 'somewhere' worldview (Slater, 2016; Williams, 2016; and for an interesting prescient pragmatic argument about similar trends in the USA see Rorty, 1998). Arguably, a major contributor to this culture of division in modern democracies is the way that knowledge has been generated, taught and consumed within UK universities, especially in the social sciences. For too long, social science has favoured the reproduction and propagation of a narrow range of 'progressive' ideas, values and outlooks among its students, through the academic orthodoxy of critical theory, and the derision of ideas and perspectives that do not fit this orthodoxy (Williams, 2016). This has shaped a rising generation of elite actors who have little tolerance for alternative perspectives. We need only reflect on the treatment of those citizens who voted for Brexit and Donald Trump to see this intolerance in action; these citizens were branded as 'racist' or 'stupid' almost immediately.

This raises serious questions about what the social sciences can do to change this culture and foster more democratic attitudes of mutual respect, reasoned debate and attempts at understanding different perspectives (see Geiselhart's chapter 7 and Huff's chapter 8, this volume). The approach taken by the expedition of seeking to park differences and find common ground did not work in this case. Certain differences are too significant to ignore or put aside and attempts at finding the common good may merely serve to avoid difficult conversations and encounters, and ultimately this reflects the way in which dominant values and ideas are imposed over minority ones in the creation of public narratives and debate (Cooke and Kothari, 2001; Young, 1990, 1996, 1997).

Progressive and conservative worldviews have always co-existed and each has had great effect in shaping the world (Haidt, 2012); the pragmatist social scientist should feel compelled to take them both seriously. However, there is a lack of coverage and fair portrayal of conservative views and the citizens that possess them in the social sciences. For the good of democracy, we need to remedy this. Academics need to be encouraged to respect and value these beliefs and attempt to understand the experiences that give rise to them. This means listening to and attempting to understand views that might make academics feel uncomfortable. It also challenges social scientists to help articulate the views of those with whom they disagree, as a democratic good in itself. This might mean conducting interviews with the 'forgotten' citizens of the UK and USA, not as a move to deconstruct and re-interpret their sentiments from a progressive perspective, but as a way of giving them voice within the academy and wider public domain. It also means transforming universities into places where a range of conflicting, divergent and competing worldviews, beliefs and values can gain a fair hearing, rather than the knee-jerk dismissal or deconstruction that usually occurs (Slater, 2016). The pragmatic notion of multiple truths could underlie such a social science, as outlined in the rest of this volume.

## The value of community for pragmatic social science and the limits of the activist imperative

Advocates of pragmatism re-envisage university social science as a vehicle for the propagation of democracy, active citizenship and good public policy (Bohman, 2002; Boyte, 2003). Given that social scientists are already in the business of creating ideas that have powerful effects in the world (Gibson-Graham, 2008; Law, 2004), the pragmatist approach urges that these ideas are directed to ends that are rooted in the public interest of a particular community (Lake, 2017a, 2017b). Doing this well requires maximum reach in the community, embracing diversity, listening to the breadth of opinion and devising ideas that can bring that community together around a shared future (Bernstein, 2010; Putnam, 1995; Rorty, 1989; Westbrook, 1989, 1991).

The expedition sought to do this in E14, yet, as seen above, we encountered significant challenges in relation to incorporating the full range of opinion. We also faced challenges in relation to the ability of the community to engage in any type of public action. Interviews with participants exposed the extent to which many people joined the expedition simply because they wanted to build relationships with other people in their locality. As one respondent put it: "I got involved in the E14 project because I thought it was a brilliant project, a great way to connect with people and get to know people as well." A number of longer-established residents argued that people were more connected in the past and the rapid pace of local change had eroded neighbourhood relations, prompting them to get involved and do something about it. Moreover, participants reported using the story-telling project as a cover to approach their neighbours in a way that had not been possible before. Participants reported feeling emboldened to approach people they saw at school, church and other places as a result of the project and, given their geographical proximity, it then became easier to cement these relationships over time through regular encounters in the locality.

At its most basic, the E14 expedition facilitated new relationships between the participants and their neighbours, and between participants within the group. The project illustrated the extent to which place can provide the ground for the formation of relationships between local residents, even when there is rapid turnover, diversity and tension in the population (Paasi, 2003). While the project recognised that the people of E14 exemplified Massey's (2005) notion of the 'thrown-togetherness' of people in place (see also Amin, 2004), it also demonstrated the extent to which sharing space can facilitate the creation of a new shared story, however diverse the origins of each person involved (Wills, 2013).

However, in phase two of the expedition, when action teams were formed around specific issues, the lack of social connections between participants and residents more widely became apparent as a key factor preventing successful coordinated action. One action team's experience in particular serves to highlight this. A team was formed to address the issue of a group of young men hanging around a housing estate in Poplar, intimidating neighbours and engaging in anti-social behaviour such as drug taking and urinating in public stairwells.

This issue was extremely localised and specific to residents of one particular block of flats on the estate. Sabu, who lived there and took part in the expedition, tried to rally his neighbours to do something about this. He was starting from a very difficult position as he lacked deep relationships with his neighbours from which to initiate collective action to challenge the problem. His involvement in the expedition gave Sabu the confidence to knock on his neighbours' doors to start conversations about the problem and many admitted it was an issue they cared about, but he struggled to get further than this, with people fearing the risks of taking action and choosing not to get involved for the safety of their own family. Sabu ultimately failed to generate a positive response from his neighbours and the problem continued.

This example helps to illustrate the reluctance of most people to take collective action to address issues that affect them and the effort that would be needed to achieve any change. It highlights the way that most people tend to *cope* with things that are not going well in their lives. They try to get on with things and while each household in Sabu's block experienced the anti-social behaviour, they did not think of it as a problem that could be tackled by them. The problem remained painful but private, and despite his limited efforts, Sabu was not in a position to change this. The lack of relationships between Sabu and his neighbours served to foreclose the possibility of coordinated action around the issue and this aspect of the expedition highlighted the importance of having strong social relationships to facilitate publics (Dewey, 1927; Putnam, 2000).

This is an issue for pragmatic social research because without strong relational foundations and a public culture among citizens, collective inquiry and problem-solving are much less likely to happen (Barnett, 2008; Bridge and Watson, 2011). To illustrate this, Calhoun (1983) uses the example of the UK miners' strike in the mid 1980s as an example of public-formation that reflected the strong communal ties, feelings of familiarity and shared interests of the mining communities, which had been fostered over generations. Existing social relationships gave people the strength to act in a situation of high risk and uncertainty, providing a strong common identity and sense of solidarity that could then travel to shape wider debate. A similar example of this was the development of trade unionism among the dock workers in east London during the early 1900s and how this fed into the local Labour movement in which the community supported their local politicians, who they perceived to act in their interests (Booth, 2009; Butler and Hamnett, 2011).

There were no guarantees for this type of public action, but the existence of a well-connected place-based community acted as a fertile ground from which organisers and activists could mobilise people around a vision of a different future. In the 'old' East End of London people were connected through close neighbourly bonds, with extended families inhabiting the same geographical area, facilitating connections and a sense of familiarity among neighbours. People were also united by a shared Christian faith and its associated traditions and rituals. Moreover, key social spaces such as pubs provided the settings for repeated, mundane social interactions, weaving together the lives of local people (Gavron et al., 2006; Koch and Latham, 2013; Studdert, 2016; Young and Wilmott, 1957).

Today the area is very different, having undergone major demographic change since around the 1970s, with waves of in- and out-migration fragmenting the community. The docks declined and thousands of people lost their jobs, devastating the local economy. Families that had lived in the area for generations left for better opportunities elsewhere, mainly moving to Essex and Kent. Newcomers arrived not just from South Asia, but Africa, the Caribbean and Eastern Europe, whilst new middle-class migrants arrived from Western Europe, the USA and other parts of the UK to work in Canary Wharf. E14 is now a fragmented, super-diverse place, home to various, sometimes overlapping, but often segregated communities. Social ties between neighbours are much weaker than in the past, owing to increased differences in identity, experience, rootedness and interests among individuals (Butler and Hamnett, 2011; Colenutt, 1991; Foster, 1999; Vertovec, 2007).

Within this context, the Expedition's attempts to facilitate collective action around shared issues appear somewhat naive. The social foundations needed for public formation were too weak, and all three action teams failed to achieve a clear 'win' through their efforts. Up against the power of professionals, bureaucrats and businesses, these nascent teams of citizens from different social worlds were always fighting an uphill battle. Moreover, this experience raises important questions about the 'activist impulse' that underpins much pragmatic thought and its application in social science.

In part, the focus on collective action reflects the particular roots of pragmatic ideas as they developed during the late nineteenth and early twentieth century, encompassing the traditions of liberalism and utilitarianism, Protestantism and progressivism. Lamenting the space vacated by the once-powerful social gospel, the early pragmatists expressed a faith that everyday democracy would provide the grounds and mechanisms through which to ferment civic virtue and a new moral order (Dewey, 1920 [1957]; Putnam, 1995; West, 1989; Westbrook, 1991). As Dewey (1920 [1957], xxxiv) wrote when reflecting on his mission to reconstruct philosophy in the wake of growing secularisation, he was responding to the "challenge to develop a theory of morals that will give the world positive intellectual direction … in developing the practical – that is, actually effective – morals which will utilize the resources now at our disposal to bring into the activities and interests of human life, order and security".

In his vision, Dewey saw inquiry as providing a mechanism for the creation of ideas about society that paralleled the self-correcting model of science developed in the wake of Darwin's arguments about adaptation. Rather than providing metaphysical certainties, philosophy was to be reconstructed to help people adapt to their changing environment. To be human was to be provoked to inquiry and this creative intelligence was about learning through doing, having new experiences and developing the resources to change the world.

There is, of course, something profoundly un-pragmatic about the development of a pragmatic approach to social research that is pre-committed to this vision of creative intelligence and the importance of inquiry. Despite loud proclamations of anti-foundationalism, pragmatists sometimes appear to be advocating a foundational approach to doing social research (Cavell, 1989; Diggins, 1998; Fish, 1989; Wolfe, 1989). As we have seen, there is a commitment to the community of inquiry, to the self-mobilising activist who is able and willing to join these communities, and to the forward-looking spirit that might motivate such engagement.

Yet, without adequate social infrastructure and relational foundations, collective action at a scale to secure meaningful change is near impossible to achieve. Moreover, reflecting on the case of E14, it is our argument that it is this imperative for action, change and progress that is (in part at least) to blame for the breakdown of community in the area. Post-war slum clearance programmes of the British Labour government fragmented tight-knit, working-class communities; open-border migration policies have enabled high flows of in-migration of people from starkly different cultures and places to the area, and free market economic and housing policies contribute to demographic change and population churn, and promise further community break-up and change over time. Whilst pockets of community and local connection do still exist, E14 today is characterised by a sense of transition, instability and constant change. For pragmatists, this should pose serious questions about the future of democratic life for the areas' citizens.

In this regard, the E14 expedition had much in common with other academic-led projects that deploy participatory research methods to co-produce ideas for change with insufficient attention to securing the power needed to generate change (Harney et al., 2016; Pain and Francis, 2003). Our research has led us to become sympathetic to less activist-oriented versions of pragmatism as well as conservative ideas that reject any necessary association with problem-solving and progress (Cahoone, 2002; Lasch, 1991). Clearly, there are dangers in the activist impulse, and much to be celebrated about being left alone to get on with living and loving rather than being told what to do (Oakeshott, 1962; Studdert and Walkerdine, 2016). Our experience with the E14 Expedition chimes well with these views and we would argue that there is real value in re-focusing pragmatic research less as a tool to form publics for action, and more to promote and develop the conditions that allow for democratic engagement and renewal. This would demand attention to the diversity of experience and opinion, and of listening to and disseminating a diversity of views, without any imperative to action. Should the process identify ways in which people want to act around their concerns that would be welcome but not imperative to pragmatic success.

Indeed, in Rorty's (1991) re-invention of pragmatism, the focus was shifted to the creation of new public narrative rather than seeking to root this narrative in the labours of a community of inquiry. Rorty developed a bifurcated understanding of the private and public in which "the demands of self-creation and of human solidarity [are] ... equally valid, yet forever incommensurable" (Rorty, 1991, xv). Private irony was ill-suited to the public good but, for him, human solidarity was "to be achieved not by inquiry but by imagination, [by] the imaginative ability to see people as fellow sufferers" (Rorty, 1991, xvi). As he put it: "If one takes the core of pragmatism to be its attempt to replace the notion of true beliefs as representations of 'the nature of things' and instead to think of them as successful rules for action, then it becomes easy to recommend an experimental, fallibilist attitude, but hard to isolate a 'method' that will embody this attitude" (Rorty, 1991, 65–6).

This spirit informed Rorty's interventions into American politics in which he advanced the process of 're-description' or creating 'new vocabulary', in order to foster solidarity for the public good (see Barnes, Chapter 5, this volume). This vision of pragmatic scholarship no longer relied on Dewey's problem-solving publics or communities of inquiry but rather advocated deploying an emotionally charged narrative to create a better world (Rorty, 1991, 1998). While some have tried to defend a form of democratic realism or naturalism as the basis from which new ideas can emerge (Bernstein, 1983, 2010; Kloppenberg, 1989; Putnam, 1992, 1995; Westbrook, 1989), Rorty and others prosecuted a linguistic pragmatism that is realised in community but not produced by any particular community of inquirers (Brandom, 2009; Malachowski, 2010). This approach reflects Dewey's commitment to liberal democracy, and is more akin to his own political activism in a wide range of organisations and journalistic writings (Barnes, 2008; Westbrook, 1991), without adopting his approach to inquiry.

As a result of our experience, we would argue for a two-pronged approach in pragmatist social research. One prong would follow Rorty's lead in helping to create narratives that value the very things that make democracy possible: relationships, community, tolerance and respect for alternative views. Such narratives might appear to be more conservative than the approaches currently favoured and deployed within the social sciences, and whilst we are not calling for the clocks to be turned back to the 'good old days' of tight-knit communities of tradition, there is much to learn and value from communities, past and present, where social infrastructure helps enable everyday civic engagement and lays the foundations for potential collective action. As a counter to the dominant 'anywhere' narrative that shapes Western democracies, in which progress, free movement of people, progressive ideology and political dogma are championed, a more conservative approach that sought to protect community, familiarity and stability might heal some wounds and better protect our democratic inheritance.

Coupled with this approach is the second prong: the need for more engagement with citizens in the creation and articulation of ideas, beliefs and values, some of which might make us uncomfortable, to enrich public discourse and help develop public narratives that are based upon and can resonate with the lives of ordinary people. This type of social science might place less emphasis on *immediate* problem-solving action as is often evoked in arguments for community-based inquiry or participatory research, but rather situate the university and its scholars as a conduit for sharing situated knowledge and experience as part of the democratic process (indeed, we have made similar arguments in relation to the role of growing numbers of community–university partnerships that can help to facilitate this, see Harney and Wills, 2017).

Committing to this kind of social science would predict change happening over generations, rather than the months or years we might more usually expect. Embedding research and scholarship in relationships, and in relation to the particular field in which social scientists find themselves, requires a long-term perspective and will depend upon relationships. However, the potential prizes are much bigger than those attached to current forms of research, and it would require challenging certain established orthodoxies in knowledge generation and social action. This approach could help to achieve some of the promises of pragmatism old and new.

## Note

1   Participants took part in four workshops over a period of three months in which they engaged in a series of discussions among themselves around the 'story of E14'. Between workshops, participants were asked to think about and write their own personal story, and talk to at least five people from the E14 area to find other stories that they were willing to share. Stories were chosen that highlighted positive instances of local people acting to make a difference, no matter how 'big' or 'small'. The stories were written by participants and sent back to the people who shared them to validate them before being compiled in the book.

## References

Agugu, D., Al-Aza, Z., Binboga, Z. et al. https://issuu.com/e14stories/docs/e14_our_stories_sp_160515 (accessed 30 January 2020).

Alinsky, S. (1971) *Rules for radicals: A pragmatic primer for realistic radicals.* New York, NY: Vintage Books.

Amin, A. (2004) Regions unbound: Towards a new politics of place. *Geografiska Annaler B*, 86. 1, 33–44.

Barnes, T. (2008) American pragmatism: Towards a geographical introduction. *Geoforum*, 39, 1542–54.

Barnett, C. (2008) Convening publics: The parasitical spaces of public action, in K. Cox, M. Low and J. Robinson, eds, *The SAGE handbook of political geography.* London: SAGE, 403–17.

Bernstein, R. (1983) *Beyond objectivity and relativism: Science, hermeneutics and praxis.* Philadelphia, PA: University of Pennsylvania Press.

Bernstein, R. (2010) *The pragmatic turn*. Cambridge: Polity Press.

Bohman, J. (2002) How to make a social science practical: Pragmatism, critical social science and multi-perspectival theory. *Millennium: Journal of International Studies*, 31, 3, 499–524.

Booth, J. (2009) *Guilty and proud of it: Poplar's rebel councillors and guardians 1919–25*. Pontypool: Merlin Press.

Boyte, H.C. (2003) A different kind of politics: John Dewey and the meaning of citizenship in the 21st century. *The Good Society*, 12, 2, 1–15.

Brandom, R. (2009) When pragmatism paints its blue on grey: Irony and the pragmatist enlightenment, in C. Kautzer and E.A. Mendieta, eds, *Pragmatism, nation, race*. Bloomington, IN: Indiana University Press, 31–45.

Bridge, G. and Watson, S. (2011) Reflections on publics and cultures, in G. Bridge and S. Watson, eds, *The new Blackwell companion to the city*. Oxford: Wiley Blackwell, 379–89.

Bunge, W. (1969) The first year of the Detroit Geographical Expedition: A personal report, in D. Peet, ed., *Radical geography: Alternative viewpoints on contemporary social issues*. London: Methuen and Co Ltd, 31–59.

Bunge, W. (1971) *Fitzgerald: Geography of a revolution*. Cambridge, MA: Schenkman Publishing Co.

Butler, T. and Hamnett, C. (2011) *Ethnicity, class and aspiration: Understanding London's new East End*. Bristol: Policy Press.

Cahill, C. (2007) The personal is political: Developing new subjectivities through participatory action research. *Gender, Place and Culture*, 14, 3, 267–92.

Cahoone, L.E. (2002) *Civil society: The conservative meaning of liberal politics*. Oxford: Blackwell.

Calhoun, C. (1983) The radicalism of tradition: Community strength or venerable disguise and borrowed language? *American Journal of Sociology*, 88, 5, 886–914.

Cavell, S. (1998) What's the use of calling Emerson a pragmatist?, in M. Dickstein, ed., *The revival of pragmatism: New essays on social thought, law and culture*. Durham, NC: Duke University Press, 72–80.

Chwalisz, C. (2015) *The populist signal: Why politics and democracy need to change*. London: Rowman and Littlefield International Ltd.

Colenutt, B. (1991) London Docklands Development Corporation – has the community benefitted?, in M. Keith and A. Rogers, eds, *Hollow promises: Rhetoric and reality in the inner city*. London: Mansell, 31–41.

Cooke, B. and Kothari, U. (2001) The case for participation as tyranny, in B. Cooke and U. Kothari, eds, *Participation: The new tyranny?* London: Zed Books, 1–15.

Dench, G., Gavron, K. and Young, M. (2006) *The new East End: Kinship, race and conflict*. London: Profile Books.

Dewey, J. (1920 [1957]) *Reconstruction in philosophy*. Boston, MA: Beacon Press.

Dewey, J. (1927 [1954]) *The public and its problems*. Athens, OH: Swallow Press and Ohio University Press.

Diggins, J.P. (1998) Pragmatism and its limits, in M. Dickstein, ed., *The revival of pragmatism: New essays on social thought, law and culture*. Durham, NC: Duke University Press, 207–31.

Fish, S. (1989) Afterword, truth and toilets: Pragmatism and the practices of life, in M. Dickstein, ed., *The revival of pragmatism: New essays on social thought, law and culture*. Durham, NC: Duke University Press, 418–33.

Foster, J. (1999) *Docklands: Cultures in conflict, worlds in collision*. London: UCL Press.

Fraser, N. (1989) Another pragmatism: Alain Locke, critical 'race' theory, and politics of culture, in M. Dickstein, ed., *The revival of pragmatism: New essays on social thought, law and culture*. Durham, NC: Duke University Press, 157–75.

Fraser, N. (1990) Rethinking the public sphere: A contribution to the critique of actually existing democracy. *Social Text*, 25/26, 56–80.

Gavron, K., Dench, G. and Young, M. (2006) *The new East End: Kinship, race and conflict*. London: Profile.

Gergen, K. (2015) From mirroring to world-making: Research as future forming. *Journal for the Theory of Social Behaviour*, 45, 3, 287–310.

Gibson-Graham, J.K. (2008) Diverse economies: performative practices for 'other worlds'. *Progress in Human Geography*, 32, 5, 613–32.

Goodhart. D. (2017) *The road to somewhere: The populist revolt and the future of politics*. London: Hurst and Company.

Haidt, J. (2012) *The righteous mind: Why good people are divided by politics and religion*. London: Penguin.

Harney, L., McCurry, J. Scott, J. and Wills, J. (2016) Developing 'process pragmatism' to underpin engaged research in Human Geography. *Progress in Human Geography*, 40, 3, 316–33.

Harney, L. and Wills, J. (2017) *Infrastructures for impact: Community-university partnerships in the USA and UK*. Queen Mary, University of London: Mile End Institute. www.qmul.ac.uk/mei/news-and-opinion/archive/items/report-highlights-how-universities-can-enrich-their-neighbourhoods.html (accessed 30 January 2020).

Heynen, N. and Barnes, T. (2011) Foreword to the 2011 edition: Fitzgerald then and now, in W. Bunge, ed., *Fitzgerald: Geography of a revolution*, 2nd edn. Athens, GA: University of Georgia Press, vii–xv.

Inglehart, R. and Norris, P. (2016) Trump, Brexit, and the rise of populism: Economic have-nots and cultural backlash, *Harvard Kennedy School Faculty Research Working Paper Series*. https://papers.ssrn.com/sol3/papers.cfm?abstract_id=2818659 (accessed 30 January 2020).

Kloppenberg, J.T. (1989) Pragmatism: An old name for some new ways of thinking?, in M. Dickstein, ed., *The revival of pragmatism: New essays on social thought, law and culture*. Durham, NC: Duke University Press, 83–127.

Koch, R. and Latham, A. (2013) On the hard work of domesticating a public space. *Urban Studies*, 50, 1, 6–21.

Lake, R.W. (2014) Methods and moral inquiry. *Urban Geography*, 35, 5, 657–68.

Lake, R.W. (2017a) Urban Geography Plenary Lecture: On poetry, pragmatism, and the urban possibility of creative democracy. *Urban Geography*, 38, 4, 479–94.

Lake, R.W. (2017b) For creative democracy. *Urban Geography*, 38, 4, 507–11.

Lasch, C. (1991) *The true and only heaven: Progress and its critics*. New York, NY: W.W. Norton and Co.

Lasch, C. (1994) *The revolt of the elites: And the betrayal of democracy*. New York, NY: W.W. Norton and Co.

Law, J. (2004) *After method: Mess in social science research*. London: Routledge.

Malachowski, A. (2010) *The new pragmatism*. Durham: Acumen.

Massey, D. (2005) *For space*. London: SAGE.

Menand, L. (2011) *The metaphysical club: A story of ideas in America*. New York, NY: Flamingo.

Oakeshott, M. (1962) *Rationalism in politics and other essays*. London: Methuen and Co Ltd.

Paasi, A. (2003) Region and place: Regional identity in question. *Progress in Human Geography*, 27, 4, 475–85.

Pain, R. and Francis, P. (2003) Reflections on participatory research. *Area*, 35, 1, 46–54.

Pile, S. (1995) "What we are asking for is decent human life": SPLASH, neighbourhood demands and citizenship in London's Docklands. *Political Geography*, 14, 2, 199–208.

Putnam, H. (1992) *Realism with a human face.* Cambridge, MA: Harvard University Press.

Putnam, H. (1995) *Renewing philosophy.* Cambridge, MA: Harvard University Press.

Putnam, R.D. (2000) *Bowling alone: The collapse and revival of American community.* New York: Simon and Schuster.

Rorty, R. (1989) *Contingency, irony, solidarity.* Cambridge: Cambridge University Press.

Rorty, R. (1991a) *Objectivity, relativism, and truth: Philosophical papers, Volume 1.* Cambridge: Cambridge University Press.

Rorty, R. (1991b) The professor and the prophet, The American evasion of philosophy: A genealogy of pragmatism by Cornel West: A review. *Transition,* 52, 70–8.

Rorty, R. (1998) *Achieving our country: Leftist thought in the twentieth-century.* Cambridge, MA: Harvard University Press.

Schutz, A. and Miller, M. (2015) (eds) *People power: The community organising tradition of Saul Alinsky.* Nashville, TN: Vanderbilt University Press.

Slater, T. (ed.) (2016) *Unsafe space: The crisis of free speech on campus.* London: Palgrave Macmillan.

Studdert, D. (2016) Sociality and a proposed analytic for investigating communal being-ness. *The Sociological Review,* 64, 4, 622–38.

Studdert, D. and Walkerdine, V. (2016) *Rethinking community research: Inter-relationality, communal being and commonality.* London: Palgrave Macmillan.

Torode, J. (1994) Dogfight in the Docklands: John Torode joins the 'islanders' of the British National Party as they campaign to take over a traditional Labour stronghold. *Independent,* 29 March. www.independent.co.uk/voices/dogfight-in-the-docklands-john-torode-joins-the-islanders-of-the-british-national-party-as-they-1432370.html (accessed 22 May 2017).

Vertovec, S. (2007) Super-diversity and its implications. *Ethnic and Racial Studies,* 30, 6, 1024–54.

West, C. (1989) *The American evasion of philosophy: A genealogy of pragmatism.* Basingstoke: Macmillan.

Westbrook, R. (1991) *John Dewey and American democracy.* Ithaca, NY: Cornell University Press.

Westbrook, R. (1989) Pragmatism and democracy: Reconstructing the logic of John Dewey's faith, in M. Dickstein, ed., *The revival of pragmatism: New essays on social thought, law and culture.* Durham, NC: Duke University Press, 128–40.

Williams, J. (2016) *Academic freedom in an age of conformity.* Basingstoke: Palgrave Macmillan.

Wills, J. (2012) The geography of community and political organisation in London today. *Political Geography,* 33, 2, 114–26.

Wills, J. (2013) Place and politics, in D. Featherstone and J. Painter, eds, *Spatial politics: Essays for Doreen Massey.* Oxford: Wiley-Blackwell, 135–45.

Wolfe, A. (1989) The missing pragmatic revival in American social science, in M. Dickstein, ed., *The revival of pragmatism: New essays on social thought, law and culture.* Durham, NC: Duke University Press, 199–206.

Young, I.M. (1990) *Justice and the politics of difference.* Princeton, NJ: Princeton University Press.

Young, I. M. (1996) Communication and the Other: Beyond deliberative democracy, in S. Benhabib, ed., *Democracy and difference: Contesting the boundaries of the political.* Princeton, NJ: Princeton University Press, 120–35.

Young, I.M. (1997) Together in difference: Transforming the logic of group political conflict, in L. McDowell, ed., *Undoing place?* London: Arnold, 332–42.

Young, M. and Wilmott, P. (1957) *Family and kinship in East London.* London: Routledge and Kegan Paul.

## Part IV

# Disciplinary applications in pragmatic research

# 10

# Ecological crisis, action and pragmatic humanism

## Meg Holden

### Introduction

This chapter envisions a pragmatic approach to the development of social science scholarship. It seeks a way for scholarship to manoeuvre in between the poles of humanistic and post-humanistic responses to crisis; I will describe this approach as a pragmatic anti-anti-humanism. As a starting point emblematic of the pervasive sense of crisis that we face today, I focus on the global ecological crisis. In attempting a response to this crisis, a post-humanist turn has been a common response of those concerned about dire warnings of ecological losses. Post-humanism paints our over-reliance on anthropocentric justifications and on human social, political and economic institutions as primarily responsible for environmental losses. That is, we are in crisis because our dreams are ignorant of humanity's dependence on non-human nature. To make a difference, we need to displace these dreams with alternative holistic ecosystems-based thinking.

In opposition to this stance is the stance, predominant in political ecology, that the most effective way to engage environmental politics is to make environmental concerns fit into the demands and workings of politics. That is, we should accept that human dreams will be human dreams, and leverage what ecological sensibilities exist at the heart of these dreams towards more sustainable outcomes. On the one hand, scholars are advocating a post-humanism and on the other, a more explicit form of humanism. In this chapter, I advocate a more pragmatic response whereby action in the face of crisis reflects the particular state of affairs (or what Dewey would call 'the situation' (see Bridge, this volume)).

As far as ecology is concerned, the excesses of humanism comprise the assumption of substitutability of human ingenuity, spirit and technology for natural, non-human resources, their functions and powers. Humanists tend to diagnose problems and devise solutions that involve growth – growing more and bigger, growing smarter and wiser. In many manifestations of these arguments, there are no limits. To ecologists, on the other hand, this denial of limits constitutes a dangerous arrogance that means we will lose natural resources like clean air, living soil and fresh water, and ultimately lose life itself. Ecologists consider it their role to shake humanists out of their ruinous dreams. Deep ecologists, in particular, can be considered outright anti-humanists, endeavouring to put the lie to the dream of limitless growth once and for all.

Of course, the danger of a humanist way of thinking and acting in the world does not extend only to ecological problems. We can understand the dangers of humanism without referring to the world 'without us'. Indeed, the schism between humanists and anti-humanists constitutes a culture war much more than it represents an ecological war. As is evident in political developments all over the world, this cultural and ideological battleground is set to deepen yet further, and this will be felt in the academy as much as the street. Pragmatism, however, does offer a different way forward. Drawing on the humanism of Hannah Arendt and from the American pragmatic tradition of John Dewey and William James, I argue for a pragmatic humanism that can overcome such divisions through collective efforts to address our crises, not least those facing the planet.

## The post-humanist ecological position as first presented to me

The syllabus for my second-year biogeography course, taught by Professor David Duffus at the University of Victoria, in British Columbia, had the usual series of readings, lectures and assignments, but also directed us to read two books side by side as a sort of meta-assignment for the semester. The professor went about his lectures and tutorials without overt reference to these books, but he behaved nonetheless as if he had placed a timer on his head. The timer was counting down to the expected awakening of the class when we finished reading. Without addressing what he expected of us directly, the prof took on the aura of Rumpelstiltskin, waiting for the consequences of the mischief he had wrought to sink into our young heads.

Much like Rumpelstiltskin, so certain the queen could never guess his name, Prof. Duffus's mischief was to cause us students to see that what we were being educated to become was utterly different from what we thought. The two books were Daniel Botkin's (1990) *Discordant harmonies: A new ecology for the 21st century*, and David Ehrenfeld's (1978) *The arrogance of humanism*. Both were written by ecologists for non-scientists, both sounded an alarm about ecological crisis of global proportions, and both offered heretical treatments of biological and ecological science. Botkin took aim at the climax theory of ecology, the notion that nature, left alone, without human disturbance, tends towards a

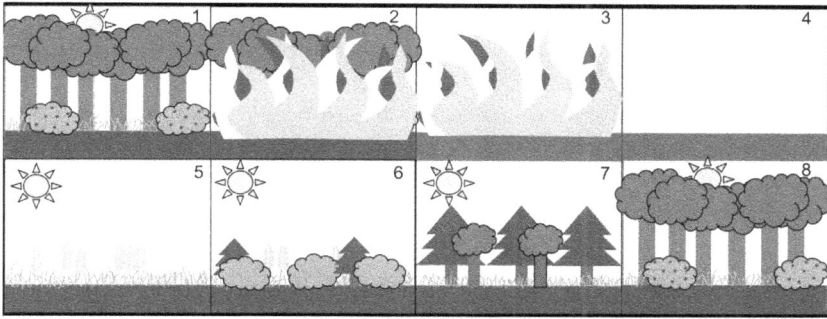

*Figure 10.1*   An illustration of 'climax theory' in ecology

singular climax state, theoretically sustainable for all time (Figure 10.1). For Ehrenfeld, the focus was on the arrogance of permitting humanism to enter into one's scientific efforts, resulting in the contamination of curiosity and thirst for knowledge, core to the scientific model, with the political and social hubris "that humans can solve any problem and overcome any difficulty, given time and resources enough" (as per the book's synopsis). Both of them made the case for anti-humanism, albeit with different shades of argumentation.

The anti-humanist ecologists say: enough with humanism's excesses and delusions of living life with more dreams than limits. They say: the only hope we hold of repairing the damage done by humanist models of problem-solving is to renounce growth metaphors and force our models of life and human action to operate within limits.

As we students finished reading the two books, we did indeed start to rub our eyes and gaze around at one another, compromised and shamed, suspicious of what humanist values lay within that one's dreadlocks, another's hemp notebook, another's button-down shirt. What was the intended purpose of the skills we were learning in this university degree programme: true inquiry or humanistic conceit? What future were we working towards? How could we respond to the world we could now see as divided along humanist–anti-humanist lines?

The implication was that those who seek to benefit ecological health had better spend time learning about the 'real' natural world and the basic facts of life, and eschew humanism. The world of politics was for the misguided, arrogant and delusional; it was the world of the past.

### Post-humanism

Botkin and Ehrenfeld served as my introduction to what I have come to know as post-humanism. Within the Western environmental movement post-humanism is often traced to the Meadows et al.'s 1972 *Limits to growth*. Within political theory, a post-humanist turn is associated with the many ways in which people and politics are implicated in ecological destruction, and it has generated efforts to increase recognition and respect for social and ecological harmony (Brulle, 2000; Grief, 2015; King, 1981; Offe, 1989; Plumwood, 2006). This post-humanist stance has mobilised people around a more or less abstract ideal of 'holistic ecology'. The basic intuition of holistic ecology is that capitalism and modernity are jointly to blame for the ravages that society has wrought on the planet and, therefore, to steer humanity towards its holistic development potential, ecological principles need to take priority over social and economic ones in organising human groups and institutions. The approach is to elaborate an ontological commitment to ecological science and to derive from this, with a good dose of humility, an ecologically holistic ethos. Post-humanism is a perspective that supports holistic ecology. It advocates that people recognise their true limits and proper place within the biophysical community and strive to be "plain member[s] and citizen[s]", as opposed to "conqueror[s] of the land-community" of this otherwise natural world (Leopold, 1968, 204; and Owain Jones presents this argument more fully in the following chapter).

### Humanism reborn for tackling ecological crisis

In diametric opposition to post-humanism is the argument that the most effective way to engage environmental politics is to make environmental concerns fit with the demands and workings of politics. To some critical political ecologists and their allies, holistic ecology can only take concerns for the non-human environment so far, and it will never be central to politics when framed this way because "no matter how important the work that has been done … ecological questions are still taken as peculiar to one specific domain of concerns, not as the core of politics" (Latour, 2011). In this view, ecological crises fail to mobilise sufficient counteraction to avert the next crisis, not because people and politics are arrogant and insufficiently in tune with ecology, but because ecological crises have not been approached in the political manner needed to compete successfully with other political priorities. The answer, to these critics, is not to strike a deeper or harder line of ecologically informed thinking and action. The answer is to reframe ecological crises as those whose resolution is essential to the pursuit of civilised, political life (see Purdy, 2015).

A major motivator driving this approach is the understanding that it is not possible to separate what is human from what is ecological. Because of the blurred boundaries between human and non-human, we can never overcome the limits of our own nature. Historically oriented environmental scholars like William Cronon (1995) have disputed the very conception of a human–nature divide, instead seeing American history in particular as clearly constituted by people-and-nature. Bruce Braun (2002) is among those to follow this line of thinking, working to demonstrate how the very notion of a pristine, old-growth forest is always political. More recently, Anna Tsing (2015) has crafted such a story line from the commoditisation of matsutake mushrooms, in order to develop a form of political ecology that doesn't pretend that humans can now leave nature alone. Recognising the unavoidably human nature of the ecological crisis, this response advocates the development of better metaphors and more effective politics as ways to respond to ecological crisis today. If the answer of the post-humanists is 'ecology first!' then the answer of the post-holistic humanists is 'politics first!' In what follows, I seek to find a 'third way' between these two camps, outlining a pragmatic anti-anti-humanism that can chart a course to ecological health.

## The pragmatic way forward

In what follows, I demonstrate how the tradition of pragmatism offers a way forward that can respect the wisdom expressed by both groups of thinkers, in ways that reflect the situation that I think we are currently facing on the ground. I seek to develop an approach that is neither naive nor excessively optimistic about the prospects for pro-human, pro-social and pro-ecological change. Recognising the powerful challenge of the post-humanists, however, I advance with care. There are critical questions about how our humanism is amenable to the kind of transformation that we could pragmatically – and ecologically – agree to be progress.

The case that I construct will back away from questions of ecological crisis per se. I draw first upon the deep humanism of Hannah Arendt, and the distinctions she makes between labour, work and action as the three ways of being in the world. I then draw from the American pragmatic tradition to develop a pragmatic humanism that can be applied going forward, responding to the environmental crisis as well as the wider human condition.

## Arendt's humanism as the grounds to proceed

In *The human condition* (1958), Arendt offers a tripartite scheme for categorising people's three ways of being in the world: as labouring animal, as worker-craftsperson and as active citizen or member of the polis. These three ways of being, the distinctions among them and the way in which they have been confounded in dominant theories of economics and sociology offer an enormous resource for understanding the transformative possibilities within human and non-human nature and culture.

First, Arendt explains labour as a mode of being that is aligned with the biological motor of life and that really is no different a mode of being for humans than it is for any other animal. As such, labour is core to human life in the very same way that it is core to all life: we labour that we may maintain our metabolism, be alive to face the new day, reproduce our life conditions and meet our bodily demands. Recognising this nature of our daily labour, ancient philosophers – Arendt relies heavily on the Greeks – did not spend too much time on questions of labour. Labour was considered messy, fleeting, never-ending and anyway uninteresting in that it did not really distinguish humans from other animals. The Ancient Greek philosophers were more interested in characterising and glorifying the acts of work, *homo faber*, which were different from labour because they were optional to the continuation of life, but which some people chose to do anyway. Work was understood to separate people from other animals, who spent almost the entirety of their time fulfilling biological demands. Work also could be distinguished from labour because while labour created no products that could outlive the stream of life, work did. Works are by definition the enduring products of human hands that can outlast their makers. We all need to keep ourselves clean and fed, and no matter how good a job we do at these tasks on any given day, the same quantity of this labour remains for us to do tomorrow. Not so, however, for the tables we craft or the books we write. Arendt clarifies the distinction between the perishable, consumable products of labour, that never lose the sense of being wrought from nature, and the durable, non-consumable products of work in which the work done by the human hand is much more apparent than the natural resources that marked their beginnings: "the grain never quite disappears in the bread as the tree has disappeared in the table" (Arendt, 1958, 103). This serves as a first means of resolving the boundary problem noted by the humanists discussed above; the boundary between what is truly human and what is truly nature can be made clearer if we can effectively distinguish between labour and work.

Arendt takes some pains to illustrate this distinction between work and labour, despite the fact that it is ultimately the third mode of being, action, which is her primary focus. She does this in order to illustrate the crucial error made in confounding work and labour during the birth of modern economic ideas, by thinkers such as John Locke, Adam Smith and Karl Marx. Indeed, modern and industrial society has mistakenly characterised almost all work as labour, because capitalism as an ideology has depended upon workers taking up within their employment the same sense of labour that they have in maintaining their households; a sense of labour that can never be finished. The embedding of capitalism has depended upon the biological, evolutionary metaphor of an endless cycle of growth, tending towards an ever-temporary, ever-more-profitable climax. At the same time, capitalism depends upon the ability of work, not labour, to create things that endure outside the cycle of life – principally, money.

In revealing the conceptual distinction between work and labour and its confoundment within modern economics, Arendt makes quick work of explaining the devastating effects of capitalism for human societies, and for non-human ecology as well. This muddying of the distinction between labour and work generated problems for workers, who have come to see work more and more as all-consuming. This is a favourable situation for capitalists, but not so for the quality of human lives. At the same time, this confoundment is harmful in terms of the fate reserved for ecology under capitalism. Arendt explains the problem that nature meets under capitalism by saying: "From the viewpoint of nature, it is work rather than labour that is destructive, since the work process takes matter out of nature's hands without giving it back to her in the swift course of the natural metabolism or the living body" (Arendt, 1958, 100). When nature is considered as an input to a process of work rather than labour, the limits of natural systems can be ignored while their components are over-extracted and over-worked to feed production. This recognition of the danger of ignoring the limits of growth, along with the political economic purpose of removing essentially natural resources from the flow of life's labour without correctly identifying the different situation of work, gets to the root of the problem of the ecological crisis.

For Arendt, the key element that differentiates both work and labour from the third mode of being, action, is that both work and labour are primarily private activities. Action, by contrast, assumes and demands the public realm, which for Arendt constituted both a physical space and a means of reasoning. The 'products' of action in speech and in deeds, which together constitute the fabric of human social and political relationships and affairs, are reduced to thoughts – 'labour' – or, if written down in stories or poetry – 'work' – if they happen in the private rather than the public sphere. Left in private, actions not only lack the tangibility of other things, but are even less durable and more futile than the things we produce through labour for immediate consumption. For Arendt, public action was so significant that she considered it to be equivalent to a 'second birth' – equivalent in importance to our actual birth because it marks our belonging not in the world of ecology, of life itself, as does our initial birth from our mothers, but our birth into the company of our fellow human beings. A life of action would have many iterations of such births as each person initiates many new attempts to create commonality with fellow people, always with indeterminate ends, over their lifetime. At the same time, however, Arendt recognised that no one could live in this public realm all the time – our ability to be physically in public space and to subject our thinking to public scrutiny can be stretched through practice, but not exhaustively so. Action in any given context depends upon the willingness and ability of the human actors in question to engage together in the presence of others and to subject their ideas and decisions to the scrutiny of others; to move towards the common world and the making of common sense (Arendt, 1958). Thus Arendt describes the scene of action she has in mind as a table situated between people interacting around it, that is both situated in the specificity of the acts being undertaken, and contingent in terms of the qualities of what and who might come together or fall apart as the action progresses. She explains: "To live together in the world means essentially that a world of things is between those who have it in common, as a table is located between those who sit around it; the world, like every in-between, relates and separates men at the same time" (Arendt 1958, 52).

Arendtian thought offers two keys to the pragmatic humanism that I am seeking, by which I mean a path that is capable of respecting the critical wisdom of ecological thinking while also guiding action to mount a response. The first key is to recognise that humans and other forms of life are not distinguishable to the extent that all life shares a common sense of labour, but that humans and other ecologies are distinguishable to the extent that only people engage in work. Adequate recognition of this distinction holds promise for clarifying the stakes and terms of debate about ecological crisis: we cannot reasonably afford to put the needs of non-human nature first in matters of labour, because in these matters, we humans are subject to the same exigencies of life as are all other life forms. On the other hand, when it comes to matters of work, Arendt gives us clear reason to make different kinds of allowances for non-human nature than we do for ourselves, because the essence of work is to remove non-human nature from the flow of life for human benefit. Clarifying the distinction between the labour involved in all life and the work involved in producing that which is intended to outlast the life of the human worker could help determine which kinds of ecological concerns are best folded into human political debate and which are better guided by an assertion of the demands of ecological processes over those of human invention. In the realm of transportation, for example, the principle of mobility may be something that we, as labouring animals who need mobility to meet our daily life needs, cannot relinquish to other animals who also need mobility, or at least not without healthy political debate. Surely, however, in the interest of preserving a stable climate and generating more and healthier livelihood opportunities, we can give up the great works of mobility driven by internal combustion engines – automobiles, airplanes – to prioritise works that are more ingenious because they are less harmful to life itself.

The second key is the Arendtian notion of action, the mode of being most conducive to world transformation. Action in Arendt's formulation invites and requires a public realm or polis and common sense comprising the justification of ideas. The public realm envisioned is not a particular location, necessarily, but "the organization of the people as it arises out of acting and speaking together ... no matter where they happen to be" (Arendt, 1958, 198). By common sense, Arendt means speech that gives voice to the considerations made and reasons for action: "The action he [sic] begins is humanly disclosed by the word, and ... becomes relevant only through the spoken word in which he identifies himself as the actor, announcing what he does, has done, and intends to do" (Arendt, 1958, 179). Arendt viewed common sense as a sixth sense, one that individuals could cultivate not by thinking alone, which she characterised as labour, but by thinking together with others, and thus attaining enlarged judgement, beyond either their own animal labourer needs or their own assimilation of worldly works within biological cycles. Acting with common sense in the public realm, in turn, would have the effect of enlarging actors' judgement. So equipped, repeat actors could hone their skills, increase their reach into the public, generate shared political ideas and discern between ideas that would advance the common world and ones that would not. Such adept actors could develop in part through education, certainly, but also crucially through cosmopolitan associations sufficient to discuss life and the world with a broad swath of diverse people. Such associations can develop "an intuitive feeling for worldliness" within us that fits us into and makes possible a common world with a growing horizon of inclusion.

Arendt (1958, 9) goes as far as to call action "the one miracle making faculty of man [sic]". At the same time, what happens around the 'table' of Arendtian action can generate alienation, exclusion and disenfranchisement when the conditions for achieving worldliness appear too difficult. Arendtian action is at once the most promising and the most dangerous mode of being. The triumph of a particularly virulent and twisted form of humanism in the twentieth century has demonstrated this danger and its terrible consequences in the excesses of nationalism, hatred, ecological destruction and war (Ferguson, 2006). The extreme political temptation of hubris, exacerbated in a world in which reasonable limits are ignored, is a direct outpouring of this brand of humanism. Based on this history, humanism may yet drive the destruction of civilisation and even the breakdown of planetary systems conducive to human life. This is certainly the sort of conclusion that has been reached by some ecological thinkers (Kunstler, 2005; Rockström et al., 2009; Weisman, 2007). What possible defence can pragmatic humanists offer, in the face of these facts? Is it not necessarily delusional, or in denial of these facts, to continue to pursue or promote humanism of any kind?

## Towards a pragmatic humanism

Building on Arendt's approach, a pragmatic humanism is cognisant of the arrogance and horrors of humanism, and yet it cannot help but continue to dream and give birth to actions that include a progressively larger swath of humanity (and Rorty's later scholarship exemplifies these concerns, Rorty, 1999). In this section I draw on a range of thinkers to outline six propositions for a pragmatic humanism to advance the miracle-making faculty of action.

*Justify action based upon 'experienceable existence'.* The worst excesses of humanism today come from justification through generalisation and a rush to judgement. In general terms, a 1.5 degree Celsius increase in global average temperature, a 50 cm rise in sea level, an 18 per cent decline in species richness do not sound like a devastating price to pay for persisting on a development path that is benefiting billions of people. The generalisation is deceiving, however, and the pragmatic answer is to identify the specificity and contingency of all action. In this way, pragmatic action is Arendtian: practical judgement and action are the embodiment of a pragmatic approach. As much as philosophers write as if they could eschew "the perils of uncertainty" (Dewey, 1981, 358) by cognitive means, a pragmatic approach seeks certainty not from individual cognitive tricks but instead from accrued experience and situated judgements, shared in public. While this position involves foregoing the notion of a unifying explanation for any phenomenon from an authority on high, such an approach provides hope that justified action may forge new, unexpected relationships and ideas, from different starting points, renewed over time. Dewey (1981, 376) held this to be essential to any notion of human progress: "We should regard practice as the only means (other than accident) by which whatever is judged to be honorable, admirable, approvable can be kept in concrete experienceable existence."

***Foster institutions that are accountable for the trust we must put in them.*** Institutions serve an essential pragmatic purpose in social life. To Arendt, institutions embodied political life by setting the terms for common acts, guaranteeing rights to participants and arriving at situated agreements upon the common good of actions and rights. In the pragmatic conception, the importance of institutions can be understood as a reflection of the broader importance of habits, which are, in essence, mechanisms to balance against the unpredictability of individual impulses and intentions (see Cutchin, this volume). Institutions add to the value of habits when they embed transparency of purpose and process, permitting some measure of recourse to improvement when expectations are not met.

The key institution for pragmatists is democracy itself. By democracy, Dewey (1981, 622) meant "the idea of community life" and individual free associations with an interplay of different groups that are free to the extent that they seek not to oppress one another. To Dewey, the improvement of the institutions of democracy would come via improvements in the articulation of a more fulsome view of the public interest, made more authoritative to the extent that more members of the public could articulate it. The key barrier to this path to institutional improvement was: "discovering the means by which a scattered, mobile and manifold public may so recognize itself as to define and express its interests" (Dewey, 1981, 622).

The key institutions of democracy, to Dewey, were institutions of education. Moreover, he did not see public education as limited to the school and education for democracy comprised "all modes of human association, the family, the school, industry, religion" (Dewey, 1981, 621). For Dewey, an educational institution was any institution that would assume the tasks of "producing the habits of mind and character, the intellectual and moral patterns that are somewhere near even with the actual movements of events". Producing these habits meant equipping people with the courage to face an indeterminate social future, while facing the facts of life as they found them.

This task of institution-building via education was the challenge of instilling within people a sense of intelligence as something which could be increased in individuals to the extent that it is fostered in more people, and put together. This task is neither bureaucratic drudgery nor the sort of thankless charitable duty performed by the fortunate for the benefit of the less fortunate. Achieving a notion of intelligence as a social asset, and education as a tool for the expansion of our sense of the social world, is a means for those who aspire to think, to think better, because this achievement is perhaps the only means to bring new ideas into the public view. This is how Dewey thought of the task of education and the responsibility of the body politic to the institutions of education, and his excitement with the possibilities of this work was immense: "Given a social medium in whose institutions the available knowledge, ideas and art of humanity were incarnate … the average individual would rise to undreamed heights of social and political intelligence" (Dewey, 1981, 652).

***Address the pursuit of happiness and well-being as part of the labour of life, not the preserve of great works.*** Core to any humanist manifesto, a notionally limitless quest for happiness should not be quelled within society; to attempt to do so would seem both pragmatically disingenuous and impossible. At the same time, to fail to place limits on this quest would be irresponsible to the competing desires and divergent histories of others. The pragmatic middle ground here is the case for the public quest of "ever more novel, ever richer, forms of human happiness" (Rorty, 1999, 31). In Arendtian terms, this shift could be considered a kind of extraction of the pursuit of happiness and well-being from the largely capitalist and materialist domain of work, where it is available only to a few, and a rapprochement of happiness with the labour of life, limited only by the terms of life itself.

Dewey thought of resituating the quest for happiness as a recognition that: "Thought, desire and purpose exist in a constant give and take of interaction with environing conditions" (Dewey, 1981, 647). Other people should be considered a part of these "environing conditions", and a part about which we are destined to remain ever partially blind. James describes the plight of the individual with respect to others, and our connected but different needs to seek happiness, this way: "We have unquestionably a great cloud-bank of ancestral blindness weighing down upon us, only transiently riven here and there by fitful revelations of the truth … Our inner secrets must remain for the most part impenetrable by others, for beings as essentially practical as we are necessarily short of sight" (James, 1977, 646). There is space to inspire more people to seek to be part of the common task of diverse and multiple ideas of human happiness and achievement of destiny within this labour.

***Use the language of experience in discourse.*** It is not possible, warns Rorty (1999, 94), to "philosophize one's way into political relevance". Just the opposite: a retreat of specialists to conversations only between other specialists is a symptom of retreat from the demands of action, and the adoption of an anaemic, 'spectator' view of the utility of scholarship. This view is also key to a move towards Arendtian action, the move to create a common world and common knowledge. The work of building common sense together implies an abandonment of much of the specialised language and method of disciplinary scholarship. The eschewal of specialised language is the price that intellectuals in particular need to pay for participation in active life. They gain, in turn, more power to their ideas as they hit the ground of action in the common world. As Rorty (1999, 27) put it: "To get along in utopia … intellectuals will have to tone down their rhetoric." If the invocation of utopia is too much to swallow, James (1977, 651) articulated the same idea this way: "The more we live by our intellect, the less we understand the meaning of life."

*Inhabit the public realm more often.* While the public realm needed for action did not, to Arendt, correspond to any particular type of place, it nonetheless needed two key elements to function for action. First, it had to be of a nature that would reduce the barriers to participation for newcomers and longstanding participants in public life, to make such action increasingly normal, non-heroic and tempting with an offer of intrinsic rewards for participation. The public realm in ancient Athens, Arendt (1958, 197) specifies, "was intended to enable men [sic] to do permanently, albeit under certain restrictions, what otherwise had been possible only as an extraordinary and infrequent enterprise for which they had to leave their households … to multiply the chances for everybody to distinguish himself, to show in deed and word who he was in his unique distinctness". To continue the work of building the public realm, intellectuals need to continue the work of expanding the sense of openness of the public realm to ensure their potential for distinctiveness. This has a spatial dimension, to be sure; but it also has a communicative dimension, aligned with number 4 above. To a pragmatist, this is core: "There can be no public without full publicity in respect to all consequences which concern it. Whatever obstructs and restricts publicity, limits and distorts public opinion and checks and distorts thinking on social affairs" (Dewey, 1981, 633–4). At the same time, it is the capacity to advance and maintain an argument that stands a chance of persuading others, rather than the space for many to create their own specialised echo chambers of unreasoned positions. The argument that is pragmatically needed, and that can never be decisively concluded, is the argument about what sorts of arguments can be persuasive to more people, in more types of public realms, and how. When we inhabit the public realm more often, in different configurations, we experience more of the process and the means by which a majority comes to be a majority, a vocal minority a vocal minority, the places and messages on which they might mix, and everything in between.

Connected to this, the second element that the public realm needs to offer is a public record, which connects this point to a principle mentioned earlier, about supporting democratic institutions. We need some means of ensuring that what transpires in public action may have the possibility of being remembered. In a context of radical ontological pluralism such as the world of ideas is faced with today, this work is essential in order to make actions accountable to public memory.

***Pair dreams with a better sense of public memory.*** The opportunity to dream, tell stories and imagine a different future are key sources of the kind of human happiness referred to above. They are aspects of a kind of humanism in which we could build pride in our common actions. While few talk openly of chasing dreams as a legitimate pursuit in critical social sciences, a pragmatic path supports renewed interest in creating common imaginaries through engaged action, as a way of locating and understanding the partially overlapping worlds of those who are engaged. At any rate, encouragement of dreaming as dreaming is socially preferable to the encouragement of forming hardened and fast ideological positions, and it is this latter climate that seems more common in the world of public ideas today (see Gieselhart, this volume). Such efforts in imagining can mobilise a pluralisation of existing understandings of intentions and directions for action. These efforts also reinforce a new sense of limitlessness on the pragmatic path that is still embedded in a real context of the limits that life imposes; in Rorty's (2004, 12) words, it represents a commitment that: "a life that is not lived close to the present limits of the human imagination is not worth living". This task of imagining new kinds of dreams represents a de-valorisation of the typical approach to dreaming as introspective "self-examination and self-knowledge" and an opening up of "the idea of enlarging the self by becoming acquainted with still more ways of being human" (Rorty, 2004, 13). It is also a democratic communication strategy, as dreams exist in the world of the possible but improbable, so that we can expect people who may advance a dream in a communicative setting to be more open to compromise and reconsideration as the communication progresses.

Imagining may seem like a purely descriptive exercise, but, from a pragmatic perspective, it is in fact the key means by which a constantly evolving public is made more real through the accumulation of common experiences. Such actions can attach our individual complaints, hardships and aspirations to larger, more public scales and arguments as well. The process of reflection via public articulation of dreams can animate and grow public space and build more active habits of debate. On the other hand, dreaming and imagining the future can be a double-edged sword, with the sharp edge felt most painfully by those who have been most disillusioned in the present. Better means of remembering and accounting for the past and its injustices can help make dreaming more palatable in the future. "The method of democracy – inasfar as it is that of organized intelligence – is to bring these conflicts out into the open where their special claims can be seen and appraised, where they can be discussed and judged in the light of more inclusive interests" (Dewey, 1981, 657). Imagining the criteria by which a better future should be judged is a task in which all should participate.

## Conclusion

In this chapter, I have presented the polarity of positions in understanding the global ecological crisis. At one end, post-humanists seek to prioritise non-human nature and natural processes, and at the other, humanists seek to reconceptualise politics to better include nature as part of human deliberations. Reasoned views from both poles were articulated in order to clarify the nature of the impasse, and the importance of seeking resolution in order to generate more effective action. This chapter has highlighted the inescapability of humanism, as well as its perils. Looking at the facts, we know that the living world might well be much better-off 'without us' and that our humanism has been used to justify innumerable acts of cruelty and injustice. At the same time, we know that we have a human need for hope in our own future as part of the world and dreams of the good that human agency may generate in the future. Taking this situation into account, my task has been to make a case for a pragmatic approach to humanism. To do this, I drew upon the thoughtful and critical humanism of Hannah Arendt, who offers a structure to guide this approach in her tripartite view of ways of being in the world through labour, work and action. I then built on these foundations in order to develop six propositions for pragmatic humanism that can guide social scientists and political activists in our action in common. Pragmatic thought allows us ways to limit the worst excesses of humanism without abandoning the spirit of the humanist impulse that drives people to create a more fulfilling life. These six propositions are as follows:

1    Justify action based upon 'experienceable existence'.
2    Foster institutions that are accountable for the trust we must put in them.
3    Address the pursuit of happiness and well-being as part of the labour of life, not the preserve of great works.
4    Use the language of experience in discourse.
5    Inhabit the public realm more often.
6    Pair dreams with a better sense of public memory.

While critical social scientists may consider this pragmatic humanism to be naive, there is much to be gained in situating ourselves and our work within the excesses and evils, as well as the successes and glories, of the human experience. In fact, it would be pragmatically irresponsible of us not to try.

## References

Arendt, H. (1958) *The human condition.* Chicago, IL: University of Chicago Press.
Botkin, D. (1990) *Discordant harmonies.* New York, NY: Oxford University Press.
Braun, B. (2002) *The intemperate rainforest: Nature, culture and power on Canada's West Coast.* Minneapolis, MN: University of Minnesota Press.

Brulle, R.J. (2000) *Agency, democracy and nature: The US environment movement from a critical theory perspective*. Cambridge, MA: MIT Press.

Cronon, W. (ed.) (1995) *Uncommon ground: Rethinking the human place in nature*. New York. NY: W.W. Norton.

Dewey, J. (1927 [1981]) The search for the Great Community, in J.J. McDermott, ed., *The philosophy of John Dewey*. Chicago, IL: University of Chicago Press, 620–43.

Dewey, J. (1929a [1981]) Escape from peril, in J.J. McDermott, ed., *The philosophy of John Dewey*. Chicago, IL: University of Chicago Press, 355–71.

Dewey, J. (1929b [1981]) Philosophy's search for the immutable, in J.J. McDermott, ed., *The philosophy of John Dewey*. Chicago, IL: University of Chicago Press, 371–88.

Dewey, J. (1935 [1981]) Renascent liberalism, in J.J. McDermott, ed., *The Philosophy of John Dewey*. Chicago, IL: University of Chicago Press, 643–65.

Ehrenfeld, D. (1978) *The arrogance of humanism*. New York, NY: Oxford University Press.

Ferguson, N. (2006) *The war of the world: Twentieth-Century conflict and the descent of the West*. New York, NY: The Penguin Press.

Grief, M. (2015) *The age of the crisis of man*. Princeton, NJ: Princeton University Press.

James, W. (1977) "What makes a life significant", in J.J. McDermott, ed., *The writings of William James: A comprehensive edition*. Chicago, IL: University of Chicago Press, 645–60.

King, Y. (1981) Feminism and the revolt of nature. *Heresies*, 13, 12–16.

Kunstler, J.H. (2005) *The long emergency: Surviving the converging catastrophes of the twenty-first century*. New York, NY: Atlantic Monthly Press.

Latour, B. (2011) "It's development, stupid!" or how to modernize modernization. www.bruno-latour.fr/sites/default/files/107-NORDHAUS&SHELLENBERGER.pdf.

Leopold, A. (1968) *A Sand County almanac*. New York, NY: Oxford University Press.

Meadows, D., Meadows, D., Randers, J. and Behrens, W.W. (1972) *The limits to growth*. Zurich: The Club of Rome.

Offe, C. (1989) Reflections on the institutional self-transformation of movement politics: A tentative stage model, in R.J. Dalton and M. Kuechler, eds, *Challenging the political order: New social and political movements in democracies*. Cambridge: Polity Press, 232–50.

Plumwood, V. (2006) Feminism, in A. Dobson and R. Eckersley, eds, *Political theory and the ecological challenge*. Cambridge: Cambridge University Press.

Purdy, J. (2015) *After nature: A politics for the Anthropocene*. Cambridge, MA: Harvard University Press.

Rockström, J. et al. (2009) A safe operating space for humanity. *Nature*, 461, 472–5.

Rorty, R. (1999) *Achieving our country: Leftist thought in twentieth century America*. Cambridge, MA: Harvard University Press.

Rorty, R. (2004) Philosophy as a transitional genre, in S. Benhabib and N. Fraser, eds, *Pragmatism, critique, judgment: Essays for Richard J. Bernstein*. Cambridge, MA: Massachusetts Institute of Technology Press, 3–28.

Tsing, A. (2015) *The mushroom at the end of the world: On the possibility of life in capitalist ruins*. Princeton, NJ: Princeton University Press.

Weisman, A. (2007) *The world without us*. New York, NY: St. Martin's Thomas Dunne Books.

# 11

# Pragmatism, anti-representational theory and local methods for critical-creative ecological action

## Owain Jones

### Introduction

This chapter explores the way that pragmatic approaches offer hope for developing the interventions needed to respond to the ecological crisis, and the wider crisis that is modern knowledge. The overall argument is that pragmatic approaches, along with a family of non- and anti-representational approaches, are inherently creative. They embrace the fact that they are generative of the world and within the world. They are ecological philosophies of change and innovation and this places them at odds with modern knowledge which, with its reductive and representational traits, is apolitical at best and deeply immoral, destructive and anti-ecological at worst.

Even when a seemingly successful example of modern life, such as an affluent, peaceful, well-appointed neighbourhood of a modern city, looks like a wonder of 'civilisation', it disguises the fact that this is the era of 'ecocide', when the hidden forces and systems of economy, technology and power that have brought that wonder into being also produce deeply toxic fallout in other places and other times. There is an understandable desire to create spaces of happiness and individual and family/community comfort in which to live, but the febrile nature of consumer capitalism relentlessly pushes us to do so in narrow, individualised ways, while awareness of the ecological implications (the ecological footprints of our everyday life/consumption) is denied us. Those sceptical about the need for transformative approaches to knowledge, politics and ethics must consider seriously the history of this and the last century, and ask themselves if they are happy with business as (more or less) usual.

Another way of looking at this is to say that modernism is an anti-ecological form of knowledge both in its impact on ecology – or the three ecologies set out by Félix Guattari (2000, and see below) – *and* in its reductive stances. Pragmatism and related non-representational approaches, in contrast, are potentially ecological forms of knowledge that embrace the interconnectivity of all things and have an evolutionary understanding of how the earth and cosmos advance through space-time in a burgeoning becoming of which they are part.

In this chapter, I seek to highlight the links between pragmatism and more recent theoretical developments such as non-representational theory (NRT) and actor–network theory (ANT). I argue that there is a particular power in pragmatism as a prophetic orientation to the future that highlights the necessity for action, and this can get a bit lost in the more recent non-representational approaches to theory and academic practice. I suggest we need to fully embrace the creative pragmatic capacities of these approaches and arrive at a position of avowedly *anti*-representational theory (ART).

Those who have espoused pragmatism and NRT claim that the need for change is urgent and the stakes are high. It is not hard to argue that we are living through the crash of the modern project both in terms of ideas about knowledge production and the social formations, politics and ethics produced therein. However, the modern project is a vast body of action encompassing great diversity and momentum, and the crash involves breaking many things, such as ecologies, landscapes, non-modern cultures, communities, and human and non-human individual well-being around the earth. But many compartments and functions of modernism remain very much intact in isolated and heavily protected pockets of success and security. Most advanced-country, middle-class elites live in these bubbles seeking to defend their interests. In what follows, I set out the provocations of the ecological crisis and previous calls for pragmatic responses to it, and then show how these calls have remained unheeded as we push ever deeper into the era of ecocide. Then a reading of pragmatism and NRT is offered to elaborate on some of their key shared traits. The idea of local, ecological, creative, radically incremental methods is discussed, pointing to some brief examples in the conclusion.

## The provocations of ecological crisis and the need for a pragmatic response

In 1991, Jacque Emel wrote an editorial for *Environment and Planning D: Society and Space* entitled 'Ecological crisis and provocative pragmatism'. This short essay, which has inspired and stayed with me ever since, makes a compelling case for a pragmatic approach to theory and knowledge creation in an era of ecological crisis. Emel described the ecological crisis that had crystallised since the 1960s (at least in the vision of those who were looking), an obvious marker being

Rachel Carson's *Silent spring* (published in 1962), and she highlighted the failure of critical thought to engage with the crisis intellectually and practically:

> Western rationality, instrumentalism, utilitarianism, privatisation, commodification, patriarchy, urbanisation, nationalism, regionalism, sedentary agriculture, medicine, consumerism, state planning – there must be hundreds of processes, events, and logics that have contributed to increasing ecological degradation. Many can be subsumed under the umbrella of 'capitalism', but they must all be faced and interrogated where theory meets practice. If we refuse to simplify the complexity and contradictions of living in nature, we may not equivocate on the enormity of the step from critiquing existing economies, disciplines, logics, and structures of power to describing a desirable future and defining a pathway toward achieving it. (Emel, 1991, 385)

Emel gathered many of the problematics she highlighted under the umbrella of capitalism. That certainly made sense insofar as many of the chronic socio-ecological problems we face are being driven by industrial extraction, production and waste; globalised financial markets; and the drive towards ever-higher consumption by a still increasing global population. But questions remain about the relationship between modernity and capitalism. Are the underlying drivers of global-scale unsustainable practices embedded more in the ideologies of modernity? Is capitalism itself an outworking of the logics of modernity, which include notions of rationality, human exceptionalism, the state, colonialism and the individual? Capitalism has indeed been named as a key *institution* of modernity, their exact historical relationship being the focus of much debate (Goody, 2004).

The first key point I take from Emel's argument is that dominant forms of modernity – be they neoliberal or market socialist – are not only systemically unsustainable, but systemically highly toxic to human and non-human co-flourishing. This is the terrible situation we (citizens of the modern, developed world), and others, find ourselves in. The very fabric of our everyday lives – and the institutions and systems that make that up – are toxic to earthly well-being. As Donna Haraway perceives it:

> It's more than climate change; it's also extraordinary burdens of toxic chemistry, mining, depletion of lakes and rivers under and above ground, ecosystem simplification, vast genocides of people and other critters, etc., etc., in systemically linked patterns that threaten major system collapse after major system collapse after major system collapse. (Haraway, 2015, 159)

A second point of note in Emel's essay is the idea that there are many sites of pressure and possible action to at least begin to resist and reverse the situation with which we are presented. Local, tactical and radically incremental actions are needed throughout the networks of globalised modern society in the hope of somehow generating systemic change. We need new ways of doing things. These might be new in terms of prevailing modern practices or might also be old ways reworked. For example, there are many calls for non-modern, indigenous 'fourth world' knowledges in relation to nature–society relations to be heeded as lessons for more sustainable models of what knowledge and critical enquiry and practice in nature–society relations are and can be (e.g. Clapperton, 2016).

The move away from the model of modernity was, in essence, the call of the classical pragmatists at the beginning of the twentieth century in the face of what they saw as the stultifications of philosophy. Then the neo-pragmatist revivals of the late twentieth century sought to refresh that legacy (Kloppenberg, 1998). The grip of modern knowledge is tightly bound up with structures of state, capitalist elite power, certain theologies, and assumptions of what humans actually are. Huge amounts of energy are expended keeping all this in place. How to recognise this, and then to challenge and disrupt it, is perhaps the underlying drive of various forms of poststructuralist and 'non-representational theory' (see Thrift, 1999).

The key argument here is that modern knowledge and key outworkings of it – in particular, capitalism, human exceptionalism and reductive forms of science and technology – are the frames which have ushered in the era of eco-cide. A whole range of alternative, non-modern, non-representational, pragmatist thinking has sought to counter this. Now the call is for these alternative legacies to be taken up as forms of knowledge creation more widely. This is not esoteric or indulgent academic argument-making: the stakes are about as high as they could possibly be. As another non-modern thinker, Michel Serres (1995), puts it in his book *The natural contract*:

> The Earth speaks to us in terms of forces, bonds, and interactions, and that is enough to make a contract. Each of the partners in symbiosis thus owes, by rights, life to the other, on pain of death. (Serres, 1995, 3)

The social contracts (such as they were) of modernity broke the contracts humans have with the earth: death is, indeed, the outcome.

## The era of ecocide

A few years before Emel's editorial, Félix Guattari wrote:

> The Earth is undergoing a period of intense techno-scientific transformations. If no remedy is found, the ecological disequilibrium this has generated will ultimately threaten the continuation of life on the planet's surface. Alongside these upheavals, human modes of life, both individual and collective, are progressively deteriorating. Kinship networks tend to be reduced to a bare minimum; domestic life is being poisoned by the gangrene of mass-media consumption. (Guattari, 2000, 27)

He added:

> Political groupings and executive authorities appear to be totally incapable of understanding the full implications of these issues. Despite having recently initiated a partial realization of the most obvious dangers that threaten the natural environment of our societies, they are generally content to simply tackle industrial pollution and then from a purely technocratic perspective, whereas only an ethico-political articulation – which I call ecosophy – between the three ecological registers (the environment, social relations and human subjectivity) would be likely to clarify these questions. (Guattari, 2000, 27–8)

Many of the authors of environmental philosophy and politics books from the 1960s onwards set out the situation (even before the full extent of climate change and extinction rates were widely known), and asked, what is to be done? Emel, Guattari and many others (the deep ecologists, the ecofeminists, the political ecologists), more or less a quarter of a century ago, not only set out demands for critical-creative practices to confront the dire situation we find ourselves in, but pithily summarised those situations in eco-social terms. It was Guattari's translators/introducers that described the overall crisis as being one of 'ecocide' (Pindar and Sutton, 2000, 3), which echoes the horrors of the genocides of the twentieth and previous centuries, but on a planetary, biospheric, pan-species, pan-culture scale.

Somehow, there has been no *meaningful* response in terms of tectonic shifts in politics, culture, economy and human identity in the developed world where the vast bulk of the damage is generated. We are trapped in the momentums and trajectories of modernity and particularly its manifestations in neoliberal, globalised consumer capitalism, and geopolitical ideological conflicts, that either resist change or make the political circumstances for it impossible. Bruno Latour famously proclaimed *We have never been modern* (1993) in terms of the ecological basis of life, but the dominance of modernity as an ideological reading of life (blind to ecology) and the knowledge practices it rested upon has allowed the proliferation of terrible monsters.

The fact that 'we' (developed world consumer citizens and powerful elites) have known about the situation but nothing has really changed, prompts Isabelle Stengers to say:

> We do, however, know one thing: even if it is a matter of the death of what we have called a civilization, there are many manners of dying, some being more ugly than others. *I belong to a generation that will perhaps be the most hated in human memory, the generation that 'knew' but did nothing* or did too little (changing our lightbulbs, sorting our rubbish, riding bicycles…). But it is also a generation that will avoid the worst – we will already be dead. I would add that this is the generation that, thirty years ago, participated in, or impotently witnessed, the failure of the encounter between two movements that could, together, perhaps have created the political

intelligence necessary to the development of an efficacious culture of struggle – those who denounced the ravaging of nature and those who combated the exploitation of humans. In fact, the manner in which large environmental movements have adhered to the promises of 'green' capitalism is enough to retroactively confirm the most somber of suspicions. But the retroactive justification should not erase the memory of a missed opportunity, of a blind division from which the capitalist sirens haven't failed to profit. Capitalism knows how to profit from every opportunity. (Stengers, 2015, 10–11, emphasis added)

As already suggested, we are trapped because the established ideological, economic, theological and epistemological elite systems devote huge amounts of power, energy and violence to not only protecting their positions of (narrow) benefit, but integrating them ever more fully into the everyday life of all those living on our planet, often at the expense of life itself.

And where are the academics – the 'critical thinkers' – in this? Have things changed since Emel's expressions of concern? Has academe been bravely battling away against this unfolding disaster or are we, as a collective, part of the elite political and epistemological systems locking modernity in place for our own short-term benefit? Sadly, it would appear that very little has changed but there are resources in the pragmatic tradition still to be mined (Coles, 2016).

## A pragmatic reading of pragmatism and NRT moving towards anti-representational theory

Pragmatism offers a radically different way of approaching knowledge creation and practice. It constitutes an *attitude* to scholarship that is needed to break out of the bubble of modernity inhabited by advanced societies including most of the endeavours underway within our academic institutions. The turn away from representation and claims about 'truth' as the grounds and the goals of knowledge is a move away from static, impossible-to-achieve, fundamentalist positions, which can be so destructive in whatever field of discourse they occur (Latour, 2005). These are some of the many traits that pragmatism shares with NRT.

### Defining NRT

In his key work that summarises NRT, Thrift (2008) sets out its background and key features. This takes time, as NRT is, like pragmatism, a different attitude to knowledge and theory, it reflects a different *culture,* and to describe it is not a simple task. There are many elements, variations and applications to be covered (see also Anderson and Harrison, 2011). Thrift (2008, 5–18) sets out seven key traits of NRT which in turn have numerous facets. In summary these are that NRT: engages with the 'onflow' of life and is a creative part of it; radically questions any notion of stable self-knowable individuality; concentrates on practice and (relational) action; argues that all the preceding takes place with and through a world teeming with things which combine and recombine in hybrid assemblages (which form new sites in their action); takes an experimental and questioning stance towards knowledge and life; advocates that affect and sensation are foregrounded in creative readings of situations; and suggests that new forms of ethics and politics are possible if the flow of the world is confronted and engaged with an NRT stance. Overall, NRT advocates process-based thinking rather than object-based thinking, embracing the particular rather than chasing the dream of the general and the universal. It is very much in and of life, and its shared traits with pragmatism are evident.

Indeed Thrift's earlier (1999) genealogy of NRT shows it stretching back through the twentieth century, starting with the work of the proto-pragmatists Heidegger and Wittgenstein, and including the later work of poststructuralists such as Deleuze and Derrida. The non-modern approaches within this family tree of process-orientated creative approaches to knowledge have made much progress in parts of social sciences, humanities and elsewhere in the academy, but remain a minority stance.

With the exception, perhaps, of certain recent 'post-truth' political enterprises, the realisation is not yet widespread that the world is there to be constructed. Theories can be thought of as tools to be used in constructing a plural world that is understood to be made of 'relational materialism ... an imbroglio of heterogeneous and more or less expansive hybrids performing not one but many worlds' (Thrift, 1999, 319). NRT seeks to reconfigure knowledge-making and associated practice in ways which can critically and creatively engage with the very dynamic troubled world, where tragedy and beauty, to paraphrase Thrift (2008), swirl and dance together through everyday life and space in an extraordinary and often bewildering *pas de deux*.

## Pragmatism and NRT

As outlined in the introduction of this book, pragmatism emerged in late-nineteenth-century America and was influenced by a number of the profound scientific, technological, philosophical and political developments of the time. Louis Menand (2001) names Darwinism, the development of statistical methods, the horrors of the American Civil War, which (rather than the First World War) was the first industrial war of mass slaughter, and the growth of democracy as key influences. Pragmatism's birth in the fulcrum of early modern America gives it a flavour of being made in 'the new world' which was clearly a world in (violent) creation. The declaration of American independence had happened only a century earlier, and the modern peoples of America were consciously making a new nation. Thus pragmatism's American heritage brings with it much baggage. There are of course the terrible histories of colonialism, genocide and early forms of ecocide in America – it was, after all, the epitome of the modern state. This history perhaps created 'blind spots' in early pragmatism, which may also account for the indifference and even suspicion that pragmatism has received within European, particularly French, philosophical circles (although see Boltanski and Thévenot, 2006).

There is a creative 'will to power' in American modern history which became a founding principle of pragmatism. The world is to be made, not revealed and accepted. Cornel West (1989) sees this emerging from the work of Ralph Waldo Emerson who was interested in the mythic self which could be built in nineteenth-century America. According to Rorty (1991a, 26), although Emerson was a significant influence on Friedrich Nietzsche, the latter's "will to power" was "more secular" than Emerson's and the early pragmatists were more communal than Emerson and Nietzsche. This is a critical aspect of pragmatism's political potential and an important point of difference with other bodies of theory.

Charles Sanders Peirce, William James and John Dewey are usually considered the founding thinkers of pragmatism. However, key ideas were derived not only from Emerson but other philosophical and ideological traditions such as the work of J.S. Mill, some aspects of utilitarianism, liberalism and democracy, the process philosophy of Alfred Whitehead and Henri Bergson, and logical positivism. In turn, pragmatism has subsequently influenced, or anticipated, several key philosophical authors and movements. Wittgenstein, Nietzsche and Heidegger, and poststructuralism more generally, are often claimed to show pragmatist tendencies (Rorty, 1991a) and the connections between pragmatism and deconstruction have been explored (see Derrida, 1996; Mouffe, 1996). Mouffe makes the point that both approaches seek to pursue progressive politics and ethics within democracy, but without founding them on rationalism and universalism, as the Enlightenment thinking of Habermas and others has sought to do (Mouffe, 1996, 1).

I believe that NRT, and all the more specific applications employed therein (Anderson and Harrison, 2011), are being, and should be, used in a generally pragmatist sense. Pragmatism and NRT can be understood not as a theory or even a set of theories, *but rather as an attitude towards theory and knowledge*. Theories are tools to be used, even metaphors to be used if we feel they are useful to us. They are not tools for revealing the world but for intervening in it.

Thus pragmatism and NRT are part of the same 'family' of thinking that has stood outside representational ontologies. The neo-pragmatism of Rorty, and those who took him up, has been deemed to be too ironist, liberal, white, American and middle-class to be palatable to those seeking radical philosophical, political and ethical approaches (and Bjørn, 2009 offers both a summary of Rorty's work and critiques of it). This is unfortunate, for pragmatism offers a profound challenge to representational thinking. In *Philosophy and the mirror of nature,* Rorty (1979) challenges modern knowledge's fundamental trait of seeking to represent an objectively known world through correspondence theories which claimed to have reached 'the truth of the matter'. The problems with this are that: a) in the end, absolute proof and truth are very slippery concepts, and (modern philosophical) attention ended up fixated on that slipperiness rather than on real world problems; b) any theory of 'objective truth' presents a deterministic model of knowledge that assumes that the world is fixed as it is presented to us, and that we have to live with the consequences; and c) even if one could produce a comprehensive, undisputed account of the world (i.e. hold a mirror up to nature) *one would still have to decide how, and why, to act in the world, and to consider the consequences of action*. Rorty's view was that pragmatism sought to set aside the mirror and instead focus on the question of actions and their consequences in creating the world.

Pragmatism is, in a way, a relativist approach, and Barbara Thayer-Bacon (2002) labels it as 'qualified relativism'. It operates on the basis that the search for fixed, objective truths is not a useful way of thinking about knowledge aspirations and practices, and suggests that there are other useful grounds on which to build. Pragmatism tries to show that this kind of relativism, contrary to often expressed doubt (for example, Bassett, 1999), does not undermine the efficacy of intellectual effort nor cut it adrift in terms of political and ethical opportunities. Rather, it does the reverse. This is important for those who want to use knowledge for change, whether in relation to oppressive social relations or a more sustainable future.

It is significant that the later articulations of pragmatism have heritages of development and use by 'outsiders' in mid-twentieth-century American academia and society (and beyond). Despite its genesis in colonial America and white middle-class male elites, it was adopted by both feminist thinkers and black and Jewish intellectuals in the era of severe prejudice in mid- to late-twentieth century America. A number of feminist thinkers (Fraser, 1995; Siegfried, 2001; Sullivan, 2001) deployed pragmatist stances (see Saegert, this volume). Cornel West, himself a prominent black scholar, and the architect of 'prophetic pragmatism' cited by Emel, stresses that the emergence of pragmatism as a philosophy used by minority scholars reflects America's social and political history with "its revolutionary beginning and its slave-based economy" (West, 1989, 5).

These efforts are instructive as they have served to act as an alternative space for post-poststructuralist feminism and critical race studies where more emancipatory forms of anti-essentialist thinking can develop. Those who have an interest in theory and knowledge which claims to make a difference have turned to a doctrine "whose common denominator consists of a future-orientated instrumentalism that tries to deploy thought as a weapon to enable more effective action" (West, 1989, 5).

Making clear and developing linkages between NRT and pragmatism serves a number of purposes for social and human sciences. First, it places NRT in a wider intellectual movement away from representational knowledges and the systems employed to build and defend them. Second, it should ensure that NRT is not treated/greeted with quite as much 'shock of the new' as is sometimes the case (see for example, Hayden Lorimer's (2005) summary of NRT's reception in cultural geography). Third, it adds weight to the NRT initiative which still faces much misapprehension and suspicion (as is also true for pragmatism). Fourth, it opens up the complex and diverse pragmatist and neo-pragmatist canon as a resource for those seeking ways forward within a number of areas raised by NRT, not least in terms of ethics, politics, epistemology and methods. Here, I offer some thoughts on how pragmatism and NRT can be combined and further energised by taking a more avowedly anti-representational stance to the practices of research, knowledge-making and social action.

### Anti-Representational Theory (ART) and ecology

Creativity is at the heart of the idea of ART, as the acronym is intended to imply. The fundamental aim is to intervene creatively, in collective formations. I believe that this chimes with the more radical versions of pragmatism as set out by Emel. ART also differs from NRT in part because the latter sought, to a large degree, to simply step away from representation (thus its prefix 'non'). But representation and the politics and knowledge systems to which it is aligned are very powerful formations which are aggressively defensive and defended. Thus radical theory cannot simply step away from representation; it needs to confront it more directly and, as such, I am advocating an antithetical stance. Indeed, since its inception in late-nineteenth-century North America, some strands of philosophy, including pragmatism, have pursued anti-representational (rather than non-representational) ontologies and epistemologies. As Richard Rorty describes it: "Nietzsche was as good an anti-Cartesian, *anti-representationalist*, and anti-essentialist as Dewey. He was as devoted to the question 'what difference will this belief make to our conduct?' as Peirce or James" (Rorty, 1991b, 2, emphasis added).

   Life is, or should be, an inherently creative process. Evolution, quantum and Newtonian physics, and chemistry, are all creative processes. Ecology is inherently creative in so far as *life* on earth is the product of evolutionary ecology and the burgeoning of forms and relations that make up the astounding richness of collective life of earth. And this is, in part, why ecocide is so breathtakingly shocking and upsetting. This is, after all, the only known, complex creative living biosphere *in the universe*, even after an increasingly thorough exploration of our own solar system and wider efforts to search for extra-terrestrial life. Ecocide is not only the eradication of ecology; it is the unravelling of creativity. Halting and reversing ecocide is a means of allowing creativity to flourish in ever-emerging eco-social formations. The sciences that describe differing chemical, physical, mathematical, biological processes of such becoming should not be seen as representations but rather as creative extensions of such processes.

   ART reflects this feeling of a world of burgeoning creativity and it is centred on collective, generative co-creation rather than the work of the 'lone artist' creator (and, as such, it echoes the collective sensibilities of pragmatism). It is interested in responding to site and situation creatively with a whole range of resources as expanded upon in the following section.

## Local methods and radical incrementalism (resisting ecocide through creative ecological action)

To return to Emel's editorial (1991), she sets out how pragmatist thinking is a key resource for a critically-creative, experimental, non-foundational, collective endeavour, which can break down the barriers that often enclose academic institutions. Emel stresses that it is these aspects of provocative pragmatism (as she terms it), focusing on the 'front-line' of ethics and politics, that distinguish it from the critical pragmatism of Rorty. As she puts it, "explanation and diagnoses are encouraged to focus down to levels where transformation can occur" (Emel, 1991, 389). Thus ambitions of 'grand theory' are transformed into ambitions for small acts of intervention and, in making this case, Emel concludes:

> every tool available must be employed to turn the tables on entrenched power: cunning, wit, parody, science and all manner of sleight of hand. Provoking, subverting, reinterpreting, unsettling, the pragmatic tactician must tack back and forth – between theory and practice, publics and academics, politics and culture. (Emel, 1991, 338)

All this, I suggest, amounts to a form of radical incrementalism where the focus of action is at the local level. The 'local' may be either or both topographical and topological (i.e. local in terms of geographic place or local in terms of networked connectivity). We must move towards the creative, collective, ecologically founded principles of becoming. Many others have made this case too (see Jones, 2008 for a summary), but provocative pragmatic ART is a call to action.

I advocate the adoption of 'random' or ad hoc methodologies, as expounded by W.G. Sebald and others, as a way of doing things differently so that creativity can be co-created with(in) the weave of the mesh-world: a way of critically-creatively engaging with the ecological fabric of becoming. The current confluence of geographic methods and art practice (a form of ART) which has grown so markedly in recent years (see Hawkins, 2015) provides a material example of a way to undertake the local, site-/situation-specific methods needed to work in any given place and time.

To resist and reverse ecocide we need ecologies of local initiatives of eco-social resistance and creative flourishing. There are very many examples one could point to. The problem is, however, that the energy and power in the destructive systems still far outweigh the energy and power in these alternatives. Of course, we need effective action on the strategic, national and international governmental levels too. But that will only emerge, or have more chance to emerge, from a change in culture, and culture is enacted within the living fabric of everyday (local) society. As noted thinkers on environmental change such as Lawrence Buell (1995) and Mary Midgley (1996) have argued, transformative change will come from imaginative, creative transformations of the underpinning cultural 'norms' of everyday life.

Projects which focus on collective action for eco-social flourishing at the community level can be found everywhere. In both rural and urban settings, there are initiatives which seek to develop community, enhance individual well-being (or at least lessen the traumas of displacement and violence), grow local food and care for wildlife in creative, collective forms of practice. One example is the work of the artist Luci Gorell Barnes, who lives and works in Bristol, UK, but who also speaks 'into' the academic world of geography at conferences and in co-authored papers. Luci runs a number of projects in deprived areas of the city, working mostly with women refugees and asylum seekers who are often challenged in their circumstances of seeking to flourish in an alien setting. One project called 'Companion Planting' seeks to co-produce "activities based around organic gardening and creative practice" (see Gorell Barnes, 2018). Such initiatives are *anti-ecocide*, as they seek to care for individual people, local communities and local biodiversity, and to do so by creating novel assemblages of eco-social hospitality and flourishing.

### The importance of ecology

Sebald, a writer credited with breaking literary moulds with a series of startling books from 1990 until his untimely death in 2001, commented: "I have slowly learned to grasp how everything is connected across space and time" (2013, 149). This is then an ecological view. It corresponds to more 'classical' senses of ecology in which "interconnection is a touchstone of ecology, *everything* that occurs in any given part of an ecosystem will affect the rest, often in unexpected ways" (Armiero and Sedrez, 2014, 4, emphasis in the original).

If this understanding of interconnections is pushed beyond notions of ecology as a 'natural science', it poses a root-and-branch challenge to modern knowledge. It demands creative, collective knowledge practices which can be termed ART. Antecedents to these ways of more holistic, creatively ecological thinking can be seen in Alexander von Humboldt's *Views of nature* (see Wulf, 2015) and similarly in pragmatism, which was strongly influenced by Darwin's great works that had only emerged a few decades previously (see McGranahan, 2017; Rogers, 2009).

The energy and meaning of unfolding collective life is seen in the pulsing mesh of relational transactions which form it, rather than the objects or the physical matter which seemingly make up the mesh. These are better understood as congealed agency; a seemingly stilled formation in material becoming (Barad, 2007). This is a processual view of becoming, in line with non-representational thinkers such as Brian Massumi (2010). Massumi draws extensively on Whitehead (and other process philosophers) and makes explicit links to the pragmatism of William James. As he explains, his approach to thought

> combines elements of James's radical empiricism with Whitehead's process philosophy with the poststructuralism of Deleuze and Guattari with chaos and complexity theory. The resulting perspective converges with Isabelle Stengers' vision of a non-judgmental political ecology of knowledge. An expansive ethics of relationality, of mutual differential belonging, is the natural correlate of an expanded culture of empiricism. (Massumi, 2010, 177)

If the world is one of ecological becoming, or the 'mesh-world' that both Ingold (2011) and Timothy Morton (2010) (differently) outline, then any research/knowledge act is a creative intervention in that meshwork that reverberates in and on both space and time.

There are also threads of connection to actor–network theory and the *Dingpolitik* of Latour (2005), which forms through and around networks, collectives and 'issues of concern', where the more-than-human are given voice, where political assemblies are of multiple form, and where there are not grand narratives of succession, but many streams of politics flowing at once in "a pixelization of politics" (Latour, 2005, 1). This means a breaking up of politics into sites of local action. This has ecological possibilities; and indeed, Latour insists on the need for the ecologicalisation of politics itself.

This is a 'local' method which, as Marcel Hénaff puts it, reflects the requirement for: "a [new] procedural methodology, taking seriously the *particularities of the sites*, the unpredictability of circumstances, the uneven patterns of landscapes and the hazardous nature of becoming" (1997, 72, emphasis added). Perloff (1996) sees a similar bent in Wittgenstein's (later) methods, in which his rejection of 'straight lines' is a compositional as well as an epistemological principle, his own 'conclusions' never being more than tentative, open and to-be-revised.

### Beyond representation to ART

These related ecological and processual views of the becoming world show why knowledge cannot be simply 'representational'. They show instead why knowledge is, or should be, generative. Any knowledge act is folding novelty into the becoming world; thus the world is anew. The pragmatist stance is to actively embrace this aspect of inquiry as intervention and to judge the value of any thought or action by its consequences. This is repeated over time collectively, experimentally and thus incrementally, but with radical impulse in so far as the conditions of the now are far from ideal and need changing. A utopia might need no transformative politics, but a dystopia most certainly does.

Everyone and everything are always somewhere in the mesh-world, located within a series of relations running in different registers and over a span of space-times or 'scales'. This is where 'local' methods come in because every situation is unique in its detailed becoming. A method applied or an idea developed in one context might not work in another because the meshwork of forces and associations in play is different in each case. Creative-critical methods seek to embrace the contextuality and contingency of each situation. The artistic method embraces this in so far as art does not seek to be replicable or generally applied but seeks to respond to the situation at hand.

One of the guiding principles of NRT is that it is 'a machine for multiplying questions and thereby *inventing new relations between thought and life*' (Thrift, 2004, 71, emphasis in the original). This is why those who seek representational answers find NRT so alien as it seeks to be more-than-representational (Lorimer, 2005), but this needs to be seen in the wider, radically incremental process of creative becoming. In this approach you ask questions and you try things. What will it be like if we think or do this? Or, we have tried this and we have shared and discussed that, now what will it be like if we try this alternative? When pushed to anti-representational positions, one arrives at the fully pragmatist stance, as set out by Rorty and many others; this is about embracing the idea that all knowledge acts are creative and are making the world anew with all the risks and possibilities that this entails. Representation is perhaps an understandable desire for fixed ground, for certainty, for a clear view of the frozen terrain of some moment or other. But these are illusions, the ghost in the machines of modernist knowledge – including reductionist science.

So where does this get us politically? Out of creative-critical actions at the 'local' level, if enough energy is generated, larger-scale change might come. As Rebecca Solnit explains:

> This [the possibility of transformative bottom-up change] will only matter if it's sustained. To sustain it, people have to believe that the myriad small, incremental actions matter; that they matter even when the consequences aren't immediate or obvious. They must remember that often when you fail at your immediate objective – to block a nominee or a pipeline or to pass a bill – that even then you may have changed the whole framework in ways that make broader change inevitable. You may change the story or the rules, give tools, templates or encouragement to future activists, and make it possible for those around you to persist in their efforts. (Solnit, 2017)

## Conclusion

Robert Burch notes that: "According to Peirce, the most fundamental engine of the evolutionary process is not struggle, strife, greed, or competition. Rather it is nurturing love, in which an entity is prepared to sacrifice its own perfection for the sake of the wellbeing of its neighbor" (2006, 1). This is the idea of "agapeism", that "growth comes only from love", as Peirce (1893, in Menand, 1997, 52) described it more than one hundred years ago. This is a profound insight reflecting the power of the pragmatic tradition of thought; love as a creative, collaborative, ecological force.

And along with love, solidarity with those who face tragedy has emerged as a central focus of pragmatism: "human struggle sits at the centre of prophetic pragmatism, a struggle guided by a democratic and libertarian vision, sustained by moral courage and existential integrity" (West, 1989, 228). Given the history of America, the social focus here is understandable, but we need to push it to include recognition of the importance of ecological solidarity, and to question the modern settlements in which we live.

The Invisible Committee asserted: "Two centuries of capitalism and market nihilism have brought us to the most extreme alienations – from ourselves, from others, from worlds. The fiction of the individual has decomposed at the same speed that it was becoming real. … It's with an entire anthropology that we are at war. The very idea of man" (The Invisible Committee, 2009, 16). This reflects the ecocide of the three ecologies – biodiversity, non-modern cultures and the psychic ecologies of the self – as outlined above in this chapter.

To return to the start, the situation we are in is grave. And it is so in two related senses: the devastation we now are facing; and the fact that the established political elites seem to fail utterly to see these risks. A previous Chancellor of the Exchequer of the UK government, George Osborne, stated that "he held out the hope that Britain will become the richest country in the G7 industrialised group of nations by the 2030s" (Wintour, 2015). At the same time, scientific reports were also in the media warning of the collapse of soil health and food production, and the rise of sea levels to the point when the UK becomes an archipelago of islands by the end of the twenty-first century. The science in the latter cases is uncertain but, even if partially correct, Osborne's capitalist, neoliberal dream of being the richest global economy is just a dream – or, rather, a nightmare.

There are those who argue that this view is 'doom-mongering', a product of the prevalence of rolling news and the outing of some undoubtedly severe global issues previously hidden. Under modernity, industrialism, capitalism and the spread of liberal democracy, it is argued, billions have moved out of extreme poverty and conflict and, to some extent, out of the grip of certain common, preventable diseases, and gender and race oppressions. In other words, 'Modernity as progress' has delivered and is working (see, for example, Pinker, 2018). But these views fail to recognise the joined-up nature and the meta-ecology of these significant trends: the progress modernity has made in the ways suggested is the same force that – at the same time – is undermining the socio-ecological fabric that underpins everything by the effects of its fallout (see Gray, 2007).

Looking at modernity from the 'outside', West argues that many figures of the pragmatist tradition have, in differing ways, attempted to face up to the tragedy of the world. Pragmatism "confronts candidly individual and collective experiences of evil in individuals and institutions" (1989, 228), while, at the same time, retaining a balancing affirmation of hope. West claims that prophetic pragmatism:

> Tempers its utopian impulse with a profound sense of the tragic character of life and history. This sense of the tragic highlights the irreducible predicament of unique individuals who undergo dread, despair, disillusionment, disease, and death and the institutional forms of oppression that dehumanize people. (West, 1989, 228)

All this, of course, can and should be extended to considerations of the non-human world, and it is urgent we act, and act creatively, now.

## References

Anderson, B. and Harrison, P. (2011) *Taking-place: Non-representational theories and geography*. London: Routledge.

Armiero, M. and Sedrez, L. (2014) Introduction, in M. Armiero and L. Sedrez, eds, *A history of environmentalism: Local struggles, global histories*. London: Bloomsbury.

Barad, K. (2007) *Meeting the universe half way: Quantum physics and the entanglement of matter as meaning*. Durham, NC: Duke University Press.

Bassett, K. (1999) Is there progress in human geography? The problem of progress in the light of recent work in the philosophy and sociology of science. *Progress in Human Geography*, 23, 1, 27–47.

Bjørn, R. (2009) Richard Rorty, *Stanford Encyclopedia of Philosophy*. https://plato.stanford.edu/archives/spr2009/entries/rorty/ (accessed 5 June 2018).

Boltanski, L. and Thévenot, L. (2006) *On justification: Economies of worth*, trans. C. Porter. Princeton, NJ: Princeton University Press.

Buell, L. (1995) *The environmental imagination, Thoreau, nature writing and the formation of American culture*. Cambridge, MA: Harvard University Press.

Burch, R. (2006) Charles Sanders Peirce, *Stanford Encyclopedia of Philosophy*. https://plato.stanford.edu/entries/peirce/ (accessed 5 June 2018).

Carson, R. (1962) *Silent spring*. Boston, MA: Houghton Mifflin.

Clapperton, J. (2016) Indigenous ecological knowledge and the politics of postcolonial writing, in J. Clapperton and L. Piper, eds, *RCC Perspectives: Transformations in Environment and Society: Environmental knowledge, environmental politics*, 4, 9–16.

Coles, R. (2016) *Visionary pragmatism: Radical and ecological democracy in neoliberal times*. Durham, NC: Duke University Press.

Derrida, J. (1996) Remarks on deconstruction and pragmatism, in C. Mouffe, ed., *Deconstruction and pragmatism: Simon Critchley, Jacques Derrida, Ernesto Laclau and Richard Rorty*. London: Routledge, 77–88.

Emel, J. (1991) Ecological crisis and provocative pragmatism. *Environment and Planning D: Society and Space*, 9, 384–90.

Fraser, N (1995) From irony to prophecy to politics: A response to Richard Rorty, in R.B. Goodman, ed., *Pragmatism: A contemporary reader*. London: Routledge, 153–9.

Goody, J. (2004) *Capitalism and modernity: The great debate*. Cambridge: Polity Press.

Gorell Barnes, L. (2018) *Companion planting – continuing the allotment project*. www.lucigorellbarnes.co.uk/companion-planting-continuing-the-allotment-project/ (accessed 13 June 2018).

Gray, J. (2007) *Black mass: Apocalyptic religion and the death of utopia*. London: Macmillan.

Guattari, F. ([orig. French 1989] 2000) *The three ecologies*. London: Athlone Press.

Haraway, D. (2015) Anthropocene, Capitalocene, Plantationocene, Chthulucene: Making kin. *Environmental Humanities*, 6, 1, 159–65.

Hawkins, H. (2015) Creative geographic methods: Knowing, representing, intervening. *Cultural Geographies*, 22, 2, 247–68.

Hénaff, M. (1997) Of stones, angels and humans: Michel Serres and the global city. *SubStance*, 83, 59–80.

Ingold, T. (2011) *Essays on movement, knowledge and description*. London: Routledge.

The Invisible Committee (2009) *The coming insurrection*. Los Angeles, CA: Semiotext(e).

Jones, O. (2008) Stepping from the wreckage: Geography, pragmatism and anti-representational theory, special issue on Pragmatism and Geography, eds N. Wood and S. Smith. *Geoforum*, 39, 1600–12.

Kloppenberg, J.T. (1998) Pragmatism: An old name for some new ways of thinking?, in M. Dickstein, ed., *The revival of pragmatism: New essays on social thought, law, and culture*. Durham, NC: Duke University Press.

Latour, B. (1993) *We have never been modern*. London: Harvester Wheatsheaf.

Latour, B. (2005) From Realpolitik to Dingpolitik – or how to make things public, in B. Latour and P. Weibel, eds, *Making things public: Atmospheres of democracy*. Cambridge, MA: MIT Press, 14–41.

Lorimer, H. (2005) Cultural geography: The busyness of being 'more than representational'. *Progress in Human Geography*, 29, 1, 83–94.

Massumi, B. (2010) Too-blue: Colour-patch for an expanded empiricism. *Cultural Studies*, 14, 2, 177–226.

McGranahan, L. (2017) *Darwinism and pragmatism: William James on evolution and self-transformation*. London: Routledge.

Menand, L. (1997) *Pragmatism: A reader*. New York, NY: Vintage Books.

Menand, L. (2001) *The metaphysical club: A story of ideas in America*. New York, NY: Farrar, Straus and Giroux.

Midgley, M. (1996) *Utopias, dolphins and computers: Problems of philosophical plumbing*. London: Routledge.

Morton, T. (2010) *The ecological thought*. Harvard, MA: Harvard University Press.

Mouffe, C. (ed.) (1996) *Deconstruction and pragmatism*. London: Routledge.

Peirce, C.S. (1893) Evolutionary love. *The Monist*, 3 (January), 176–200.

Perloff, M. (1996) *Wittgenstein's ladder. Poetic language and the strangeness of the ordinary*. Chicago, IL: Chicago University Press.

Pindar, I. and Sutton, P. (2000) Introduction, in F. Guattari, ed., *The three ecologies*. London: Athlone Press, 1–20.

Pinker, S. (2018) *Enlightenment now: The case for reason, science, humanism, and progress*. London: Penguin.

Rogers, M. (2009) *The undiscovered Dewey: Religion, morality, and the ethos of democracy*. New York, NY: Columbia University Press.

Rorty, R. (1979) *Philosophy and the mirror of nature*. Princeton, NJ: Princeton University Press.

Rorty, R. (1991a) *Consequences of pragmatism*. Hemel Hempstead: Harvester Wheatsheaf.

Rorty, R. (1991b) *Essays on Heidegger and others: Philosophical papers volume 2*. Cambridge: Cambridge University Press.

Sebald, W.G. (2013) *A place in the country*. London: Penguin.

Siegfried, C.H. (2001) *Feminist interpretations of John Dewey*. University Park, PA: Pennsylvania State University Press.

Serres, M. (1995) *The natural contract*. Ann Arbor, MI: Michigan University Press.

Solnit, R. (2017) Protest and persist: Why giving up hope is not an option. *Guardian Online*, 13 March. www.theguardian.com/world/2017/mar/13/protest-persist-hope-trump-activism-anti-nuclear-movement (accessed 5 June 2018).

Stengers, I. (2015) *In catastrophic times: Resisting the coming barbarism*. Paris: Open Humanities Press.

Sullivan, S. (2001) *Living across and through skins: Transactional bodies, pragmatism, and feminism*. Bloomington, IN: Indiana University Press.

Thayer-Bacon, B.J. (2002) Using the 'R' word again: Pragmatism as qualified relativism. *Philosophical Studies in Education*, 33, 93–103.

Thrift, N. (1999) Steps to an ecology of place, in D. Massey, P. Sarre and J. Allen, eds, *Human geography today*. Oxford: Polity, 295–352.

Thrift, N. (2004) Intensities of feeling: Towards a spatial politics of affect. *Geografiska Annaler*, 86, B, 57–78.

Thrift, N. (2008) *Non-representational theory: Space, politics, affect*. London: Routledge.

West, C. (1989) *The American evasion of philosophy: A genealogy of pragmatism*. London: Macmillan.

Wintour, P. (2015) Britain can become world's richest major economy, says George Osborne. *Guardian Online*, 14 January. www.theguardian.com/politics/2015/jan/14/britain-richest-country-world-george-osborne-fiscal-policy (accessed 11 June 2018).

Wulf, A. (2015) *The invention of nature: The adventures of Alexander von Humboldt*. London: John Murray.

# 12

# Pragmatism and contemporary planning theory: Going beyond a communicative approach

*Ihnji Jon*

## Introduction

The word 'planning' contains so many implications that it is not easy to define it in a few sentences. According to Healey (2009), planning is a governance practice that not only concerns existing relations but also opens up future possibilities for improving the conditions of human co-existence. In this sense, planning includes the tasks of today and the future. The tasks assigned to planning in the past were much clearer than is the case today. We used to assume, with certainty, that we could analyse and understand the problems of today and that we would be able to model and predict the future. As decades went by, however, trust in rational reasoning was challenged by historical events that could not be explained by calculative techniques of modelling and prediction. Wars, economic depression, riots and environmental hazards have made us realise that our rational understanding of the world was never a complete representation and that our prediction of the future was often proven to be wrong. Planners discovered the dilemmas inherent in instrumental rationality and accepted the limitations of quantitative methods and other systematic analytic techniques to depict the world and predict the future (Innes, 1995). Such recognition prompted uncomfortable questions: Why plan at all when our understanding of today is limited and our idea of the future is so uncertain? What *is* planning when we cannot picture where we wish to arrive through our plans?

Acknowledging the limits of our capacity to grasp and control the world is related to a pragmatist attitude towards truth, which emphasises the fallibility of our knowledge of the world. Pragmatists questioned transcendental, timeless bases for establishing truth and belief, and raised doubts about the 'logical positivist' version of scientific inquiry that sought out objective truths and universal laws (Harrison, 2002; Healey, 2009). Such an anti-essentialist perception of 'truth', I argue here, is the central characteristic of contemporary planning theory. Contemporary planning ideas, despite differences in their orientation, share a rejection of the existence of *the* truth and of any certainty about what is happening today and will happen tomorrow. Planning in this sense does not expect or envision a specific type of future. Its concern, rather, is on the contextual experience of 'what to do' in the here and now. What planners have in mind is a set of practices and orientation, not one eventual end point.

This chapter argues that pragmatism has much to offer contemporary planning theory and practice and in what follows I discuss the influence of pragmatism on contemporary planning thought and introduce a new reading of pragmatist planning that can enhance theory and practice in future. Contemporary planning theory has been dominated by debates about communicative and radical planning approaches. Although these two branches of planning theory seem to be very different from one another, I argue that there are important similarities to be observed when viewed through the lens of pragmatism. I then demonstrate how importing pragmatism to planning can help us go beyond communicative or consensus planning (Healey, 2009; Forester, 2012), in order to develop pragmatic planning theory that is able to fully embrace the plurality of the social. By drawing on ideas from current pragmatist philosophers (Bernstein, 2010; Fraser, 1998; Macke, 1995; Shalin, 1992), I underline pragmatism's prioritisation of experiential knowledge over linguistic representation, in an attempt to show how a new reading of pragmatism can better reflect the social plurality recognised by proponents of agonistic and radical planning theories. As such, this chapter provides a pragmatic critique of communicative/consensus planning, while also facilitating greater recognition of the importance of pluralism and agonistic social conflicts in planning. Introducing this approach is important primarily because it expands our horizon of what is considered to be a pragmatic approach to planning practice. While theorists have suggested developing a 'post-consensus' or 'post-collaborative' approach to planning theory (Bacqué and Gauthier, 2011; Bond, 2011; Brownill and Parker, 2010), there has been little effort to engage with pragmatism in the development of these ideas. A pragmatic approach to planning has an important emphasis on experiential knowledge and impassioned action that firmly acknowledges the plurality of the social and negates the possibility of a unitary, overarching public. Despite their apparent differences, this kind of pragmatism chimes with the core idea of agonistic and radical planning theories, as outlined in more detail below.

## The shared pragmatism of communicative and radical planning theory

In this section, I introduce two major branches in the contemporary planning theory literature: communicative planning and radical planning theory. In these brief introductions, the difference between the two bodies of literature stays apparent: while communicative/consensus planning focuses on rendering planning processes more inclusive and fair, highlighting how planners can be good mediators in the battle of different interests, radical planning attempts to go beyond the conventional roundtable approach to planning so as to more seriously recognise and valorise the plurality of the social. However, as I discuss below in more detail, these approaches also share important characteristics that are central to pragmatic thought: their focus on arriving at a temporarily per-fect moment, rather than achieving a final, modernistic, perfect utopia that reflects the 'truth'.

### *Communicative planning*

Introduced by Healey (1996 [2003]; 2009), Forester (1999, 2006, 2012) and Innes (1995), communicative planning's focus on democratic communication within a community is based on the assumption that open, transparent discus-sion on the subject of concern constitutes the practice of democratic planning (Forester, 1999, 2006, 2012; Healey, 1996 [2003], 2009; Innes, 1995), the result of which should be respected as what pragmatists call truth as being 'what works for us' (Scheffler, 1974). Dewey's pragmatism was especially sceptical of the role of experts in democratic communities (Bernstein, 1998, 149) because he rejected the assumption that any group of individuals has the sole expertise to make the judgements and decisions that have impacts on our everyday lives. Openness, fallibility of knowledge and ongoing criticism are the virtues that Dewey highlighted as being important in a democratic community.

Yet if planners are sceptical about expert knowledge, then on what basis are planners supposed to plan? Healey and Forester, the leading communicative planning theorists, escape this dilemma by focusing on procedural validity. An outcome can be justified if the process of producing it was open, transparent and democratic. They lean towards the importance of process – or how we get to an agreement - whether or not the outcome was fair. Healey (2009) discusses how to make the process of inclusionary argumentation fairer and more reason-able, taking the example of legal procedures in court. This critical standard, however, is not applied to the outcome or the substance of the agreement. As long as the procedure or discourse was under the supervision of reflexive cri-tique to ensure that it was fair and inclusive, the planners' job is done and the kind of agreement reached does not matter. According to Forester, the consensus-building framework must be attentive not just to getting agreements or getting things done but to the legitimacy and transparency of producing agreements (Forester, 2012).

### Radical planning

Radical planning theory attempts to incorporate power and conflict into the planning framework because attempts to establish a rational consensus may result in a thin agreement around the lowest common denominator of agreement (Allmendinger, 1999). The introduction of a radical planning approach began from Hillier's (2003) trenchant critique of communicative/consensus planning, which revealed the dilemma of the consensus-building framework, arguing that it fails to guarantee a constructive (and not shallow) agreement due to the power relations embedded in communication and which reflect the conflicts, antagonisms and contradictions that lie at the heart of any society (Tajbakhsh, 2001). Following on from such criticisms, writers such as Hillier (2008), Purcell (2013), Newman (2011), Boelens (2010) and Boonstra and Boelens (2011) have proposed new approaches to planning that go beyond consensus-driven planning. Writers such as Purcell (2013), Newman (2011) and Boelens (2010) have focused on the roles of social movements and citizen-driven autonomous action as alternatives to government-driven initiatives in planning. For instance, Boelens (2010) introduced an 'actor-relational approach' (ARA) to underline the importance of acknowledging the planning initiatives led by actors beyond the traditional governmental structures. He argues that the ARA approach is not about different actors with divergent interests meeting halfway to sacrifice their ideals: as he puts it:

> the point is not to formulate an objective, vision or plan, which then has to be implemented in trade-offs, whether in a participatory, public-private or collaborative way. The point is to refocus on the actors in space themselves, to follow their existing and/ or evolving networks and to analyse if it is necessary or possible to (re) connect or translate these actor-networks into more suitable, robust, resilient spatial programs, in such a way that they themselves would benefit. (Boelens, 2010, 556)

These arguments overlap with an earlier tradition of radical planning, developed by writers such as Soja (1997) and Sandercock (1998) who focused on the 'eradicable differences' that exist in any community. Such approaches call for more attention to addressing the plurality of the social, which can lead to a valorisation of social conflicts (agonism) as well as alternatives to government-driven planning (Pløger, 2004; Sørensen, 2014). Radical planners acknowledge the plurality of the social and many of them draw on Chantal Mouffe's (1999) writings on agonism. Mouffe argues that honouring the existence of conflicts or *agons* is essential for plural democracy as such conflicts signal the limits of politics done in the name of 'the' public. As Laclau and Mouffe (1985 [2000], 192) argue: "there is no radical and plural democracy without renouncing the discourse of the universal and its implicit assumption of a privileged point of access to 'the truth', which can be reached only by a limited number of subjects". From this point of view, the active defence of plural democracy is necessarily associated with the self-organisation of different social collectives because these self-organisations are manifestations of a plurality of social life.

The aim of radical planning is, therefore, not to reach for a shallow consensus that reinforces existing power relations, nor to eliminate the conflict through verbal consensus that necessarily obscures the plurality of the social. But this raises the question of what is left for the role of the planners? According to Newman (2011), radical planning does not seek a revolution that aims to overthrow existing power and create an alternative society. This type of revolution ultimately fails because there is no one perfect alternative society and every revolutionary project of creating a new society should be seen as a utopian illusion. Rather, for radical planners, the goal is to initiate self-ordering, autonomous action from below. Examples vary but it is essentially about everyday autonomous practices (such as grassroots mobilisations) by ordinary people and in this form of social change, ordinary people are encouraged to take up the project of governing themselves (Purcell, 2013; see also Deleuze and Guattari, 1972 [1977], 1980 [1987]). Moreover, such activity is about an ontology of becoming, as opposed to an ontology of being. This is about the process of change rather than reaching a particular goal; as Purcell (2013, 22) suggests, radical planning "insists that objects in the world are continually in the process of becoming something else, that reality is a continual unfolding of events that do not necessarily move towards a larger end goal". What planners have in mind here is not a single, normative, fixed vision of a future but a continuously changing desire to move towards more autonomous, self-ordering, pluralistic and democratic urban space. Within this perspective, radical planning is not a practice with a stable, specified goal; rather, it is a dynamic, constantly changing experiment that welcomes uncertainty. This approach to planning, therefore, is realistic and pragmatic. We no longer dream of a revolution or a plan that will produce utopia; rather, we should continuously look for our own utopia by constantly trying to act in the present. Nobody knows in advance what this utopia will look like. We may reach it temporarily, but it will continuously change as we keep escaping institutionalised power. In short, radical planning theory looks for moments, glimmers or ruptures of temporary triumphs and temporary revolutions. No matter how long they last, such events become part of a continuously changing movement against top-down order and control.

The way in which towns and cities can be planned in reflection of these radical planning ideas has been explored by several writers (Balducci et al., 2011; Boonstra and Boelens, 2011; Hillier, 2008; Nyseth, 2012). Their arguments address how to engage the public more effectively in planning processes, rather than merely hosting roundtables or public hearings, and how to take account of the roles played by different actors in the process of planning; and they develop an actor–network approach to planning where planners first observe what the range of potential actors can achieve for themselves before government intervention.

### Bridging the gap between communicative and radical approaches to planning via pragmatism

These brief summaries demonstrate both similarities and differences between these two bodies of contemporary planning theory and practice. There are significant differences between consensus building and radical planning, especially in terms of their ideals regarding the role of planning. Consensus building sees planning as a communicative activity employing language and discourse to foster the possibility of coexistence as well as working together despite our differences. Radical planning, on the other hand, incorporates power and conflict into the planning framework; it aims to escape from any form of institutionalised power; and it encourages direct, autonomous, self-ordered movements. Despite their differences, however, the two approaches meet each other in relation to the pragmatic idea of truth. Both were born in a rejection of transcendental truth or a single vision of the future and both welcome plural perspectives and visions of how different futures may unfold.

Consensus building focuses on the story-telling *process* of arriving at agreement. According to this framework, what really matters is the fact that different parties came together and *made an effort* to create a satisfying outcome for all participants. With the best effort, it may be possible to reach an agreement from which all parties can benefit, but it is never guaranteed. The role of planners is *not* about promising the socially good outcome but creating a *stage* that enables a discussion despite the differences. However, each case is different and there is no one approach to consensus that suits all situations. Planners pursuing a communicative approach celebrate their temporary achievements in relation to each individual case when it occurs, but they are continuously searching for those temporary moments of success and not one kind of success that is *the* answer for all. Planning here is about contextual experience and decision-making, rather than securing a concrete goal.

Radical planners adopt a similar approach. They reject the idea of one single utopia and end-point of organisation. In this vision, there is no fixed destination but, rather, a series of temporary triumphs such as workers occupying their factory or Egyptians taking over the public square in a moment of utopian rupture within the present (Newman, 2011). Instead of pursuing a single utopia or a fixed outcome, radical planning involves autonomous, self-ordered movements that provide glimmers of a social revolution that comprises "a profound transformation of the existing order of society" (Purcell, 2013, 25). This approach radically departs from the consensual approach to planning but both approaches understand planning to be contextual and dependent upon circumstances. The rejection of transcendental truth and the idea of planning as being dependent upon contextual experience are both factors very much in line with pragmatic thought, as explored in the following section, below.

## How pragmatic planning goes beyond the communicative approach

### *A pragmatic critique of communicative/consensus planning*

Many scholars looking at the potential to apply pragmatic ideas to planning have drawn sustenance from Habermas's theory of communicative action (Forester, 1989, 1999; Hoch, 2007; Healey, 2009). However, Harrison (2002) has noted that Habermas's theory cannot be equated with pragmatism and that "at best, it represents a highly selective reconstruction of some parts of pragmatist theory" (Joas, 1988, as cited in Harrison, 2002, 162). Similarly, Shalin (1992) noted how the Habermasian understanding of pragmatism, with its selective focus on communicative rationality, "shows little sensitivity to other facets of pragmatism" (Shalin, 1992, 237). Building on these efforts to differentiate Habermas's theory from early pragmatism, in this section I argue that the consensus approach can be criticised on pragmatist grounds by highlighting the aspects of pragmatism that were neglected in Habermasian theory of communicative action. In a departure from discursive communicative action and consensus-building theory, which are fundamentally based on creating the right kind of rules and therefore the ideal speech environment for discursive deliberation, my ideas are based on the existence of social solidarity that is gradually constructed through people's historical *experience* through shared activity. Drawing from Shalin's (1992) critique of Habermasian pragmatism and Macke's (1995) attempt to connect pragmatism with French postmodernism, I criticise the communicative approach because its focus on verbal consensus tends to disregard the fact that there can be more than one form of consensus and action within a community and that verbal agreement itself is not a prerequisite for tangible (or practical) outcomes. Going further, focusing on pragmatism's emphasis on pluralistic community and to engage in action, I contend that a pragmatic understanding of democracy is essentially agonistic - which allows us to see conflict not as a hurdle to overcome but as a source of energy that drives collective actions and experiences.

A contemporary reading of early pragmatism underlines its emphasis on lived experience as the context for the practice of communication. Shalin (1992) objected to the Habermasian understanding of pragmatism because, in the theory of communicative action, "what pragmatists call 'experience' has shrivelled into verbal intellect" and its emphasis on thinking (consciousness, understanding, cognition) shows little appreciation for the larger context of material practice (Shalin, 1992, 254). In contrast to the Habermasian approach that prioritises the cognitive form of universality above all others and "inadvertently devalues human experience as merely private and intellectually mute", pragmatists believe that "to divest reason from living experience is to disembody it. . . When thinking leaves experience far behind and escapes into theoria, it is likely to lead practical action astray" (Shalin, 1992, 255). As Dewey puts it, the "conclusion is not that the emotional, passionate phase of action can be or should be eliminated in behalf of bloodless reason. More 'passions,' not fewer, is the answer. . . Rationality, once more is not a force to evoke against impulse and habit. It is the attainment of a working harmony among diverse desires" (Dewey, 2008a, 136).

Consequently, Shalin suggests that the theory of communicative action leaves out what pragmatists call embodied or concrete reasonableness (Alexander, 1987, Rochberg-Halton, 1986; Shalin, 1992). Macke (1995) has similarly argued that Dewey's concept of experience is not qualitatively or perceptively different from some forms of French phenomenology and postmodernism in that they both saw 'passion' as the driver through which we can find the birth of meaningful art, reason and experience. Macke discussed how impassioned experience, a concept drawn directly from Dewey (Dewey, 2008b, 295), can be interpreted as a somatic experience that underlines the limit of linguistic expression or communication: "in the space of such a moment, we are both shaken from the fragile foundation of the infinite (language's false promise, its tragic heaven) and riveted to the astonishing, enveloping, and exorbitant encounter with the speechlessness that reminds us of our ultimate limit" (Macke, 1995, 164).

Macke contends that Dewey's pragmatism is "an inquiry into the limits of communication", an inquiry that relates to "the vitality of speechless primary experience" (Macke, 1995, 164). Bridge (2004) also cites Dewey's remark that "a universe of experience is a precondition of a universe of discourse. . . Although lived experience may exceed the boundaries of discourse, our expression of it usually, and our discussion of it always, cannot" (Dewey, LW: 74, quoted in Bridge, 2004, 73). Accordingly, Habermasian communicative action, the fundamental basis of the consensus approach in planning, can be criticised via this pragmatic insight that emphasises the importance of lived experience and embodied action, which subsequently highlights the limits of instrumental communication. This notion also explains why more weight should be placed on practical, material actions and emotions than on verbal consensus, as explained further below.

The consensus approach regards verbal discourse as a practical action in itself, because securing agreement can eventually lead to actions that can solve problems (Forester, 1999) and because consensus building is a learning process that fosters mutual understanding (Healey, 1996 [2003]; Innes and Booher, 2000). However, the idea that the act of trying to reach a wider consensus is practical is questionable since it presumes that a meaningful, material or practical action can be best achieved through a discursive consensus. Following

Shalin's (1992) example, we can expose the limits of a focus on communicative consensus by asking "if we choose to understand Bach by reading the music sheets rather than by listening to his fugues" (Shalin, 1992, 262). We don't know, until it is actually played, why discussions over certain notes on a musical score would matter in practice. Therefore, each recital, played via a unique interpretation of the score, is valued as a valid attempt to narrow the gap between theory and practice, however much each interpretation disagrees with any other. Similarly, the importance of material action is highlighted in pragmatism because we don't know how the current social climate will affect, enhance or distort the implementation of our ideas until they are actually practised. As Shalin (1992) noted, Habermasian communicative action demands unequivocal commitment to a consensus before taking any action, which is a far cry from a pragmatic focus on uncertainty and the importance of context.

Embracing uncertainty about society and our experience of it is an important step in differentiating pragmatism from the approach of communicative rationality. In the context of defining a democratic community, Bernstein (1998) noted that when Dewey spoke of the 'Great Community', he did not think of a single homogeneous community. Instead, "it is (the) ideal of a community of democratic communi*ties*" (Bernstein, 1998, 148, emphasis added) where individuals are responsible for forming and directing activities in a diversity of groups. Dewey was sceptical of the melting pot metaphor and declared that "the theory of the melting pot always gave me rather a pang" (Bernstein, 1998, 148). His notion of community, accordingly, is essentially pluralistic (Bernstein, 1998, 148). Based on pragmatism's focus on pluralism as well as its emphasis on material action, there is scope for understanding planning through the lens of pragmatism, moving beyond the limits of the consensus approach.

While communication helps us to understand one another, groups with different values and ideals do not need to arrive at a consensus or to compromise their fundamental differences in order to take action or undertake new initiatives. Pragmatism's concept of pluralistic community can be interpreted as acknowledging plural consensuses and plural actions within a community, especially given the emphasis on material actions over discursive communication. Dewey did not think that rational discussion alone is "sufficient to bring about genuine social reform" (Bernstein, 1998, 149); for Dewey, social problems are "resolved by releasing human energies so that people will be able to *act* for themselves" (Putnam, 1990, 1695, emphasis added).

The examples of pragmatic action discussed by Kloppenberg (1998) are more than just the act of discourse itself, and include the labour of building a playground or investigating historical controversy. In other words, if we are a group of people (small or large) who have already come to a consensus to take a certain action, we do not have to dilute the essence of our group's identity and belief in order to achieve a wider consensus through verbally persuading other groups with fundamentally different values from ours, which would most likely result in 'standardisation favourable to mediocrity' or the 'melting pot' that Dewey objected to. Diluting different identities and beliefs for the purpose of making wider consensus is not 'pragmatic' because these (undiluted) identities and beliefs are the main drivers of plural, impassioned actions advocated by pragmatism. In other words, a sheer collection of more 'yeses' from more types of people is not a prerequisite for collective action and the resulting experiences, which means that a group does not have to be larger, or a consensus does not have to be wider, for it to produce impassioned social action. Prioritising practical action over verbal consensus can be referred to as achieving a "pragmatic certainty" (Rosenthal, 1986, 59) in our behaviour to engage in material action, which means that we have to move beyond symbolic (or, in this case, discursive) actions in order to pragmatically accomplish narrowing the gap between knowledge and reality.

A pragmatic understanding of democratic polity is essentially agonistic and stresses the value of conflicts. Bernstein notes that the early pragmatists including James and Dewey "never subscribed to the belief that there can be a 'final' reconciliation or resolution to all social conflicts" and they accepted that "the agonistic quality of democratic politics is intrinsic to creative democracy" (1998, 153). By emphasising "the *fertility* of conflict and dissonance" among the plural groups (Bernstein, 1998, 155, emphasis added), pragmatist pluralism "accentuates the limits of theoretically grounded consensus and highlights the productive properties of dissent" (Shalin, 1992, 262). Strong identities, values and ideals of each group, which are in some cases hard to negotiate, certainly reflect more radical differences between groups, and while these differences are the reasons for conflicts and struggle, it must not be forgotten that they can also fuel each group's collective action, through which their everyday experience of democratic action is augmented.

Dissent is "the first sign that communication was uncoerced and that participants expressed themselves freely" (Shalin, 1992, 263) and pragmatism's emphasis on pluralism as well as prioritising engagement in actions over verbal agreements helps us realise that conflicts are not just a hurdle to overcome but in fact are a product of the differences (in identities, values and ideals) that can give rise to active engagement and impassioned actions. Differentiating yourself from others provides you with a firm identity that gives you energy to act. In other words, the existence of radically different groups is not necessarily a negative sign in participatory democracy; it is a proof that these groups would not remain as mere followers of what they have verbally agreed, but can become active entrepreneurs for developing their own creative initiatives to be followed by their actions.

This is why an agonistic understanding of democracy rooted in pluralism, difference and conflict is not just a pessimistic critique of communicative action but can be interpreted as a pragmatic approach that underscores the importance of struggles among divergent values and ideals. Accordingly, the positive and

even productive role of conflict has been discussed by agonist-inspired planning theorists. Flyvbjerg (1998), for example, has argued that it is important to
value the social conflicts that produce valuable ties and provide modern democratic societies with the strength and cohesion they need, such that "social
conflicts are the true pillars of democratic society" (Flyvbjerg, 1998, 209).
Recently, Sørensen (2014) underlined the value of conflicts in governance and
planning, especially regarding the productive role of conflict in creating the
institutional conditions that can result in pluricentric governance. At this point,
conflict is not only inevitable or irreducible but also an essential factor that
renders democracy more democratic (see also Featherstone, 2008; Norval,
2007). Therefore, the task before us is not to smooth out differences that exist
among us but to devise ways in which we can harness the energy that comes
from these differences, and to consider a point of conflict as an opportunity to
bring out creative initiatives and augmented voluntary actions.

### Going forward: importing a new reading of pragmatism to planning

Building on the pragmatic insights about experience, pluralism and conflict, it
is clear that pragmatism can inspire new planning approaches that go beyond com-
municative/consensus planning. In the field of planning theory, a pragmatism-
influenced planning is often equated with communicative planning ideas that
are largely dependent on Habermasian ideals of communicative rationality
(Forester, 2012; Healey, 2009). But there is a lot more that pragmatism can offer
planning. Here I discuss some pragmatist ideas that could be particularly
important in advancing contemporary planning theory going forward.

What has been overlooked in introducing pragmatism to the field of planning is pragmatism's position on language versus experience. Bernstein (2010),
an avid advocate of reviving Dewey's pragmatism, criticised the linguistic turn
in pragmatism, arguing that its extensive focus on discursive action limits our
access to wisdom derived through experience. Bernstein noted that the linguistic turn is problematic because, above all, it "slides into linguistic idealism,
which tends to lose contact with the everyday life world of human beings and
fails to do justice to the ways in which experience … constrains us" (Bernstein,
2010, 152). In short, with the shift from experience to language, knowledge
claims cannot be verified by lived experience as they are in Dewey's experimental logic (Waks, 1998).

Similar worries have been expressed by feminist pragmatists, such as Kruks
(2001), who argued that effective feminist politics requires "hold[ing] onto the
concepts of experience and attending to the ways in which experience can
exceed discursivity" (Kruks, 2001, 133). She presents domestic violence as an
example that is "not only discursively constituted but also lived 'from the inside
out'" (2001, 138). In relation to that, it may be helpful to consider how Bernstein (2010) confronted the political theorists who criticised Dewey for his

overly optimistic view on participatory democracy. In advocating for Dewey, he distances Dewey's ideas from "some versions of 'deliberative democracy'" that "tend to exaggerate the role of rational persuasion in democratic politics". Bernstein argued that:

> there is a tendency to overemphasize the role and potential power of rational argumentation. Dewey was never happy with the way in which philosophers and political theorists characterized reason – especially when they sharply distinguished reason from emotion, desire, and passion. Intelligence is not the name of a special faculty. Rather, it designates a cluster of habits and dispositions that includes attentiveness to details, imagination, and passionate commitment. What is most essential for Dewey is the embodiment of intelligence in everyday practices. (Bernstein, 2010, 85)

While pragmatism's emphasis on experience could reveal the limits of today's planning practices that are often dominated by discursive actions, it may also have something to say about rational planning thoughts. Taking a cue from pragmatists' emphasis on experience, planners recognise different types of intelligence and knowledge that aren't necessarily measurable or objectifiable yet they provide the depth of wisdom which can only come from our embodied experience. An example includes customary management in natural resource management, where planners do not necessarily impose scientific measures to protect the watershed but listen to the ideas and wisdom within indigenous communities that have built up their own knowledge through living in and with the watershed. This might provide some points of reconciliation between expert-driven planning and democratic planning. Expert-driven, *a priori* knowledge is bound to have limitations that come from not being verified by experience, and different knowledges formulated by individuals through their lived experience – what may be considered "democratic knowledge" (Jasanoff, 2003) – are needed for pragmatic purposes of creating positive impacts on the lives of citizens. Conversely, some forms of expert knowledge may be cherished not because of their objectivity but because it can be derived from planners' years of experience in working with communities and learning from the consequences of certain decisions. Such perspectives can lead to planning practices that place more importance on history and learning from previous experiences, whether of other cities or of their own failures and successes.

Bernstein (2010) discusses some ethical consequences of James's pragmatic pluralism, asserting that "pragmatic pluralism is not relativism" (2010, 55). One has to recognise that James's advocacy for plural and pluriverse perspectives was an important theoretical stepping stone that provided support for his political engagements, such as his activism against imperialism, monism and the intolerance that fuelled the epidemic of lynchings of African Americans. And the legacy of his pluralism continued, as those pluralistic insights have been the source of countering racism, religious intolerance and xenophobia that were so prevalent in the USA in the years leading up to and following the First World War.

The impacts of such ethical consequences of pragmatic pluralism can be observed today, especially with regard to African American studies and feminist studies. In her essay 'Another pragmatism', Fraser (1998) noted the relevance and importance of the pragmatist Alain Locke's demystifying of race to today's effort to revive pragmatism. Locke's lectures (1916 [1992]) demonstrated how race is a product of the practices of power, and that the notion of superiority is formed by the political fortunes of a group and not by any intrinsic or inherent qualities with respect to social culture. In short, racial categorisation can be understood as "the offspring of domination" (Fraser, 1998, 164). Locke focused on power inequalities as the producer/creator of differences and therefore provided a contrasting point that highlights the limits of communicative/consensus theorists who have focused on Habermasian understanding of pragmatism. Locke's work shows us that pluralism can be a source of activism that not only condemns homogenisation, but also underlines the fact that "the systematically dominated social groups have pragmatic political needs for solidarity that differ from the needs of others" (Fraser, 1998, 173).

These ideas challenge our conventional notion of dealing with difference or what it means to abide by the principle of pluralism in democratic planning. If participatory planning – roundtables and public meetings organised by the government – is what democratic planning is all about, then pursuing pluralism in this context would mean listening to each other and attempting to understand each other's different positions. On the other hand, if we take on the perspective that pluralism is a kind of social activism that attempts to address the unequal distribution of power pervading our differences, perhaps democratic planning for planners is not just about organising roundtables but also about analysing and acting upon those differences and the ways they are produced through systematic inequalities in power relations.

## Conclusion

This chapter has argued that pragmatism has much more to offer planning than is often suggested by advocates of communicative/consensus planning theory and practice (Forester, 2012; Healey, 2009). I have drawn on ideas from contemporary pragmatist philosophers who prioritise experiential knowledge and action over the Habermasian emphasis on communication and consensus that has been widely adopted in planning. By recognising the plurality of social life, pragmatism can also endorse the ideas developed by radical planning theorists. In the first part of this chapter, I showed how communicative/consensus planning and radical planning have a common thread; both of them reject the ideas of universal truth and expert-led governance. However, in contrast to radical planning, communicative/consensus planning theory fails to recognise the plurality of the social. In this context, pragmatism has much to offer in bridging the gap between these approaches. Early pragmatists embraced the plurality of the social and they acknowledged different identities, values and beliefs as drivers of impassioned action. Radical planning's focus on the way in which conflicts are generative to democracy (see Flyvbjerg, 1998; Pløger, 2004) is in fact pragmatic in the sense that it recognises the role of different experiences and perspectives in generating collective action. I suggest that a new reading of pragmatism, drawing from Shalin, Macke, Bernstein and Fraser, can lead to a new kind of pragmatic planning theory that actively addresses the plurality of the social, and the inequalities on which this is based.

Pragmatism can inspire the planning theory to go beyond the limits of communicative and consensus planning. With an emphasis on material action and pluralism, pragmatists such as Shalin, Macke and Bernstein have criticised the dominance of Habermasian communicative action in pragmatism, arguing that it constitutes only a partial picture of what early pragmatists such as Dewey and James envisioned. I have provided a critique of communicative planning based on these ideas in order to suggest how a new reading of pragmatism can enrich planning theory and practice. This new version of pragmatic planning needs to valorise knowledges that come from actual lived experiences, whether of citizens or of planners. It also needs to recognise the extent to which social differences reflect systematic social and economic inequalities. These ideas can help planning theorists develop a more progressive version of pragmatic planning that recognises the generative value of pluralism and agonistic conflict in planning.

## References

Alexander, T.M. (1987) *John Dewey's theory of art, experience, and nature: The horizons of feeling*. Albany, NY: SUNY Press.

Allmendinger, P. (1999) 'Beyond Collaborative Planning', paper presented at AESOP conference, Bergen, 7 July.

Bacqué, M.H. and Gauthier, M. (2011) Participation, urbanisme et études urbaines. *Participations*, 1, 36–66.

Balducci, A., Boelens, L., Hillier, J., Nyseth, T. and Wilkinson, C. (2011) Introduction: Strategic spatial planning in uncertainty: Theory and exploratory practice. *Town Planning Review*, 82, 5, 481–501.

Bernstein, R.J. (1998) Community in the pragmatic tradition, in M. Dickstein, ed., *The revival of pragmatism: New essays on social thought, law, and culture*. Durham, NC: Duke University Press, 141–56.

Bernstein, R.J. (2010) *The pragmatic turn*. Cambridge: Polity Press.

Boelens, L. (2010) Theorizing practice and practising theory: Outlines for an actor relational approach in planning. *Planning Theory*, 9, 1, 28–62.

Bond, S. (2011) Negotiating a 'democratic ethos' moving beyond the agonistic–communicative divide. *Planning Theory*, 10, 2, 161–86.

Boonstra, B. and Boelens, L. (2011) Self-organization in urban development: Towards a new perspective on spatial planning. *Urban Research and Practice*, 4, 2, 99–122.

Bridge, G. (2004) *Reason in the city of difference*. London: Routledge.

Brownill, S. and Parker, G. (2010) Why bother with good works? The relevance of public participation(s) in planning in a post-collaborative era. *Planning Practice and Research*, 25, 3, 275–82.

Deleuze, G. and Guattari, F. (1972 [1977]) *Anti-Oedipus: Capitalism and schizophrenia*, trans. R. Hurley, M. Seem and H. Lane. New York, NY: Penguin.

Deleuze, G. and Guattari, F. (1980 [1987]) *A thousand plateaus*, trans. B. Massumi. Minneapolis, MN: University of Minnesota Press.

Dewey, J. (2008a) *The middle works, 1899–1924, volume 10: 1935*. J.A. Boydston, ed. Carbondale, IL: Southern Illinois University Press.

Dewey, J. (2008b) *The later works, 1925–1953, volume 10: 1916–1917*. J.A. Boydston, ed. Carbondale, IL: Southern Illinois University Press.

Featherstone, D. (2008) *Resistance, space and political identities: The making of counter-global networks* (Vol. 103). Chichester: John Wiley and Sons.

Flyvbjerg, B. (1998a) *Rationality and power: Democracy in practice*. Chicago, IL: University of Chicago Press.

Forester, J. (1989) *Planning in the face of power*. Berkeley, CA: University of California Press.

Forester, J. (1999) Dealing with deep value differences, in L. Susskind, S. McKearnan and J. Thomas-Larmer, eds, *The consensus building handbook*. Thousand Oaks, CA: SAGE: 463–93.

Forester, J. (2006) Making participation work when interests conflict. *Journal of the American Planning Association*, 72, 4, 447–56.

Forester, J. (2012) On the theory and practice of critical pragmatism: Deliberative practice and creative negotiations. *Planning Theory*, 12, 1, 5–22.

Fraser, N. (1998) Another pragmatism: Alain Locke, critical 'race' theory, and the politics of culture, in M. Dickstein, ed., *The revival of pragmatism: New essays on social thought, law, and culture*. Durham, NC: Duke University Press, 157–75.

Harrison, P. (2002) A pragmatic attitude to planning., in P. Allmendinger and M. Tewdwr-Jones, eds, *Planning futures: New directions in planning theory*. New York, NY: Routledge, 157–71.

Healey, P. (1996 [2003]) The communicative turn in planning theory and its implications for spatial strategy formation, in S. Campbell and S. Fainstein, eds, *Readings in planning theory*. Malden, MA: Blackwell, 237–55.

Healey, P. (2009) The pragmatic tradition in planning thought. *Journal of Planning Education and Research*, 28, 277–92.

Hillier, J. (2003) 'Agon'izing over consensus: Why Habermasian ideals cannot be 'real'. *Planning Theory*, 2, 1, 37–59.

Hillier, J. (2008) Plan(e) speaking: A multiplanar theory of spatial planning. *Planning Theory*, 7, 1, 24–50.

Hoch, C.J. (2007) Pragmatic communicative action theory. *Journal of Planning Education and Research*, 26, 3, 272–83.

Innes, J. (1995) Planning theory's emerging paradigm. *Journal of Planning Education and Research*, 14, 3, 183–9.

Innes, J.E. and Booher, D.E. (2000) Indicators for sustainable communities: A strategy building on complexity theory and distributed intelligence. *Planning Theory and Practice*, 1, 2, 173–86.

Jasanoff, S. (2003) Technologies of humility: Citizen participation in governing science. *Minerva*, 41, 3, 223–44.

Joas, H. (1988) The unhappy marriage of hermeneutics and functionalism. *Praxis International*, 8, 1, 34–51.

Kloppenberg, J.T. (1998) Pragmatism: An old name for some new ways of thinking, in M. Dickstein, ed., *The revival of pragmatism: New essays on social thought, law, and culture*. Durham, NC: Duke University Press, 83–127.

Kruks, S. (2001) *Retrieving experience: Subjectivity and recognition in feminist politics*. Ithaca, NY: Cornell University Press.

Laclau, E. and Mouffe, C. (1985 [2000]) *Hegemony and socialist strategy: Towards a radical democratic politics*. London: Verso.

Locke, A. (1916 [1992]) *Race contacts and international relations: Lectures on the theory and practice of race*. Washington, DC: Howard University Press.

Macke, F.J. (1995) Pragmatism reconsidered: John Dewey and Michel Foucault on the consequences of inquiry, in L. Langsdorf and A.R. Smith, eds, *Recovering pragmatism's voice: The classical tradition, Rorty, and the philosophy of communication*. Albany, NY: State University of New York Press, 155–76.

Mouffe, C. (1999) Deliberative democracy or agonistic pluralism? *Social Research*, 66, 3, 745–58.

Newman, S. (2011) Postanarchism and space: Revolutionary fantasies and autonomous zones. *Planning Theory*, 10, 4, 344–65.

Norval, A.J. (2007) *Aversive democracy: Inheritance and originality in the democratic tradition*. Cambridge: Cambridge University Press.

Nyseth, T. (2012) Fluid planning: A meaningless concept or a rational response to uncertainty in urban planning?, in T. Nyseth, ed., *Advances in spatial planning*. London: InTech, 27–46.

Pløger, J. (2004) Strife: Urban planning and agonism. *Planning Theory*, 3, 1, 71–92.

Purcell, M. (2013) A new land: Deleuze and Guattari and planning. *Planning Theory and Practice*, 14, 1, 20–38.

Putnam, H. (1990) *Reason, truth and history*. Cambridge: Cambridge University Press.

Rochberg-Halton, E. (1986) *Meaning and modernity*. Chicago, IL: Chicago University Press.

Rosenthal, S.B. (1986) *Speculative pragmatism*. Amherst, MA: University of Massachusetts Press.

Sandercock, L. (1998) The death of modernist planning: Radical praxis for a postmodern age, in M. Douglass and J. Friedmann, eds, *Cities for citizens: Planning and the rise of civil society in a global age*. New York, NY: Wiley, 163–84.

Scheffler, I. (1974) *Four pragmatists: A critical introduction to Peirce, James, Mead and Dewey*. London: Routledge.

Shalin, D.N. (1992) Critical theory and the pragmatist challenge. *American Journal of Sociology*, 98, 2, 237–79.

Soja, E. (1997) Planning in/for postmodernity, in G. Benko and U. Strohmayer, eds, *Space and social theory: Interpreting modernity and postmodernity*. Oxford: Blackwell, 236–49.

Sørensen, E. (2014) Conflict as driver of pluricentric coordination. *Planning Theory*, 13, 2, 152–69.

Tajbakhsh, K. (2001) *The promise of the city*. Berkeley, CA: University of California Press.

Waks, L.J. (1998) Experimentalism and the flow of experience. *Educational Theory*, 48, 1, 1–19.

# 13

# Exploring possibilities for a pragmatic orientation in development studies

*Alireza F. Farahani and Azadeh Hadizadeh Esfahani*

## Introduction

Doing development work and being reflective is a frustrating and confusing matter. Every decision in the field or in policy circles, or in interaction with academics, can be extremely challenging. If you have been through a rigorous critical education and you still want to do something to improve the material living conditions for people who have not benefited or have been harmed by prevailing development discourses, policies and practices, you are faced with dilemmas. If the desire to make a difference was missing, it would be easy to find an academic research or journalistic job, sit in your intellectual armchair, take a sip from your cup of tea and work through the mass of articles and books that criticise development or any initiative that has tried to improve the material conditions and lived experiences of the poor, disenfranchised and excluded. You would be part of the intellectual game that makes a good moral life for yourself; you have detached yourself from the amoral, dirty and inappropriate discourse and practice of development while also declaring an ambition to achieve the total social transformation and alternative modernity/development that will benefit the poor, disenfranchised and excluded on a completely different level.

On the other hand, if you are not cynical about the development industry and seek to find employment in the field, you could secure a job with an international agency, non-governmental organisation (NGO), charity or government or, even better, become a consultant who could take projects from all. You would have a busy life marketing and delivering projects (and climbing up your career ladder), and you would probably feel tired after a tedious work trip or a challenging facilitation or evaluation meeting. But simultaneously, you would feel a sense of achievement from helping the poor and using your skills. And, if you get some mixed messages about your project being somehow damaging (e.g. building a dam and facilitating the eviction of rural inhabitants displaced by construction of the dam) or being derived from intentions other than delivering good (e.g. stirring up conflict for geopolitical reasons, such as espionage or inflaming ethnic/religious divides) or you see that all you have done was wiped away with the simplest change of conditions (e.g. the imposition of new sanctions), you could blame it on the lack of information, support, institutions, finances and/or social/human capital in the target society. You could even ask for Rostow's (1959) help to claim that the people are not yet at the stage to take flight; or deploy Kuznets's insights (Dasgupta et al., 2002; Martinussen, 1997) to convince yourself that this is temporary, they will reach and bypass the peak if they push more; and maybe Diamond (1997, 2005) and Sachs (2015) could help to blame it on nature, weather and geographical latitude. Again, you would have a fabulous personal life working with nice, selfless and politically correct people in international development, all of them concerned about and dedicated to the poor, so much so that they are paid many times more for holding a passport from the West and working in the lands of the rest (Hall, 1996).

The two comforts described above – armchair theorising and non-reflexive developmental action – are understandable responses to the challenges posed by the dominant discourse about development ('big-D' development) and its counter narrative (which can be characterised as 'little-d' development). 'Big-D' development can be understood as a post-Second World War project of intervention in the 'Third World' that emerged in the context of decolonisation and the Cold War, and has been continued with globalisation (Hart, 2001; McMichael, 2011). 'Little-d' development has developed as a counter narrative that focuses on 'post-development' with an emphasis on non-intervention (Escobar, 2008; Jakimow, 2008). The comfort gained from taking non-reflexive action described above is associated with big-D development and is most commonly associated with the modernisation and globalisation projects pursued by international agencies, international businesses and dominant powers underpinning mainstream economic thinking. Big-D development also recruits representative democracy as its preferred institutional arrangement and it largely restricts the assessment of experiments in development to the satisfaction of economic growth.

In contrast, little-d development is associated with armchair theorising and focuses on the underlying processes driving development and, more recently, the representations of certain countries as 'underdeveloped' (Escobar, 1995, 2008; Jakimow, 2008). Little-d development relies on different accounts developed from Marxist and/or poststructuralist philosophies and hence there is a spectrum of ontologies and epistemologies underpinning these views. With dystopian perspectives on the condition of development, progress is denied or postponed until after total social transformation and/or revolution (Jakimow, 2008).

One can't say which of these alternatives – armchair theorising associated with little-d development or conventional non-reflexive developmental action informed by big-D development – is better, but both would be relatively comfortable compared with trying to practise 'reflexive development' (Jakimow, 2008), which is an approach to development that is more aligned with pragmatic principles. In this challenging environment, pragmatism provides some guiding principles to help navigate reflexive development which demands: (1) a non-relativist anti-foundationalism comprising "systematic understanding of complex influences and contexts that shape knowledge" and attention to the "metis" of local practice (Jakimow, 2008, 315; Scott, 1998); (2) reflexive practice that targets power dynamics based upon a dynamic and process-oriented approach to social reality (Hickey and Mohan, 2005; Peet and Hartwick, 2009); (3) learning to learn from and engage with local knowledge in the development process in a way that cherishes experimentationalism for progress (Brohman, 1995); and (4) participation of marginal voices and a shift in the location of the expert by celebrating a deep, creative and radical democracy (Jakimow, 2008; McFarlane, 2006).

With these insights, pragmatism can contribute to the development of a form of reflexive development practice that allows you to remain sane and do something useful. In this chapter, four dilemmas in the field of development are introduced and connected to broader difficulties in doing development which relies on big-D and little-d perspectives as well as efforts to practise reflexive development. Drawing on examples from Iran regarding the production of development documents, overconsumption of water resources, restricted approaches to learning due to imitation of developed countries, and coping with the ailments of representative democracy, four principles from pragmatism will be utilised to help overcome these dilemmas and draw up new guidelines for development practice. The chapter concludes by suggesting how development theorists and practitioners can utilise pragmatic thinking in action-oriented reflexive development practice.

## Pragmatism: A non-relativist, anti-foundationalist approach to inquiry in development policy-making and practice

Development policy-making and practice never falls short of producing archived documents that are read by few – if any – readers. It seems that some of these documents are produced for the sole reason of making colourful shelves in the offices of directors and lengthening the CVs of development practitioners. While this phenomenon itself signals a detachment from action and departure from the primacy of practice (Bernstein, 2010), it also illustrates an inadequate universal and foundationalist approach to knowledge and knowledge production for development. Moreover, development policy-makers and directors are always greedy for models and cookbooks. 'What is your model?' is a popular question in development circles (Bebbington and Kothari, 2006; Kothari, 2005; McFarlane, 2006a, 2006b; Wilson, 2006). Practitioners respond to this demand for models and cookbooks by referencing this or that organisation's or scholar's approach to development. Models are important in articulating your position and assisting others to understand your approach but also for stereotyping and putting a halt to inquiry. From there, things get easier to judge.

However, this reality reflects a deeper epistemological problem: formulaic thinking and decision-making. This epistemological problem is primarily the outcome of the dominance of empiricist and positivist thinking (Archer et al., 2013; Sayer, 2000). Education in development and beyond has prosecuted the idea that "the social world could be shown to be a composite of a number of behavioural regularities which would eventually be described by social laws akin to those of natural science" (Sayer, 2000, 4). Thus development practitioners are looking for a formula to which they can put data to produce the magical strategy or formulation for development practice. This might be about the target group that they must focus on or about the actions they should take in that target group. Formulaic thinking has all the characteristics of a foundationalist approach to knowledge production. It is based on "timeless pre-existing perfect forms" (Barnes, 2008, 1544). Even further, formulas make complex realities, events and situations into perfect or ideal forms in order to process them. They rely on transcendental truths. They work with ideas that exist in a geographical and temporal vacuum (Barnes, 2008).

Formulaic modernisation suggests that for development in a place like Iran's Sistan and Baluchistan Province, for example, people need electricity, agricultural technology, water transmission systems, electricity lines and gas pipelines, hospitals, schools, roads, airports, factories and, more recently, hotels (to attract tourists) and the internet. This formulaic approach applies to all places and ignores the internal dynamics and local knowledge that shape the culture of the region. The Paulo-Freire-style conscientisation about the existence and formative role of habit, convention and local institutions doesn't come out of the formulas that development cookbooks provide. Alternatively, it is through participative processes of knowledge creation and collaborative inquiry into the contingent local norms that a critical consciousness towards transforming these habits is generated.

Moving beyond formulaic thinking doesn't mean that anything goes: it is not relativism. As Rorty asserts, this is not to say that "every belief on a certain topic, or perhaps any topic, is as good as every other" (Rorty, 1982, 166). An idea is good when it is useful and enables the participants to accomplish their targeted goals and makes possible a social agreement. As Barnes (2008) maintains, "knowledge claims are justified through social practice and within a community" (2008, 1549). A development agent is either an outsider to the target community (without any magical formula) or rises from inside a community with a socially emergent agenda. In the former case, if a social agreement is not achieved and the agent fails in creating a consensus, he/she has no reason to stay. In the latter case, s/he should attempt to communicate with others and convince fellow citizens of a mutual solution.

While philosophers such as Bernstein, Rorty and Brandom have attempted to develop sophisticated answers (Bernstein, 2010, 53–69 and 106–24) to the problem of "substituting artificial static constructs [formulas] for the actual flow of experience [community based practices]" (2010, 56), practitioners can move on from this "intellectualist fallacy" (2010, 56) and work with an alternative approach to the contextual production of knowledge. Pragmatism reminds development practitioners to avoid the trap of transcendental, atemporal and placeless models and frameworks. There are no pre-determined fixed solutions for the ailments of underdevelopment to be applied in every instance. In each situation, the contingencies and circumstances will mean that the people affected by and involved in the situation should define the issue, explain the problem, search for solutions and develop new ideas.

Contrary to formulaic thinking, participatory and community-based practice develops solutions in context. Reaching socially agreed solutions is part of the development process that could lead to production of knowledge and new concepts. Involvement of local people in the process of articulating the issue and looking for solutions facilitates the implementation of local change. In development you should not expect a universal model or perfect formula that you can act on to achieve targeted goals. Instead, you need to monitor the situation continuously, shape conversations among local actors constantly and develop ideas contingently. As pragmatism insists, solutions emerge contingently and experimentally in response to particular situations. Ideas and solutions are utensils or tools suitable for a specific situation and they might lose their usefulness over time and location. They might even become obstacles in new situations. They must be analysed in the new situation to cope with the new conditions.

## Pragmatist ontologies and a solution to the problem of hopelessness

The way in which the reproduction and transformation of the social world is understood has consequences in relation to the scope of hope. Hopelessness grows in response to the challenges of the current condition and the impossibility of realising a desired condition. A moving and motivating analysis of what the social realty is widens (or narrows) the window of opportunity for transforming the situation. Pragmatism, with its animating ontology, provides hope; not a sweet dream or wishful thinking about the current condition of the social world; and not a mirage, which will never be realised, but something more practical, developed in place. The water crisis in Iran is in a condition of hopelessness but pragmatist ontologies can help to unearth seeds of hope within this condition.

Iran has a serious water problem (Madani et al., 2016). The roots of the problem are in historical layers of modernisation (AghaKouchak et al., 2015; Madani, 2014) including: the Shah's white revolution (Katouzian, 2006) of the 1960s, which, in tandem with inheritance laws, replaced feudal-type land ownership with constantly shrinking rural agricultural land; state-controlled water governance that cultivated excessive dam construction; corrupt land grabs by the ruling class; exponential growth in the number of deep water wells in the past three decades; and jobless and environment-insensitive growth, especially in the 2000s, which amounted to a return to smallholder market-oriented (rather than livelihood-based) agricultural production. At present, Urmia Lake at the cross section of East and West Azerbaijan and several other lakes and rivers are in a dismal state of drying out. In several provinces such as Fars, Esfahan, Khorasan, Hamedan and Kerman, farmers and industries have excessively absorbed underground water resources, and tensions over water management projects have turned into daily news: Esfahani farmers have smashed the water pipelines to Yazd; Ahwazi citizens have protested against the transfer of water from Karun to Zayandeh river; Azerbaijan has recently experienced salt storms from the dried Urmia lake; and several industrial cities in the Western half of Iran experience numerous polluted days, not from urban/industrial pollutants but due to dust storms rising from dried rural areas.

The prevailing discourse in coping with Iran's water problems points to more, deeper, modernisation, new technical solutions (such as bringing Caspian Sea and Oman Sea waters to the central plateau), shifts in individual water consumption behaviour, pricing disincentives and better governance (Madani, 2014). Few want to focus on the complicated local dynamics of each water crisis, or on breakthrough changes in collective water consumption behaviour, or the political economy underlying established livelihoods. The major response has been abandonment, either physically, by migration, or mentally, through ignorance. The problem seems too big, too complicated, with too many conflicting beneficiaries to cope with, and proposed solutions don't spark enthusiasm. Deterministic depictions of the situation provide no room for hope and alternative approaches are needed.

Pragmatism was a response to the disappointment, damage and hopelessness that the civil war created in American society (Barnes, 2008). By employing a process-oriented, open-ended and context-specific spatio-temporal approach, pragmatism undermined the sense of universal progress, and absolute truth imposed by deterministic views that dominated society. It emphasised the contingency of the world, implying that there should be continuous endeavours for change. Pragmatism as Dewey describes it represents the world "as being in continuous formation, where there is still place for indeterminism, for the new, and for a real future" (Hickman and Alexander, 1998, 12). Pragmatism is a response to the overdetermined world of rationalist thinking. Hence, for pragmatists, contingency is an opportunity, not a threat (Barnes, 2008, 1546), for improving the living conditions of the poor, the disenfranchised and the excluded.

Pragmatism stresses the importance of time in understanding and responding to social problems. This is represented in conceptualising experience, situation, contingency and the importance of learning. For instance: "Experience is an interaction of organism-environment which has both spatial and temporal dimensions" (Bernstein in Dewey, 1960, xxxix), and the open-endedness of temporality ensures the possibility of hope. But the most significant aspect of temporality and dynamism in pragmatism relates to the conceptualisation of self-action, inter-action and trans-action (Cutchin, 2008). As Bridge (2013, 305; see also this volume) asserts:

> Dewey moved away from the idea of interaction which suggested that the elements or organisms interacting were fixed or rounded out, rather 'transaction' captured their ongoing co-constitution. Organisms were in process and for humans this meant experiencing provisional identities subject to revision and constituted by the multiplicity of their relations with the environment.

In contrast to trans-action, self-action relies upon an inherent capacity for activity by an entity that acts under its own powers, and inter-action takes place among entities that were already formed (Bernstein in Dewey, 1960). This appreciation of time and relationships between organisms, human agents and components on one hand, and the environment on the other hand, highlights the reproduction and transformation of agents and structures over time as a consequence of their interaction (Archer, 1995). Transaction conceptualises both structural and agentic generative mechanisms of social constellations and it doesn't reduce them to one another nor collapse them into one generative mechanism (Archer, 1995; Archer et al., 2013; Giddens, 1984). In transactions, structures and agents are products of prior interactions and they emerge out of these exchanges. But, because they occupy and operate at different tracts of time, they are distinguishable from each other (Archer, 1995; Elder-Vass, 2010). The reproduction and transformation of structures and agents can be captured by a dynamic, time-sensitive, cyclical theorisation of their exchange (Archer, 1995; Bhaskar et al., 2013). Transaction exactly provides this type of interface. In a transaction "the components themselves are subject to change; their character affects and is affected by the transaction. They are not independent: they are phases in a unified transaction" (Bernstein in Dewey, 1960, xl). The task for development is the identification and cultivation of transactional spaces in which reflexivity and "reflexive intelligence" can develop (Barnes, 2008;

Bernstein, 2010). In little-d development, there is no hope for change because everything has been set in advance by deterministic structures and the possibility of meaningful change is denied. In big-D development, there is an unrealistic confidence that individuals can do anything and if they don't become successful, they should be blamed since they have not tried hard enough, they do not have enough creativity, they have not activated the entrepreneur spirit and, thus, individuals are responsible for any failure or success and there are no other resources for change.

Moreover, reflexive intelligence is the pragmatist name for reflexivity (Archer, 2009; Farahani, 2013) as a heterogenous process based on social conditions and agentic responses. When Peirce talks about reflexivity and internal dialogue, he talks about the conversation between I (present self) and you (future self). When Mead talks about internal dialogue, he talks about the conversation between I (present self) and me (past self) (Wiley, 2009). Both consider time in their approach to reflexivity in ways that include the past and future (Wiley, 2009). Wiley combines these two views and argues for conversation among the I, me and you, arguing that this is where hope blossoms. The possibility of overcoming the temporality of the interplay between structure and agency is created by inner speech where a temporal approach to social reality incorporates the determinable effects of past activities on the current situation, as well as the indeterminacy manifested in the basic irreducibility of the present to future activities. This emergentist perspective makes possible an interpretation of the past, estimating the future, and shaping performance in the present, in an interplay with structures.

In the example of Iran's water problem, instead of demonising dams and engineers, investing in huge technical fixes, setting nation-wide policies for increasing the price of water or injecting government money for creating jobs that supposedly reduce the consumption of water, policy-makers should identify spaces of transaction in which it is possible to consider the problem with a range of the people involved. Take the example of Urmia Lake. A change in agricultural water consumption is inevitable but poor rural farmers should be the last to be blamed and victimised. The socio-technical systems and economic and livelihood activities that have been set up upstream are fixes for the benefit of inhabitants of Tabriz, the richest city in northwest Iran and a major loser of the drying lake due to sand/salt storms. These beneficiaries are the ones who must transform investment behaviours from land grabbing in the region to lower-profit investments in less water-consuming agricultural production, change collective consumption behaviours (including increasing demand for local products) and support the change of water use and employment activities in the upstream rural areas (based on the will and satisfaction of these rural inhabitants). Through community-based planning, solutions for changing agricultural water consumption by promotion of rural tourism and production of local food in higher-end markets have been suggested, but their successful transformative implementation is dependent on further funding from, and a change in consumption behaviours in, higher-value markets of the region (e.g. Tabriz). In other words, Tabriz should be involved in solving the problem that was created for its benefit in the first place but has turned into its environmental crisis later, rather than focusing only on the least powerful group, the rural farmers.

While Big-D development focuses on a sweet dream that change happens through continuous self-action endeavours of individuals (including entrepreneurial activities and technical fixes) and little-d development suggests direct confrontation between social movements and established power relations and governance systems in agricultural value chains to change the resulting interactions, a pragmatic-reflexive approach looks for real social hope in spaces of transaction between agents and structures, in concrete situations.

## Continuous learning and experimentation for progress

In the realm of development, learning and knowledge have re-emerged as central to contemporary debates and dialogues since the early 1990s (Escobar, 1995; Ferguson, 1990; Ferguson et al., 2010; McFarlane, 2006; Mehta, 1999; Stiglitz, 1999; Stone, 2003; World Bank, 1999). The rise of learning and knowledge as part of contemporary development theory and practice stems from three contributions. First is a realisation of the shortcomings of developmental economics regarding knowledge and learning that has determined the knowledge agendas of the World Bank, USAID, UNESCO and many other mainstream developmental activities since the late 1990s (Stiglitz, 1999; UNESCO, 2016; Wilson, 2006; World Bank, 1999). In this literature, 'knowledge gaps' and 'information failures' are prominently recognised as a source of market failure, and knowledge has been limited to a rational, technical, objective, universal and instrumental phenomenon that can be transferred somewhat unproblematically to/from places. Currently, and as an extension of this approach to knowledge, the most popular approach to experimentalism in development is experimental (randomised) economics (Banerjee and Duflo, 2009; J-PAL, n.d.; World Bank, 2015), which evaluates the effect of interventions on randomised test communities before assigning technical fixes to larger populations. This is closely related to Big-D development.

Second, little-d development scholars have increasingly highlighted how knowledge and learning are socially constructed through power relations (e.g. see Cooper and Packard, 2005; Escobar, 1995; Jakimow, 2008; Mehta, 1999). Here, attention to knowledge and learning in the critical (post-)development literature has focused on the social construction of (power-)knowledge that highlights the role of discourse as an apparatus of control. Post-development literature tends towards a focus on hegemonic and enduring conceptions of knowledge in development that ignore agency and romanticise local and indigenous knowledge and social movements (Escobar, 2008; Jakimow, 2008; Radcliffe, 2005).

Third, there has been a re-engagement with critical pedagogy for cultivating emancipatory and participatory learning processes in development. This work draws inspiration from Freire's (1970) foundational work and realises the transformative possibility of local knowledge creation processes through pedagogical initiatives that seek to overcome power imbalances in local communities (Chambers, 1994, 2005; Hickey and Mohan, 2005; Hope and Timmel, 1984; Scones, 2009). Here, the bankable conception of knowledge as something that is patiently received, memorised and repeated and leaves the receivers with a lack of creativity and transformation is criticised. This approach to learning and knowledge is often criticised for its neglect of power relations and tendency to homogenise local communities, with a lack of evidence for successful scale-up (Cooke and Kothari, 2001; Cornwall, 2003, 2008; Hickey and Mohan, 2005).

While the big-D development approach to knowledge dominates the field of developmental practice in Iran, the major counter discourse is related to the little-d development approach in which insufficient attention is paid to the participatory approach to learning and knowledge. The dominant discourse of development in Iran is illustrated below in the words of Mahmud Sariolghalam, the highly referenced Iranian development celebrity, University of Southern California graduate, top-ranking university professor and lecturer, World Economic Forum member and previous presidential adviser:

> Development is a universal and accomplished human affair. It is not influenced by countries, geography, or culture, rather it follows specific principles. It is a phenomenon that has reached a formulaic and mathematical form and like engineering and medical science it has a definite framework... It is capable of being Googled... we can easily utilise the results that the rest of the world has accomplished...the other fact is that if we want to achieve in this field we need to focus on elites. We have two roads for development: either the society decides or the elites A society can decide that has associations, parties, and awareness and has some sort of certainty about its issues and the world... in all countries that have developed outside of the West such as Malaysia, Singapore, South Korea, and China, decision making for progress has been restricted to political and intellectual elites. (Sariolghalam, 2014)

This passage highlights many differences between a conventional, positivist, formulaic, modernist, elitist, individualistic, colonial account of development and what counts as alternative, reflexive, people-centred, participative and indigenous development. Sariolghalam restricts decision-making about development to elites and hence prioritises a formulaic and (Habermasian) deliberative account of learning. This is contrary to pragmatist thought, which "locates politics in the everyday experiences of ordinary people" (West, 1989, 213). As Elkjaer (2009) illustrates in detail, experience for Dewey is not equivalent to knowledge, it is not subjective, or oriented towards the past, isolated mere action. Rather, it is closer to what we conceptualise these days as practice (Bourdieu, 1984; Wenger, 1998):

> experience is the relation between individuals and environments, subject and worlds ... experience is both the process of experiencing and the result of the process. It is in experience, in transaction, that difficulties arise, and it is with experience that problems are resolved by inquiry. (Elkjaer, 2009, 75)

The process of experimental inquiry is central to the conception of learning for Dewey. In contrast to Sariolghalam, who finds development a universal affair, in pragmatist thought a felt difficulty, conflict, discrepancy or situation that necessitates reflection and inquiry and thus demands a disruption of ordinary or habitual (i.e. non-reflective) experience is the point of departure for experimentation. Hence, development starts from the current livelihoods and daily practices of the excluded, marginalised and poor. Thus development is a product of context, shaped by a country's institutions, geography and culture: "The locus of the difficulty is in the situation" (Bernstein, in Dewey, 1960, xxviii). Situation is the "contextual whole" (1960, xxviii) that consists of "objects and events" (1960, xxviii) that are internally related, and a focus on understanding the specific spatial and temporal circumstances that produce and reproduce the situation is necessary for reaching a productive solution. Solutions emerge in order to transform the situation through engagement and a constructive reflection on the situation. Hence "there is always an element of adventure or risk in suggestion" (Dewey, 1960, xxix) of solutions; they are not given, formulaic and mathematical. Finally, solutions need to be tested in thought and in action and can't be imported simply by utilising the results that the world has accomplished.

Experience, practice and learning have taken a long road after Dewey. As Elkjaer (2009) suggests, "the pragmatist perspective on learning can elaborate contemporary learning theory by being linked to the notion of practice-based learning as introduced by Jean Lave and Etienne Wenger" (Elkjaer, 2009, 74) and their conceptualisation of learning in 'communities of practice' (CoPs) (2009, 87). Learning that is co-constitutive with being and becoming (identity), membership (belonging) and meaning takes place in communities through a gradual process, whereby the newcomer learns initially by "legitimate peripheral participation" (Wenger, 1998, 100). Wenger (1998, 2010) utilised the concept of community of practice (CoP) to describe the processes of learning at work in an assortment of communities that he identified as CoPs (e.g. families, student groups, staff of a workplace). This social, emergent, activity-oriented and contextual description of ongoing practices provides an approach which is useful for studying multiple CoPs that strive for development.

In conclusion, it should be restated that by bringing practice-oriented reflexive learning to the fore of development, the production, reproduction and transformation of human agents, CoPs and institutions take a central role in developmental praxis. A pragmatist conception of learning paves the way for the engagement of experts and people in the process of development. The detachment of people from the development process, and related learning and reflexivity, separates and disconnects people and leaves no space for further collaboration and participation, offers no reason for effort and sacrifice and restricts a sense of belonging and ownership. Instead of attempting to find final conclusions and best solutions, pragmatism gives focus to partial spatio-temporal solutions that address the critical aspect of felt difficulties (not ultimate solutions) and encourages reflection on the result and re-examining of the transformed situation, for a new inquiry.

## Practising deep democracy as a cure to development elitism

Development and democracy have a convoluted relation (Fung and Wright, 2003; Heller and Evans, 2010; Przeworski, 2000). A major reason for this is the way democracy has been conceptualised and measured. The discourse that currently prevails about democracy is focused on the role of representatives who are generally selected by the aggregation of individual votes to represent the people. While there have been some innovations to the ways in which representatives are selected (e.g. electoral systems, weighted representations and representative shares), they are nevertheless based on the same logic. The degree of association between representational democracy and (big-D) development shows that democracy and development are not necessarily correlated (Przeworski, 2000). A deeper look at representational democracy illustrates that such versions of democracy in action are often not far from an oligarchy. Pessimistically looking at this, it can be argued that elites have been successful in inventing a technology that superficially involves the masses and creates the illusion of democracy while making sure that the order of a hierarchical society (both within nations and globally) prevails (Lake, 2017; Rancière, 2014). Below, three suggested alternatives for moving beyond representative liberal democracy are distinguished and analysed with respect to pragmatic ideas.

First is the Habermas-inspired solution of deliberative (dialogic) democracy. This alternative/supplementation to representational democracy is a conservative sweet dream that is very compatible with the current liberal democracy. Habermas argues that a true dialogue between politicians and technocrats in an ideal speech situation in which both sides are "freed from the influence of specific problems" is the way forward for extending the possibility of the rule of people over themselves. This Habermas-inspired (Green, 1999; Hadizadeh Esfahani, 2013; Holden, 2008) deliberative democracy is brought to the development literature by Evans (2006; Heller and Evans, 2010) and Sen (2000) when they tackle the nature of preferences in development models and argue that to get the preferences right, they should be "arrived at through open public discussion" (Evans, 2006, 96). Putting this argument into dialogue with institutional theories of development highlights that "figuring out concrete institutional mechanisms for instantiating open and public discussion" becomes the central problem of development (Evans, 2006, 97). Habermas, Evans, Sen and Nussbaum pursue public dialogue and democracy that is dependent on elites not the subjects of development; rather, the people are absorbers of the dialogue and deliberation that has happened among academics, philosophers and social scientists or communities of practice of development practitioners. Hence, the right to define what is citizenship is denied or at least confined to exclude the subjects of development.

This turn towards deliberative democracy, rights and citizenship has been inserted in the big-D approach of international development agencies (Cornwall and Nyamu-Musembi, 2004). As Manzo (2003, 438) asserts: "Rights based development does little to empower either critics of neo-liberal development or the intended beneficiaries of the development – be they people or states … In the name of human rights … adjusted states [to neoliberal conditions] are being subject to novel methods of international surveillance and forms of conditionality". It is only a sweet dream that people, and more impossibly, elites, have serious dialogue by leaving their politics at the gates of the ideal spaces for dialogue as Habermas envisions. A realistic alternative to representational liberal democracy needs to consider the tensions and ruptures ingrained in politics and social transformation. Deliberative democracy is unqualified for such necessity.

Second is anarchistic, populist or absolute democracy that is best identified in the work of Hardt and Negri (2005) and Deleuze and Guattari (1980 [1987]) and is reliant on interpretations of the work of Foucault, Gramsci and Lefebvre (Purcell, 2013). Here, democracy is described as living in a state-less and structure-less world. The distinction between constituent and constituted power is turned into a value-laden differentiation: the former, desired, and the latter, forbidden. The mass of the people, 'the multitude', "can act, create, and produce life on their own" (Purcell, 2013, 13). Democracy, as autogestion, is desired, because within it people actively take up the project of managing their own affairs for themselves. Using Rancière's framework, populist democracy can be described as living in a constant state of potential rupture. In this worldview, after the multitude takes over, institutions (including laws) are degraded to tools that are under control of the multitude. The rights advocated here (e.g. right to the city, right of autogestion) are differentiated from liberal democratic and deliberative rights. Here, rights are points of departure towards overthrowing the structures. In this narration of democracy, Foucault's concepts of governmentality, discourse and power-knowledge are interpreted one-sidedly without any consideration of his ideas on the governance of the self (Ettlinger, 2011). This alternative to representational democracy is a mirage that haunts proponents of little-d development. It motivates and inspires for progress but, on the ground, it promises another failed experiment similar to the twentieth-century's statist-socialism or short-lived revolutions of the Arab Spring.

The third alternative is a pragmatist alternative of creative democracy (Bernstein, 2010; Lake, 2017; West, 1989), deep democracy (Green, 1999) and radical democracy (Bernstein, 2010). Dewey develops the idea of democracy "as an ethical form of life" as a normative consequence of humans being more than "isolated non-social atoms" (Bernstein, 2010, 72). Dewey pulls democracy out of the vertical understanding of power as he contradicts the idea that "(1) democracy is only a form of government; (2) government is simply that which has to do with the relation of subject and sovereign, of political superior to inferior; (3) democracy is the form of government in which the sovereign is the multitude of individuals" (or "numerical aggregation") (Bernstein, 2010, 72). Dewey also was critical of "democratic elitism" and the argument that, in the face of the complexity of social problems and the manipulation of individuals by mass media, "the wisdom of an intelligentsia", which has the responsibility to make wise democratic decisions, is necessary. Further than Dewey, pragmatists such as Rorty and Bernstein have also clashed with Habermas's ideal speech situation, which for them is just a sophisticated variant of the "Platonic urge" (Barnes, 2008, 1550) for truth. Dewey also argued that whatever expert knowledge was required for understanding situations, it wasn't the experts who should take over debate and it was up to democratic citizens to judge and decide (Bernstein, 2010, 75). Hence, as Lake (2017) argues, an ethic of radical equality applies equally, for Dewey, as a theory of democracy and as a mode of interpersonal behaviour. For Dewey the ideal of democracy was thoroughly associated with the ideal of community. It is in the "deeply democratic community" that democracy is realised:

> Dewey's transformative prescription calls for revitalising the face-to-face local community, understood as diverse lives interconnected and sustained by full and free communication, because this is the birthing place of the democratic desire, the testing place for social inquiry, and the launching place for a broader translocally dispersed "public". Dewey's call is not for a nostalgic and impossible return to times of simpler technologies, narrower aspirations, and more limited opportunities. (Green, 1999, 57)

Dewey was under no illusions about perils of "the corporate mentality", "the fetishism of individualism", the harm of "pseudo-liberalism", the destruction of laissez-faire, "the institutional apparatus of government and macroeconomy" and the "eclipse of the public" as "elite-controlled mass-communications media" distorted public opinion (Bernstein, 2010; Green, 1999). But he did not see democracy taking place at the polls. Rather, democracy was a way of life. Hence, he insisted that "unless local communal life can be restored, the public cannot adequately solve its most urgent problem: to find and identify itself" (Dewey, 1927, 216).

Development's take away from these considerations is that, while the ailments of representative democracy are real and should be dealt with, the way to progress doesn't come from either an elitist or a populist route. Rather the focus should be on deepening democratic community life. Instead of moving towards more complicated institutionalised layers of representative democracy, the focus should be on creating space for enabling more direct democracy. New technologies could be a resource if they are used towards deepening democracy and dialogue (for example, by creating a possibility of continuous, online voting as a replacement or supplement for occasional elections). Policy and activism should focus on new venues of direct democratic decision-making (e.g. participatory budgeting, community-based planning and grassroots territorial governance) instead of dismantling the democratic institutions at work, drawing back to populist mirages or conservative new forms of representation (e.g. changing representation from counties, to districts, to provinces, or the number of representatives).

This guidance is pertinent for the current disarray regarding democratic participation in city councils (CCs) in Iran and the assistant city councils (ACCs) experiment in Tehran. CCs include elected officials who are responsible for overseeing the activities of the city's planning, budgeting and supervision of local activities as well as selecting the mayor. Despite the significance of the institutions and discourse underpinning the establishment of CCs after the Islamic revolution, the formation of CCs was postponed until the late 1990s. The experience turned into a disaster, especially regarding Tehran's CC and its experimentation with setting up ACCs, which became forums for rent seeking, disagreement and tedious debates, and led to the distrust and disappointment of voters. As a consequence of low participation at polls (and election politics in Iran afterwards), CCs in major metropolitan areas fell into the hands of the conservatives for three consequential turns. ACCs, which were set up for creating a space for direct involvement of citizens by electing their neighbourhood representatives, turned into another layer of representative democracy and became venues for fraudulent elections, growth machine politics, real estate entrepreneurship, spreading the hegemony of petty religious discourses, and every kind of corrupted relations between local bullies and municipal bureaucrats including vote-purchasing. With the sweeping victory of reformists in 2018, heated debates have emerged about continuation, modification or dissolution of ACCs.

A pragmatist solution for this dilemma builds on the participatory budgeting experiments in Latin America (Fung and Wright, 2003), the success (as well as failures) of Tehran neighbourhood renovation offices, which employed facilitation techniques for fostering participation and community building to rebuild deteriorated buildings and were successful in increasing participation by citizens (Hadizadeh Esfahani, 2017), the support for more inclusive local identity building and substantive citizenship activities of Tehran's neighbourhood centres, and Tehran social activist experiences at the neighbourhood scale (Hadizadeh Esfahani, forthcoming). This highlights the possibility of a modified direct democratic engagement of citizens through a rearrangement of the structure, regulations, competencies and practical mechanisms of ACCs. ACCs can turn into venues of direct democracy and a place for experimenting with transformative processes at the neighbourhood scale with the highest potential for face-to-face dialogue. But they also need to be accompanied by empowered, skilled and well-funded executive bodies that act as facilitators for the dialogue, planning and funding, and implementation process. This approach departs from the modernist big-D inspired revitalisation processes that ignore and erode local identities, belonging and participation. It also moves beyond the little-d inspired advocacy and cultural approach, which focuses on increasing awareness but doesn't lead to enduring, sustainable transformation of neighbourhoods and their institutions.

## Conclusion

The relation between pragmatism and development studies can at best be described as emergent. In this chapter, we have tried to present pragmatism as a non-relativist anti-foundationalist guide for inquiry in development studies in order to transform a quest for transcendental, atemporal and placeless models and frameworks towards socially oriented, contingent and community-based knowledgeability (Wenger-Trayner and Wenger-Trayner, 2014). Moreover, we have joined Bridge's (2013) and Cutchin's (2008) endeavours to attend to the importance of transaction as underpinning the emergent spatial and temporal interplay of structure and agency in the context of development (see also Bridge, this volume). Furthermore, we have carried pragmatic thought into recent debates about practice-oriented conceptualisations of learning that can guide development praxis. Consequently, development is located in communities of practice as the social, emergent, activity-oriented and contextual place of developmental praxis. Finally, we have argued for creating and cultivating venues for direct democracy for a deep, creative and radical democratic position against the backdrop of populist and elitist inclinations.

As a field of research and practice, development studies is conceptualised by dichotomies of big- and little-D development (Hart, 2001) that reflect other dichotomies such as modernisation/dependency, development/post-development, participatory/exclusionary, indigenous/exogenous, top-down/bottom-up and immanent/imminent (Hickey and Mohan, 2005). In this chapter we have explored these dichotomies and suggested new directions for development studies by employing the above-mentioned epistemological, ontological, practical and politically extended pragmatic principles.

For Iran, pragmatism offers hope even as the country is targeted by warmongering as the shadows of a third Persian Gulf war grow. As its people live through elitist, neoliberal environmentally tragic, uneven and authoritarian development, and as hopes for a nonviolent, inclusive, people-centred, balanced, multicultural and indigenous development become foggy, pragmatism offers hope. It directs attention towards deepening democracy, it strategically relocates developmental endeavours to reflexive learning in the everyday experiences of ordinary people, and it guides meaningful and practical inquiry.

## References

AghaKouchak, A., Norouzi, H., Madani, K. et al. (2015) Aral Sea syndrome desiccates Lake Urmia: Call for action. *Journal of Great Lakes Research*, 41, 1, 307–11.

Archer, M.S. (1995) *Realist social theory: The morphogenetic approach*. Cambridge: Cambridge University Press.

Archer, M.S. (ed.) (2009) *Conversations about reflexivity*. New York, NY: Routledge.

Archer, M., Bhaskar, R., Collier, A., Lawson, T. and Norrie, A. (eds) (2013) *Critical realism: Essential readings*. London and New York, NY: Routledge.

Banerjee, A.V. and Duflo, E. (2009) The experimental approach to development economics. *Annual Review of Economics*, 1, 1, 151–78.

Barnes, T.J. (2008) American pragmatism: Towards a geographical introduction. *Geoforum*, 39, 4, 1542–54.

Bebbington, A. and Kothari, U. (2006) Transnational development networks. *Environment and Planning A*, 38, 5, 849–66.

Bernstein, R.J. (2010) *The pragmatic turn*. Cambridge: Polity.

Bourdieu, P. (1984) *The logic of practice*. Stanford, CA: Stanford University Press.

Bridge, G. (2013) A transactional perspective on space. *International Planning Studies*, 18, 3–4, 304–20.

Brohman, J. (1995) Universalism, Eurocentrism, and ideological bias in development studies: From modernisation to neoliberalism. *Third World Quarterly*, 16, 121–40.

Chambers, R. (1994) The origins and practice of participatory rural appraisal. *World Development*, 22, 7, 953–69.

Chambers, R. (2005) *Ideas for development*. Sterling, VA: Earthscan.

Cooke, B. and Kothari, U. (2001) *Participation: The new tyranny?*, Vol. 1. London: Zed Books.

Cooper, F. and Packard, R. (2005) The history and politics of development knowledge, in M. Edelman and A. Haugerud, eds, *The anthropology of development and globalization: From classical political economy to contemporary neoliberalism*. Malden, MA: Blackwell Publishing, 126–39.

Cornwall, A. (2003) Whose voices? Whose choices? Reflections on gender and participatory development. *World Development*, 31, 8, 1325–42.

Cornwall, A. and Nyamu-Musembi, C. (2004) Putting the 'rights-based approach' to development into perspective. *Third World Quarterly*, 25, 8, 1415–37.

Cutchin, M.P. (2008) John Dewey's metaphysical ground-map and its implications for geographical inquiry. *Geoforum*, 39, 4, 1555–69.

Dasgupta, S., Laplante, B., Wang, H. and Wheeler, D. (2002) Confronting the environmental Kuznets curve. *Journal of Economic Perspectives*, 16, 1, 147–68.

Deleuze, G. and Guattari, F. (1980 [1987]) *A thousand plateaus*, trans. B. Massumi. Minneapolis, MN: University of Minnesota Press.

Dewey, J. (1927) *The public and its problems*. New York, NY: Holt.

Dewey, J. (1960) *On experience, nature, and freedom*, ed. R.J. Bernstein. New York, NY: Liberal Arts Press.

Elder-Vass, D. (2010) *The causal power of social structures: Emergence, structure and agency*. Cambridge: Cambridge University Press.

Elkjaer, B. (2009) Pragmatism: A learning theory for the future, in K. Illeris, ed., *Contemporary theories of learning: Learning theorists… in their own words*, Vol. 1. London and New York, NY: Routledge.

Escobar, A. (1995) *Encountering development*. Princeton, NJ: Princeton University Press.

Escobar, A. (2008) *Territories of difference: Place, movements, life, redes*. Durham, NC: Duke University Press.

Ettlinger, N. (2011) Governmentality as epistemology. *Annals of the Association of American Geographers*, 101, 3, 537–60.

Evans, P. (2006) *Extending the 'institutional' turn*. Research Paper (113). World Institute for Development Economics Research.

Farahani A.F. (2013) *Socio-reflexive regional learning in the Khorasan (northeast Iran) saffron cluster*. Simon Fraser University Master of Urban Studies thesis. Vancouver, BC.

Ferguson, J. (1990) *The anti-politics machine*. Cambridge: Cambridge University Press.

Ferguson, J., Huysman, M. and Soekijad, M. (2010) Knowledge management in practice: Pitfalls and potentials for development. *World Development*, 38, 12, 1797–1810.

Freire, P. (1970) *Pedagogy of the oppressed*. New York, NY: The Seabury Press.

Fung, A. and Wright, E.O. (2003) *Deepening democracy: Institutional innovations in empowered participatory governance*, Vol. 4. London and New York, NY: Verso.

*Geoforum* (2008) Special issue: Pragmatism and geography, 39, 4, 1527–1624.

Giddens, A. (1984) *The constitution of society: Outline of the theory of structuration*. Berkeley, CA: University of California Press.

Green, J.M. (1999) *Deep democracy: Community, diversity, and transformation*. Lanham, MD: Rowman and Littlefield Publishers.

Green, J.M. (2008) Pragmatism and social hope: Deepening democracy in social contexts. New York, NY: Columbia University Press.

Hadizadeh Esfahani, A. (2013) Exploring people-centred development in Melbourne Docklands redevelopment: Beyond physical development and collaborative planning. Simon Fraser University Master of Urban Studies thesis. Vancouver, BC.

Hadizadeh Esfahani, A. (2017) Urban renewal in Tehran's neighbourhoods: Displacement or potential for identity-building and place-making?, in *Urban Transformations*. Routledge, 155–69.

Hadizadeh Esfahani, A. (forthcoming) Neighbourhood as a site of policy and activism: Exploring citizenship, belonging, identity building in Tehran's neighbourhoods. Clark University PhD thesis. Worcester, MA.

Hall, S. (1996) The west and the rest: Discourse and power, in S. Hall, D. Held, D. Hubert and K. Thompson, eds, *Modernity: An introduction to modern societies*. Cambridge, MA: Blackwell, 184–227.

Hardt, M and Negri, A. (2005) *Multitude: War and democracy in the age of empire*. New York, NY: Penguin.

Hart, G. (2001) Development critiques in the 1990s: Culs-de-sac and promising paths. *Progress in Human Geography*, 25, 4, 649–58.

Heller, P. and Evans, P. (2010) Taking Tilly south: Durable inequalities, democratic contestation, and citizenship in the Southern Metropolis. *Theory and Society*, 39, 3–4, 433–50.

Hickey, S. and Mohan, G. (2005) Relocating participation within a radical politics of development. *Development and Change*, 36, 2, 237–62.

Hickman. L.A. and Alexander, T.M. (1998) *The essential Dewey, Vol. 1: Pragmatism, education, democracy*.

Holden, M. (2008) Social learning in planning: Seattle's sustainable development codebooks. *Progress in Planning*, 69, 1, 1–40.

Hope, A. and Timmel, S. (1984) *Training for transformation: A handbook for community workers*: Gweru: Mambo Press.

Jakimow, T. (2008) Answering the critics: The potential and limitations of the knowledge agenda as a practical response to post-development critiques. *Progress in Development Studies*, 8, 4, 311–23.

Jamal Abdul Latif Poverty Action Lab (J-Pal). www.povertyactionlab.org/ (accessed 2 April 2018).

Katouzian, H. (2006) *State and society in Iran: The eclipse of the Qajars and the emergence of the Pahlavis*, Vol. 28. New York. NY: I.B. Tauris.

Kothari, U. (2005) Authority and expertise: The professionalization of international development and the ordering of dissent. *Antipode*, 37, 3, 425–46.

Lake, R.W. (2017) On poetry, pragmatism and the urban possibility of creative democracy. *Urban Geography*, 38, 4, 479–94.

Madani, K. (2014) Water management in Iran: What is causing the looming crisis? *Journal of Environmental Studies and Sciences*, 4, 4, 315–28.

Madani, K., AghaKouchak, A. and Mirchi, A. (2016) Iran's socio-economic drought: Challenges of a water-bankrupt nation. *Iranian Studies*, 49, 6, 997–1016.

Manzo, K. (2003) Africa in the rise of rights-based development. *Geoforum*, 34, 4, 437–56.

Martinussen, J. (1997) *Society, state and market: A guide to competing theories of development*. London: Zed Books.

McFarlane, C. (2006a) Knowledge, learning and development: A post-rationalist approach. *Progress in Development Studies*, 6, 4, 287–305.

McFarlane, C. (2006b) Crossing borders: Development, learning and the North–South divide. *Third World Quarterly*, 27, 8, 1413–37.

McMichael, P. (2011) *Development and social change: A global perspective*. London: SAGE.

Mehta, L. (1999) From darkness to light? Critical reflections on the World Development Report 1998/99. *The Journal of Development Studies*, 36, 1, 151–61.

Peet, R. and Hartwick, E. (2009) *Theories of development: Contentions, arguments, alternatives*. New York, NY: The Guilford Press.

Przeworski, A. (2000) *Democracy and development: Political institutions and well-being in the world, 1950–1990*, Vol. 3. Cambridge: Cambridge University Press.

Purcell, M. (2013) *The down-deep delight of democracy*. Malden, MA and Oxford: John Wiley and Sons.

Radcliffe, S.A. (2005) Development and geography: Towards a postcolonial development geography. *Progress in Human Geography*, 29, 3, 291–8.

Rancière, J. (2014) *Hatred of democracy*. London: Verso.

Rorty, R. (1982) *Consequences of pragmatism: Essays, 1972–1980*. Minneapolis, MN: University of Minnesota Press.

Rostow, W.W. (1959) The stages of economic growth. *The Economic History Review*, 12, 1, 1–16.

Sachs, J.D. (2015) *The age of sustainable development*. New York, NY: Columbia University Press.

Sariolghalam, M. (2014) A thesis for the development of Iran. https://sariolghalam.com (accessed 2 April 2018).

Sayer, A. (2000) *Realism and social science*. London: SAGE.

Scoones, I. (2009) Livelihoods perspectives and rural development. *Journal of Peasant Studies*, 36, 1, 171–96.

Scott, J.C. (1998) *Seeing like a state: How certain schemes to improve the human condition have failed*. New Haven, CT: Yale University Press.

Sen, A.K. (2000). *Development as freedom*. New York, NY: Knopf.

Stiglitz, J. (1999) Public policy for a knowledge economy. *Remarks at the Department for Trade and Industry and Center for Economic Policy Research*, London, 27 January.

Stone, D. (2003) The "knowledge bank" and the global development network. *Global Governance*, 9, 1, 43–61.

UNESCO. (2016) Global network of learning cities. http://learningcities.uil.unesco.org/home (accessed 3 February 2016).

Wenger, E. (1998) *Communities of practice: Learning, meaning, and identity*. Cambridge: Cambridge University Press.

Wenger, E. (2010) Communities of practice and social learning systems: The career of a concept, in C. Blackmore, ed., *Social learning systems and communities of practice*. New York, NY: Springer, 179–98.

Wenger-Trayner, E. and Wenger-Trayner, B. (2014) *Learning in landscapes of practice: Boundaries, identity, and knowledgeability in practice-based learning*. New York, NY and London: Routledge.

West, C. (1989) *The American evasion of philosophy: A genealogy of pragmatism*. London: Palgrave Macmillan.

Wiley, N. (2009) *Inner speech and agency*, in M.S. Archer, ed., *Conversations about reflexivity*. Routledge.

Wilson, G. (2006) Beyond the technocrat? The professional expert in development practice. *Development and Change*, 37, 3, 501–23.

World Bank. (1999) *World Development Report 1998–99: Knowledge for development*. Washington, DC: World Bank Group.

World Bank. (2015) *World Development Report 2015: Mind, society, and behavior*. Washington, DC: World Bank Group.

# Part V
# Conclusion and postscript

# 14

# The quest for uncertainty: Pragmatism between rationalism and sentimentality

*Robert W. Lake*

Insecurity generates the quest for certainty. (John Dewey, 1929 [1988], 203)

Anyone claiming to tell me the absolute truth is demanding from me unquestioning submission. (Gianni Vattimo, 2014, 77)

Indignation is not yet politics. (Graham Harman, 2014, 31)

## Introduction

Anyone engaged in the pursuit of knowledge confronts daunting challenges posed by incommensurable definitions of truth, the destabilising threat of uncertainty, the lure of dogmatism and authoritarianism, and the seductive power of sentimentality – and all this quite aside from the political sand traps and institutional impediments that can thwart academic scholarship. As illustrated by the contributors to this volume, pragmatism offers a way through these multiple challenges. How and why it does so bears careful scrutiny, especially in light of the growing crisis of collective confidence in our knowledge and its production today. In this brief concluding chapter I attempt to clarify some of the challenges facing the production of knowledge in the social sciences and to highlight the contributions that can be made by the pragmatic tradition in general, and this book in particular.

## Finding certainty in an uncertain world

We opened this book with a discussion of Dewey's (1929 [1988]) book *The quest for certainty*, in which he sought to offer a new way of thinking about ideas, their development and their application. Dewey argued that the search for certainty may propel attempts to "propitiate the powers" that determine one's destiny through, for example, attachment to superstition, or what he referred to as "ceremonial rite and magical cult" (Dewey, 1929 [1988], 3). Since the Enlightenment, however, superstition has been at least partly replaced by faith that knowledge provides the means to bring destiny under control. Not just any knowledge counts as certain, of course: guesswork, conjecture, unfounded assertions or mere opinion are no improvement over ecclesiastical pronouncements or spiritual premonitions. What counts as knowledge in the tradition of Descartes, Bacon, Locke and Newton, is invariant, universal, law-like and timeless knowledge that "has a rational, necessary and unchangeable form'" (Dewey, 1929 [1988], 67). Knowledge of this sort rests on the belief that the world precedes our knowledge of it (what Arendt (1978, 23) called the "two-world theory") and that it comprises statements that necessarily correspond with that antecedent reality. This is what Richard Rorty (1999, 15) called the "unwobbling pivots" of knowledge on which certainty and security depend.

In Stephen Toulmin's (1990) magisterial recounting of the history of modernity, the seventeenth-century's embrace of Cartesian rationality was far from a random invention of "lonely individuals in separate ivory towers" but instead was a desperate response to the political, social and theological chaos of the Thirty Years' War, an apparently endless conflict of religious doctrines that resulted in the slaughter of more than a third of the population of Europe. Understood in this context, Toulmin observes, Cartesian rationalism provided society with "a real hope of *reasoning* their way out of political and theological chaos, at a time when no one else saw anything to do but continue fighting and interminable war" (Toulmin, 1990, 71, emphasis in the original). From Newton's Laws of Thermodynamics to Adam Smith's laws of the markets to Marx's inevitable dictatorship of the proletariat, the formulation of universal, invariant and predictable knowledge promised certainty and security in the face of chaos. This was the "escape from peril" that Dewey cited as the title of the opening chapter of his book. "A contributing cause," Dewey explained, "was found in the harshness, cruelties and tragic frustrations of the world of action. Were it not for its brutalities and failures, the motive for seeking refuge in a higher realm of knowledge would have been lacking" (Dewey, 1929 [1988], 234).

## Seeking consolation in the promise of progress

If the certainty of Cartesian rationalism seeks to establish order on the battlefield of chaos, it also offers the condition for and guarantee of progress in the future. Belief in the possibility of progress rests on the tenet that knowledge of the world grants the power to improve it, and knowledge is power because understanding opens the door for rectification. If progress entails the ability to identify, address and rectify a problem, then the representation of a problem reveals the path to its solution. Faith in the revelatory power of knowledge (Barnett, 2018) is manifest in the expectation, for example, that exposing exploitation, domination, inequality or injustice necessarily reveals the path and paves the way for their elimination. This, after all, was Marx's powerful call made in the opening of his *Theses on Feuerbach* (1888 [1976], 1) to combine understanding with action: "Philosophers have hitherto only interpreted the world in various ways; the point is to change it".

Faith in the possibility of progress has endured even as recent critical theorists have rejected the rationalists' assumptions of distanced objectivity and effaced the God's-eye view with positionality, plurality, multiplicity and difference. There are rationalists and critical theorists alike who subscribe to the spectator theory of knowledge and the correspondence theory of truth, even while advancing divergent, even incommensurable, epistemologies through which to access the particular truths congruent with their respective ideologies and worldviews (Lake, 2014). Whether approaching the world from a critical or a rationalist perspective, knowing how things work is assumed to reveal how they might work better.

Consistent with the quest for certainty, however, the obduracy of representation lies in its emotional and consolatory significance (Vattimo, 2014). In this regard, the knowledge practices of both rationalists and critical theorists can be no less ritualistic than the superstitions and ceremonial rites displaced by the Enlightenment. Like any religion's promise of redemption in the next life as compensation for pain and suffering in the present, belief in the possibility of progress is profoundly and existentially reassuring (Gray, 2007). Reliance on the certainty of eventual rectification makes the awareness of suffering possible, without which it seems that only hopelessness and despair would prevail. Deborah Nelson (2017, 8) has called this the "master narrative of human perfectability", arguing that it provides a comforting defence against the yawning abyss of either despondency or nihilism. The impassioned, often indignant, documentation of iniquity that occupies much academic scholarship is both motivated and enabled by a controlling faith that, as Nelson remarks, "every source of pain is ... already located somewhere on the path to (its) elimination" (Nelson, 2017, 8). The reassurance provided by the promise of perfectability fuels recurrent slogans of revolutionary change. Nelson (2017, 28) quotes Simone Weil's remark that "Revolution, not religion, is the opiate of the people," explaining that "revolution is a painkiller because it promises a world free of blind necessity ... in which suffering will somehow be excluded", and this despite the unforgiving record of history in which the desired revolutionary correction is somehow always promised in the future but never realised today (Gray, 2007; Vattimo, 2018) while the suffering continues unabated.

The lure of progress through knowledge is seductive, producing not certainty (an ultimately impossible standard to attain in any event) but, rather, the *feeling* of certainty as a reassuring antidote to doubt. The claim to possess certain knowledge or truth produces subjective reassurance and provides a source of psychic comfort for those in the know. For Toulmin (1990), the claim to certainty was as much a selling point for the Cartesian rationalists as was their substantive ability to explain empirical phenomena in the world. And as Dewey (1929 [1988], 181) similarly concluded, "Thinking … ceases to be an effort to effect change in the objective situation and is replaced by various devices which generate a change in feeling or 'consciousness'". This is about knowledge providing a psychic curb against the insecurity and doubt that are inevitable when living in a complex ecosystem that will always defy our mastery of it (Latour, 1993; see also Jones, Chapter 11, this volume).

## Navigating the slippery slope of authoritarianism

Graham Harman (2014), channelling Bruno Latour, describes two forms of authoritarian knowledge that can be produced in the quest for certainty; one based on a purported privileged access to truth, which he calls 'Truth Politics', and a second, called 'Power Politics', based on the ability to impose truth on the world. Truth Politics, as Harman describes it, relies on the claim to have found knowledge of underlying antecedent truth – to have succeeded, in other words, in realising the correspondence theory of truth – and it comes in both Left and Right versions. On the Left, Truth Politics purports to have uncovered a truth that is otherwise obscured and distorted by relations of power and domination. It proceeds by speaking 'truth to power' to unmask the falsity of appearance on behalf of the claims of the weak (Harman, 2014, 2; see also Gray, 2007; Nelson, 2017). On the Right, Truth Politics asserts the priority of elite and specialised expertise, whether the Platonic "superiority of philosophers over the masses" (Harman, 2014, 2), Francis Bacon's anti-democratic elitism (Leary, 1994) or William Easterly's "tyranny of experts" (2013). Both Left and Right versions of Truth Politics share the beliefs, situated in the spectator theory of knowledge, that antecedent truth is available to be found; that it is obscured either by the deceit of the powerful or by its inherent complexity; and that knowledge politics comprises the confrontation of contending parties, each claiming to possess exclusive, authoritative knowledge of the 'real' by virtue of their unique and privileged perspective (see also Arendt, 1972). As Vattimo (2014, 71) concludes, "[i]f there is an objective truth, there will always be someone nearer to it than I am, someone who will arrogate to themselves the right and the duty to impose it on me. Everywhere you look, you see authoritarianism grounded in claims of a metaphysical kind."

Power politics, in contrast, denies the existence of an underlying or antecedent truth and asserts that truth is whatever power dictates it to be. Power Politics also comes in Left and Right versions, with the identity politics of the Left claiming, as Harman (2014, 3) describes it, that identity and desire are "infinitely creative" self-expressions that must be free to assert themselves unhindered by external constraint, and the post-truth politics of the Right asserting that "alternative facts" are those that power announces them to be (Geiselhart, Chapter 7, this volume; see also Flyvbjerg, 1998).

Both Truth Politics and Power Politics rely on authoritarian claims of exclusive and privileged access to knowledge that countenances no opposition. In Truth Politics, Harman explains, the interests of the powerless are always more valid than those of the powerful, and in Power Politics the reverse is often the case. In neither instance is the assertion of knowledge amenable to debate, dissension or the voicing of alternative viewpoints. Thus the quote I used at the start of this chapter: "Anyone claiming to tell me the absolute truth is demanding from me unquestioning submission" (Vattimo, 2014, 77). Openness, inquiry and learning are stifled when the authoritarian claim that 'there is no alternative' prevails. Both forms of authoritarian knowledge "short-circuit politics by trying to silence their enemies once and for all, whether by proofs or by force" (Harman, 2014, 108). In the face of authoritarian dogmatism, knowledge becomes both the vector and the victim of struggle in which only rhetorical force determines the outcome. Toulmin's description of the battle for intellectual supremacy in the seventeenth century applies equally today:

> The argument became active, bloody, and strident. Everyone now talked at the top of his voice … and the need for toleration no longer won a hearing. In the circumstances, the best that 'men of reason' could do was outshout the … dogmatists, and find a way of beating them at the game of 'invincibly proving' their fundamental beliefs. (Toulmin, 1990, 79)

## Choosing an affect

Any would-be scholar engages in the production of knowledge through the prism of their chosen attitude towards uncertainty, contingency and doubt. Among the catalogue of attitudes available, several can be readily rejected as both individually and collectively self-defeating. A nihilistic fatalism in the face of doubt justifies irresponsibility, whether in the form of unrestrained licentiousness or hermetic withdrawal from the world, and equates with a kind of moral disingenuousness in which the acceptance of anarchy and chaos can be "immensely satisfying" because it combines the certainty of failure with "the absolute comfort of being morally superior" (Harman, 2014, 115).

A related and equally self-defeating form of withdrawal and disconnection is the retreat behind artificial walls of identity or ideology, circling the wagons to create the semblance of security and certainty via the exclusion of difference and the erasure of contestation. This may take the form of a descent into victimhood in which the "solidarity of pariah groups", in Arendt's controversial phrase (Nelson, 2017, 76), offers the seductive reassurance of certainty when one's situated understanding is valorised and certified in the reflected experiences of group identity. A similar yet even more destructive form of disengagement and disconnection results from the seductive comfort of ideological solidarity achieved by insulating oneself from the premises and demands of belief systems different from one's own. Nelson conveys Mary McCarthy's complaint that "ideological solidarity eliminate(s) unpredictability by providing a largely fantastical but soothingly coherent theory of experience and narrative of the future" (Nelson, 2017, 76). Such ideological comfort imposes a cost in foreclosing the possibility of alternative futures not compatible with one's preferred ideology even if circumstances demand that people shift their ideas. Mott and Cockayne (2017, 11–12) explore the constraining effects of ideological solidarity within the academy, finding that bibliographic citations in scholarly publications all too often "resonate with our own intellectual positioning", reflecting "the desire for an intimate community indulging in the shared comfort of the familiar".

Drawing from the writing of Hannah Arendt, Susan Sontag, Simone Weil and others, Nelson offers an escape from the seductions of consolatory thinking in a resolute, albeit harsh, rejection of sentimentality in favour of a disciplined confrontation with the pain of life, unencumbered by theoretical abstraction, obfuscation and associated certainties. In Nelson's (2017, 71) terms, "the realist accepts the pain of reality, no matter how extreme … and concedes control over the future. The only way to become a realist … is to cultivate suspicion of intellectual and psychological comfort in whatever forms we find them". Richard Rorty (1999, 193) echoes this approach when he says that "the more metaphysically comfortless and morally insignificant our vocabulary, the likelier we are to be 'in touch with reality'" and thus able to address that reality rather than being distracted by our feelings about it.

Abjuring comfort need not require the abandonment of hope but this, too, is fraught with peril. Hope and the expectation that things *can* get better must be distinguished from optimism, the claim that things *will* get better. The latter returns us to the Enlightenment's reassuring belief in the inevitability of perfectability, which requires, in turn, a commitment to predictability and the denial of uncertainty. Hope, in contrast, involves accepting the complexity and contingency of the world while grasping the recognition that uncertainty leaves open the *possibility* for improvement as well as the *probability* of deterioration. In this vein, however, Shannon Sullivan (2017) makes a compelling case for "setting aside hope", which she calls a "cruel optimism" in the face of Black American experience of injustice. Hope for an eventual end of racial injustice, in Sullivan's view, displaces attention from the immediate need to address current circumstances in order to "deal with the present reality instead of working toward a hoped for but unattainable future" (Sullivan, 2017, 232).

## What does pragmatism bring to the production of knowledge?

In its disciplined rejection of consolatory thinking, pragmatism brings us face-to-face with the problematic situations we encounter in the world. In its confrontation with the world, unprotected by abstraction, dogmatism, sentimentality or certainty, pragmatism demands that we turn our attention to the problems at hand. Located within any number of 'problematic situations', the pragmatist finds herself transformed from spectator to agent and no longer merely able to cast blame but now required to act (see also Young, 2011).

In *The quest for certainty,* Dewey developed an eloquent defence of 'experimental intelligence' via social inquiry as a means to transform a problematic situation into a more desired state under unavoidable conditions of contingency and uncertainty. Experimentation proceeds through the application of collective intelligence to change the situation, assess the effect of the change and determine whether the change constitutes an improvement or not. While intelligence constitutes the ability to direct change in the most promising directions given past experience and future expectations, the outcome of action will be uncertain until it has happened. In the experimental reasoning that we introduced in our opening chapter: "An idea in experiment is tentative ... conditional, not fixed and rigorously determinative. It controls an action to be performed, but the consequences of the operation determine the worth of the directive idea" (Dewey, 1929 [1988], 230). For Dewey, "Intelligence is as practical as reason is theoretical (and) we can afford to exchange a loss of theoretical certitude for a gain in practical judgment" (1929 [1988], 170).

As illustrated by the contributions to this volume, the cultivation of experimental intelligence demands a reckoning with the production, status and use of knowledge as we know it today. It encourages a move beyond critique to engagement in the process of social inquiry that seeks to develop experimental proposals for action (Cutchin, Chapter 2; Harney and Wills, Chapter 9). It involves a shift from monologic representation of an antecedent reality to dialogic deliberation to observe, participate in and reflect upon the process of social engagement in which experimental intelligence is brought to bear to address problematic situations in the world (Bridge, Chapter 3; Fuller, Chapter 4; Huff, Chapter 8; Jon, Chapter 12). It grounds experimentation as a collective, deliberative and situated process rather than a solitary encounter with truth (Geiselhart, Chapter 7; Holden, Chapter 10; Jones, Chapter 11; Farahani and Esfahani, Chapter 13). These processes of experimentation and deliberation also require effective modes of communication within and beyond the inquiry, mobilising new ideas in 'conversational politics' that employ Rorty's practice of re-description through various means (Barnes, Chapter 5).

This approach to knowledge production requires an openness to multiple and variegated ontologies and perspectives to enrich the conversation and increase the probability of success (Saegert, Chapter 6). Moreover, this pragmatic orientation transcends topical specialisations and disciplinary boundaries, offering a framework and an approach to knowledge production that is not restricted to a particular substantive field (as illustrated by the range of disciplines, geographical homes and topics addressed by our authors). Pragmatism finds certainty in its openness to contingency, its rejection of consolatory obfuscation, its repudiation of authoritarianism and its affective embrace of political possibility. The production of knowledge through the affordances of pragmatism offers the last, best hope for, in Dewey's words, imagining a better kind of life to be led.

## References

Arendt, H. (1972) On violence, in *Crisis of the Republic*. New York, NY: Harcourt Brace.

Arendt, H. (1978) *The life of the mind*. New York, NY: Harcourt.

Barnett, C. (2018) Geography and the priority of injustice. *Annals of the American Association of Geographers*, 108, 2, 317–26.

Dewey, J. (1929 [1988]) The quest for certainty, in J.A. Boydston, ed., *The later works, 1925–1953, volume 4: 1929*. Carbondale, IL: Southern Illinois University Press, 3–250.

Easterly, W. (2013) *The tyranny of experts: Economists, dictators, and the forgotten rights of the poor*. New York, NY: Basic Books.

Flyvbjerg, B. (1998) *Rationality and power*. Chicago, IL: University of Chicago Press.

Gray, J. (2007) *Black mass: Apocalyptic religion and the death of utopia*. London: Macmillan.

Harman, G. (2014) *Bruno Latour: Reassembling the political*. London: Pluto Press.

Lake, R. (2014) Methods and moral inquiry. *Urban Geography*, 35, 5, 657–68.

Latour, B. (1993) *We have never been modern*. Cambridge, MA: Harvard University Press.

Leary, J. (1994) *Francis Bacon and the politics of science*. Ames, IA: Iowa State University Press.

Marx, K. (1976 [1888]) *Theses on Feuerbach*. Amherst, NY: Prometheus Books.

Mott, C. and Cockayne, D. (2017) Citation matters: Mobilizing the politics of citation toward a practice of 'conscientious engagement'. *Gender, Place & Culture*, 24, 7, 954–73.

Nelson, D. (2017) *Tough enough: Arbus, Arendt, Didion, McCarthy, Sontag, Weil*. Chicago, IL: University of Chicago Press.

Rorty, R. (1999) *Philosophy and social hope*. London: Penguin.

Sullivan, S. (2017) Setting aside hope: A pragmatist approach to racial justice, in S. Dieleman, D. Rondel and C. Voparil, eds, *Pragmatism and justice*. New York, NY: Oxford University Press, 231–46.

Toulmin, S. (1990) *Cosmopolis: The hidden agenda of modernity*. Chicago, IL: University of Chicago Press.

Vattimo, G. (2014) *A farewell to truth*. New York, NY: Columbia University Press.

Young, I. (2011) *Responsibility for justice*. New York, NY: Oxford University Press.

# 15

# Who's afraid of pragmatism?

## *Clive Barnett*

Whenever a dispute is serious, we ought to be able to show some practical difference that must follow from one side or the other being right.

William James, *Pragmatism: A new name for some old ways of thinking*

### The uses of Pragmatism

The essays in *The power of pragmatism* draw on the canon of first-generation
Pragmatist thinkers, primarily John Dewey, alongside William James and
George Herbert Mead, as well as on Richard Rorty's more recent iconoclastic
anti-representational pragmatist revivalism. One might ask, however, in what
respects the problems addressed by this philosophical tradition are the same
problems faced by practising social scientists today. With this question in mind,
it is worth looking at how *The power of pragmatism* throws light on the problems
faced by social scientists that Pragmatism, with a big P, appears able to resolve.
There are, it seems, at least three areas in which Pragmatism is thought to be
able to make some practical difference to social research.

The first of these areas concerns the repository of concepts that Pragmatism
offers to social scientists. Dewey's account of habitual qualities of human action
(Chapter 2), the centrality of the notion of the situation to Dewey's account of
inquiry (Chapter 3) and the recovery and application of Mead's account of the
inter-subjective dimensions of self-formation (Chapter 4) all demonstrate how
Pragmatism remains a source for innovative concepts that challenge and extend
contemporary debates about embodiment, conduct and action. What emerges
across the discussion of these foundational Pragmatist concepts is what one

might call a broadly *environmental* imagination, if by that is understood a concern with placing aspects of human life which are often theorised in atomistic ways in a holistic network of interactive (or, in Deweyan terms, 'transactional') relationships. The importance of attending to the milieux in which human life unfolds is demonstrated throughout this collection: in the focus on the emplacement of action in urban worlds (e.g. Chapter 4, Chapter 5, Chapter 8); in ecological spaces (Chapter 10, Chapter 11); in mediated networks of communication (Chapter 3); in situated spaces of learning (e.g. Chapter 6, Chapter 7, Chapter 9); and in networks of professional expertise (Chapter 12, Chapter 13).

The second theme running across *The power of pragmatism* is a political imperative, reflected in discussions of various methodologies of assertively engaged and experimental social research (e.g. Chapter 5, Chapter 9, Chapter 11). The consistent emphasis is upon not treating people as mere data points, but as active participants in a work of collective inquiry. It is this inclusive ethos that is also taken to be central to the democratic credentials of Pragmatism (e.g. Chapter 2, Chapter 9, Chapter 13). Of course, Pragmatism is not the only tradition of thought that informs practices of research that approach people as the active subjects of their own lives – a hermeneutic imagination is, after all, foundational to social science since Max Weber. And this raises the question of whether contemporary social science actually needs the kind of strictly philosophical warrant provided by Pragmatism. And in asking this question, it is helpful to notice two distinct challenges facing champions of the relevance of big-P Pragmatism to social science.

The first is the challenge of distinguishing Pragmatism from markedly different traditions of thought in a way that really matters to social science. It is not as if modern social science has ever been committed to the Platonic ideals of Truth that Pragmatism is quite good at puncturing. As it is actually practised, social science is not besotted with the Cartesian quest for certain foundations and nor does it hold to a spectator theory of knowledge. Like the rest of science, it is shaped by a fallibilistic commitment to learning through error. The second challenge is that of identifying what is genuinely distinctive or original about avowedly Pragmatist approaches in contrast to other traditions of thought that also hold to what might be called small-P pragmatist themes, such as an inter-subjective account of the self, or the priority of practice in warranting knowledge claims (it was Marx, for example, who asserted the practical 'this-sidedness' of matters of truth).

These two challenges are at the core of the third recurring theme running through *The power of pragmatism*, which is the status of claims to knowledge in social science research. This issue is discussed at length in the editors' Introduction, and it also runs through chapters discussing, for example, the nature of the practical knowledges deployed in planning practices (Chapter 12), development initiatives (Chapter 13) and educational contexts (Chapters 6, 7 and 9), as well as discussions of post-truth media publics (Chapter 7). Perhaps the fundamental question for any critical engagement with Pragmatism in social science is whether this tradition warrants the jettisoning of epistemological concerns completely (the perspective most often supported via an appeal to Rorty's neo-pragmatism), or whether it recasts epistemological questions – including questions of truth – in more modest ways. When looked at in the round, debates in contemporary Pragmatist philosophy suggest that the problem of *getting things right* remains the central concern of this tradition (see Misak, 2013).

The emphasis in Pragmatism on the practical relevance of knowledge runs the risk of substituting urgent assertions of political relevance or claims of democratic inclusivity for the task of thinking through difficult epistemological questions. One of the more important contributions of Pragmatism is to reorient epistemological discussions of knowledge and truth around normative issues of appraisal, evaluation and judgement, and to do so without reducing the former to the latter (there might, after all, be quite a lot of knowledge involved in being good, virtuous, in living well). So, while it is easy to think that Pragmatism affirms that truth is just 'what is good in the way of belief', this simple-sounding maxim is not meant to solve anything. Rather, it opens up the problem of criteria. And this problem is not simply a matter of arriving at an agreed set of criteria against which one might judge the value (not utility, surely) of knowledge claims. It is a matter of slowing down and thinking about how criteria work (Cavell, 1979).

## Living Pragmatism

There is now a well-established narrative around Pragmatism, most explicitly articulated in Louis Menand's (2001) collective biography of the first generation of thinkers, in which the most important feature of this tradition of thought is a shared aversion to dogmatism in matters of knowledge, politics and religious observance. This historical reference point also provides the basis for the interpretation of Pragmatism as a broadly liberal, progressive tradition. But Pragmatism is a living tradition of thought, one that exceeds the classical canon of Dewey, James and Peirce (Bernstein, 2010; Talisse and Aikin, 2011). Pragmatism is, also, a contested tradition, with more radical edges (for example, the early work of Cornel West), as well as central philosophical disputes, not least over the validity of Rorty's hegemonic account of pragmatism. And in fundamental respects, the lesson of this living tradition is that classical Pragmatism needs reappraisal and augmentation if it is to act as an aide to understanding contemporary problems facing social inquiry.

The vibrancy of contemporary philosophical debates about Pragmatism raises the question of whether it is, in fact, even possible any longer to delimit Pragmatism as a distinct tradition. After all, if Pragmatism is characterised, as suggested by Hilary Putnam (1995), by the primacy it accords to practice in matters of knowledge and truth, then the question arises of who, among influential philosophers whose work circulates in social science, doesn't count as a pragmatist? Was Wittgenstein a pragmatist? What about Heidegger? (Does it matter?) If an emphasis on practice is meant to be its defining feature, Pragmatism loses much of its distinctive shape. Part of the problem arises from the fact that, in academic debates, 'practice' tends to be invoked as a diacritical term, defined in contrast to, and in favour of, some other term, especially Theory. The idea that practice acquires its value by not being 'theoretical' loses some of its gloss once one notices the importance of the idea of abduction in the work of Charles Sanders Peirce, the granddaddy figure of American Pragmatism. Abduction, for Peirce, was the first step in any inquiry, and refers to "all the operations by which theories and conceptions are engendered" (Peirce, 1957, 237). Abduction is the imaginative, creative, dimension of inquiry, a kind of educated guesswork that suggests that 'mere' theory might be rather more important to Pragmatist inquiry than is often supposed (see Swedberg, 2014, 101–6; see also the editors' Introduction).

A better contrast to make is that between the practical and the technical. This is a crucial distinction in the social theory of Habermas, for example, in which the practical always involves some reference to reasons for action, rather than simply instrumental application. But this is a distinction that interrupts any easy assimilation of critical theory and Pragmatism, precisely because the latter tradition does often seem to hold to rather instrumental ideas about the primacy of practice.

In short, the commitment to the 'primacy of practice' only raises the question of how Pragmatism differs from lots of other traditions of social thought. There is a risk of painting too narrow a picture of the world from which resources for thinking practically can be drawn. On the other hand, and more to the point perhaps, practice is not necessarily a very important concept in Pragmatism. It is *experience* that is the central concept, understood not as an attribute of an isolated consciousness squaring off against a passive external world, but as a shared and interactive phenomenon. This observation suggests that we should suspend the simple affirmation of the practical over the theoretical, in order to be better placed to notice what is most distinctive about a broadly small-P pragmatist inflection identifiable in contemporary social theory (see Joas and Knöbl, 2004). And perhaps the best way of appreciating what is distinctive about this small-P pragmatism is to examine some of the family resemblances between Pragmatism with a big-P and other streams of modern social thought.

For example, one might note the evident affinity between Dewey's concern with inquiry as a matter of responding to problematic situations and Michel Foucault's account of problematisation (Barnett and Bridge, 2017; Koopman, 2011). Here, what links Pragmatism to Foucault's work is a common concern with investigating the role that practices of truth play in the world.

One might also recall, again, that there is no more influential source for thinking in terms of the primacy of practice in social science than Marxism.

The importance of Marx's emphasis on 'human sensuous activity' is best captured by Merleau-Ponty's (1973, 50) definition of *praxis*, the notion that became so central to strands of dissident Marxist thought in the twentieth century: "The profound philosophical meaning of the notion of praxis is to place us in an order which is not that of knowledge but rather that of communication, exchange, and association". Here, the point of an emphasis on the practical lies in thinking of issues of cognition and knowing as thoroughly social, historical, and no less prone to objective analysis for all that.

And by way of one final example, the importance of the French tradition of 'pragmatic sociology' lies not simply in preferring the concrete to the abstract, nor even of moving from an individualistic focus to a more collective imagination. It lies in addressing the challenge of acknowledging the irreducible dimension of normativity that defines practices *as* practices (Boltanksi and Thévenot, 2006; see also Rouse, 2007).

There are, of course, other connections one can make between big-P pragmatism and other practically oriented approaches to inquiry. But by noting the pragmatist resonances in these three fields, one can begin to glean the outlines of what is most significant about taking a small-P pragmatist approach. First, there is an emphasis on how truth emerges as an issue in relation to *problems* of human coordination, cooperation and living in common. Second, there is a sense that knowledge is a thoroughly *social* phenomenon, emergent around commonly experienced difficulties. And third, there is a sense that the *normative* capacity to judge, to evaluate and to give and receive reasons is an irreducible element of practical knowledge.

And this characterisation of small-P pragmatism brings us back to the issue of how to best appreciate the proposition that the truth status of knowledge is warranted by elaborating on the consequences of holding this or that belief. James held that "The true is the name of whatever proves to be good in the way of belief, and good, too, for definite, assignable reasons" (2000, 38). The first part of that proposition is what is most often emphasised in readings of canonical Pragmatism. But it's the second part that is much the most interesting. In thinking through the problem of giving and receiving reasons (to use the terms of Robert Brandom's neo-Analytical pragmatism) when weighing up the consequences of a belief, what is opened up to analysis is a world of *conflicting* interests and possibilities.

The suggestion that what is good in the way of belief is a matter open to reasoned judgement therefore helps address one of the bugbears of any social science treatment of Pragmatism, which is the oft-repeated assertion that Pragmatism does not deal very well with structural forms of power. In fact, power shows up in pragmatism as a concept concerned with capacities to act, rather than in terms of relations of domination – as power-to, rather than power-over (see Allen, 2016). One can find this sense of power, for example, in Dewey's (1927) account of public formation, in which the extension of interactions across time and space enhances the collective capacity to address a wider web of issues (see also Chapter 3). This sense of power might not, still, satisfy someone who does think that relations of domination are important matters of concern. But there is no reason, in principle, why one might not develop an analysis of domination from this prior sense of power as a capacity to act (it is, for example, the concern of James Bohman's pragmatist-inflected democratic theory (see Barnett, 2017, 231–6)).

James's reference to the need for reasons in deciding upon what is good in the way of belief suggests the implicit sense of conflict lurking within Pragmatism's headline commitment to the pluralism of human activities. Perhaps what is most needed, then, is a more agonistic sense of collective life than one often finds in interpretations of canonical Pragmatism (see Barnett and Bridge, 2013). And here it is worth pausing, and acknowledging the limits of Pragmatism's constitutive sense of optimistic confidence – confidence both in rendering old philosophical problematics redundant, and confidence in the capacity of collective action to resolve pressing issues. Stanley Cavell (1998) once charged that neither Dewey nor James took the threat of scepticism seriously, preferring to dissolve metaphysical 'Cartesian' worries about other minds or knowledge of the external world into the reassuring certainties of collective practice. From Cavell's perspective, dismissing the threat of scepticism as a metaphysical error amounts to a failure to acknowledge the tragic dimensions of human life. A similar sort of charge can be levelled at Mead, who acknowledged the affective dimensions of human action, but worked hard to neutralise the wilder implications of this affirmation (see Leys, 1993).

Cavell is resistant to the overly energetic invocation of action and practice in Pragmatism, at the cost of the need for patience and reflection. But what's most at stake in his criticism are two different understandings of experience, that most central of Pragmatist concepts. Pragmatism tends to displace notions of individualist rationality into collective practices. Cavell wants to hold to some aspect of experience that resists full rational articulation, and that therefore remains irreducibly singular and personal (see Donatelli et al., 2010). And behind this contrast, there is a deeper difference in perspectives on the status of individuality. One reason that Pragmatism appeals to social scientists is precisely because of its critique of individualism. But it might also risk over-socialising the self. Cavell wants to affirm the irreducibility of the self to its conditions of social formation, an affirmation that serves as a source for an ordinary dimension of agonism in human affairs that challenges social scientists' satisfaction in socialising every aspect of human life as well as easy invocations of 'Democracy' as the solution to any and all political conundrum.

The essays in this collection testify to the creative potential of a living tradition of thought. The horizon of future inquiry into the value of big-P Pragmatism and small-p pragmatisms lies in negotiating between overly socialised views of the social (for example, in cultural theories of the social construction of subjectivity or non-representational theories of affective atmospheres) and under-socialised views of the individual (for example, in economics or psychology). Big-P Pragmatism's value lies in part in its emphasis on the social dimensions of knowledge, on how problems arise and resolutions are arrived at through practices of collective interaction. But it is also a tradition of thought that affirms the irreducible pluralism of human life. And this pluralism, it should be said, is more of a problem than is often acknowledged. It calls for a more serious consideration of sharing as an inherently divisive activity (see Barnett, 2016). Taking pluralism seriously involves attending to problems of cooperation, coordination and organisation *as* problems. And this requires giving more attention to the normative practices of evaluation, judgement and verification through which different ways of proceeding are assessed, warranted and contested.

## References

Allen, J. (2016) Pragmatism and power, or the power to make a difference in a radically contingent world. *Geoforum*, 39, 1613–24.

Barnett, C. (2016) 'We're all in this together', in A. Ince and S.M. Hall, eds, *Sharing economies in times of crisis: Practices, politics and possibilities*. London: Routledge, x–xiv.

Barnett, C. (2017) *The priority of injustice: Locating democracy in critical theory*. Athens, GA: University of Georgia Press.

Barnett, C. and Bridge, G. (2013) Geographies of radical democracy: Agonistic pragmatism and the formation of affected interests. *Annals of the Association of American Geographers*, 103, 1022–40.

Barnett, C. and Bridge, G. (2017) The situations of urban inquiry: Thinking problematically about the city. *International Journal of Urban and Regional Research*, 40, 6, 1186–1204.

Bernstein, R.J. (2010) *The pragmatic turn*. Cambridge: Polity Press.

Boltanski, L. and Thévenot, L. (2006) *On justification. The economies of worth*. Princeton, NJ: Princeton University Press.

Cavell, S. (1979) *The claim of reason: Wittgenstein, skepticism, morality and tragedy*. Oxford: Oxford University Press.

Cavell, S. (1998) What's the use of calling Emerson a Pragmatist?, in M. Dickstein, ed., *The revival of pragmatism*. Durham, NC: Duke University Press, 72–80.

Dewey, J. (1927) *The public and its problems* New York, NY: Henry Holt & Co.

Donatelli, P., Frega, R. and Laugier, S. (2010) Pragmatism, transcendentalism, and perfectionism. *European Journal of Pragmatism and American Philosophy*, II-2, 1–11.

James, W. (2000) *Pragmatism and other writings*. London: Penguin Books.

Joas, H. and Knöbl, W. (2009) *Social theory*. Cambridge: Cambridge University Press.

Koopman, C. (2011) Genealogical pragmatism: How history matters for Foucault and Dewey. *Journal of the Philosophy of History*, 5, 3, 533–56.

Leys, R. (1993) Mead's voices: Imitation as foundation, or, the struggle against mimesis. *Critical Inquiry*, 19, 277–307.

Menand, L. (2001) *The metaphysical club: A story of ideas in America*. New York, NY: Farrar, Straus and Giroux.

Merleau-Ponty, M. (1973) *Adventures of the dialectic*. Evanston, IL: Northwestern University Press.

Misak, C. (2013) *The American pragmatists*. Oxford: Oxford University Press.

Peirce, C.S. (1957) *Essays in the philosophy of science*. New York, NY: Liberal Arts Press.

Putnam, H. (1995) *Pragmatism: An open question*. Oxford: Blackwell.

Rouse, J. (2007) Social practices and normativity. *Philosophy of the Social Sciences*, 37, 1, 46–56.

Swedberg, R. (2014) *The art of social theory*. Princeton, NJ: Princeton University Press.

Talisse, R. and Aikin, S. (eds) (2011) *The pragmatism reader: From Peirce through the present*. Princeton, NJ: Princeton University Press.

# Index

Page locators in bold refer to tables; those in italics refer to illustrations.

EU authorised representative for GPSR:
Easy Access System Europe, Mustamäe tee 50,
10621 Tallinn, Estonia
gpsr.requests@easproject.com

www.ingramcontent.com/pod-product-compliance
Lightning Source LLC
Chambersburg PA
CBHW051954270326
41929CB00015B/2647

"In a world in which ideological boundaries are increasingly impermeable and cross-political debates mere shouting matches, pragmatism offers not just an escape but entry into a world of mutual respect, justice and democracy. This book is a contribution to hope at a time when despair seems unavoidable."
Robert A. Beauregard, Professor Emeritus, Columbia University

"This book offers a timely message about how a living tradition of thought can embrace a world of uncertainty and competing truths without itself seeking guarantees. Genuinely multidisciplinary, the collection champions a political stance as much as a philosophical one: the pressing need to create shared, collective responses to the social, political and environmental challenges that confront us today."
John Allen, Professor Emeritus, Open University

"This excellent book offers a vital approach to knowledge as a collective and participatory process of experiment and action for an unstable and complex world. A diverse set of outstanding authors offer innovative insights on a wide range of fields, including geography, politics, environmental studies, economic development and urban planning."
Peter Sunley, Professor of Economic Geography, University of Southampton

This book advances a pragmatist sensibility for social inquiry in which truth and knowledge are contingent rather than universal, made rather than found, provisional rather than dogmatic, subject to continuous experimentation rather than ultimate proof, and verified through their application in action rather than in the accuracy of their representation of an antecedent reality.

The contributors explore the power of pragmatist approaches to inform a practice of social inquiry and knowledge production that is problem-oriented, community-centred, democratic and experimental. *The power of pragmatism* offers a way to address contemporary challenges and mobilise the practice of inquiry and knowledge production to discern what John Dewey referred to as "a sense for the better kind of life to be led."

Jane Wills is Professor of Geography at the Centre for Geography and Environmental Science (CGES) and the Environment and Sustainability Institute (ESI), at the University of Exeter, UK. She is based on the Penryn campus in Cornwall.

Robert W. Lake is Professor in the Edward J. Bloustein School of Planning and Public Policy and a member of the Graduate Faculties in Geography and Urban Planning at Rutgers University, USA.

Image: An adaptation of Blanchard's full 1906 Chicago map, part of the David Rumsey collection (2018). Andrew Taylor via Wikimedia Commons (CC BY SA 4.0).

Cover design: Daniel Benneworth-Gray

Manchester University Press

ISBN 978-1-5261-6719-4
90000
9 781526 167194
www.manchesteruniversitypress.co.uk